TRIAL:

STRATEGY AND PSYCHOLOGY

John Nicholas Iannuzzi

PRENTICE HALL
Englewood Cliffs, New Jersey 07632

Prentice-Hall International (UK) Limited, *London*
Prentice-Hall of Australia Pty. Limited, *Sydney*
Prentice-Hall Canada, Inc., *Toronto*
Prentice-Hall Hispanoamericana, S.A., *Mexico*
Prentice-Hall of India Private Limited, *New Delhi*
Prentice-Hall of Japan, Inc., *Tokyo*
Simon & Schuster Asia Pte. Ltd., *Singapore*
Editora Prentice-Hall do Brasil, Ltda., *Rio de Janeiro*

10 9 8 7 6 5 4 3 2

Library of Congress Cataloging-in-Publication Data

Iannuzzi, John Nicholas
Trial strategy and psychology / by John N. Iannuzzi.
p. cm.
Includes index.
ISBN 0-13-953670-1
1. Trial practice—United States. I Title.
KF8915.I36 1992
347.73'7—dc20
[347.3077]

92-5180
CIP

ISBN 0-13-953670-1

90000>

9 780139 536700

PRENTICE HALL
Professional Publishing
Englewood Cliffs, NJ 07632

Simon & Schuster, A Paramount Communications Company

Printed in the United States of America

FOREWORD

A trial is many things. In Chapter 1, a trial advocate is compared to one of those performers at the circus who smiles nonchalantly as he or she works feverishly to keep many plates spinning simultaneously on the tips of long sticks.

Keeping the law, the facts, the jury, the judge, the adversary, the Record, a view of the appellate court all spinning simultaneously while smiling nonchalantly for the audience (read jury), is exactly what the trial advocate does.

But unlike the circus performer, the advocate has one distinctly different, and far more vexatious ingredient in the mix of his or her performance: an adversary who attempts to dislocate, to derail, to undermine, to thwart every spin, every move of the advocate.

If you were to liken the trial advocate to a surgeon attempting to suture a patient on the operating table, you also would have to imagine a adverse (should this read perverse?) surgeon standing on the opposite side of the table, just as deftly, just as quickly attempting to pull out each suture, parrying each move attempted by the advocate.

What other profession is there in the world where an equally trained, experienced opposite number strives on every turn to deter you from accomplishing what you attempt as champion on behalf of your client?

And you can't even look worried or concerned while you are being unstrung. Indeed not. The instant the jury sees you struggle, appear to be making an effort, appear concerned, that's the instant that the jury begins to think that perhaps you are working too hard to make your point; perhaps the need for such effort is an indication that your client has something to hide, is not worthy, therefore, of their support (verdict).

What sort of perverse activity is this, where even the appearance of difficulty in the accomplishment of what you are doing—despite the fact that there is that adversary on the other side attempting to thwart your every move—is a sign of weakness.

Oh well. This is the profession you sought, and you must want to do well at it. This, in part, is the purpose of this book: To assist you in knowing, then anticipating, and then deftly placing each piece of evidence on the scale that is the jury.

In addition, this book points out to trial advocates looking to sharpen their skills a true understanding of the trial, the actual psychology that lies beneath the surface of the trial. For it is in just such understanding that the advocate begins to move more quickly, more precisely in the arena of the courtroom, eluding the thrusts and lunges of the adversary, the idiosyncrasies or predispositions of the Court, and the resistance or hesitance of the jury.

You do not have to absorb this book at one sitting. Nor should you read this book once through, and set it down, forever, sure of all the information that it contains. This book is a gathering of the knowledge and techniques of the trial that have been honed and polished for many years, even lifetimes, of many advocates. I have attempted to put together an amalgam of the thoughts and techniques of those advocates I have known and admired personally, and those of whom I've read because they were before my time. You may even get a smattering of the techniques employed by the eloquent Cicero as he strove to enlighten and persuade—without appearing to be doing so—the Roman Senate more than 2000 years ago.

When you face a trial task, pick up this book, even a few minutes before you walk into the courtroom to begin the trial session. Let the words and the concepts flow over you like water from a waterfall. You do not have to try to get wet while standing beneath a cascade; nor do you have to memorize the words of this book. Let them flow over you, try to understand their meaning, rather than memorize them by rote. The more you understand the psychology and the technique of the trial, and then fuse them into your own style, the more comfortable you will feel. In this way, the true advocate in you—not me, not the other trial advocates whose styles and ideas are here to suggest to you a style and technique of your own—but your ideas and your own style will surface.

Don't be hidebound by the ideas and techniques suggested here. Take them, use them, and carry them to new heights, there to plant your style as a banner for others who watch you, admire you, remember and imitate you.

Always try a case as well and as hard as your ability allows. There are no unimportant trials. If it were unimportant you wouldn't be trying it; your client wouldn't retain a lawyer just to go through unimportant efforts. And always keep in mind the words of Joltin' Joe DiMaggio, when asked why he labored so intensely in each and every game as a New York Yankee. He said, "There may be somebody in the stands that's never seen me play before."

About the Author

JOHN NICHOLAS IANNUZZI has been an active trial lawyer for 29 years. His father, Nicholas P. Iannuzzi, was an active trial lawyer for 32 years.

The author has tried all types of cases, civil as well as criminal, in jurisdictions throughout the United States. He has handled more homicide cases in the New York City area than any active practicing attorney in that jurisdiction.

In addition, the author is an Associate Adjunct Professor at Fordham University School of Law, teaching Trial Advocacy.

Mr. Iannuzzi's other published books include *Cross Examination: The Mosaic Art,* published by Prentice Hall, as well as six novels of which several have been translated into many languages and published throughout the world.

Mr. Iannuzzi is listed in *Who's Who in American Law,* and *Who's Who in the World.*

CONTENTS

1

BECOMING A TRIAL PRO

WHAT IS A TRIAL?

A trial is many complex and unseen things. When you see a fine trial lawyer working, although what he or she does and says may seem effortless and smooth, merely flowing from a font in the top of his or her head, the lawyer is, in fact, working hard as hell to make it seem as if he or she is doing nothing.

Like the man in the circus who keeps many plates simultaneously twirling on the tip ends of long sticks, a trial lawyer must keep many different and separate aspects of a case going at the same time.

Nobody said it was easy. And if you think it's easy, if you think that you can just stand up in front of the judge and jury and extemporize, spout whatever comes into your head and that will carry the day, that you don't have to prepare, work hard, read this book no further. Go and do it. When that fails, come back and read this book.

When you're up in front of that jury, thinking feverishly what do I do next, how do I contain the loose cannon witness who's on the stand, what evidence do I have to bring in to counter this testimony, just remember, all trial lawyers have to solve all the same problems. The fine trial lawyer did it before the trial began.

A TRIAL IS A MOSAIC: ASSEMBLE THE PIECES

A mosaicist takes little pieces of stone, precious or otherwise, and assembles them into a beautiful picture. At the beginning, an observer doesn't know what the picture will be. Indeed, the artist may work one area for a while, then another, so that the picture being created does not reveal itself easily. But it is there, developing as the mind of the artist conceives it. At the end of setting all the pieces in place, the artist finally reveals the total picture he had in mind all along.

So, too, a trial is begun with one witness, then a document, then another witness, perhaps another, each adding certain nuances or aspects to the fabric of the trial. To the casual observer, each witness may, at first, seem totally disconnected to the others; but in the mind of the advocate, ever watchful of the flow and energy of the trial, a picture is emerging.

Ordinarily, even in what we call a "one-witness" case, there is other evidence, a technical witness, peripheral witnesses who set the stage, and exhibits and documents that support the testimony of the main witness.

A trial, then, is the amalgamation of many pieces of evidence, witnesses, documents, exhibits, arguments, blended carefully by the advocate. Each piece of the picture must be laid into the framework of the trial, so that at the end, at the Summation, the advocate can call upon each of the fragments to weave together a fabric of irresistible strength and logic to carry the day for his or her client.

TRIAL IS CIVILIZED BATTLE

In days of yore, champions did physical battle with sword and axe before a host of attending citizens to resolve disputes. The patron whose champion vanquished the opposing champion was declared the winner of the dispute or controversy.

Today, opposing champions still prepare strategies and counterstrategies, store weapons, and, using all the force both can muster, attempt to vanquish their patron's enemies. The only difference is that their weapons are words and ideas, the battle-field is a courtroom, the attending host is a jury, and the victor gets a verdict rather than the head of the slain opponent.

Although in a different setting, today's battle is just as ferocious as when fought with thrust and parry of sword. Each adversary attempts to destroy his opponent's troops (witnesses) and ultimately to assail the fortification (case theory) erected by that opponent.

If you're lucky, occasionally, you can see a magnificent battle between a brilliant advocate and an equally clever witness, toe-to-toe, cheek-to-jowl, locked in combat, thrusting and parrying each other's best offense. It may be bloodless, but it is ferocious combat.

TRIAL IS ALSO DRAMA

A trial is not just a brutal, uncontrolled beating administered to an opponent. For in that pummeling there is the danger that the observers (jurors) will be repelled by your savage attack, or, for whatever reason, drawn sympathetically to your opponent.

For example, suppose in an accident case the defendant is an old woman who really shouldn't have been driving her car down crowded Fifth Avenue in the midst of pre-Christmas shopping traffic.

But driving she was. And she did cause an accident; no question about that.

Now, you are the plaintiff's counsel, and you stand to sear the venerable defendant on cross-examination after she testified on direct to explain her position. With righteous incivility for the malefactor, you tear into that old lady with venom, sarcasm, and hammer blows.

Beware!

The jury may throw you and your client out of court because you are an insensitive oaf. Even though you were in the right!

Thus, trial masters must take into consideration the sensitivities of their audience (jurors) so that what is presented fits comfortably into the minds of the audience. Don't cause your audience to close down its collective mind to a valid issue or argument because of an insensitive presentation. There is in a trial, therefore, a need for a tastefully orchestrated presentation of the evidence to your audience.

In the theater, audiences render their opinion in box-office receipts. A jury is an audience that renders its opinion in a verdict.

The advocate is the producer, director, wardrobe keeper, in short, the chief cook and bottle washer, rolled up into one person during the presentation of the trial drama.

The aim and purpose of this drama is, as in any drama, to make a presentation that will convince, persuade, move, educate the audience. If the presentation is interesting, exciting, enthralling, convincing, then you are moving in the right direction. If the presentation is boring, dreary, illogical, and puts your audience to sleep...well, you can't very well hope to move an audience that has slumbered off—even if their eyes are open.

Thus, in addition to being in control of the facts, you have to make sure that this drama of yours builds logically and interestingly. You must try never to lose your audience nor to offend that audience. Be careful. The audience may identify with a witness you are attacking, and, in the end, the audience may render a negative verdict in retaliation for your boorish handling of something you didn't even consider to be part of the case.

Indeed, there have been cases where the jury has rendered a negative verdict in retaliation to the overzealousness of the judge.

Of course, if the witness you attack is the sleaze of the world, the jurors will take vicarious satisfaction in your pounding the vulgarian into the floor.

In the end, that jury that you may have thought to be a thoughtless collection of faces truly has the capacity, as representatives of all the citizens of your jurisdiction, to make the system work beautifully, rising to the occasion to cut through the slick, the clever, that which is intended to deceive, and render what it was intended to render, a fair and just verdict.

Don't be insensitive to the jury's sensitivity.

TRIAL IS PSYCHOLOGY

You may be getting the idea that a trial is a complex amalgamation of many parts, that the advocate must be adept at many disciplines.

You're right. And we're not finished yet.

Yet another facet of a trial is the psychology of the trial. As in all of life, there is psychology involved in a trial. For example, the jury may be impressed with the handsome, gray-haired judge who has a nice smile and manner. That judge, as every advocate in the courthouse is aware, is a perfect monster. But the jury looks upon him as a father or upon her as a mother image, clothed with the authority of the State. What that judge says or instructs goes a long way. And you'd be foolish not to take that into consideration in handling your case.

The same is true for the jury's first impression of that clean-cut, dashing prosecutor, or the slick weasel of an ambulance-chasing plaintiff's advocate, or the wily, crafty, criminal defense advocate. Their very appearance and demeanor affects the jury.

Al Julian and Harry H. Lipsig, the well-known and successful New York trial lawyers, each went out of his way to create the right psychological picture during trial. Although each was well able to afford a fine wardrobe and an elegant briefcase, their clothing during trial would always be the same, tending-toward-the-shabby "trial suit," and their files were carried in common red-welt file envelopes. As they got on in years they would sometimes play the dodderer before the jury, even before the judge, sometimes almost forgetting what they were talking about. All this was intended to gain the indulgence of the jury, get the jury to strain to be helpful, to be kind to the struggling advocate and his cause.

Indeed, if you would meet one or the other of these foxes while you were on trial, he would more than likely look at your suit, shake his head, and say, quite seriously: "that's not a trial suit."

The reason for this is that these experienced trial lawyers believed that everything that goes on in a courtroom—not only every word you say, but the way you say it, the way you appear as you say it—affects the jury. Therefore, while they would be in a courtroom, everything they did, the way they stood and walked, was carefully analyzed before they did it.

There are those lawyers, who while their adversary's main witness is testifying on the stand, appear to be falling into a somnolent state, head drooping, eyes occasionally closing. Don't be fooled! They're catching every word, just as precisely and carefully as you please, but they are attempting to transmit to the jury a state of boredom, lack of care, as if to convey to the jury: This isn't significant, important testimony; this is boring.

Other times the crafty trial lawyer conveys other emotions: tragic response to her infant plaintiff's sad injury, hesitating with emotion in the midst of the direct to let the jury ponder what was just said. Or silently shaking her head to express shock or dismay at the tactics of her adversary.

What? You say this is play acting, and you're a serious trial lawyer? Well, if you're really serious, you'll have to come to grips with reality. No one said you were to be an obvious, flagrant fraud. But you can be aware of psychology of the juror. Jurors are human beings, currently engaged in the judicial process. Their response to external stimuli remains, despite the fact that they're on the jury. Rather than permit a negative influence, rather than permit an adversary to sway the jury with subtle reactions and manners, you'd best be aware that no one in the trial setting is totally stripped of his or her humanity or response to that which surrounds him or her.

Of course, mere psychology won't carry the day over sheer, overwhelming evidence. But the combination can be devastating.

Thus, you must remember that not only what you say but the way you say it before the jury is important. As the trial unfolds, the jury can be favorably impressed with an advocate who is obviously prepared, is respectful of the Court, trying hard to be truthful and honest; who each time he or she opens his or her mouth, speaks with knowledge and fairness. Even if you fly into the face of the Court—which happens occasionally—the jury can understand, even commiserate with the respectful, brave advocate attempting to protect a hapless client.

Knowledge of the Latest Law Is Essential

If there weren't substantial reason to make what seems to be a very obvious statement, the statement wouldn't be made. Unfortunately, there are many who, having passed the Bar, prefer not to read cases and do research, who consider that they know the law and are satisfied with their knowledge.

The fact of the matter, as any serious trial lawyer can tell you, is that you must keep up with the latest cases on the subject matter in which you specialize, particularly those cases that relate to evidence and trial work. In the midst of all that a trial lawyer does (see above)—battling the adversary, putting together a mosaic, balancing the psychology of the courtroom—you must know the law.

To those would-be trial lawyers who just want to have a six-gun and go into the middle of the street and shoot it out with an adversary, who want to leave that mild, sedentary law book stuff to those who can't take the heat of battle, all I can say is beware. Everything that is done in a courtroom has to be gauged around the law.

If you don't know the law, you can't know where you're going. It is the law that is the basic chart for your actions. If you don't know what the law is, you're adrift in a horizonless sea.

So, in addition to everything else that you have to keep in mind as you twirl through your trial as if there's nothing to it, you have to temper everything toward the legal goal that you have set for yourself. Most particularly, you have to be aware of the rules of evidence and shape the direct or cross-examination based thereon.

If the Court refuses to permit you to proceed along a legal path, substantively or procedurally, that you believe is absolutely correct, you must proceed as best you can, ALWAYS protecting the record for later Appellate Review.

All this, while making it seem before the jury that you are doing nothing, nothing at all.

Only Go to Trial When You Have To

A trial is an ordeal that is necessary where there are disputed issues of fact. A trial is not a pleasant excursion that everyone should experience and enjoy. Where there are no issues of fact in dispute, there is no triable issue, and there should be no trial.

What is the point of the foregoing?

To dispel the romantic attachment of some advocates to the idea of going to trial, being a trial lawyer.

Never fight a battle you don't have to. In every battle, there's a 50/50 chance you may lose. I'm not suggesting that you should walk away from a battle with your tail between your legs. I am saying, however, that you shouldn't walk around with a chip on your shoulder either, looking for any battle you can stir up.

Your function as a trial lawyer is to protect your client's interests, even at the cost of some personal publicity you might get during a sensational trial, even at the risk of seeming as if you don't want to fight. To win without fighting is a far more difficult task than to rush in with a knife between your teeth, a sword in each hand, looking for a fight.

The same principle applies in cross-examination, which is the grout that holds the trial together: Don't get involved in a cross-examination unnecessarily. In the section on cross-examination later in this book, I indicate that the best cross-examination is one that never takes place. Where the witness on the stand gives no testimony against your client, where the testimony fits comfortably into your overview of the trial, don't cross-examine.

Your function as a trial lawyer, as a cross-examiner, is to further your client's interests. Where those interests are furthered by your sitting on your seat and doing nothing, you are fulfilling your function.

Trial work and cross-examination were not designed merely to hone your trial skills. They are not forums in which you can dance and display your cleverness, your deft thrusts and parries, to the detriment of your client.

In short, a trial is not the venue in which you serve your client up like a tennis ball.

SHORT DEFINITION OF A TRIAL

I made this analogy before, but it seems the perfect description of a trial, so I proffer it again.

A trial advocate is like the performer in a circus who keeps many plates turning on individual, tall sticks. She or he gets three or four plates twirling, then a fifth, rushing back to the first, second, third, and fourth to give them a bit more spin, then puts up a sixth. That's the way you may begin to feel in the midst of a trial, keeping many plates on sticks spinning at the same time. Your plates are the facts, the law, the psychology, the drama, the record.

Did someone tell you it was going to be easy?

2

THE TRIAL BOOK

WHY BOTHER REMEMBERING?

Yes, of course you can remember everything about each of your cases, and you can store all that information in your head. You're a great rememberer. Which may mean that you have quite a large mental capacity. But wouldn't it be far better to use that capacity to think great thoughts, to creatively think about your cases, rather than to be a storehouse used only for sorting and rummaging?

Supposedly, Einstein indicated that he never remembered anything he could look up. Even if Einstein didn't say that, it is a commendable idea. Why waste the brain capacity to store and remember something—even unconsciously used brainpower—if you could simply leaf through an inanimate book that has a greater capacity for exact storage than that great brain of yours.

A justice of the New York Supreme Court, Hon. Peter McQuillan, recently was kind enough to hear the oral motion arguments of some of my law school students. During the session, he made a remark that I think bears repeating, it goes right to the heart of what I am now trying to tell you. Judge McQuillan was trying to advise the students that letters, written memos to your adversary, copy to the Court, or vice versa, were far better to preserve a point than was an evanescent telephone message that evaporates in the air and can be denied or disputed. In a phrase, Judge McQuillan said: "A short pencil is better than a long memory."

A homely little message, but it speaks volumes—and can save volumes of appellate work if adhered to. For the trial advocate, that inanimate, but most helpful place to store trial information is in a book, a Trial Book.

WHAT IS A TRIAL BOOK?

A Trial Book is a loose-leaf, or some other replacement-page book that is composed of (a) your permanent trial reference material, and (b) your current case trial information.

PERMANENT TRIAL REFERENCE MATERIAL

As you research cases, from time to time you will come across decisions, appellate or otherwise, that bear upon trial work: a decision regarding hearsay; another about when certain information about a trial witness falls into the category of proscribed collateral matter; another about declarations against penal or economic interests; the collateral source doctrine, which relates to whether or not information about a pension or insurance proceeds are admissible in evidence to influence (diminish) a jury's damage award; another concerning what is a record kept in the course of business, when it is admissible, and what weight such business record has before the jury. These, and a myriad of miscellaneous decisions, depending on the main field of your trial work, are decisions that are likely to arise time and again.

And because of their recurrence or specific interest to you, you should make a copy of these pertinent decisions or holdings, add them to your index of cases, and store them in a section of your Trial Book. Then, when on trial such an issue arises, you may very well have the latest case right on hand to show to the Court and resolve the issue straightaway.

> ***NOTE:*** *Your capacity to produce the latest cases relating to the subject matter of your current trial may be very impressive psychologically to both the Court and your adversary. Your preparation will show that you are fully prepared for the battle and will alert your adversary that he or she is in for a hell of a struggle.*
>
> ***ANOTHER NOTE:*** *As time goes on, other cases may be decided on the same issue. Replace the older or outmoded decisions with the latest decisions, so that your Trial Book is always up to date.*

CURRENT CASE TRIAL INFORMATION

Beginning in the next chapter, you will start to put a case together for trial. You will start by talking to your client, getting the facts of the case and getting the documents to back up those facts. You will be speaking to witnesses; you will be taking witness statements. And each and every item that you investigate must be recorded or preserved in your Trial Book.

Each witness should be given his or her own section in the book where you either record the facts volunteered to you by your own witnesses or where you record information from which you will develop your cross-examination if that witness is an adverse witness.

When you put together the direct examination of each witness, it should be written out and kept in the section of the Trial Book for that witness. Thus, when you are ready to produce that witness, you will have your script before you and will not be "winging" it from the top of your head.

When your task is to cross-examine a witness, analyze all the information, prior statements, and investigative memos relating to a particular witness. Cross-reference that information in that witness's section of your Trial Book, so that, together with the direct examination that you will record almost verbatim, you can put together your cross-examination script. For both recording the direct examination and a cross-examination script, see cross-examination, infra.

As you develop more facts about the case, these facts should be added to the Trial Book in the appropriate section so that each and every item of information about the case is carefully preserved.

Reports, documents, investigations, memoranda, specific case law researched for the trial—all should be kept in their own section.

Exhibits, too, premarked, should be kept in the book, both the original AND A COPY so that you are prepared to submit the original in evidence and will still have a copy for your own reference.

In short, your Trial Book is the compilation of the complete trial, witnesses, anticipated direct testimony, cross-examination, research, and exhibits, all kept together in one place so that your trial flow shall be uninterrupted BECAUSE YOU ARE PREPARED—NOT IN YOUR HEAD, BUT IN YOUR BOOK, IN WRITING, READY TO GO.

3

TO GET THE FACTS, GET THE WITNESSES

YOU MUST KNOW WHAT THE CASE IS ABOUT

Now that you have a Trial Book, it's time to begin to fill that book with information about the case you're going to try.

In most instances, the first contact of any sort that the trial advocate has with a case is when the prospective client, the aggrieved party, whether that party is a potential plaintiff or a defendant, comes to your office seeking your advice. Before that, except for what the advocate may have read, heard, or seen in the media (which is very often inaccurate and put together in the most dramatic, not always the most precise fashion), the advocate has no awareness that a litigation even exists.

Then, someone seeks the aid of counsel and asks for that counsel to become his or her trial advocate. What the case is about is the first question you want answered.

CLIENTS LIE

There is no better way, no better source to begin to find out about the case at hand than by plumbing the knowledge of your client.

Keep carefully in mind, however, that clients often do not tell their prospective advocate the unvarnished truth about their case.

Perhaps it isn't really lying. Perhaps, in an attempt to win the prospective advocate's confidence and dedication to her cause (of action), the client somewhat gilds the lily to convince the advocate of the righteousness (and profitability) of the prospective cause.

Perhaps the preceding statement is too uncharitable, too harsh. The reason that the rendition of the case first given by the client to her proposed Paladin is somewhat askew may be more elemental: The client has already convinced herself of the favorable rendition of the facts and is now only repeating what she has already caused herself to believe.

Whatever the reason, oftentimes clients do not, at first, give the true picture, the true facts to their advocate.

Of course, it is not an absolute that the client will lie, will smooth or modify the facts when she first tells you her rendition of the case. It is, however, important that you keep that possibility very much in mind when you talk to your prospective client.

PLOY #16

Sometimes it is helpful and time saving to use Ploy #16 when talking to your client at the second or third meeting that you have with her, particularly, but not exclusively, in a criminal case.

By this second or third meeting, the client feels comfortable with you—otherwise, she would have sought other counsel before this. And the client also feels that you have properly dedicated yourself to her cause—otherwise, you would have opted out of the case yourself. Thus, the client may now be willing to tell you the straight, unvarnished facts. In addition, you have begun to investigate the case on your own, and you now know more about the case. Trying to "con" you is no longer going to work.

Ploy #16 begins by assuring the client that you wish to put forward the most formidable, impregnable case possible—for both your sakes. In order to do that, however, you advise the client that you have to know the true, unvarnished facts. You further advise the client that you are willing to accept and work with whatever facts—favorable or not—that the client submits to you. However, you warn your client most earnestly, if you put together a case built on banana oil (embellished facts), plaintiff or defense, both you and your client are liable to end up slipping on your briefs.

Advise your client that a wily adversary is liable to destroy a case built on false information right in the client's face, right in front of a jury. Advise the client, further, that it will be her face, her case blown to bits—not yours. You will go on to your next case. The client is the one who will end up without recompense for injury, or paying unnecessarily for injury caused, not being redressed for wrong, or doing time for the crime.

And now for the essence of Ploy #16, the *sine qua non* that makes this ploy a formidable truth getter.

Advise the client further that if she has any idea of embellishing or twisting the true facts, since she doesn't know the law, her attempt to fabricate a new structure may be undermined by ignorance of the essential elements of the case. Tell the client that if she will tell you the absolute, unvarnished truth, then, indeed, you would know exactly what it is that you have to do, what facts have to be twisted, what version of the facts should be presented to your adversary, the Court, and, ultimately, the jury.

With this, your client may—only may—tell you the true facts. You may peel off some of the gilding the client may have applied to get you to take the case. Remember, I said *may* have applied. The client may have told you the truth in the first instance. However, use Ploy #16 anyway, just to make sure that you have the true facts.

> ***NOTE:*** *You are NEVER—and I mean NEVER—to help your client manufacture a false case. Never, never get involved in such activities. Ploy #16 is merely intended to smoke out the true facts so that you will know exactly what the case is about and whether or not you want to stay in the case.*

DO NOT PUT YOUR CLIENT'S STATEMENTS IN WRITING

After you have obtained your client's ultimate version of the events of the case—more that has been inadvertently forgotten will trickle out as you go along—you must now obtain the supporting facts, the names of the witnesses, their names and addresses, the locations involved in the case, and the documents that support or undercut your client's position. In short, you want to know—and record in your Trial Book—all the facts you client knows about the case.

However, *do not write out your client's version of the case in your Trial Book.*

Why is that, you ask, since that may be the most significant information in the case?

The reason for this lack of memorialization of your client's version of the case is that the written statement of a party is discoverable. Don't create a document that you will later have to turn over to your adversary, and with which your adversary may later batter your client on cross-examination.

And don't think that if you write out such a client statement, and thereafter, kind of accidentally-on-purpose fail to turn over such a document to your adversary, that you have saved yourself.

First, I do not advocate dishonesty. Second, it may come out during the development of the case, or on the cross-examination of your client, that there is such a document. Don't be in the unenviable position of being called upon, before the jury, to produce a document that you should have turned over long ago, that you obviously had tried to hide. Being caught red-handed in a deception (read cover-up, and remember Richard M. Nixon) magnifies the harm of trying to conceal such a document immeasurably. How much better off you are to be able to reply truthfully that there is no such document in existence.

More significantly, nothing could be more damaging than for your adversary to take apart—or appear to take apart—your client's trial testimony *using her very own prior statement,* a statement that *you* set to paper and preserved in your file.

Of course, you can write your own synopsis or impression of the case after listening to your client. But this synopsis should just be your notes, your *work product* and not purport to be a verbatim—or any sort of—statement of your client. It should be a rendition of your own thoughts about the case, a work sheet from which to go forward with other investigation.

INTERVIEW ALL WITNESSES

Each person with knowledge of the case must be interviewed thoroughly. Ordinarily, the main witnesses, the ones who were closer to the incident, the ones with the most knowledge of the circumstances, should be interviewed first. The interviews of these witnesses may give you better insights and may lead to other facets of the case, other witnesses, and other means to develop the case.

> ***A CAUTION:*** *In some situations, the main witnesses may be hostile to your client's cause. A* hostile witness, *in terms of our art, may be defined as anyone harboring a view of the facts or of the evidence that is inconsistent with your trial posture. Before encountering such hostile witness, you may want to first interview the lesser witnesses in order to be forearmed with facts and information to counter, parry, dilute the initial antagonism of this hostile witness(es).*

REDUCE "OTHER" WITNESS STATEMENTS TO WRITING

Remember the previous admonition that you should not reduce your client's statement to writing. A party and a witness, however, are two very different persons, and are treated accordingly.

You do not memorialize your client's statement—in addition to not wanting to memorialize a statement that can be used to whip your client on cross-examination—because your client, the party-witness, is accessible to you at any time. You can confer with and discuss the case with your client at any time you wish.

Moreover, it is a violation of the canons of ethics for an adversary, or his or her investigator, to contact your client without your knowledge or permission. Therefore, you know that your client is not going to be sniped at by the other side without your knowing about it.

An ordinary witness, on the other hand, is fair game for both you and your adversary. Either you, or your adversary, have to reach out for the nonparty witnesses in order to interview them, in order to get their version of the facts. As such, you want to get the less-accessible, ordinary witness's statement securely reduced to writing, memorialized, fixed for the future so that later on you need only open your Trial Book to accurately refer to and work with the information supplied by the witness(es).

Another reason to get an ordinary witness's statement on paper is to have it "set," get it on paper, so that if and when your adversary interviews that witness, the witness will have to advise your adversary of the prior statement—and its contents—and will likely, therefore, have to stick to the same version.

Another reason you want a prior statement of the ordinary witness is to be able to whip the witness with such statement on cross-examination in the event that your adversary somehow causes that witness to give statements that differ from the statement given to you.

RECORD THE WITNESS'S STATEMENT— EVEN IF HOSTILE

As indicated earlier, you may find that a witness to an event gives a statement of the events that is not helpful to your client. I am not saying that this witness's statement is purposely contrary to that told to you by your client. Rather, the main course of evidence may show that your client is quite vulnerable or liable in the situation at hand. While it is devoutly to be wished that you always represent clients in the right, it may happen on occasion that your client is in the wrong. That may be precisely why your client has sought your help.

Your responsibility in this situation is the same as if your client is entirely in the right: find out what the case is about, counsel and advise, and guide and direct your client to the safest, most protected harbor available.

The witnesses you encounter who give renditions of the facts that are contrary to the version your client has recounted to you may not actually be hostile to your client, they may merely be honest, direct, and accurate. Not all honest, direct, and accurate witnesses are hostile. For trial purposes, however, and in terms of our art, witnesses who agree with your side of the case are not hostile. All the others are.

Whatever the witness's version of the case, reduce it to writing and have it signed by the witness.

Why, you ask, would you want to have a written hostile witness statement? For two reasons: to memorialize it and to contain it.

By recording the hostile statement in writing, you reduce the damage of the hostile witness to a known quantity, to a set scenario. You know what you are dealing with. Additionally, the hostile witness is thereafter going to be hard-pressed to embellish his or her version of the facts. It will be difficult for your adversary to induce the witness to alter his or her story to make it *even more harmful* to your client.

Moreover, by memorializing the hostile statement, you may later use that recorded statement on cross-examination as a prior inconsistent statement should the witness alter or deviate from his or her story while testifying. Oftentimes, despite the best efforts of your adversary, a witness's trial testimony may deviate, in greater or lesser measure, from a prior pretrial statement. When this happens, you can get some cross-examination mileage from using the prior recorded inconsistent statement to show that the adverse witness is inconsistent, is inaccurate, and therefore, you hope, noncredible. For a complete discussion of the kinds and use to be made of prior inconsistent statements, see the chapter on cross-examination, infra.

EVEN A NONSTATEMENT SHOULD BE WRITTEN

On occasion, a person who was at or near the scene of an event, whether he or she is truthful or not, has no recollection or information that can be useful to your cause. Either the witness didn't see or hear anything, or can't remember what he or she saw or heard. Despite this lack of useful information, the negative (not hostile) statement should be reduced to writing.

You say you now understand why we wrote out the hostile statement, but why bother with a negative statement?

For exactly the same reason that you took down the hostile statement. So that the nonwitness cannot, by fickle subsequent recollection, or by the inducement or importuning of your adversary, suddenly become a hostile witness with damaging information. By having the negative or nonstatement in writing, you have a cross-examination arrow to twang at the witness should the witness suffer from a sudden recollection of damaging information.

Of course, the nonwitness may have a sudden recollection of favorable information. When this happens, naturally you must reduce this to writing, as well, in order to avoid the possibility of another attack of recurrent amnesia—whether or not this amnesia is the result of the inducement or importuning of your adversary.

In the event that a nonwitness has a sudden recollection of favorable information, you should include in the second (now nonnegative) statement some reference to his or her prior negative recollection (and statement) and the basis for his or her current recollection. The reason for this is that you are laying the foundation to defend against the possibility that your adversary also had the sagacity to read this book and also had taken a prior negative statement from the witness.

THINK AS YOUR ADVERSARY WILL

Always think your position, your evidence, your witnesses through to the point of what your adversary would do to this witness; what would you do to this witness if you had the opposite case; how would your adversary cross-examine this witness; how would *you* tear apart this witness. In doing this precautionary projection, you can envision what steps you have to take to protect both yourself and your client from the anticipated assault of your adversary.

> *A NOTE: When I refer herein to the inducement and importuning of your adversary, I do not suggest that all adversaries are dishonest: Remember, you are an adversary to your adversary. Nor do I suggest that all witnesses are fickle or dishonest. However, your adversary, by deft interview and probing of a witness, may be able to stir gremlins of recollection that may result in the witness modifying his or her prior version of the events.*

WRITE IT OUT FOR THE WITNESS

When taking a statement from a witness, it is perfectly acceptable, even preferable, for you—or your investigator—to write out the witness's statement in your own handwriting as it is being told. Witnesses are often reluctant to speak to lawyers or investigators; they don't want to "get involved."

Surely, then, these witnesses are going to be even more reluctant to write out a statement for you.

The fastest and smoothest way to take a statement, therefore, is to ask questions, listen to the answers, and as you are going along, write out the statement.

Don't ask the witness if you can write out what they are saying. Just write it out, as if you are simply making notes for yourself. As you are going along making these notes, you should ask questions, then add to, alter, or change what you are writing. Thus, the witness, who is watching you write, waiting for you to finish writing before he or she goes on to the next sentence, becomes involved in the preparation of the statement.

You may gather from what has been indicated earlier that I prefer to take witness statements myself, rather than to rely upon an investigator. The reason for this is that I know what I want for the trial. I see the statement prospectively, not as an end in itself but as a piece of evidence to be used for cross-examination.

An investigator, as good as he or she may be, may not be adept at cross-examination and all of its nuances and may not, therefore, get exactly what you might have included or wanted in the statement.

Moreover, by being there, listening to and hearing the witness's capacity to think and to articulate as well as the capacity to testify calmly and accurately, you are gauging his or her capacity to weather cross-examination by yourself or by your adversary. This gauging, thus, helps you to determine if you really want to call this witness as your own. It also helps you to comprehend better both the strengths or weaknesses of your case, or of the case you are fighting.

Just as a record on appeal misses the blood and sinew of the trial room and the nuances of live testimony, so too does a written statement miss the vibrancy, or lack of it, of the witness in person.

Trial work is a hands-on activity. The personal approach may give an extra dimension to your sense of the case. If, however, you find your investigator takes a statement to your total satisfaction, then by all means let the investigator take the statements.

DON'T MENTION THE WORD TESTIMONY

If you want to see a case of instant amnesia, tell the person you are interviewing that you shall want them to come to court someday in the future to testify. In the wink of an eye, the knowledged witness, with the facts at his or her fingertips, becomes unsure, hesitant, forgetful, you name it.

Therefore, do not mention the word testimony as you are taking a witness's statement. As I've already indicated, while you are interviewing the witness and writing out a statement of the salient information imparted by that witness, from time to time read the written statement to the witness, asking the witness if you have accurately recorded what he or she has said so far. The witness is now becoming part of the memorialization process. This is important, because when you are finished taking the statement, you are going to ask the witness to sign the statement.

And, often, witnesses are reluctant to sign statements.

That shouldn't be surprising. Witnesses are often reluctant about giving even an oral statement. So you must be tactful, schmoozing the shy witness a bit at a time into talking. As you talk, take out your pad. Begin to make notes. Then begin to read your notes to the witness. You are now involving the witness in the statement, setting the stage for the final request to sign the statement.

Why, you ask, are witnesses reluctant to sign a statement? They are not always. Some witnesses are not at all reluctant to give or sign a statement. These are often people who are involved—by friendship, outrage, or like point of view—with your cause, or with your client's cause. For these nonreluctant witnesses you need no special technique to obtain a statement.

But there are often independent, disinterested witnesses who wish to remain exactly that, independent, disinterested, uninvolved. Yet, regardless of that witness's personal feelings, you may need that witness for trial. You must, therefore, undertake to convince the witness that the mere making of a statement is neither painful nor difficult.

Try to convince the witness that by taking the statement you will probably not have to talk to him or her again, nor will you have to interview him or her again. The statement, once in your file, may be the end of the witness's involvement in the case. The implied threat that you may have to come back to talk to the witness again may very well be the impetus for the witness to give you a statement, just to be rid of you and get back to what he or she was doing.

Surely you understand that if the witness shows hesitation or reluctance to the mere giving and signing of a statement, a mention to that person that he or she may have to come to court and testify may cause the witness to flee at double time behind a locked door.

Indeed, many witnesses will tell you outright they will *not* come to court.

Don't panic!

When a witness shows reluctance to come to court to testify, don't throw up your hands, walk away, and forget about the witness as useless.

Indeed not. Go along with his or her attitude. Tell the reluctant prospective witness that you are only doing an investigation, that you are just interested in getting the facts for your file, and that you are not interested in his or her testifying. That is the truth. For the moment, that is. Tell the witness that at this time, you are *really* just investigating, just trying to find out who would be a good witness and who would be a necessary witness.

Thus mollified, the reluctant witness will be more willing to talk to you, more willing to give you a statement that will result in your leaving him or her alone and out of this litigation.

What good is taking information from a witness who has already told you that he or she will not come to court to give evidence?

First, you may get insight into the case: you may get the name or identity of other witnesses who can supply the same sort of information and who will be willing to come to court.

Second, have you ever heard of a subpoena? Once you have the witness's statement safely reduced in your handwriting and subscribed with the witness's signature, you can subpoena that reluctant person to the trial.

Of course, the witness is going to be annoyed, sometimes *very* annoyed, with a subpoena. Blame the subpoena on the judge, the system, the rules. Then show the witness their prior statement—not the original, only a copy, in case he or she wants to rip it up. Most witnesses will reluctantly succumb to the system, to the majesty of the law. They will reluctantly take the stand and testify to what is contained in the statement you took from them previously.

At worst, the Court will assist you in forcing the person to take the stand. This is not the best situation, having a totally reluctant witness being forced into the witness chair. But, as a last resort it may be necessary. And, since you have the prior signed statement in hand, even if the reluctant witness has a faltering memory you can usually bring him or her back to reality with a display of this prior statement. For more details on the handling of witnesses and the use of prior inconsistent statements, see direct examination and cross-examination, infra.

MAKE MISTAKES: HAVE THE WITNESS'S ENDORSEMENT

While you are writing out the statement, make at least one, perhaps two mistakes per page. These mistakes you then have to strike out. Later, when you ask the witness to read and sign the statement, have him or her initial the mistakes as he or she goes along.

Why?

To avoid the situation where the witness says he or she may have signed the statement but didn't actually read its contents before affixing his or her signature to the bottom thereof.

With the initials in place in the text above, and with the signature below, the witness is really going to be stretching the jury's imagination by stating that he or she didn't read the statement before initialing each of the mistakes in the body of the text as well as signing the bottom of each page of the document.

YOU WANT MORE THAN A SIGNATURE

Not only do you want initials at every mistake and a signature on the bottom of each page, you also should have the witness write out the following in his or her own writing on the bottom of each page:

> *"I have read the above two [however many] pages, and they are true.*
>
> *Signature. Date.*

The reason for the preceding being written in the hand of the witness is that you have more visible proof of the witness's actual endorsement of the document than just his or her signature. You have an entire positive statement concerning the contents of the document, indicating in his or her own hand that the witness actually read the document and that the document contains a truthful account of the events that it purports to describe.

In the event that the witness, through forgetfulness, error, or vindictiveness, or through the blandishments of your adversary, does not testify as to the facts previously related to you, you will be able to whip out the signed statement and use it to refresh recollection, to cow the witness back into line (with the piece of paper staring the witness in the face, ordinarily the witness will realize the futility of recalcitrance), or to beat the witness by using the signed statement as a prior inconsistent statement.

Obviously, all of this has to do with a reluctant witness whom you have called or want to call to the stand. If your adversary has called the witness to the stand, that witness is to be considered hostile rather than reluctant.

You may be further concerned about calling a reluctant witness to the stand because of the old chestnut that you can't impeach your own witness, one that you have called to the stand.

The federal rules of evidence (see evidence chapter, infra.) has changed that old rule, now permitting any party to impeach any witness, whether that party has called the witness to the stand or not. As these federal rules have already been adopted *in toto* by more than 30 states, and as the list is growing steadily stronger, there is hardly a jurisdiction where you will be impeded in jogging the memory of the reluctant witness that you have called to the stand with a prior, written inconsistent statement.

How is a jury going to look at such reluctant testimony, you ask? Why would you put a reluctant witness on the stand?

Certainly, you would prefer to have a cooperating, easy witness to help support your case. But rather than nothing, the reluctant witness will serve.

Moreover, the reluctance of the witness often disappears and evaporates in the presence of the jury. It is quite difficult for a witness to indicate to a jury that he or she doesn't remember certain facts, particularly when confronted with a document that the witness previously signed, even inscribed in his or her own hand, attesting to the fact that the witness indeed did read the statement and that what he or she read was true.

A jury is going to look with very jaundiced eye at the testimony of such a witness and will credit the prior statement—given at a time when there was no litigation imminent and given in a leisurely manner—as the probable truth of the matter.

SIGNED, SEALED, AND DELIVERED

The reality is, over time, the witnesses to an event do not change. But the witnesses's perceptions of an event may change. Perhaps such change is just natural attrition of memory. Or it could be a change in affection for your client, a change of allegiance. But, just as those memorable words in the song "Diamonds Are a Girl's Best Friend"—"square shape or pear shape, those rocks don't lose their shape"—are true, witnesses' statements that you have memorialized, written, and had signed and initialed don't lose their shape, either, and they go a very long way in stemming the shifting of the sands of the case.

Moreover, with all that there is to do in a case, there is no need to carry around in your head various amorphous statements of what you believe the witnesses told you.

Use Einstein's theory; not his theory of relativity, but that theory already mentioned, the one about Einstein never bothering to remember anything he could look up. Why bother using your memory power to catalogue and remember, to carry around a statement that could very easily be reduced to writing so that it remains unchangeable and readily available for study, reference, and use at any time?

Get the Rest of the Witnesses

Now that you have the statement of witness #1, who has described the event, the participants, and the sequence of the occurrence, go out and get the rest of the witnesses. And take their statements, as many as you can round up.

Remember, it doesn't matter what they say; write it down, record it, and have them sign and initial it.

One Good Witness Is Enough

It isn't necessary to have 20 or 30 witnesses. Indeed, be grateful for one good witness to an event. You are looking for quality information that will become evidence in your upcoming trial, or that will at least become ammunition in your disposition of the case. Don't look for numbers of witnesses. Look for whatever there is. Look for the real thing. A trial is not a numbers game. Sure, it would be nice to have 20 witnesses, all of whom saw exactly the same thing. Just as you read this, however, doesn't it just slightly occur to you that there's hardly an event that has occurred in the history of the world that 20 people could or would describe in exactly the same way? Such a display of uniformity would immediately make you think, hey! This thing is being staged, rehearsed. And it would make a jury think the same thing.

Besides, a trial lawyer is like a surgeon. He or she works with what he or she has, determines what has to be done, does it, and closes it up.

Work with what you have and get it together as tightly wrapped as you possibly can.

When you've done all of that, other witnesses may become available as you go along, and you will add their statements to your Trial Book as you obtain them.

Put It in Your Trial Book

Each witness should occupy his or her own section in your Trial Book. Give each witness a tab and his or her own special section. Put in the witness's statement. When you begin to put together your script for the direct examination of that witness, it will, likewise, be placed in that witness's section. If it is an adverse witness, you will write out your cross-examination script and place it in this section.

If there is additional information about that witness, if there are things to do in connection with that witness, if there are exhibits that have to be introduced through that witness, all should be placed in that witness's section of the book.

Now you're getting organized.

On to the next witness and further analysis of the case.

4

WHAT AM I GOING TO PROVE?

THE CARDINAL TRIAL QUESTIONS

Armed with the witness statements and with any documents, photographs, or objects suggested by and through those statements, you are now ready to answer the most important questions, the cardinal questions that must be asked and answered in every trial setting.

These cardinal trial questions are not to be asked of your own witnesses on direct. Nor are you going to ask them of your adversary's witnesses on cross.

The cardinal questions you must ask for every trial are:

What do I have to prove?

How will I prove it?

What is my adversary going to prove on his or her case?

How is my adversary going to prove his or her case?

These are not idle questions. Nor are they simplistic, sophomoric questions. These questions are at the heart, the essence, of any and every trial.

A HUMAN WITNESS IS NEEDED FOR EVERY IOTA

As you begin to answer the first of the cardinal questions, keep ever in mind that not an iota of evidence, other than that for which there is a stipulation or which is admitted by judicial notice, can be introduced into any trial without a live witness taking the stand and testifying to sufficient information (foundation) to introduce that evidence.

So the trial lawyer, having gained preliminary facts and information from his or her client, or from the witness(es) to an event, must analyze and gauge the overall picture of the case, the dimensions of it, and must then determine what the case is about, what has to be proven, what evidence shall be necessary to prove it, and, most important, what witnesses are available to introduce the testimony, documents, or evidence necessary to prove the case.

PLAINTIFF'S ADVOCATE MUST PROVE

Whether it is a civil or a criminal litigation, the person or entity who or which complains, who or which has a grievance, voices a wrong, or drafts the complaint is the plaintiff.

It is a matter of everyday knowledge that in a civil action, the party with the grievance or complaint is regularly called the plaintiff.

Equally so, the prosecutor in every criminal action represents a complainant, a plaintiff, whether that plaintiff is called the People, the government, the commonwealth, or whatever. That governmental entity is also a party-plaintiff.

And, regardless of whether it is a criminal or a civil case, it is the plaintiff who bears the burden of proof, that is, who must present sufficient evidence not only to establish the complaint but to establish that complaint to the extent of the weight of evidence prescribed by law.

Without sufficient evidence to sustain the particular burden of proof, at the end of the plaintiff's case a defense advocate will certainly move to dismiss the plaintiff's case for failure of proof. And, without so much as introducing a weather report, the defense shall take the day if the judge decides that, indeed, there has not been enough proof presented, enough meat to sustain a cause of action cognizable under the law.

DEFENSE ADVOCATE UN-PROVES

Once the plaintiff's advocate has successfully met his or her burden of making out a prima facie case—a case that, if not refuted or countered is sufficient to fulfill plaintiff's burden of proof and is sufficient to prove the defendant's liability—it then falls upon the defense advocate to undo and unmake, to dilute and lighten the weight of plaintiff's evidence.

You've often heard that the plaintiff has the burden of proof, the responsibility of proving a case, and that this burden never shifts to the defendant. This, of course, is true, whether the plaintiff's burden is beyond a reasonable doubt, as in a criminal case, or a preponderance of evidence, as in a civil case.

It is common to hear the Court's charge or admonition to a jury in a criminal case that the defendant needs do nothing, needs submit no evidence, needs not testify, or do anything else in the case. The full duty and responsibility to prove a case rests totally with the plaintiff/prosecutor. Failure of sufficient proof by the plaintiff/prosecutor is fatal to the case against the criminal defendant.

You civil practitioners might well remember that the same theory applies to civil cases. That is, it is the full burden of the plaintiff—somewhat less heavy, to be sure—to prove the case. The civil defendant, like the criminal defendant, needs do nothing, needs prove nothing, needs testify to nothing if the plaintiff fails in his or her burden of proof.

Remember, also, that if a prima facie case is proven by the plaintiff, though the defense advocate may be called upon to submit evidence, the thrust and aim of the defense case is not to prove a case, but to "un-prove" the plaintiff's case, to remove some of the weight of evidence that has been proffered by the plaintiff.

In short, the defense does not have the burden of proving anything. The defense has the burden of un-proving, of diminishing the weight or significance of the evidence submitted by the plaintiff. If successful, the defense's diminution or shrinking of the plaintiff's evidence leaves the plaintiff short of his or her burden or responsibility of proof.

The plaintiff may, of course, come forward again in rebuttal, not to add additional weight that might have been brought out on the plaintiff's direct case, but to counter the shrinking process of the defense, thus revitalizing the significance of the weight of evidence previously submitted sufficiently enough to still carry the day.

Of course, turn and turnabout being fair play, the defense is also given the opportunity to rediminish and reshrink the rebuttal case of the plaintiff in what is called the sur-rebuttal.

As in the defense case-in-chief, the sur-rebuttal is not to prove, but to disprove, to diminish, to dilute plaintiff's evidence. And just as the plaintiff's rebuttal is not a chance to put in evidence that which has been overlooked on the case in chief, the sur-rebuttal is only to counter what was put in by the plaintiff on rebuttal.

REBUTTAL—A LIMITED PURPOSE

So a trial is not an endless process of back-and-forth submissions of evidence, a plaintiff may not utilize rebuttal as an opportunity to submit evidence that should have been introduced on the direct case, a new and another bite at the apple. Rather, rebuttal is intended only to afford a plaintiff an opportunity to present evidence to counterbalance the shrinking and dilution effected by the defense during its turn at bat.

If a plaintiff attempts on rebuttal to add totally new weight to the case—new evidence, something that should have been done on the direct case—which evidence does not directly counterbalance something submitted by the defendant on defendant's case, a proper objection to the Court that such attempted submission is improper shall likely be sustained.

Anticipating a Rebuttal Is Permitted

While a plaintiff cannot introduce wholly new evidence on rebuttal that does not directly counter evidence submitted by the defense, such rule does not preclude plaintiff from anticipating, through careful, thoughtful analysis of the defense case, what the defense will necessarily present on its case and hold back some evidence from the direct case for use on rebuttal.

Of course, this is a calculated risk. For, if plaintiff's anticipation was incorrect, if the defense does not present the anticipated evidence, then that which was held in abeyance cannot be presented by plaintiff in counterpoint. No point was proffered to be countered, and the plaintiff cannot, therefore, introduce that which was held back.

Then again, however, if the defense didn't present the evidence that plaintiff anticipated, perhaps the defense put in a meager, shoddy case. In such circumstance, plaintiff probably doesn't need the extra arrow reserved for the coup de grace. But it doesn't hurt to analyze, anticipate, and be ready to counterattack.

Defendant's Sur-Rebuttal

It's been said that what's sauce for the goose, is also sauce for the gander. Therefore, the defense is also permitted an opportunity to rebalance the scales of evidence on sur-rebuttal.

But, again, the rules of evidence restrict any evidence submitted at this stage of the trial only to that which counters the evidence brought forward by the plaintiff on rebuttal.

Any attempt by the defense to submit new evidence that does not specifically and directly attack the plaintiff's rebuttal evidence, that could and should have been brought out on the defense's case, can properly be objected to. Usually, the Court shall sustain such an objection.

NOTE: A Court may in its discretion permit a plaintiff or a defendant to submit on rebuttal or sur-rebuttal further evidence that should ordinarily have been submitted on that party's case-in-chief.

In effect, the Court is permitting the party presenting such evidence to reopen his or her case.

Thus, if you forget something on your main case, and if it is essential to the outcome of the case, if it significantly affects the trial, you should have no hesitation whatever in requesting the Court to give you a further opportunity to reopen your case. The Court may, in the interest of justice, permit same.

Of course, your adversary is going to object. As you stand to make the application, remember that you miss a hundred percent of the birds at which you never take a shot.

TO DEVELOP A CASE YOU MUST KNOW THE LAW

I have previously mentioned the necessity of the Trial advocate knowing the law. And, you'll see, I'll repeat it often.

The witnesses that you have now interviewed have given you a wide-angle view of the entirety of the case. This view of the case has permitted you to ask yourself the cardinal trial questions enumerated earlier.

The answers to these cardinal questions shape the body of work that you have to do throughout the rest of the trial.

You cannot answer these cardinal questions, however, and you cannot determine what you have to prove, what your adversary has to prove, until you are fully aware of the latest law that governs the particular area of litigation into which this case falls.

In short, you cannot go forward another inch until you research the law.

Wait a second, you say, I'm not an appeals lawyer; I'm not one of those studious types who spends my time holding up books in the library. I'm a trial lawyer, a gun slinger. I want action, not books.

For a complete discussion of the necessity of the trial lawyer to master the law as well as the facts, see Chapter 5, infra. However, to permit us to continue our present discussion, you must instantly come to grips with the fact that litigation is not a mere compilation of facts and a jump in the water. Litigation is a very precise construction of facts within the specific requirements of the law. Without the law, you can't even begin to imagine what sort of fortress to construct.

PLAINTIFF ADVOCATES' CONSIDERATIONS

As he or she researches the law for the particular case at hand, the advocate for the plaintiff must determine what legal theory has been violated and what redress the law provides to recompense his or her client.

To those would-be advocates who shudder at the thought of having to crack a book, who want only to grab a file to go into Court, who want to stand in front of judge or jury to display virtuoso trial techniques with only silvered tongue and golden words standing between their clients and the juggernaut of the law, be advised that your wits and your tongue alone are not sufficient protection for your client.

Indeed, you might very well be committing malpractice to attempt to represent a client without being fully prepared and conversant with the latest developments in the law.

You cannot be an excellent trial advocate without being an excellent *lawyer.* There is no such thing as a nonlawyer advocate.

Lawsuits are fought within the parameters of the law. It would be a dreadful pity, indeed, to dissipate all that marvellous virtuoso energy you are confident you have, slashing and hacking a path through the jungle of facts, only to find that you have forged a path to an abandoned site, an outmoded fortress, teetering on a precipice overlooking a vast wasteland.

WHAT MUST I PROVE?

What the plaintiff's advocate must prove is easy.

You must prove every element of the cause of action or crime that you have alleged in the charging or accusatory instrument.

Moreover, every element of every cause of action or charge contained in the charging instrument must be proven to that measure required by the civil or penal law, to wit, by a preponderance of evidence in the civil law or beyond a reasonable doubt in the criminal law.

THE CHARGING INSTRUMENT

The real, and far more difficult question to answer, therefore, is not what must I, plaintiff's advocate, prove, but what causes of action, what crimes shall I include in the charging instrument?

The answers to these questions shall shape the entire litigation for all time. And the answers to these questions come from your overview of the facts, the research of the law that you've completed, and from the availability of witnesses or evidence you have with which to prove sufficient facts to support those anticipated elements of the charge that you are going to include in your charging instrument or complaint.

Remember, it is not what you wish, will, want, desire to prove that may be permitted to control the charging instrument. What controls what you put in the charging instrument is what you shall, factually and objectively, be able to prove, based upon the potential evidence that is, or shall be, available.

Litigation is not made up of wishes or dreams. True, it may be formed along the lines of what the courageous litigator sees the law ought to be, what the law is evolving into or is tending to be, based upon the most recent decided cases that have come down from the appeal Courts.

But while litigation may have novel theory as its form, those theories must be supported with hard evidence, facts, witnesses, documents, exhibits to pass the muster standards that are being enunciated by those appeal Courts.

In short, the evidence that you have available to you, as it jibes with the known or currently forming body of law on this issue, is the ultimate arbiter of what charges or causes of action are to be included in the charging instrument. If you can't prove the elements of the charge you wish to level at the defendant, then don't charge that violation of the law. Restrain yourself now, or the Court will dismiss the charge at a later date for failure of evidence.

Contrapuntally, the elements of those charges or causes of action that you have envisioned to include in the charging instrument determine or frame what it is that you have to prove, what facts are needed to prove your anticipated case.

In choosing what causes of action, what charges, to include in the charging instrument, therefore, you must work with what factually exists, the rules of evidence, the current law.

For example, if a homicide occurs but there are no witnesses, just a dead body and a pistol on the ground next to it, without something more, without an Admission, without forensic evidence of some sort, there may be no possibility whatever—despite your suspicions—despite the very real fact that there is a dead body in the morgue—to form a charging instrument against the suspected perpetrator.

Take the same body; take away the pistol. Throw in the fact that you have several witnesses who can attest to the fact that the deceased had been in a bar, drinking heavily with a buddy. After a while, the two men had some hot words. The two, the deceased and his or her buddy, stepped out into the street for a convivial fistfight. Someone passing by sees a fist fight, sees one man strike the other; one falls, one runs. The passerby can identify the clothing of the person he saw running from the scene. People in the bar positively identify the two men, including the clothing they were wearing. The dead body is positively identified as one of the two men.

It may not be an airtight case, but it certainly seems to tend toward a provable case of involuntary homicide. The prosecutor might think about charging intentional murder—but it doesn't appear from the above factual pattern that such a charge is appropriate. The prosecutor would be better off not reaching too far beyond the evidence just to have a gravely serious charging instrument.

As we all know, a charging instrument is just an allegation, an accusation; it is not evidence, and it does not become evidence merely by reducing it to writing. You're better to charge what you can prove, and prove it, than to overcharge, only to end up standing in front of a jury with a baseless piece of paper.

Go back to the first set of circumstances recited earlier: The sole evidence is the body and the pistol. Add that the deceased's brother-in-law had been in town that day, threatening to kill the deceased the moment that he saw him, displaying a pistol that looked very much like the weapon found on the street. Add the fact that the brother-in-law was seen immediately after the homicide driving from town at very high speed. Perhaps now, by circumstantial evidence, a charge of intentional murder may reasonably lie.

A man is walking along a busy thoroughfare. A tire of a passing car runs over a large steel bolt that had fallen into the middle of the street from another vehicle that had coursed along the same road moments before. By catching the edge of the bolt, the tire of the second car causes the bolt to flip into the air, striking the passerby in the eye, causing him to be blind in one eye.

Very substantial injury, but no liable person or entity. What can be charged in the charging instrument? Certainly nothing against the second motorist who did not see the bolt, nor cause it to be in the street. The driver of that vehicle had no notice or even awareness of the bolt being in the street.

Now, add the fact that the local utility company had men working in the street all day. The workers had folded their tents only moments before the event. Tired after a day's work, one of the workers left several similar bolts right next to the manhole (person-hole) in which the workers had been working. Because of its unique configuration, the bolt is clearly identifiable as the property of the utility company. Do you have at least a colorable cause of action now? Of course. Not against the motorist whose tire flipped the bolt in the air, but against the utility company.

Thus, the facts form the charging instrument. The elements of the charges contained in the charging instrument form what you have to prove.

HOW WILL I PROVE THOSE ELEMENTS?

Once you have resolved the answer to the first cardinal question, you have to answer the second: How will I prove the elements?

This question may be more difficult to answer than the first. You now have to determine how you can prove each element that composes the cause of action that you, as plaintiff's advocate, have decided to pursue.

But decide you must, now, even before the charging instrument is drawn.

You cannot wait until later to decide how you are going to prove the case. It is not enough just to want to bring the case, the cause of action. You must decide before you plead a cause of action if, indeed, you can prove it.

If you can't prove it, don't plead it.

And before you plead it, you must, step by step, in your mind and in your Trial Book, lay out the steps you will take, the witnesses you will call, the documents you will use, the exhibits you will introduce, to prove the case you are about to allege.

Remember, unless there is a stipulation, a self-authenticating document, or the Court takes judicial notice, no evidence whatever, not a photograph, not a document, not a bumper or bumper sticker gets in evidence without some human being taking the witness chair and articulating, through your deft questioning, a testimonial foundation for the introduction of that item of evidence.

What do I have to prove, therefore, can be replaced as the operative question by another question: Which witness can I call to the stand to prove this element of the case; whom can I call to introduce that piece of physical or documentary evidence?

You must have answers to these questions or you do not have a law suit that you can prove.

WHAT MUST MY ADVERSARY PROVE?

Once you have determined what you have to prove on *your* case-in-chief, and the witnesses or means by which you are going to prove it, you have still two more cardinal questions to answer, two more steps to undertake and resolve in your preliminary analysis of the litigation.

The third cardinal question is: What must my adversary prove? You must determine what it is that your adversary must necessarily or will probably prove, what he or she will introduce to counter, to dilute, and to minimize your evidence.

Your purpose in doing the analysis of your adversary's defense, of course, is to countermove in advance, eliminating as much weakness from your case as possible *before* you even draw the charging instrument.

In the case of a defense advocate, the case analysis is done in reverse. You already know what the plaintiff intends to prove. You have the charging instrument. Still, you must analyze that charging instrument and determine what your adversary necessarily must prove and how, more than likely, he or she shall prove it. Defense counsel must then determine what evidence shall have to be produced to diminish, to dilute, and to undermine the plaintiff's evidence. It is only after the defense advocate determines what his or her adversary's case is all about and what the adversary must necessarily prove that the defense can undertake to counter and to parry that evidentiary thrust.

To determine what your adversary is going to prove is fairly simple. Put yourself in your adversary's place. Determine what it is that you, or any, advocate would have to prove to support the opposite case. What are the elements of the opposite case? What are the points of law that apply?

After all, there are finite and specific elements that have to be proven to support any theory of law. The law, although ever changing, is fairly measurable as it relates to any particular issue on any particular day. Moreover, the facts are also fairly measurable, the avenues of defense are finite, the number and names of witnesses are imaginable and ascertainable. Determine what you would do to undermine the plaintiff's case if you were your adversary; what law, what facts would you bring to bear?

Once you do this, you shall know what your adversary is more than likely going to try to prove.

HOW IS MY ADVERSARY GOING TO PROVE HIS CASE?

Once you make an educated determination about your adversary's case, what he will likely attempt to introduce to counter your case, you then have to determine what evidence he is going to use to prove that case.

It's not hard. Think of what witnesses must be brought in—by your adversary, by yourself, by anyone—to support the proofs that face your adversary.

Sure, there are several possible combinations to prove each element. Okay. Think of what those combinations are. You can't specify precisely what your adversary is going to do. But you can surely make an intelligent estimate of just what is going to be done to prove the opposite case. What stipulations might your adversary request? What items of Judicial Notice will he probably request? What documents will self-authenticate?

Since you are investigating the same case, since the witnesses to a case are equally determinable, available, and investigable by both sides, with diligence you can determine what both sides of the case are about, regardless of which side you represent.

PLAN A REBUTTAL

Once you have determined not only what you are going to do, but also what your adversary necessarily must do, either in the first instance, in presenting the plaintiff's case, or to counter your case, you have to prepare a third step: counterattack; the rebuttal and the sur-rebuttal.

Do you recall previously, when I first mentioned the function of the rebuttal, I indicated that it was not a second bite at the apple, it was not an opportunity to put in evidence that which you overlooked on your case-in-chief? Recall that I also indicated, however, if you could anticipate what your adversary was going to do on the defense case, you could hold back from your case-in-chief some facts or evidence that would counter your adversary's evidence; in other words, save ammunition for the second assault you know may come.

THE TRAP

In football, there is a play called the Trap. As part of the strategy of this play, the offensive linemen set themselves in what seems to be an ordinary formation. When the play begins, however, one of the offense tackles or guards permits himself to be pushed inward, as if succumbing to the strength of his defensive counterpart. But this is a purposeful plan. As soon as the defensive man has exploded through the offensive line, thinking that he is overcoming a weakness in the offense, another offense player blocks the intruder to the side, thus opening a hole in the defense behind the onrushing player who was permitted to rush into the Trap. This leaves daylight and running room for the play that was calculated to be run through the hole created by shunting the invading defenseman to the side.

In advocacy, you can use the Trap as part of your trial strategy. While putting together whatever case you are going to present, let an area of your proposed presentation appear somewhat vulnerable. You know there is a counterargument. But purposely, don't play that card just yet. Wait until your adversary attacks the point and rushes armed with the argument of which you were aware; then cut that argument away with the counterpoint that you've saved.

Don't let the Trap appear too obvious a weakness, lest your adversary realizes that there must be a reason you are exposing that flank to his or her attack. You want your adversary to think that he or she has outthought you and cleverly discovered a weakness in your case. In this way, your adversary concentrates a good portion of his or her attack at precisely the point that *you* wanted, that you've planned, the point for which you already have the rebuttal answer and the countermove.

This legal Trap-play is not available in every case and in every situation. But look for it. You may find you can employ such strategy during preliminary motions, hearings, or during the trial itself. The reason you look to utilize such Trap strategy is that when you erect a uniformly solid fortification, a solid wall of evidence or argument for your adversary to attack, he or she may just blunder about, slashing in this direction or that, probing for any weakness that might be lurking somewhere, anywhere.

If you don't know where your adversary is likely to attack, you must dissipate your energy defending against any and all attacks, on all points of the perimeter of your case.

On the other hand, if you can attract your adversary to a point that must be attacked, for which he can find cases, a defense, your adversary must concentrate some—not all—of his or her energy in that area. If your adversary doesn't attack the vulnerable point you've put forward, then he or she loses the point by default. Anytime you can make your adversary lose a point by default or use his or her energy defending a spot you can victoriously counterattack, you are in the advantage; you are controlling the show.

Don't let your poor adversary blunder about looking for a weakness. Give him some grist for his mill. Let him cleverly discover the weakness you have apparently overlooked or misargued. Let him attack it. You have drawn the fire where you want it; you have drawn the bees to the poisoned honey.

YOU CAN BE PRETTY DARN SURE

True, an advocate can't know precisely what avenue, street, or route her adversary will take when putting together her direct case or during her rebuttal case. But you can be darn sure where she must end up, what her destination must be. After all, you are both involved in the same lawsuit. The issues are framed. Neither you nor your adversary can go wandering around two totally different areas of the countryside. You are involved in the same lawsuit, and the Court is going to restrict you to the issues that have been joined, albeit from opposite sides.

If you don't know precisely who or what your adversary is going to present to support her side of the case, be prepared for all eventualities. The routes or avenues in any lawsuit are limited. Usually there can't be *that* many alternatives. Fathom each one. Narrow them down logically. How would you do it? How else can it be done? And then be prepared for each eventuality.

If the particular case permits, try to sucker your opponent to attack an obvious weakness that you prepared in advance to defend. Such a move may not entirely carry the day, but it is psychologically beneficial—both to help shape the judge's and the jury's view of your adversary and to shake your adversary's confidence—if you can really buckle her knees from time to time on some issues.

The adversary who begins to trickle blood from the nose may not be mortally wounded, but she loses some concentration from her attack, opening herself, therefore, to other attacks.

And now, you say, what is this, a game or a serious legal matter? You'll be far better off if you consider a trial a little bit of each.

5

INVESTIGATION

VISIT THE SCENE; READ THE DOCUMENT

Depending on the particular case, there is either a scene to visit, documents to read, or some further reading and investigation that must be done at this point.

I find it preferable to undertake this further probing of the circumstances of the case *after* interviewing at least some of the witnesses. In this way, you will already be somewhat familiar with the case; you will know where and at what you should look.

If there are only documents to be read, now is the time to read them. Don't read them as if they were a novel, quickly, skimming across the pages, using your speed-reading technique. Peruse and study the documents. Immerse yourself in their meaning. This is where the case lives. And it is only by knowing each aspect of the underlying facts that you will be able to field whatever balls are going to be hit at you.

THERE IS MORE THAN ONE WAY TO INTERPRET WHAT YOUR EYES CAN PLAINLY SEE

Be alert to the fact that there is more than one approach to the litigation. If there weren't, there wouldn't be a litigation in the first place. So don't be hidebound to only one possible way in which even clear words, printed black on white paper, can be interpreted. Lawyers are amazing in their capacity to divine several meanings from the same simple words, the same simple event.

If there is a scene or place of occurrence to go to, go there. Familiarize yourself with the physical layout of where the event took place. Consider all the different possible ways in which the event could have taken place. Consider each different scenario. Try each one out in your mind. Any that are feasible are possible scenarios against which you must prepare.

LITIGATION FOLLOWS THE PATH OF IRRESISTIBILITY

It's a funny, but predictable thing. Lawsuits seem, eventually, to follow the path of irresistibility, *not necessarily the path of reality.*

Recently, a female client called our office after having been involved in a minor traffic accident. She had been stopped at a red light, behind a truck. All of a sudden, the truck *backed* up, right into the front of our client's car. It appears that the driver of the truck may have proceeded too far into the pedestrian crosswalk when he stopped at the red light. In attempting to retreat out of the designated pedestrian area, the truck driver momentarily failed to appreciate that another vehicle might have been behind him.

As the client explained what had occurred, she indicated that the driver of the truck was very apologetic, indicating that he "just had to back up," and that he was sorry to have caused the damage sustained by the client. Further, the client explained how passersby had reproved the driver for having caused the damage to our client's car by backing up.

I asked the client if she had waited for the police to arrive to make a report. She said she had not. I asked her if she took the names of witnesses who had reproved the truck driver. She said she had not. I advised her that by the time that this lawsuit was filtered through the hands of an insurance adjuster, was prepared for trial or settlement, the story would most likely—irresistibly—be modified to the effect that our client caused the accident by driving into the rear of the truck.

The client told me that was impossible. That was not the way it happened. The driver and, afterward, the owner of the truck—whom the client had called to get further information about insurance, and so forth—acknowledged responsibility.

Wait and see, said I, wait and see.

And, of course, as any of you who are reading these words already know, by the time the lawyers representing the insurance company got their hands on the case, the entire flavor of the case changed dramatically.

The client had become the malefactor, the transgressor; she had driven into the back of the truck....

DON'T BE SUCKERED OUT OF POSITION BY REALITY

Wasn't the change of the focus of the minor traffic accident above recited obvious from the outset?

Perhaps it wouldn't be to a layperson. But it would be to a lawyer who had been to town before. And, perhaps, the very fact that advocates can so easily see the obvious interpretation of the litigation by other advocates, indeed, find it predictable and, what's more, irresistible is a condemnation of the legal profession, a condemnation of the morality of lawyers. Perhaps it is.

Or is it merely an instant distillation and recognition of the foibles of humanity? Is the thought process that leads a lawyer inevitably to the ultimate logic that will be adopted by an adversary peculiar solely to lawyers? Or are the thought processes of a lawyer merely a direct skewing to the working of the human mind, a recognition of the way in which people justify their actions in everyday, common thought? Remember, advocates do not testify to the facts in court. They do not get up on the stand and introduce the evidence. They are the Virgils, not the Dantes. So the totality of the warping of reality in the cauldron of the courtroom and the lawsuit cannot become the total responsibility of the lawyers.

This discourse is not a philosophical dissertation on human nature. It is intended to open your eyes to possibilities. Thus, when you visit the scene of an event or read the documents about which the controversy revolves, armed with the statements supplied by your client or other witnesses you have previously interviewed, leave some room for appreciating where the litigation may ultimately flow, where the situs might change or move, where the events may be played out—REGARDLESS OF WHERE THE EVENT ACTUALLY TOOK PLACE.

THERE ARE TWO (2) REALITIES

Perhaps it should be put another way. There are two realities: the one of the world outside the courtroom and the other, the world inside the courtroom.

If, indeed, a witness were to describe your client as having green hair and purple skin, and the jury were to accept the testimony of that witness, then, for the purposes of the world within the courtroom, your client does have green hair and purple skin.

The world inside the courtroom does not necessarily comport to reality.

Recently, in a rape case, DNA blood-testing testimony ruled out the defendant as a possible perpetrator of the sexual assault on the victim. The victim, however, was a woman who made a good appearance, spoke softly and weepily of the tragic events—there were six women in the jury—and was quite clear in identifying the defendant as the person who had sexually abused her.

Conviction!

The jury believed the victim, regardless of the physical reality.

Therefore, look around for every possibility. Don't be closed-minded. See everything, including the fact that your client or the witnesses, whether purposely or inadvertently, may not have recalled exactly what occurred or how it occurred. Don't lock yourself into one set of facts, one locale, one anything. View the entire case and prepare for all the possible areas of attack.

PHOTOGRAPH THE SCENE

There are many truisms that are often disparagingly referred to as hackneyed clichés. In actuality, these sayings or phrases may be considered clichés by those who have failed to heed the message deduced from the many mistakes of past generations, or by persons who have a Pollyanna view of humanity as being far more worthy, sophisticated, and intellectually progressed than is the actual condition.

These clichés have lasted over ages of human vicissitudes because they have some real and abiding application to the human condition. Perhaps that which should truly be called hackneyed is the continuing discounting of prior events or experience, the entire human past, by "modern," forward thinkers as not quite as meritorious or advanced as is the current experience. In Ecclesiastes it was indicated that the more things change, the more they remain the same. We have hardly progressed except in our packaging of things. And even that keeps moving backwards.

Now for our cliché.

A picture is worth a thousand words, or a thousand trips to the scene, for more reasons than one.

When you have photographs of the scene—preferably from several different angles—you can readily and conveniently revisit the scene by hauling out the pictures to verify physical details that may come into question during future interviews of other witnesses.

Additionally, these photographs will be extremely helpful in focusing and refreshing the recollection of witnesses during interviews.

Moreover, the photographs may be very helpful to have in the office or at home as you toil through the night to find new approaches based on newly discovered or previously unnoticed details in the photographs.

And, most significantly, the photographs will "psych" your adversary and the party(ies) on the other side when they realize how prepared you are. More on this, anon.

ENLARGE AND MOUNT THE IMPORTANT VIEWS

After the photographs are developed, select the important pictures, those views that best represent the scene or scenes of the occurrence, views that will best capture for the jury the essence of how the scene looked at the time in question.

Have those important views enlarged to at least 8"x10" for better and closer inspection of the scene by yourself, your investigator, your associates, your client, and the prospective witnesses.

In addition, have the best, the real essence-of-the-event photographs enlarged further, perhaps to 11"x14", and have them mounted on cardboard for utilization during EBTs, court conferences, and the trial.

The effect of these enlargements is significant. Preparation reaps great benefits, particularly in your own psychological confidence that you are prepared and that you have, amongst other things, photographs of every aspect of the scene. You can assure yourself that no witness can be presented at the trial to describe any aspect of the scene or its environs for which you do not have a photograph to stem the creative imaginations of a witness who might have a tendency to ramble all over reality unless checked by the display of a photograph.

In other words, your photographs can limit the damage that might be done by a rambling description of the scene or some aspect of the case, given by a witness unfettered by photographs.

Moreover, the psychological effect on your adversary, and even on the Court, may have great benefit in your quests for success.

PSYCHING THE OTHER SIDE

I have already mentioned that there is significant psychology involved in litigation. If the other side—whether it be your adversary or his or her client—is awed by you or your client (okay, impressed is sufficient)—you have another potent factor working for you. The other side's mental set, the way they view you, your client, or your case may go a long way in carrying a day for you, or at least influencing that day significantly.

Thus, in addition to your sheer talent and desire to win—which is obvious from the fact that you're reading this book—if you can garner your adversary's respectful view of your talent, you'll have a veritable dynamic duo of factors working toward your ultimate success, that is, your talent and your adversary's respect thereof.

Get the psychology factor working in the litigation as soon as possible. At the first opportunity, haul out your enlarged and mounted photographs of the scene, say at a deposition or Examination Before Trial (EBT). This display, in addition to the benefit of having them available for specific use during that deposition, instantly alerts your adversary that you and your case are well prepared, are going to be even more prepared at the trial—this is only a sampling of what's coming—and that they are in for one hell of a fight.

The use of the photographs at an EBT, as I've indicated, is not only for the psychological effect. Far from it. When deposing a witness, utilize the photograph to tie down his or her story, to tie him or her down to a particular location, to tie down the events to the actual physical setting. However damaging the adverse witness's testimony might be, it is most important to tie down the events to one location to keep matters from getting worse.

When isolated by a photograph, the situs of any event can no longer shift around like mere words in the air, floating about or changed in an attempt to escape the sharp point of your cross-examining épée as it begins to unravel a witness's account of the event.

Tying down the witness at the outset, at an EBT, is a major benefit to your case. You know what the witness is talking about. You know, therefore, what you're talking about. And the witness is bound to a story and a location for that story for the rest of the litigation.

HAVE THE PHOTOGRAPHS MARKED AND INITIALED

In order to be sure that the witness has been securely restricted to one location, one locale for the significant events he or she describes at the EBT or deposition, have the photographs physically "marked" for identification (on the back of the photograph, of course) and then have the witness view the marked and identified photograph and duly note for the record specifically where in the photograph the particular event he or she is describing took place. Have the witness mark the spot, put his or her initials there. The witness is now stuck with that story, that place. And you know where you are.

You have effectively tied the witness and your adversary down to one story, one location, and it is going to be very difficult for them to vary down the line.

Some advocates may think that as a result of the careful specifying and marking of the photographs not only is the adversary tied down to that story, so are you. True. But it is far better to know the particular poison that you face and to look for an antidote than to guess where the situs may eventually turn out to be and to face a floating situs that can change at the drop of a word or two.

HAVE DUPLICATE PHOTOS MADE

At the trial, you might use a clean and unmarked copy of the photograph that had been displayed at the deposition. Keep the deposition exhibit nearby. But use a clean, fresh copy for the trial. And, at that trial, have the witness again identify the photograph and locate the event. Who knows, you may have the witness caught in a discrepancy, a variation, and may have amassed more ammunition for your attack.

If they make the same identification, locate the event exactly the same as previously, no harm. If they do it differently, you have a prior inconsistency with which to work.

No, you don't HAVE to do it with duplicates. It's just a suggestion that may work under the right conditions.

COURTS CAN BE PSYCHED TOO

In addition to using your photographs at EBTs and depositions, bring your photographs to conferences with the Court, on a motion, or on a preliminary housekeeping conference. In this way, the Court has the opportunity to see how well prepared you are, are going to be, and just how formidable your case is.

Such an impression will be helpful to you as you and your adversary attempt to settle or resolve the case. This applies to criminal as well as to civil cases.

As Courts are always interested in clearing their calendar and easing their workload, when they see a case that lends itself to settlement and resolution, one that is obviously going badly for your adversary as a result of your great preparation, the Court will—during future conferences—directly or indirectly display its feelings toward the hopelessness of your adversary's resistance to your overwhelming onslaught. Your adversary will get the message. He will know that other people see your case in the same light as he fears they will. When so august a personage as the trial judge is already impressed (read psyched) by you and your case, your adversary begins to feel less secure, less confident.

Now, I'm not suggesting that the mere taking of photographs is going to win the case for you. No. But, it is part of the preparation, inter alia, that can certainly send out the message that this case is being prepared to death, that you're going to be ready, that you're not leaving a stone unturned.

> ***A NOTE:*** *If the photographs make you realize that your case isn't as formidable as you thought it was, then taking and enlarging the photographs has yet another salutary effect. It makes you see your case for what it is—one way or the other.*

JUDGES AND ADVERSARIES REMEMBER

When you impress—psych—the Court and your adversary in one case, be assured that the Court and the adversary will remember you in the next case, the next time that you come into contact with each other.

The impression that you make on both the Court and your adversary will continue. Thus, you'd better favorably, formidably impress those with whom you come in contact during the litigation for you're going to have to be practicing in the jurisdiction a long time. One case is only a case, but more than likely you're going to be in contact with these people throughout your career. Be a lazy creature, or a sleaze, and the Court and your adversary will remember when you pass their way again.

Conversely, just think of the benefit, when they hear your name, that they know instantly that here comes a fighter, a preparer, a *real* trial advocate.

PROBE ON

Now you have interviewed your client and the other witnesses. You have visited the scene. You have photographed the scene. You have enlarged and even had some of the photographs mounted. What next?

Next, you have to get into those details that your gross examination of the case has revealed need further checking, further probing.

For example, you've seen in the photographs that all the parked cars on the street are facing in one direction. It appears to be a one-way street. This is such a simple matter for a layman. But in a Court, to establish that a street was a one-way street on a particular day is another matter altogether.

Was it a one-way street on the day of the occurrence? How will you find out? And, if it was, how do you get that fact into evidence? In addition, you see in one of the photographs that there is, right over the site of the occurrence, a street lamp. Was it working the day of the occurrence?

None of these answers, positive or negative, can prove themselves. Some evidence must be introduced, with proper foundation, to establish each of the just-mentioned items, as well as any other fact that you wish the jury to consider.

Remember what was said in earlier chapters: Nothing is received in evidence except if some human being can be called to the stand to testify about that something, to lay the foundation for documentary evidence.

In other words, you can't establish the weather on the day of the occurrence by just telling the jury, "Oh, by the way, the weather was rainy on April 15, 1989."

You can't prove to the jury that the street was a one-way street, by your telling them that it was. You can't show that the light over the scene was working on the day in question, even if you talk to the Bureau of Streets and Highways in your local jurisdiction and are told so, merely by recounting your conversation with the highway superintendent. You must not only uncover the fact but be able to establish that fact by proper evidence and live witnesses.

Yes, yes, there are some exceptions. If you can stipulate to certain facts, if the Court takes Judicial Notice of certain facts, if certain documents fall within the ambit of being "self-authenticating," you will not need a human body on the stand to do the introducing. Those exceptions, however, will not cover the vast majority of what you have to put in evidence. So now what?

FOR THE MOMENT, KEEP PROBING

Keep asking questions. Keep looking at the photographs. Keep reading the documents. Keep probing deeper into the underlying facts of the case, until you have a working familiarity with the entire fabric of the case.

Now that you have a layperson's knowledge of the facts, you have to begin working them into a trial fabric. And a trial fabric for a lawyer is quite different from a layman's view of the trial fabric. Quite different.

For in order for the facts now to be formed into the shape necessary for trial you have to:

research the substantive law;

determine what you must prove;

determine the applicable rules of evidence;

determine what evidence you will need;

determine which witnesses best suit your strategy; and, most important of all,

round up those witnesses and get their statements into writing.

HOW DO I WANT TO PROVE THE FACTS?

Well, by now you have surmised that the weather report can be introduced in evidence by obtaining a self-authenticating weather report from the National Weather Bureau or the local branch of the weather bureau. So that is *one way* you can get into evidence what the weather was like.

But, is that the way you want to prove the particular fact?

There may be several ways by which to prove a fact. For example, the weather. You can prove it with a self-authenticating weather report. Or, you can subpoena someone from the weather bureau and have him or her testify. Or, you can have your client testify about the weather. Or, you can have some other, independent witness testify about the weather.

After your search for facts, you must begin on an entirely new quest, not for what evidence there is, but for how you get it into the evidence to be presented to the jury—how do you get certain facts into evidence?

And, not insignificantly, if there are several alternatives, *which* alternative will reap the best results for you?

6

Researching the Law

Making it look easy is hard work

As was said earlier, it is romantic to think of being a consummate, lightning-fast trial slinger like Paladin, the character in the old TV series *Have Gun, Will Travel.* Just give me the file and I'll walk right up to the Bar and try any case.

If you want to make trying a case look as easy as that, you have to work very hard. The more you work, the easier the trial or hearing will be. The more you work, the more armament you have assembled, but hidden, the more casually confident you can appear.

But if a lawyer's casual attitude is exactly that, a casual serenity born out of a total ignorance of the dangers or difficulties ahead, that lawyer's client is going into court totally disarmed, disoriented, and deceived.

That old abandoned path

You can't just take a file and walk right up to the Bar. Not without *actually* knowing that the legal path along which you intend to travel is still open, still viable, still valid.

Our system of jurisprudence is alive, ever changing, dynamic. Appeals courts are handing down new decisions every day in every jurisdiction. If you don't think so, just look at the shelves of your case law books, or the shelves of your nearest law library. See how they grow!

Yet, there are those would-be advocates who refuse to look at the advance sheets, the slip-sheets. These are the lawyers who think that once they've graduated law school and passed the Bar, they're set for life as far as studying is concerned. All of you know just such a lawyer. The simple fact is that lawyer is never going to be a fine advocate. It just can't be done that way.

A good trial advocate need not be a fine appellate lawyer, need not be able to write a final brief for the Supreme Court of the United States. But he or she *must* know the law.

You cannot possibly hope to take up arms to defend your client's interests, to ferry his or her cause across a sea of trouble, if you do not know the latest direction in which the appeals courts have chartered the particular body of law involved in the case at Bar.

You must keep up with the latest law to be a trial attorney. I repeat this again, because those would be trial attorneys who hate research, who hate looking in the books, but who consider themselves quick on their feet, agile, articulate enough to handle cases without looking at the books, are committing malpractice.

Oh, yes!

Think of a doctor, a surgeon. Think of this surgeon as he or she thinks lawyers think of doctors—as a fit subject of a lawsuit for some act of misfeasance, malfeasance, nonfeasance.

If a client came to you to tell you that a surgeon had performed an operation but had not read a book or an article in a medical journal since she got out of medical school, had not utilized, had not even been aware of the latest techniques of modern surgery, you would be ready to flay the surgeon, literally prepared to slice off her skin for that act of blatant malpractice.

Would you consider as a valid excuse that the new technique was in use for only one year? Would you advise your client to forbear suing the surgeon because the technique the surgeon had used had been the normal method of performing the particular operation *until* the new, totally revised method was discovered and used by other surgeons? Would you be impressed with the logic that the new technique was written only in specialized medical journals intended for surgeons, and this particular surgeon was so busy cutting people that she hadn't had time to read the issue that included the article on the new technique?

Hell, no!

Let's go further. Is it acceptable for a pediatrician—who never performs surgery—not to keep up with the latest pediatric surgical procedures? Would you as trial counsel to your clients not hold liable the family pediatrician who was unaware of the latest surgical procedures, who was not sufficiently versed in pediatric surgery to be able to advise his patients' parents as to whether or not the advice of a pediatric surgeon was proper or would be necessary or beneficial for their child.

You can bet your briefs you'd put the name of the family pediatrician on the caption of the malpractice suit right next to that of the surgeon.

How then, could any trial lawyer worth any amount of salt not be up on the law? What excuse is there for such a disinclination to know what is absolutely essential? The answer is simple. There is no excuse—none whatever.

THE APPEALS COURTS CHANGE PROCEDURE, TOO

Please spare yourself the convenient logic that as a trial lawyer you don't have to know every aspect of every bit of the substantive law; that you can steep yourself in the particular substantive law involved in a trial on an as-needed basis.

The appeals courts are not only, each day, handing down decisions that change the substantive law. In procedural law, the rules of evidence are constantly being changed, modified, distinguished, and eliminated as well.

> What are collateral matters; when can you inquire into collateral matters?
>
> When can you inquire into prior bad acts; prior similar acts?
>
> Despite being hearsay, when can you, nevertheless, inquire about certain nonparty statements?
>
> Can you, or can you not, impeach your own witness?

Even if you know the answers to the preceding questions today, that doesn't guarantee that the highest court in your jurisdiction hasn't reinterpreted the rules governing such procedures yesterday, that the rules won't change today as a result of the latest decisions from appeals courts.

And you can't be a success as yesterday's lawyer. You must be today's lawyer, ready to champion your client with today's applicable law. You can't rest on your laurels here. If you want to, if you insist on being a seat-of-the-pants trial lawyer, stay home. Do your client a favor. Don't take his or her case.

It doesn't change that fast

From time immemorial, the law has been known not to move precipitously. It moves, but not with spasms or fits and starts, prodded by whims and fancies. Not all the time, anyway. "The laws delay" is of Shakespearean vintage, and that's not the first reference to the stealth with which the law overtakes the currency of thought.

Thus, there's plenty of time for those with sufficient interest to keep up with the latest outpourings of the appellate courts. For those who refuse, who do not deign to do so, there is no time whatever.

Change the law yourself

If you are up on the law and come into contact with an area of resistance, a legal theorem that you believe is illogical, out of date, not in keeping with contemporary knowledge or thinking, then tilt at it, fight to change it.

How can you change the law yourself? Once you are keeping up with the law, you may find that the law should go further in a particular area. This usually occurs when you have a case and you cannot find the law to support where you think it should go to protect your client.

If you can get there by logical, legally tenable step upon step, then you should be able to put together a legal argument, based upon precedent, logic, and knowledge to support your position.

For example, in more ancient times—not that long ago—the law did not provide for recovery for injuries to infants *en ventre sa mere*, injuries to unborn fetuses who were not *in esse* at the time of the incident.

Upon the advancement of medical knowledge, it became clear that a fetus, after six or seven months, could be plucked from the womb of an injured mother and nurtured outside the womb. In short, the unborn fetus *was* a being *in esse* at the time of such injury, requiring only nurture and shelter to grow into full bloom. Thus, the law in effect at the time of the above medical discovery had to progress, had to move forward, to provide recovery for this being *in esse* who was merely yet unborn.

The lawyer who was ultimately successful in bringing about the change from nonrecovery to recovery for such an unborn being *in esse* had to mount a fight against a bulwark of outmoded law. But obviously there was a change made, based upon advancement in thinking, supported by logical legal tenet.

Subsequently, medical knowledge advanced yet again. It was determined that all that a person shall be is passed on to the fetus at the very moment, the instant of conception. All the attributes, intelligence, coloring, ultimate height, ultimate weight, ultimate everything of the being are genetically fixed for all time at the instant of conception. The mother, thereafter, provides only shelter and nurture to the fetus. The fetus, in turn, with shelter and nurture will grow into an adult human being.

Is not the fetus, therefore, a being *in esse* at the very moment of conception, lacking only shelter and nurture to grow into an adult human? Under such medical and factual reality, should there not be recovery for any injury to any fetus, no matter at what time in gestation such injury occurs?

The intrepid and innovative advocate, armed with knowledge and the legal principle of logical progression supported by precedent, may be able to convince a Court at *nisi prius*, or an appellate Court, that further advance is necessary and proper.

But, you can't advance to the next step of the law if you don't even know where the law is today. Thus, you must know the law. Study the law. And then you can become, or hope to become, a great and innovative advocate.

> ***A PUZZLEMENT:*** *If, indeed, a person driving a car and striking a 20-week pregnant woman might be liable to that unborn being in esse for injuries sustained, does then the Court, as Parens Patriae, have an obligation to protect the continued existence of that being in esse independent of the individual preference of the pregnant woman?*

Clever Advocates Versus Knowledge

There are those, as they read these very words, who believe that the above admonition about knowing the law is for others, not for them. These are the geniuses who readily believe that they are cleverer than clever, that they are too swift to be left at the gate holding their briefs; that their cerebral legerdemain will carry them through whatever.

Wrong!

The most inarticulate adversary, unkempt and hardly able to make himself understood, armed with the latest decision from the appellate Court that shows, as a result of a decision last week in the appellate Court, that your lawsuit is without merit, will overwhelm empty, albeit stylish, advocacy every time.

Well, perhaps I shouldn't be too sanguinary; almost every time. Sometimes, a local favorite might be given an edge—despite the law—by a local trial judge. But there are appeals courts. And whatever advantage a local favorite might have with judge, clerk, or jury in the local venue, such advantages have a way of evaporating in the calm, quiet appellate halls.

Moral: He who knows the law is more *likely* to win.

SOMETIMES THE JUDGES DO NOT KNOW EITHER

The moral stated here should be plain and clear. Merely because you know what the current law is doesn't mean that you will necessarily win the day or the trial.

There are those instances where the law that has recently been handed down from the high courts has not come within the scrutiny or awareness of the judge who is presiding at your trial.

Just because a person is a judge and wears a black dress doesn't mean he or she is omniscient, or even a well-versed lawyer, or is keeping up with the latest developments in the law.

To ensure against just such happenstance, bring the law along for the benefit of the judge. Write a compelling Memorandum of Law for the judge. Let him or her read and become familiar with the current trend of the law.

There are also those situations where the judge is just not disposed to your case—or you—or your client. This does not imply venality, just humanity. Judges, for those of you who are skeptics, are just people, just like everyone else. Sure, they should overcome their petty views, likes and dislikes—so should everyone—and dispense evenhanded justice. But that's not always the case.

You may find yourself up against the proverbial brick wall, unable to move that wall by argument, cajolery, exhortation, or anything else. The Court may be plaintiff or prosecution-minded. The Court may be defense minded. The Court, just like other people, may have troubles with carbuncles or the IRS on the very morning that you are trying the case. Whatever the reasons, don't expect it always to go well for you or your cause, even when you think you have the law on your side.

What to do?

That's easy, of course. Make a clear and concise record for appeal. On this subject, see the chapter on protecting the record, infra.

> ***CAUTION:*** *Don't think that you made a clear and concise record merely because, in your mind, you cerebralized that you wanted to make a record. Don't think you made a record because you've offhandedly, vaguely alluded to the point of law you want to preserve. A record*

must be specific; it must be specifically articulated. Don't be shy. That's what the record is for; that's what appeals courts are for.

SECOND CAUTION: *If the judge refuses to permit you to make a record, make a record of the fact that the judge refused to let you make a record. That's record enough.*

KNOW PROCEDURAL EVEN MORE THAN SUBSTANTIVE

It is not sufficient to know only the substantive law in order to be successful at trial; you must know and digest even more finely the procedural law as well.

After all, the procedural law and the evidentiary rules are the same, or pretty much the same, regardless of the subject matter of the particular issues on trial. That goes for criminal as well as civil cases.

While there may be some specific rules applicable to particular cases, the Rules of Evidence are fairly universal in your jurisdiction. Hearsay is hearsay; business records are business records; collateral matters are collateral matters; and cross-examination is cross-examination.

Therefore, you must surely be well-versed in the procedural law.

Oftentimes, as you research various points of law, you will come across prior decisions and opinions that involve mixed questions of substantive and procedural law. The particular procedural issue elucidated may not even apply to the case at hand. But it is something that may come up in future cases. Make a note, keep the citation, add it to your Trial Book. The issue may be one that you need on your very next trial, or the next.

By the way, not only substantive cases are the subject of appeal. Many procedural issues are raised on appeal, wherein the aggrieved party has complained that true justice was not rendered because the lower Court did not permit, or did permit, what the aggrieved party believes not to have been proper.

In other words, the procedural law is constantly changing, being modified, being redefined. So you must keep up with the appellate decisions on such procedural questions as if your life, or at least your livelihood, depended on it.

It does.

RESEARCH SHORT CUT

Don't reinvent the wheel. Most often, while doing research, you will find that the appellate Court, in rendering a decision, cites various cases that agree or are distinguishable from the issue you are researching. Even though these citations are not exactly on point, they are close, they are in the same ballpark. Don't pass Go on your way directly to Jail (that's Monopoly talk); start with the citations given you in the opinion. Let the work that the judges and their staffs have done on this subject point you in a direction and to other cases in the same particular area. Use those citations you find to help you leapfrog in helpful directions and to opinions that you may have to overcome, deal with, or that may bring you to a fork in the road from which you can fashion your own legal argument.

In short, stand on the shoulders of others who have been there before you. Save your energy for battles never fought before.

Save it for your Trial Book

When you find a decision that is one that you think will be valuable to you in the future, either make a copy of the page or pages on which the particular language or holding appears or make a notation of the pertinent language and the citation. Put this in your Trial Book and keep it for future reference.

Many of the same evidentiary issues arise in diverse cases. Rather than looking something up for the moment that you need it and then discarding it, or closing those citations and your research notes with the closed file on the particular case in which the point arose, save the holding, the citation. There are better things to do with your time than to reresearch the same questions you looked up a few cases back.

Update your Trial Book constantly

Of course, an old case that is still the law is a good citation. But, if the case is good law, the issue may have arisen more recently and the old decision may even have been cited with approval in the more recent decision.

It may also be that the issue is rare and has come up on only a few occasions, on all of which occasions the case you've found has been cited.

If the citations in your Trial Book are the most recent, state-of-the-art law on the subject, then, by all means, keep them for handy reference.

However, if more recent cases have arisen or have added another nuance or wrinkle to the subject, then update your Trial Book.

Psychologically, your adversary and the Court will be doubly impressed when you merely flip to a page in your Trial Book and recite the up-to-date law on the particular subject or evidentiary rule in question. They will be impressed in the first instance that you are such a professional that you have a Trial Book and impressed in the second instance with the fact that your Trial Book is as up to date in the law as yesterday, or the day before.

The entire picture of you and your case will be that you and it are well-prepared, fully armed, ready for any turn of events.

And you are and will be.

7

WHICH WITNESSES: WHICH EVIDENCE?

LEGAL CHESS

You've already interviewed witnesses to the event. You've determined which documents were implicated in the event. You've had a photographer take pictures of every possible angle of the situs. But now trial is fast upon you. You have to distinguish the wheat from the chaff. You have to determine what is the best, most dramatic, most convincing presentation you can make to the trier of fact.

MAKE IT DRAMATIC

Yes, we're talking dramatic here. Not legal. Not strictly legal, that is. For, after all, a trial is a presentation of facts, events, with the intent to persuade the trier of fact, be it jury or judge at a bench trial, of the correctness of your presentation.

Remember what was indicated earlier: If there are no factual issues in dispute, there is no need for a trial. Thus, a trial is not to determine legal issues, but, rather, factual issues in a legal setting.

Each time you read a book, each time you see a motion picture, you are subjected to a dramatic presentation that works toward an end—hopefully entertainment or enlightenment. If the presentation is drab or dull, you quickly lose interest, close down your mind, close the book, walk out of the movie, or just sit there bored, enduring, anxious to get out.

Think of the jury as your audience, reading a book that you wrote, watching a film that you directed. Make it boring and they are going to close down, close the book on you and your case, and just sit there, fulfilling their responsibility, anxious to pan you and your presentation and go home.

On the other hand, make your presentation dramatic, interesting, persuasive, and they'll stay with you all the way.

DETERMINE THE ALTERNATIVES

So, what you now have to decide as you prepare for the actual trial is which witness, which evidence, will present the case in the most dramatic, most palatable way.

There may be only one way to present certain facts or evidence. In that case, there is no choice. However, most often there are several ways in which to make a presentation of fact, some requiring witnesses, some not. You must explore which alternatives, if any, are available to you for your presentation, and, of these, which shall likely achieve the best overall result for you case.

Each trial is different. Each jury is different. Thus, on a case-by-case basis, you have to decide if you have alternative methods of presentation, and if you do, which will impact more significantly on the trier(s) of fact.

MINIMIZING THE EVIDENCE

Assume you are a defense lawyer in a narcotics case, where the only real evidence connecting your client with the crime is a former co-defendant who has pleaded guilty and agreed to cooperate with the prosecution against your client. Your defense is that the witness is a liar, merely tarring your client with the dirty brush to gain a bargain for himself, to escape harsh punishment. You wish to show the jury that there is nothing other than the sleazy, admitted narcotics-dealing witness implicating your client and that that one witness is simply not a credible witness.

Under the circumstances, you might want to minimize the number of prosecution witnesses in order to emphasize the dearth of evidence against your client. It may, therefore, be in your interest and in keeping with your strategy to stipulate to much of the prosecution case.

Therefore, rather than force the prosecution to present credible officials to the jury, such as a narcotics agent to establish the chain of custody of the contraband to the chemist, and then the government chemist to testify as to the amount and the strength of the narcotics, stipulate to their testimony.

Since your defense is that your client had nothing whatever to do with the drugs, what's the difference how much or of what quality the drugs are? Stipulate. In the mind of the jury, the case is then reduced psychologically—there's that word again—to a minimal number of witnesses, making the cooperating witness's sleaziness more outstanding. Thus, by the lack of other witnesses, you emphasize that in order for the jury to convict they must believe the sleaze, or not. Convict on his sleazy testimony, or acquit.

CHOICES MUST BE MADE IN ADVANCE

Therefore, before you go further with your trial preparation, you must decide how the same facts, through varied presentations of evidence, can be placed in front of the trier(s) of facts in a fashion that highlights the case the way you want it. Try the case the way you want it, rather than permit a random flow of facts, a mass of legalese in which the jury can be distracted and can founder.

SAUCE FOR THE GOOSE; SAUCE FOR THE GANDER

Of course, if you were the prosecutor in the foregoing narcotics case, particularly if you felt that the cooperating witness—who is your main witness—is truly a dirt-bag, you might prefer to build the case with as many credible, unquestionable integrity witnesses as you can muster, such as the police officer who will testify that she walked the narcotics to the laboratory and the government chemist who testifies to having received the narcotics, what tests he administered, and just what quality and quantity of narcotics were involved.

This more elongated presentation has a tendency to lend strength and formidability to the prosecution presentation and therefore to lend apparent support to the cooperating witness. Thus, as prosecutor, you might refuse the offer by the defense to stipulate to the narcotics, the chemist, et al.

Let's look at some of the alternative evidentiary methods and just when they should be utilized.

SELF-AUTHENTICATION

A self-authenticating document does not require a witness to lay a foundation for its admission into evidence.

Ordinarily, by rule or statute, certain documents, because they are regularly prepared in the course of some business or activity and because such documents have not been prepared solely for the purpose of the instant litigation, can be admitted in evidence so long as they are certified by a person connected with their formulation or publication as a true copy of the particular document(s).

In this category are hospital records, weather reports, birth certificates, newspapers, telephone directories published by the telephone company, statutes, regulations, court files or records of the clerk of a court or jurisdiction.

Ordinarily, as in Federal Rule 902, the documentary evidence that is recognized to be self-authenticating is set forth in statute.

Self-authentication, however, is not always the answer to your trial needs. It may be that you wish to call a witness from the agency, hospital, or jurisdiction that produced a record, but not only for the purpose of introducing the record or document. You may want to call the witness for some other purpose that supports your scenario for the trial. By all means call that witness.

However, if you call such a witness merely to introduce a document that authenticates itself, you will be wasting your time and the Court's, and you will be putting yourself in position to be criticized by the Court for delaying or lengthening the proceedings unnecessarily.

ALWAYS READ THE SELF-AUTHENTICATING DOCUMENT

As said before, you cannot just think about evidence, you cannot just think about making a record and believe the same will be done automatically.

The same is true for self-authenticating documents. You cannot just have the document admitted into evidence because of its status as a self-authenticating document and then leave the document lying on your counsel table. You must read the document to the jury in order for the jury to know what is in the document.

If you don't read the document to the jury, you will have to rely on the jury's reading it to themselves. But as a result of your failure to enlighten them, by the time jury deliberations come about, their minds may be turned off to you, your client, and your case.

In other words, although you have technically won the evidentiary battle, you have lost the war of getting the right tone and keeping that tone going, of keeping your momentum, and your pace with the jury.

Therefore, get the jury thinking the right way about the evidence. Let them know what the evidence is.

Advocate: Your Honor, I offer into evidence Plaintiff's Exhibit 4, for Identification, the certified hospital record of St. Vincent's Hospital for Mr. Plaintiff, for a hospitalization from the 24th of April to the 2nd of May, 1990.

The Court: Have you seen this document, Ms. Adversary?

Adversary: I have, Your Honor. It is the hospital record described by Mr. Advocate.

The Court: Received then, as Plaintiff's Exhibit 4.

Advocate: I'd like to read a portion of the said hospital record to the jury, Your Honor.

The Court: Very well.

Adversary: I object, Your Honor. The document speaks for itself.

The Court: That's probably true, but for a document such as this, it's probably far easier if counsel reads that portion to the jury that he wishes to emphasize. You will have the same opportunity, Ms. Adversary.

Adversary: Then I object on the further ground that Mr. Advocate, if he does wish to read from the hospital record, should read the entire record, not just selected snippets.

Advocate: If I leave anything out that Ms. Advocate wishes in, she can read that portion to the jury, Your Honor.

The Court: No speeches, please. Yes, Ms. Adversary. You can read any portion you wish to the jury as well. Please proceed.

JUDICIAL NOTICE

Another device that permits an Advocate to eliminate a witness or witnesses from the witness list is to have the Court take judicial notice of some fact.

FRE 201 indicates, inter alia, that

> *"a judicially noticed fact must be one not subject to reasonable dispute in that it is either (1) generally known within the territorial jurisdiction of the trial Court or (2) capable of accurate and ready determination by resort to sources whose accuracy cannot reasonably be questioned."*

In addition, the FRE indicates that a Court can take judicial notice, in its discretion, whether requested to or not [201(c)]. However, when requested to by a party and when supplied with the necessary information, it is *mandatory* that a Court take judicial notice [201(d)].

That an advocate can actually *require* a Court to take judicial notice is dubious. But the wording is present in the FRE, and you can go a long way to save yourself the trouble of providing witnesses to prove facts that are not subject to reasonable dispute and that are capable of accurate and ready determination by asking the Court to take judicial notice thereof.

NOTE: Judicial notice is not restricted to laws, statutes, ordinances, or governmental regulations, although these readily fall within its scope.

Judicial notice can be had of any fact that is supportable by sources of information which cannot readily be disputed, that can be looked up in sources that cannot be questioned, that are obvious.

OTHER JUDICIAL NOTICE

In actuality, a Court can take judicial notice of anything that an ordinary person could not help knowing. When you request a Court to take judicial notice, you are merely asking the Court to recognize an obvious fact. Your request, therefore, can go beyond items like statutes and court files or those other items specifically enumerated in the FRE or other evidence statutes.

Indeed, you can ask the Court to take judicial notice of anything that is obvious and known to be correct, but that is being resisted by your adversary just to make you work harder. In other words, you can enlist the aid of the Court to cut away the expenditure of unnecessary time, to help you avoid the wasteful task of producing witnesses who will testify to the obvious.

For example, at a trial where you are using the transcript of a deposition as a prior inconsistent statement to cross-examine a witness on the stand, your adversary might arbitrarily object to the accuracy and use of the deposition, thus requiring you to call in the reporter who transcribed the deposition.

Q. Do you recall having attended a deposition on the 15th of April?

A. Yes.

Q. And do you recall having been asked these questions and having given these answers—and please let me read both the questions and the answers—so that I may ask you a question about them here?

A. Okay.

Adversary: Your Honor, I object to this use of the deposition.

Advocate: Would Your Honor take judicial notice of the fact that this deposition incorporates a stipulation permitting exactly this use of the deposition?

The Court: Don't make speeches. You may use the deposition. Continue.

Q. (Reading) "Question." What color was the traffic light as you approached the intersection?

A. "Answer." It was yellow, then turned to red.

Q. "Question." How far away from the intersection were you when the light turned red?

A. "Answer." About 100 feet.

Q. Do you recall being asked those exact questions and giving those exact answers at your deposition?

A. I don't remember exactly. That was quite a while ago.

Advocate: Your Honor, perhaps my adversary will concede that I read the deposition correctly.

Adversary: Your Honor, I think it quite improper that my adversary requests concessions in front of the jury.

Advocate: Would Your Honor take judicial notice that I read the deposition correctly?

The Court: You're not going to concede that counsel read the deposition correctly, Ms Adversary?

Adversary: No, Your Honor.

The Court: Let me see the deposition. (Reads) I take judicial notice that counsel has read that portion of the deposition exactly as it appears. Continue.

The above is a use of judicial notice quite within the statute, that saves both yourself and the Court time and difficulty. In short, you can use judicial notice to short-circuit the obvious, that which everyone knows, that which everyone should—with a degree of reasonableness—know or recognize. Oftentimes, out of zest for adversarial combat, your adversary—or you—are unwilling to focus on the easy, the simple, that which eliminates work and time. By a simple expedient—judicial notice—unnecessary work can be avoided and unnecessary witnesses can be dispensed with.

There may be many other uses of judicial notice that will arise in a courtroom. It is not necessary that the matter be a statute or other legislative fiat in order that a Court's inherent power to notice or acknowledge the obvious be invoked. Where the matter is beyond the dispute of reasonable persons, a Court can exercise judicial notice of *anything* in order to shorten the time of a trial or a hearing.

Therefore, be aware of judicial notice and use it to your advantage to eliminate unnecessary work, to save time and to work some trial strategy to your own advantage.

NOTE: *As indicated with self-authenticating documents, you may have a secondary trial strategy reason to want to call a witness to the* *stand to testify to certain facts that might otherwise be dispensed with by way of judicial notice. If that be the case, then by all means, do not ask the Court to take judicial notice, and argue against your adversary's invocation of judicial notice so that your plan of action continues.*

STIPULATION

In addition to self-authentication and judicial notice, whereby you are seeking to save trial time either by eliminating the necessity to call witnesses merely to lay foundations for the admission of evidence or to produce witnesses who will testify about matters on which both you and your adversary agree, you may eliminate proofs of those items or calling those witnesses by stipulation.

The parties can stipulate to any evidentiary matter under the sun. After all, a trial is necessary only where there are open items of facts or where there are issues that remain unresolved and undetermined. If you and your adversary can stipulate to certain facts, thus eliminating those facts or some of those facts from the need of jury determination, the Court will ordinarily not object to such a procedure.

It is not a dereliction of duty to stipulate. In fact, depending on the circumstances, it may very well be part of your strategy to stipulate.

IF IT DOESN'T MATTER—STIPULATE

You need not fight, cheek to jowl, with your adversary about every single inch of ground in the trial. For different reasons it may be to your mutual advantage to stipulate to certain facts.

Let's go back to the previous example of a narcotics trial, where you are the prosecutor. You have to bring in the police chemist to testify that she tested the narcotics that have already been introduced through the arresting officer, and that the drugs were 79 percent pure cocaine. However, before the chemist can testify about the purity of the narcotics and the steps she undertook to arrive at the finding of purity, you would have to conduct a Direct Examination of the chemist as to her qualifications as a chemical expert, as to a description of the tests that were utilized in evaluating the narcotics, and then as to the chemist's ultimate findings of purity.

On the other hand, defense counsel is contending that her client had nothing whatever to do with these drugs, that her client was and is totally innocent of the charges.

To stipulate to the testimony that the chemist might give if the chemist were to take the stand is to serve the purpose of both counsel, that is, to conserve the time of the chemist from the prosecutor's point of view while not affecting the defense case posture in the least. Yet, at the same time, such stipulation shortens the trial, permitting everyone to get on with other business sooner. In this situation, a stipulation should be very seriously entertained.

In any situation where there is evidence or facts about which you and your adversary mutually agree, unless you have a secondary purpose to have the witnesses appear, there should be no necessity to produce witnesses to introduce that evidence or proof of those facts. You should stipulate.

> ***REMEMBER:*** *This is not going to be the only case you try in your career. Don't make a career out of it. If the stipulation works to your advantage, take it, make it, use it. Don't be hidebound to some vague precept that you should not stipulate to anything that your adversary wants to stipulate to as if, by stipulation, you surrender some constitutional right of your client or some of your integrity.*

Quite the opposite. You have an obligation to yourself, your client, the Court—not necessarily in that order of priority—not to take an overly long time trying this particular case. If a matter even suggests resolution by stipulation, that fact cannot be so seriously in contention. If that be the case, stipulate to those insignificant facts, saving your energy and the focus of your case for the truly significant facts in issue.

YOU DON'T HAVE TO STIPULATE

On the other hand, you know where you are going, where your case is going, and where you want it to go. The Court and your adversary may urge you to stipulate to certain facts or to the testimony of certain witnesses. If, however, you have some secondary purpose to be served by the production of a witness, then by all means don't stipulate.

No one can make you stipulate.

SQUEEZE THE LEAST LIKELY WITNESS DRY

I have mentioned three times earlier that you need not stipulate or ask the Court to take judicial notice, nor do you need even to take advantage of self-authentication where there is another purpose that you believe further strengthens your case.

Example: You intend to introduce photographs of the scene of an accident or of a site that is significant to the litigation. What is the best way to get them in evidence?

An axiom: The easiest way is usually the best way.

And the easiest way is to get the photographs in—assuming that your adversary will not stipulate to the introduction of the photographs—is through that witness who will permit you to get the pictures into evidence with the least resistance, the witness who will not oppose or attempt in any way to hinder the introduction of the evidence.

This principle is most sharply focused when you are a defense attorney (in either a criminal or a civil case). Even though you are defense counsel, you may want to introduce photographs into evidence early in the proceedings so the jury can better understand the case as it unfolds and so you can better cross-examine the adverse witnesses that the plaintiff (prosecutor) is presenting.

In other words, you want to set the tone of the case and get your defense going while the Plaintiff is still on his or her case.

Therefore, you will want to introduce your photographs on the plaintiff's case through one of the plaintiff's witnesses. In this circumstance, you have to decide which of the plaintiff's witnesses will be the most cooperative in identifying the photographs, the documents you want to get in evidence.

Remember, the adverse witnesses are adverse to your case. They are pieces of a case that is adverse to your interests, to your position. The adverse witnesses are not merely going to lie down and let you run all over them. Being a witness is a traumatic event, and the hostility of the adverse witnesses is exacerbated by that trauma. At the very least, the adverse witnesses are wary of the cross-examiner. They are not going to be cooperative.

In this context, the witness whom you select as the conduit through which to introduce the photographs or documents should be the least likely of the available candidates for such a task. The reason for this least likely tactic is that the more important the adverse witness, the more likelihood there is that the witness will be the most difficult, the most wary, the most uncooperative of the witnesses.

Don't fight to get your photographs or your documentary evidence before the jury. Select the least adverse witness, the one who is *least* likely to be hostile and therefore the most likely to be cooperative.

WHO IS THE MOST LIKELY CANDIDATE?

Who is most likely to be the most cooperative witness? The least involved witness.

And now we come back to the reason that you refused to stipulate earlier to a certain seemingly unimportant witness.

That person whose testimony you could easily stipulate to may give you the perfect opportunity to introduce your photographs or documentary evidence. The reason that you might have stipulated to this particular witness's testimony is that the witness's position is not very adverse to the defense. The witness is, in other words, rather neutral; the witness is not hostile. Thus, the witness is the most relaxed, and most indifferent to the entire litigation and, therefore, to your cause. Moreover, your adversary has not schooled this witness extensively to resist your thrusts. Perfect.

Let's say, for example, the witness is a police officer who was the first on the scene of an accident. He didn't see the accident. He can't testify to the occurrence. He is being brought to the stand only to introduce his aided report (report of the occurrence). For these reasons, he is likely to be a candidate for a stipulation to his police report or accident report.

These very circumstances, however, make this witness the perfect candidate to introduce photographs of the scene of the accident. He's seen the site; he was there immediately after the accident; he's familiar with the scene from his experience in the particular precinct where the accident occurred. He is, therefore, the most likely candidate to be used as your truck horse, the witness to help you introduce the photographs you need for later cross-examination of the significant witnesses.

And, at the same time he will help you get your tone set before the jury, undercutting your adversary's plan to permit only testimony to set up the facts of his or her rather weak case. You, on the other hand, are willing to live with the facts, with the photographs helping you.

For these reasons, you refused to stipulate to this witness's testimony.

It may very well be that your decision not to stipulate may have been viewed with some displeasure by both the Court and your adversary. That's okay. This is not a popularity contest you're involved in. When you begin to introduce the photographs through the not-too-adverse witness your adversary proffers, your purpose in earlier refusing to stipulate will be very well understood.

Indeed, you may have only perfunctory cross-examination of the witness on the subject matter of his direct testimony. That's okay, you'll *make the witness your own* (for more on this subject, see the chapter on cross-examination, infra) and continue the examination of the witness in the new area, the foundation for introduction of your photographs.

Begin making the witness your own with a few preliminary questions to establish the witness's knowledge and experience with the scene. More than likely, the witness—as well as everyone else in the trial—is going to be somewhat surprised by the turn you've taken in the midst of what was considered to be routine testimony. But you don't want to wait until the defendant's case to get the photos or documents before the jury. And you know your adversary isn't going to introduce such photos or documents for you.

After laying the necessary foundation for the introduction of the photographs (on this subject, see the chapter on documentary evidence, infra) you introduce the photos/documents through the witness who is still wondering *why me?*

But you know why. Now you've introduced the evidence you wanted in the case, at the time you wanted it in the case, during your adversary's case, so that you can use that evidence to cross-examine, to let the jury know what the case is really about.

WHICH OF SEVERAL WITNESSES?

When you are preparing the case that you are going to present on behalf of your client, you have to determine which witness you are going to use to introduce your version of the case, or at least to introduce some of the facts that support your version of the case.

If there is only one witness, one way for you to introduce certain testimony, then of course you have no choice but to use that witness or forgo that particular evidence.

Sometimes, you will determine that a witness will make such a bad impression on the jury that you'd rather forgo the witness, or that aspect of the case.

For example, in a criminal case your client is intelligent, personable, and his version of the events is convincing. You want very much to put your client on the stand. Except, you know your adversary will belabor your client into testamentary death with questions about his previous criminal acts, even though the previous charges occurred 20 years ago when he was quite young and are unrelated to the case at Bar.

Despite the fact that your client's record isn't so bad, you know you don't want that record out in front of the jury. You are afraid that the sympathetic figure that you've built up around the defendant in the eyes of the jury will be destroyed the moment that the defendant takes the stand and it is revealed that he has a prior criminal record.

Thus, you have to decide which is the best case for you to present: the one *with* the defendant or the one *without* the defendant.

The same considerations apply to the choice of nonparty witnesses. A witness may have information to provide in the case, but that witness may be so unsympathetic and incredible, that her testimony, you fear, will be disregarded as concocted or contrived. You try in every way you know how to help the witness make a better presentation, suggesting clothing, manner of sitting, going over the testimony, pointing out your view of the witness's proposed testimony. But nothing works. This witness is going to be a disaster.

Your real fear is that this witness will not only undermine herself, but that the lack of trustworthiness of this witness is going to undermine the entire fabric of your case, the credibility of your entire case.

Do you go with the witness and risk her unsympathetic personality being flung before the jury, or do you forgo this witness?

It is a balancing that you have to do, to determine, in the overview of the entire case, do I need this witness, how is this witness going to affect the case, how will the jury react to this witness, can I get along without this witness, am I better off without this witness, is there another witness who can do approximately the same job for me without the risk of destroying the case?

These questions have to be answered by you long before the judge tells you, counsellor, call your next witness.

8

Rules of Evidence

Universality

Every trial, federal or state, civil or criminal, requires the advocate to invoke and be guided by Rules of Evidence. A trial cannot take place and an advocate cannot function without knowing these rules.

Until recently, this task was somewhat more complicated by the fact that each jurisdiction had its own peculiar Rules of Evidence, and federal courts had yet more and different Rules of Evidence.

Within recent times, however, the formidable task of knowing two or three different rules for the same evidentiary problem has been somewhat simplified. The federal Rules of Evidence (FRE), enacted in 1973, has been adopted in more than 30 states. This trend is moving inexorably toward a future where a unified set of Rules of Evidence, on both a federal and a state level, will be in place throughout the United States.

As long as you have to know the Rules of Evidence, it would be better if you knew them verbatim; each word, each comma, of every section. But who is as lucky as that? Moreover, what good would it do an advocate to know the Rules of Evidence verbatim but not know in his mind, in his gut, the essence, the concept, the theory of evidence?

The Evidentiary Essence

A trial is not a mini re-creation of real life. Trials are their own existence. The way that people conduct and manage their personal and business affairs in the lay world is not at all like the precise codified fashion in which life in the well of the courtroom is conducted.

The purpose of the Rules of Evidence is to ensure that no testimony, no fact or piece of documentary or physical evidence, is admitted into a trial unless it is as precise, as free from undue prejudice, and as reliable as the savants throughout legal time could have made them.

In short, the Rules of Evidence are intended to preserve and maintain the integrity and reliability of evidence, in antiseptic fashion, so that a trial can become a pure exercise in weighing sheer, unadulterated fact.

> ***NOTE:*** *All evidence is prejudicial; it is intended to be such. Each side in an adversarial contest submits evidence that shall indeed negatively impact, affect, prejudice the other side. Therefore, the Rules of Evidence do not protect a party and counsel from prejudice, but from undue, improper, contaminated prejudice (evidence).*

In order, therefore, to secure the integrity of evidence, the rules governing the introduction of documentary evidence require that a basic foundation need be established before a document can be received in evidence. This, of course, is to be sure that the document is not irrelevant, immaterial, or extraneous to the trial.

A trial cannot become contaminated with a separate trial within a trial to determine a collateral issue about a witness or a piece of evidence.

The rule against hearsay is intended to proscribe from the consideration of the jury testimony that cannot be chastened before a jury by a cross-examiner. If a witness were to testify to something that someone else said, then the cross-examiner would be impeded from cross-examining that statement, because the person testifying, when asked what the statement meant and why it was made, could continually hide behind the phrase, "I don't know, I didn't say it."

Thus, a declarant, the person who makes a factual statement, must make such statement in a courtroom, subject to be cross-examined, or the statement cannot be allowed into evidence as hearsay.

The use of prior inconsistent statements—there are four kinds of them—is governed by certain rules that require different foundations depending upon the reliability of the particular statement; a prior statement taken under oath, such as a deposition or Grand Jury testimony, because of its greater reliability can be used the most readily and the most easily. A statement in the handwriting of a witness or signed by a witness on some prior occasion is somewhat less reliable than one taken under oath and therefore requires somewhat greater scrutiny. Statements that were made—and testified to—by third persons require the most stringent scrutiny because the reliability of such statements is far more suspect and far more vulnerable than one taken under oath or in the handwriting of the witness.

From these examples, you should get the perception that the essence of the Rules of Evidence is integrity and precision of trial evidence.

THE FRE

The Federal Rules of Evidence, and, in the main, the rules of all those jurisdictions that have adopted the FRE, are divided into 11 Articles.

1. General Provisions
2. Judicial Notice
3. Presumptions
4. Relevance
5. Privileges
6. Witnesses
7. Opinions and Expert Testimony
8. Hearsay
9. Authentication
10. Best Evidence
11. Miscellany

These are all there are. This list is the entirety of the Rules of Evidence, the entirety of the rules by which trials are conducted—not so overwhelming an amount of words, facts and knowledge that they cannot be known with great particularity by every trial advocate.

To make it even more simple for the advocate, and therefore less forgivable if an advocate is not totally aware of the meaning and essence of each rule, is the fact that some of the articles are of lesser significance and importance to the average trial, whereas others are of great significance.

For example, rules 1, 2, 3, 5, 9, and 11 are lesser used and lesser referred to rules than are numbers 4, 6, 7, 8, and 10.

Thus, the five cardinal Rules of Evidence are covered in the following paragraphs.

RELEVANCE (Rule 401)

> *Relevant evidence means evidence having any tendency to make the existence of any fact that is of consequence to the determination of the action more probable or less probable than it would be without the evidence.*

There, in a walnut nutshell, is the definition and measure of relevance.

If a fact has a tendency to make the existence of a material issue in your case more probable, it is *relevant*, and you can mount a substantial argument that it should be admissible.

However, such fact must indeed be a fact and not something proscribed by another rule of evidence. For example, if a matter is hearsay, even if relevant it will not be admitted in evidence. If a matter cannot be established with a proper foundation, even if relevant, it shall not be admitted.

As you shall see momentarily, there are exceptions to the various Rules of Evidence, even as to the admission of hearsay under the proper circumstances.

UNDUE PREJUDICE OUTWEIGHS RELEVANCE (Rule 403)

Even if relevant, however, evidence may be excluded if its probative value is substantially outweighed by the danger of *unfair* prejudice and confusion or is misleading or a waste of time.

This, then, is the balancing test you've all heard so much about, the balancing of relevance against unfair prejudice. Even if a fact be relevant to a particular litigation, if the unfair prejudice that it may cause in the minds of the jury outweighs the fact-finding value, that evidence cannot be introduced before the jury.

PREJUDICE IS FINE; UNFAIR PREJUDICE IS NOT

Rule 403 does not mean that evidence that impacts *against* a party cannot be brought to the attention of the jury. Indeed, not. That is exactly what evidence is supposed to do, negatively impact upon an adverse party. The harder you hit, the stronger your case.

However, while you are entitled, even expected to strike blows—even harsh blows—against the adverse party and your adversary, you are *not* permitted to strike *foul* ones.

Thus, where the evidence, while somewhat relevant to the trial, has a tendency to inflame, mislead, or confuse the jury, where it is cumulative and repetitive, such evidence will be excluded.

On the other hand, a heinous crime or a gruesome injury may be presented to the jury, if indeed that is the result of the defendant's actions. But you cannot "gild the lily," unfairly creating an atmosphere that might *unnecessarily* tend to cause the jury to think ill of the adverse party or the adverse case and that might blind or stampede the jury against the adverse party.

For example, photographs of a mutilated dead body might very well, because of their gruesome content, tend to revolt the jury and turn the jury against the person who caused such a horror. They might, therefore, have a tendency to cause the jury to react by revulsion or emotion rather than by clearheaded deliberation.

If sufficient account of the injury caused by the party can be brought to the attention of the jury in some other less inflamatory way, through testimony or through a photo from a different angle, such alternative evidence is the more acceptable and less objectionable.

However, if the essence of the case revolves around the mutilation and thus, perhaps, the frame of mind of the perpetrator of such offense, then, regardless of the gruesome aspect, the photographs would have to be admitted.

Another example: photographs of a tragic injury to a child, taken at the scene of the accident, in which the child is crying hysterically, bleeding, and the mother is beside the child, in equal anguish, may be unfairly prejudicial. Later photographs, however, that are objective depictions of the injury without the pathos, that illustrate the very same injuries without wrenching the hearts of the jurors, are preferable. These latter photographs depicting the same injury, but without the sympathy-evoking, pitiful aspect and emotion, are equally relevant, and would be admitted before the bloody photographs. Indeed, a Court may exclude the bloody photos altogether, requiring the advocate who failed to obtain "proper," nondramatic photographs to rely on the testimony of the doctors to establish the injury.

ARGUE UNFAIR/LACK OF UNFAIR PREJUDICE

The judge must decide on a case-by-case basis what is properly prejudicial evidence and what is unfairly prejudicial evidence. It is, classically, a balancing of factors.

The advocate who wishes to use certain evidence must show the Court that the facts wished to be presented are properly prejudicial, that is, that they are relevant in the proof of the case, but *are not* unfairly prejudicial. In short, the evidence shows merely the facts; it is not overreaching, emotion charged, inflammatory.

On the other hand, the advocate against whom such evidence is being presented must show that the same facts can be brought in front of the jury without inflaming the jury, through the use of *other* evidence, through the use of different photographs, through different witnesses.

CONFUSION, WASTE OF TIME IS UNFAIR PREJUDICE

The balancing and exclusion of evidence has another aspect. Even if the evidence does not unnecessarily inflame or mislead the jury, but has a tendency to confuse the jury and has more of a tendency to obfuscate the issues than to clarify them, if the evidence has already been presented and is cumulative and less convincing than it is a waste of time, an advocate can argue for its exclusion from the jury's consideration.

In short, where the introduction of the evidence or the fact the adversary wishes to present in evidence is outweighed in its probative effect by some other factor, an adversary can argue that it should be excluded—even though that fact IS relevant and does bear upon the issue.

PRIOR BAD ACTS

A party's responsibility for an act is to be decided by a jury, not on that person's propensity to commit such an act, not on that person's track record relative to similar acts, but on the actual facts surrounding the particular incident in issue.

This principle is applicable to both civil as well as criminal trials. Indeed, it is tantamount to *negative* character evidence.

FRE 404(a) indicates that evidence of a person's character or trait of character is *not* admissible for the purpose of proving action in conformity therewith except if such evidence is presented by the person or party him- or herself. Then, the adversary has the right to rebut such character evidence.

Thus, unless a party introduces character evidence that that party hopes is affirmative evidence in his or her own behalf, an adversary is estopped from presenting contracharacter evidence.

As here indicated, however, there are exceptions to many rules, even the proscription against prior similar acts.

FRE 404(b) provides that evidence of other crimes or wrongs is not admissible to show the character of a person or a tendency to show that the accused may have acted in conformity with such propensity EXCEPT to show motive, opportunity, lack of mistake, lack of knowledge, or lack of intent.

For example, in a prosecution for drugs, a prosecutor cannot introduce evidence that an accused has been convicted on two prior occasions of drug-related offenses. Such evidence would be *unfairly prejudicial* to the question of whether or not the accused committed the act in question in the instant litigation.

Where the defendant denies the current crime altogether, sets up a defense that the crime never occurred at all, or that he never participated in such crime, the prosecutor cannot bolster the government's case by showing that the accused had committed similar acts on previous occasions. Such evidence would improperly cause the jury to consider the accused's guilt not on his acts in the instant case, but on a consideration of propensity; that is, if he's done it before, he has probably done it again.

PRIOR SIMILAR ACTS ARE ADMISSIBLE ON OCCASION

The preceding proscription against prior similar acts applies where a defendant presents such defense *without* personally taking the stand to testify on his or her own behalf. If the defendant does take the stand, other rules concerning prior bad or similar acts, as seen hereafter, then apply.

The law's desire to be fair should not be confused with foolishness. Where an accused, therefore, submits to a jury not the defense that the act in question never occurred, but a defense that while the event may have taken place, the accused had no knowledge thereof, that the act was unintentional, a mistake, a prosecuting advocate *may* counter such defense by showing prior similar acts by the accused, thereby negating the defense that the defendant's acts were those of a neophyte who had not realized the seriousness of the act.

> ***ANOTHER REMINDER:*** *As aforesaid, where a defendant takes the stand and testifies, the Court may or may not allow that defendant to be cross-examined about prior similar acts, for credibility purposes, based upon a pretrial determination of the relevance and age of such prior offenses.*

However, even if the defendant does not take the stand, where the defense is that the current acts were the result of inadvertence, lack of knowledge, or lack of awareness, then the Court, to keep the jury from having the wool pulled over its eyes, may permit use of the prior bad acts regardless of age or type of prior act, in order to permit the jury to properly evaluate the defendant's defense of inadvertence or mistake.

SUCH USE CAN BE AVOIDED BY THE DEFENSE

To avoid the use of similar acts against an accused, a defense advocate must, therefore, scrupulously avoid placing into issue the unintentional, unknowing participation of the defendant.

In short, character evidence cannot be introduced against a party, *except* if that party places his or her own good character before the jury or claims lack of scienter, awareness. In that case, the adversary can utilize character evidence to rebut.

For example, in a trial where a defendant is accused of bank robbery, if the defendant claims not to have been present, prior convictions of the same act cannot be introduced (provided the accused does not take the stand).

If the defendant, however, were to set up a defense that while she was present within the bank, she was an innocent bystander and that she didn't know anything that was going to happen, in that situation, even if the defendant does not take the stand, the prosecutor is in a position to properly introduce prior similar acts to show that the claim of unawareness is disingenuous.

Cross-Examination of Bad Acts Is Different

The proscription against the use of prior bad acts except where a party introduces *character* evidence is quite different, however, when a party (or witness) takes the stand to testify.

The rule remains substantially the same but is different because when a party (or witness) takes the stand his or her character for credibility, veracity, and accuracy is put on the line in a very direct way.

Therefore, a cross-examiner can inquire into *any* bad, illegal, or immoral act that the party or witness has ever caused or been engaged in, even if it is a prior crime. Indeed, a cross-examiner is permitted to go into the underlying facts of an *arrest*, even if there was an acquittal, but he or she is bound by the answers of the witness.

For example:

Q. Sir, on the 15th of April, 1991, did you assault a woman?

A. No.

Q. You didn't cause such woman serious bodily injury, on 14th street in Manhattan?

A. No.

The above cross-examiner was aware of the fact that the defendant had been arrested for and charged with the crime of assault causing serious bodily injury, but that he had been acquitted of such charge. Notwithstanding, the cross-examiner may ask about the underlying facts—not the arrest, not the trial—of the incident. But the cross-examiner is bound by the answer because of the collateral evidence rule. The current trial cannot open into a mini-trial about the witness's prior assault charges. Therefore, whatever the witness answers is binding and cannot be relitigated.

Why, then, bring this out, for the witness is bound to answer that he did not, in fact, commit such act. First, that result is not absolute or necessarily correct. With witnesses, nothing is absolute or necessarily correct. Indeed, the witness might very well answer:

> **A.** I was acquitted. (Which answer affirms the existence of such charges.)
>
> **Q.** I realize that, sir, but my question is, did you in fact assault that woman, causing serious physical injury?
>
> **A.** No.

You see, you've put information about the witness's prior bad acts in front of the jury without even getting an affirmative answer. And the jury can better evaluate the witness's credibility, even though the rules did not permit you to ask the witness if he was ever arrested, was ever charged with such act, and the jury can better evaluate even when the witness denies the event entirely.

The rule, therefore, remains, that when a witness takes the stand any bad, illegal, or immoral act can *and should* be explored to permit the jury complete latitude in evaluating the credibility of that adverse witness—even if the witness answers the propounded question by denying the accusation.

Other Purposes Are Permissible

As here illustrated, while an advocate cannot use prior similar acts or character evidence in the first instance, such facts *may* be introduced where the other side attempts to create in front of a jury a lack of knowledge or intent or tries to create a positive picture that is simply not so.

In other words, a party shall be protected from unduly prejudicial facts so long as that party does not use such protective shield as a sword with which to harm the other side.

Permissible use of otherwise proscribed facts or evidence exists in almost all areas of the Rules of Evidence. For example, because of its lack of reliability or the capacity to cross-examine the witness about what someone else said, the use of hearsay is strictly forbidden.

If a statement is admissible under some other rule or for some other purpose, however, then the introduction of that proscribed fact is permitted, even though it is hearsay.

For purposes of order, discussion of hearsay is considered in more detail in later sections.

IMPEACHING YOUR OWN WITNESSES

Often, almost by rote, advocates and judges play an old saw, indicating that an advocate cannot impeach his or her own witness. That is, the party presenting a witness vouches for the credibility of that witness and cannot be heard to impeach or besmirch the credibility of that witness.

That principle was true in the old movie, but it just ain't so now—at least not under the FRE or the Rules of Evidence in those jurisdictions that have adopted the FRE, and even in many of the jurisdictions that have not as yet adopted the FRE.

THE CHANGE

Rule 607 indicates that the credibility of a witness may be attacked by *any* party, including the party who has called the witness.

This appears, at first blush, to be the single most dramatic new change in the Rules of Evidence wrought by the FRE. To an extent that's true, only because the FRE is mostly a distillation and codification of rules that had already been in effect in many jurisdictions.

There are jurisdictions in which the Rules of Evidence had permitted such impeachment prior to the FRE. While New York is a jurisdiction that has not adopted the FRE, it has long permitted the impeachment of a witness by the party calling that witness *where that witness surprises the party by testifying to facts or circumstances adverse to the trial posture of that party.*

In other words, if the party calling a witness presents a witness who testifies contrary to that party's trial position (under New York rules) or, in general (under the FRE), that witness may be impeached by the party calling the witness in order that the jury be able to properly assess the credibility of that witness.

Thus, an advocate is not denied the capacity to present a witness with relevant evidence, merely because that witness is not totally savory or totally sympathetic to the advocate's case.

The FRE, and some other jurisdictions, has abandoned the Pollyanna approach to a trial and has recognized that there are occasions when an advocate must call a witness whose credibility may not be exemplary, whose cooperation is less than complete, but whose knowledge of the facts is unique.

IMPEACHMENT CANNOT BE ABUSED

As indicated here, many of the Rules of Evidence that proscribe certain uses of fact or evidence do allow for an exception *when there is another purpose,* where a door has been opened, where there is a need in order that the trial remain fair, or where there is a need for the jury to know more in order to render a fair and impartial verdict.

Such "other use," however, cannot be abusive, insidious, or purposely intended to abuse the concepts, of fair trial and search for the truth. For example, while impeachment is permitted of one's own witness (FRE 607), an advocate may not proffer a witness who the advocate knows has testified to certain facts adverse to the advocate's client, merely to use such adverse testimony as an excuse to get otherwise proscribed hearsay into evidence to impeach the anticipated testimony.

In other words, an advocate may not purposely introduce a witness or facts that are unquestionably contra to that advocate's client's interest merely as an artifice to impeach that witness with contradictory evidence that was otherwise impermissible.

HEARSAY—*ENFANT TERRIBLE*

Because it is the most used and abused evidence, the rule controlling hearsay is the centerpiece of any Rules of Evidence.

Let us first explore what hearsay is.

FRE 801 says hearsay is a statement other than one made by the declarant (witness) while testifying and offered to prove the truth of the matter asserted.

There's an awful lot to that definition.

First, there's the declarant. Despite some confusion as to who the declarant is, for our purposes the person who makes the original statement is the declarant.

I repeat: The person who made the original assertion of fact, not necessarily the witness on the stand, is the declarant.

The third person who testifies concerning this declaration or statement is the witness. If the declarant and the witness are the same person, ordinarily there is no hearsay. The word *ordinarily* is most important in the foregoing sentence, because the statement of a declarant, even though he or she be the witness *may* be hearsay.

Second, there's the witness—not the declarant—who testifies to the statement (a verbal *or* nonverbal assertion) of another person (declarant);

Third, there's the present statement, that is offered for the purpose of proving the truth of another person's assertion.

AN ASSERTION NEED NOT BE VERBAL

Yes, that's right, an assertion need not be verbal, yet may, nevertheless, be hearsay.

An assertion is a proffer of fact, a laying out of details in a certain order to establish reality. Notice, I have purposely stayed away from using the words "declaration" or "statement" of facts. Because an assertion is more than both of those words. Declaration and statement imply spoken word. Assertion is more. It is an indication of fact about something, whether in words or by other means.

For example, a person was not at the scene of an intersection collision at the moment it occurred. This person arrived moments later to hear the two drivers, now out of their cars, arguing as to whose fault caused the accident. At trial, this non-firsthand person is called to the stand and asked who was the driver of car #1. Wordlessly, the witness points to the plaintiff, or to the defendant.

Although not a single word is spoken by the witness, her pointing out the person who was the driver of vehicle #1 is classic hearsay!

Why?

First, because it is an assertion—an indication of the existence of a certain set of "facts"—about the happening of the above accident.

Second, and most significantly, it is NOT the assertion of the testifying witness, but is merely a repetition by that witness of certain assertions made by others (the overheard argument).

And, third, this assertion is being offered to establish the truth of the assertion.

Let's do it again. The testifying witness is not a firsthand witness who actually saw the accident or who even saw who was driving one of the cars. Remember, the two drivers were outside their cars arguing when the witness first arrived. When the witness is called to the stand, the witness is asked:

> **Q.** Who was driving car #1?
>
> **A.** (The witness points to the defendant.)

At that point, if you were the advocate for the defendant, you must stand up and object. It's hearsay.

A WITNESS'S OWN PRIOR STATEMENT AS HEARSAY

To really get a handle on understanding what hearsay is, be advised that a witness's *own* prior statement may be hearsay.

I hear you say, but I thought you said that if the declarant was the witness and could be cross-examined about her own statement that it would not be hearsay.

Almost always true.

What's really essential in the entire mix of hearsay/nonhearsay is that the witness must testify and make a PRESENT declaration about which she can be cross-examined. If a witness were to be put on the stand and would not offer present testimony, but rather, would be shown a book that the witness wrote some years before, and if she were asked questions about the text of that book, the witness would be testifying to hearsay contained in her own book.

Why?

Because the witness did not presently testify to the facts, but was merely being asked about the contents of a book—albeit one written by the witness. The book is a written, out-of-court declaration.

Thus, an out-of-court declaration, when offered for its truth through a trial witness—even a former declaration of the currently testifying witness—is hearsay and is not admissible at trial because the witness did not testify in front of the jury about that subject matter.

If, on the other hand, the author of the book is called to the stand, is asked questions about the subject matter, and testifies—even in the verbatim words that are in the book she authored—the testimony, obviously, is not hearsay, but is direct testimony and can be introduced and cross-examined.

Of course, after the author/witness testifies about the subject matter, the information contained in the book—if it is in agreement with the direct testimony, it cannot then be introduced in evidence for yet another rule of evidence: The contents of the book would be a prior CONSISTENT statement and would, therefore, be superfluous and be impermissible "bolstering." For more on this subject, see the section following relating to prior consistent statements.

THE REASON HEARSAY IS FORBIDDEN

The foregoing material, which may be somewhat confusing, has been set down so that by this time you would be begging to know precisely what hearsay is.

Let's explore why this thing called hearsay is so *verboten* in trial courts. In days of yore, juries were composed of landholders in the shire. If selected as jurors to settle a dispute, they would go about, talk to folks who were involved in the dispute or to neighbors who knew some of the facts, They would then get together with the other jurors, discuss the matter, and reach a verdict.

As it was unknown what facts the various jurors relied upon to make their determination, rules to standardize the evidence to be considered at dispute resolution proceedings (trials) evolved.

The cardinal rules of a trial are

(a) a fact witness must appear in person;

(b) must testify in open court;

(c) and must be subject to cross-examination.

While a witness who testifies to (or who offers nonverbal) hearsay appears in person and testifies, that hearsay witness *cannot be cross-examined about the assertion of another person (declarant).*

And therein lies the rub and the basis of the rule against hearsay. The nonfirsthand witness may appear in court and testify, but she *cannot be cross-examined about the statement of another person.*

Let's go back to our example of the nonfirsthand witness who was asked who was the driver of car #1 and who pointed to the defendant. This witness did not see or in any way perceive with her own senses that the defendant was actually the driver of car #1. The witness is merely repeating information that she picked up while listening to the argument between the two drivers.

The witness, therefore, cannot respond with her own perceptions about the defendant's driving of car #1 because the witness never saw the defendant drive the car. The witness is merely repeating an assertion heard and is not the person to be cross-examined. The one who made the original assertion, the one whose statement the present witness merely repeats, is the only one who can be cross-examined about the statement or assertion.

For that reason, the repeater, the nonfirsthand witness, is not permitted to make such a statement intended to prove the truth of the assertion. The original assertor (declarant) must be called or the advocate forfeits the opportunity to present that statement.

WHEN HEARSAY IS PERMITTED

Actually, hearsay is never permitted.

But you will often hear or read decisions in which it is said that hearsay is permitted under certain exceptions to the hearsay rule. Without getting into a discussion of semantics, those exceptions take the declaration *out* of the hearsay rule. What is permitted in evidence is not hearsay.

For example, a case recently decided in the Federal Court of Appeals, Second Circuit, involved a man who went to India on vacation. Just before returning, the defendant testified on his own behalf, someone he met in India asked the defendant to take a wedding suit back to a relative who was about to be married in the United States. The defendant testified that he was also told that the relative would meet the defendant at the airport and that he was a livery taxi driver and would drive the defendant to Manhattan.

Upon the defendant's going through customs at Kennedy Airport, the suit was found to contain narcotics, and the defendant was arrested. The defendant told his story to the customs agents. He attempted, in cooperation with the agents, to make a controlled delivery of the suit to the relative waiting at the airport. The relative was apprehended and interviewed by the agents. He denied that he was getting married and that he was going to give the defendant a ride to Manhattan.

At trial, the defendant, in addition to testifying, attempted to introduce through another government agent that upon a second interview, the apprehended relative admitted to an interviewing agent that he was, in fact, soon to marry and that he was, in fact, a livery car driver.

The trial court ruled that such statement by the relative elicited at trial through the interviewing agent was impermissible hearsay.

The Court of Appeals disagreed. While, indeed, the statement was an assertion testified to by a person other than the declarant, the statement WAS NOT OFFERED FOR ITS TRUTH. Rather, the defense didn't care if the statement were true or false. The statement was offered to show the state of mind—regardless of whether the statement was true or false—of the defendant in carrying the suit back to the United States. The statement was sought to show the lack of intent, the innocent motive, of the defendant, regardless of whether the statement was true or false when made to the agent.

Thus, the statement—as used—was not hearsay. It was approved for use by the Second Circuit not because it was hearsay, but exactly because it was not hearsay; it was NOT offered to prove the truth of the matter asserted.

OTHER USES THAT ELIMINATE HEARSAY

There are, in addition, under Rule 801(d)FRE, many assertions not originally made by the witness on the stand that are offered for the truth of the assertion and *are* admitted into evidence under certain and particular circumstances.

These statements are NOT hearsay.

Because of their indicia of reliability, because, from human experience through the eons, these particular types of statements can be accepted as factual, these statements do not fall within the hearsay proscription. Some of the more frequently seen of such statements, that are often referred to as exceptions to the hearsay rule, follow. There are others, with which you should be familiar. For these, see the text of Article 8, FRE in its entirety.

(a) Statement of a Party Opponent

First of all, this sort of declaration is called an Admission, rather than a statement. When you see the word Admission, it relates ONLY to the declaration of a party.

A witness, therefore, cannot make an Admission. A witness's declaration is called a statement.

The very fact that a party is just that, a party, and therefore is deeply involved in the lawsuit, available for explanation or clarification, is the reason that the declaration of that party (an Admission), in either an individual or a representative capacity, is admissible in evidence whether the said party takes the witness stand or not.

> ***NOTE:*** *There is no difficulty whatever using either an Admission OR a statement for impeachment purpose during cross-examination (see use of inconsistent statement section, infra).*

(b) Statement Made in the Presence of a Party

Following right behind an Admission as an introducable declaration regardless of whether or not the party takes the stand is a statement made by a third person *in the presence of a party*. This declaration, too, because of the prominent role played by a party in a litigation, is not considered hearsay and is admissible in evidence whether or not the party becomes a witness in the litigation.

Because human experience has come to realize that a statement made of or about the subject of the litigation, in the presence (and awareness) of a party, would not be permitted to stand *unchallenged*, a statement that impacts negatively against the litigation, *uncorrected or unchallenged* by the party in whose presence the declaration was *made* is admissible as a *tacit admission.*

Remember, we're talking about a party here. The statement had to be made in the presence of a party, not a witness.

Thus, an adverse statement, made in the presence of a party, *unchallenged* is considered to be a tacit acknowledgment of the content of the statement by a party, and is *not* hearsay. It is an Admission by Silence.

(c) Statement of a Party's Co-Conspirator

Since a conspiracy is likened to a partnership, in which each partner is deemed the agent of all other partners (co-conspirators) and in which each partner is responsible for and bound by the acts and words of all other partners, the statement or admission of a partner/co-conspirator is admissible in the same fashion as if it were the direct Admission of each of the other partners/co-conspirators. That is, it is an Admission made by an authorized agent, and thus is the Admission of the party.

However, *before such statement may be used,* the party(ies) against whom the statement is offered must be shown to be a member(s) of the partnership (conspiracy), fully familiar with the purpose and aim of the conspiracy. Once this knowledge and awareness is shown, however, the statement of any co-conspirator becomes the Admission of and binding upon any other co-conspirator/party. Thus, such statement is admissible against a party regardless of whether that party takes the witness stand.

> ***NOTE:*** *The determination of whether or not a party is a member of a particular conspiracy has now been relegated to a question of law, not a question of fact. Thus, the determination of whether or not a party is a member of a conspiracy is currently decided by the judge as a matter of law, not by the jury as a question of fact.*

(d) Excited Utterance/Present Sense Impression

These are declarations, that, in human experience are made with reflex action, before a person, party, or witness has the opportunity to think and fabricate.

These declarations ordinarily describe an event or condition while the declarant was actually perceiving the event, or immediately thereafter.

Thus, a witness who, immediately after the happening of an accident, overwrought by emotion and concern, running about screaming that someone who just walked backward into a plate-glass window is bleeding and needs help, is making an excited utterance. This, depending on its spontaneity and closeness in time to the event, could be admitted in evidence even by a third person/witness who heard the statement as it was being screamed about.

(e) Prior Inconsistent Statement

When a witness takes the stand, whether that witness be a party or a mere witness to an event, any prior inconsistent (relevant to the litigation) statement made by such witness may be introduced for the purpose of impeaching that witness. For a complete discussion concerning the four different kinds of prior inconsistent statements, their use, and the foundations necessary for each different category of inconsistency, see the chapter on cross-examination, infra.

> ***NOTE:*** *When introduced to affect credibility, a prior inconsistent statement is NOT evidence-in-chief. It is not introduced to assert the truth of the statement, but is being used to affect credibility, to show the jury that the witness may be unreliable as that witness had previously made another and different statement concerning the case.*

Depending on how such a prior inconsistent statement affects your case, you may request of the Court a limiting instruction to the jury that such statement is NOT evidence.

Such statement is also not hearsay. Why? I hope, by this time, you have the proper understanding of the proscription against hearsay. A prior inconsistent statement is not hearsay for two reasons: (1) it is not introduced for the truth of the statement, only to affect credibility; and (2) the witness on the stand can be cross-examined about his or her own prior statement.

Even where the prior inconsistent statement was made to a third person upon the proper foundation (see cross-examination, infra), the prior inconsistency is admissible *through that third person* for credibility purposes. And, as such, the third person inconsistent statement is *not* hearsay.

(f) Prior Consistent Declarations

Indicated earlier is the rule that prior inconsistent statements may fall outside the proscription against hearsay.

Prior consistent statements, on the other hand, CANNOT be admitted into evidence and are not an exception to the hearsay rule because they violate yet another rule of evidence. Prior consistent statements cannot be used by the party offering a witness because they merely bolster the testimony of the witness/prior declarant. Thus, the prior statement is superfluous and cumulative. A repetition of the same statement adds nothing to the proceedings. After all, a person saying something once or twice or five times is still the same person making the same declaration. Repetition does not make it more true, nor more cross-examinable.

For a different reason, the same prior consistent statement is not usable by an adversary on cross-examination. For example, when a party or witness testifies consistently with prior statements, that party or witness is testifying currently to certain circumstances. The current testimony can be cross-examined. The fact that the witness made prior consistent statements need not be established in order for the cross-examiner to probe the witness's current testimony.

Therefore, neither party can utilize a prior consistent statement except—isn't there always an exception?—except when the witness's testimony has been attacked as a *recent fabrication.*

Not every cross-examination, even a scathing, ripping cross-examination of a witness, that attempts to discredit that witness, is an attack of recent fabrication.

Recent fabrication, as a term or art, means that as the time for trial drew nigh the witness has changed, fabricated, his or her testimony to accommodate the position of one of the parties.

In such case, a prior *consistent* statement can be utilized and not be considered a violation of the hearsay rule to show that the current testimony of that witness is NOT a recent fabrication but is exactly what the witness had previously said on some prior occasion.

> ***NOTE:*** *The prior consistent statement, when introduced as described here, is not being introduced for the truth, but merely to show that the prior statement was previously made and, thus, that the testimony is not a recent fabrication. For this "other" reason, the prior consistent statement is not hearsay and is permitted in the limited circumstances illustrated here.*

(g) Declaration Against Penal Interest

A declaration by a party or a witness that is adverse to that person's penal interest, that is, that affirms something that would put that person at jeopardy vis-à-vis the penal law is considered a declaration against penal interest.

There is also a concomitant declaration against economic interest—a declaration that would impact negatively against a person's economic interests—that may also qualify as an exception to the proscription against hearsay.

The reason that the preceding indicated declarations may be exceptions to the rule against hearsay and therefore might be admitted into evidence whether or not the party or witness takes the stand, is that, in ordinary human experience, such statements are not made by persons unless they are true. People do not ordinarily say things adverse to themselves for fun, in jest, or to amuse an audience. Rather, humans have a tendency to boast and to puff, not to deprecate themselves. Thus, negative statements about oneself, when made, carry the human implication or indicia of reliability of the truth of such statement.

(h) Exceptions Where Witness Is Unavailable

Where a witness is unavailable, certain declarations of that witness may be used as a substitute for current testimony, where those declarations are clothed in reliability. In other words, not *every* prior statement of an unavailable witness can be admitted. It must pass other qualifying criteria.

There are several bases for a Court to declare a witness unavailable: inability to be present due to death or then-existing mental or physical illness; inability of the proponent of the statement to procure the declarant's attendance by process or other reasonable means; refusal of the declarant to testify under color of legal privilege (Fifth Amendment); or refusal of the declarant to testify despite court order; inability of the declarant to recall the subject matter of the declaration.

Under this category, depositions and prior testimony qualify as the sort of prior statements that, if available, are admissible in the absence or unavailability of a witness.

(i) Past Recollection Recorded

When a declarant has no present recollection of the subject or event, but previously had made a written memorandum or record when the matter was fresh in the witness's memory or experience, and when the memorandum or record was made accurately, such written record may be used in the examination of the witness. The written statement may not be shown to the jury, however, unless offered by the party to whom this is an adverse witness.

In other words, the witness must testify at trial that he has no current recollection of an event, but that he recalls having made a note or memorandum of the event and that when he made that note, he wrote down exactly what had been seen. Such note or memorandum may be admissible, since the witness is available to be cross-examined concerning the event and the capacity of that witness to have seen or heard what he wrote in the note.

THERE'S MORE TO THE RULES THAN THIS

This is just a smattering of what is involved in the Rules of Evidence. There are other rules and other exceptions to those rules. These should be studied, so that the advocate is familiar with all of them, knows when to use them and knows how to counter his or her adversary's attempt to use them.

They may seem difficult, confusing, too numerous to master, but they're not. As indicated earlier, there are certain rules that are significant, and when you master the essence of these rules, the real meaning and purpose of the rules, you will be well on your way to being able to understand and use them easily.

Start absorbing the essences. The trial is at hand. We're about to pick the jury.

9

DISCOVERY DEVICES

There are several methods of obtaining discovery from your adversary in order to uncover additional facts concerning the upcoming litigation and in order to better prepare yourself, your witnesses, and the case itself. We shall discuss the basics of some of these methods and devices in this chapter.

BILL OF PARTICULARS

A Bill of Particulars is a very narrow discovery device. It is intended only to amplify or expand the allegations contained in the complaint or accusatory instrument. In the main, and as as result, of course, a Demand for a Bill of Particulars is used only by defense advocates.

Where a cross claim or a counter claim is employed by the defense advocate, however, the plaintiff/prosecutor has the opportunity to Demand a Bill of Particulars.

VERY LIMITED PURPOSE

Since complaints and accusatory instruments are couched in ultimate conclusions of fact, they are almost always written in terse statements that merely present a succinct declaration of occurrence, allegations that merely hint at the underlying event. The Demand for a Bill of Particulars is intended to uncover, with specificity, more details or "particulars" concerning the allegations of the complaint.

Thus, by addressing the complaint paragraph by paragraph, the Demand for a Bill of Particulars seeks specificity of the charged event: the time; the specific place; the specific acts of negligence or criminal activity; the specifics of hospital stay, disability, out-of-pocket expenses, and so forth, all of which are alleged in the complaining document.

In the main, both procedure rules and case law in your jurisdiction shall indicate precisely what information is available by way of a Bill of Particulars. For this reason, I am not going to detail the items available to you. I am merely going to indicate that defense advocates should seek a Bill of Particulars in every case. And plaintiff/prosecutors should be careful not to permit overzealous adversaries to make excessive demands.

In any situation where you think your adversary has requested more than he or she is entitled to, or where your adversary has not responded fully or adequately, a motion to the Court may resolve the situation.

Request for Discovery

The Request for discovery, along with the Demand for a Bill of Particulars, is the other side of the initial inquiry into specifics of the lawsuit.

Here again, it is usually the defense advocate who makes the discovery demand, although in connection with discovery both sides may require certain additional facts, documents, scientific or expert test results or analyses, or a view of some physical evidence under your control.

What is sought in the Request for discovery is further details of the physical evidence supporting the allegations and charges. By the Request for discovery, the advocate seeks "all other" information that might be available but is under the control of the adversary.

A Request for discovery is not intended to send your adversary on an investigative trip on your behalf. It seeks out discovery of facts or items that are specifically under the control of your adversary or his or her client. If the facts, documents, and so forth, are available to both sides equally, by the exercise of diligence or effort, the Court will not require one adversary to supply that information, facts, documents, or whatever, to the other. Again, the items of discovery available via a Request are ordinarily enumerated in the rules of procedure for your jurisdiction.

If the items are not specified, they are nonetheless circumscribed fairly well by use and custom. Though circumscribed, they are at the same time fairly broad.

You are entitled to discover everything that is carryable, movable, studiable—except for that which is the specific work product of the adversary. In other words, you are entitled to view anything in the case that is objectively a factor in the case and that is not the specific work product—the thought processes—of the adversary in formulating a counter to your position.

If it can be studied, evaluated, put under a microscope, looked at, and if it is an objective factor in the case, you should be able to discover it.

Both civil and criminal

The Demand and the Request—get used to the difference—are available in both civil and criminal litigation.

Don't be surprised, however, you criminal defense advocates, if you get hardly anything for your demand or request.

Because there is so much at stake—your client's life, sometimes—it seems that you get very little information from the prosecutor. And the Courts ordinarily uphold such paucity.

In a civil case, on the other hand, where often only money is implicated, you can be involved in discovery proceedings for months, even years. Which just goes to show you where the heads of most of the people involved in our jurisprudence are.

For those who answer that the criminal bums (meaning the clients, not the lawyers) should be eliminated so that the good guys can go on with their life, liberty, and pursuit of happiness, I just remind you that the Constitution and the rules of criminal procedure are designed to protect the rights and lives of citizens accused of crime, not the criminals.

The only way you can protect and pamper criminals is to give them two pillows and a down comforter AFTER they are convicted by a fair trial procedure.

The day that we fail to protect our fellow citizens by insisting on a fair and complete prosecutorial procedure for all is the day that we sound the death knell for all those "good guys"—also citizens—who just want to go on with their life, liberty, and so forth. There ain't nobody going to be making or enjoying nothing in a totalitarian atmosphere where summary trials, imprisonments, and executions are the orders of the day.

When you opt for a full and fair trial for ALL, you're not supporting "them," you're supporting yourself, your own freedoms, life, liberty, and the pursuit of you know what.

Deposition

A deposition or examination before trial, an EBT, is a formal questioning of an adverse party or witness who is under the control of your adversary.

Ordinarily, the deposition is attended and recorded by a stenographer or reporter working on a stenographic machine. The recording is reduced later to a typed transcript, that is presented to the testifying witness for reading and signature.

NOTICE IS NECESSARY

Ordinarily, the deposition becomes functional when one or the other of the advocates sends a Notice to Take Deposition to his or her opposite number.

There is no specified order of taking depositions. The order is caused by the service of the notice. Whichever advocate sends the first notice is ordinarily the advocate who examines first, at the location of his or her choice.

The adversary will ordinarily send a counternotice scheduling depositions of the party or witnesses of the advocate who sent the first notice, on the same day and in the same place, to be recorded by the same reporter as those scheduled by the first notice served.

Thus, you can get home court advantage by forwarding an early notice to Take Deposition to your adversary. Indicate in the notice whom you want to examine, what documents or materials you expect the witness (or party) to bring with him or her, and the time and place that you wish to conduct the deposition.

SCHEDULE THE DEPOSITION AT YOUR OFFICE

The adversary who presents the first notice to Take Deposition has the option of selecting the site at which he or she shall conduct the deposition.

As long as you have the option of selecting the site, schedule the deposition at your office. This causes you the least amount of inconvenience and your adversary the most amount of inconvenience. In addition, it is good psychology to conduct the deposition on your home base, in surrounding that are foreign to your adversary and in which you are totally at home and comfortable.

ADVERSARIES, SELECT YOUR OWN SITE

Merely because the advocate who sent out the first notice schedules the deposition at her office does not *require* the adversary to select the same site or date for counterdepositions.

True, as I've already indicated, the adversary who is going to present her party or witness at the office or selected site chosen by the advocate who sent the first notice ordinarily opts to conduct all the depositions at the same time and place, and shall fall into scheduling her depositions to coincide.

There are various reasons for this, including an economy of time and money. As long as a stenographer is going to be taking one deposition, it is ordinarily less expensive to have that same stenographer take the other depositions at the same location in the same time frame.

Moreover, all the advocates are assembled, and it is far less time consuming to complete the depositions at the same time, or during the same time frame, than it is to have to assemble all the advocates and witnesses and stenographer again at some other place.

The adversary is free, however, to choose where and when she wishes to conduct further depositions of the witnesses or parties of the opposition.

This freedom to choose does not mean an unlimited choice of time and place. For example, the traditional place to conduct a deposition is at the office of one or the other of the adversaries. If the adversary who has been served with a notice to Take Deposition does not wish to conduct the counterdeposition at the office of his adversary, he may notice the counterdeposition at his own office on a later or different occasion.

Also, in many jurisdictions, the adversary who has been served with a notice of EBT can insist that the EBT be held at the courthouse rather than at the office of the originally serving advocate.

This change in location must be accomplished either by agreement with your adversary or by application to the Court to change the location to the courthouse or some other place that you deem to be more convenient or appropriate.

Another example of change of site of the deposition is when the notice to Take Deposition insists on the production of voluminous records or a substantial amount of equipment or machinery connected to the litigation. In this event, the advocate representing the party or person who is required to produce the said records or equipment might make application to the Court to change the site of the examination to such place or location that is more practical and convenient.

METHOD OF CONDUCTING A DEPOSITION

A deposition is handled by the advocate conducting the deposition as if she were cross-examining the witness. In other words, leading questions are permitted, as the witness is under no circumstances considered the witness of the examiner.

Unlike cross-examination, however, questions can be asked only once. If a question is posed a second time from a slightly different perspective—that might be perfectly proper on cross-examination—the attorney representing the party or witness may object to the question as having already been asked and answered.

Indeed, if the adversary insists on asking the question again, the advocate representing the witness may very well direct the witness not to answer.

When such occurs, a ruling from the Court may become necessary to clarify whether or not the witness is required to answer such question.

For this reason, it is always more convenient to be conducting the deposition in the courthouse, as obtaining a ruling is eminently more convenient when you have only to walk along a corridor or take an elevator.

If the examiner feels that the question is of such import that the deposition cannot continue, it may be necessary to suspend the deposition until the ruling is obtained, either on that day or on some other scheduled day. Naturally, it shall be necessary to have the reporter either prepare a transcript of the proceedings thus far or to accompany counsel to the courthouse so that the judge may be apprised of the exact circumstances of the proceedings to which there is an objection.

OBJECTIONS IN GENERAL

One of the "usual" stipulations into which each side commonly enters at the beginning of a deposition is that all objections, except as to form, shall be preserved until trial.

What this means, in short, is that if there is an objection to relevance or propriety of a question, the objection may be noted, the witness may answer, and an objection shall be litigated before the Court prior to trial, or when the adversary seeks to use the deposition at trial. The objection is preserved in full force, without dilution or diminution until both advocates are in front of the Court. At that time, the Court shall decide the motion as if it had just been made for the first time and shall rule as to whether or not the question is proper or should be disallowed for use at the trial.

In the event, however, that an advocate feels that the question or line of questions being asked is totally irrelevant to the litigation, then he or she *may* direct his or her witness not to answer.

This procedure, of course, may very well result in the suspension of the deposition until the Court can decide the matter. Thus, the stipulation that preserves the rights to object to the questions may be a more convenient method of getting on with it.

SCOPE OF A DEPOSITION

A deposition is a discovery device, a medium through and by which an advocate can uncover facts and circumstances about the upcoming litigation in order to prepare for trial. Anything relevant to the litigation, therefore, is proper subject for questioning.

A deposition is not, however, the time or place for delving into the credibility of the witness. Since credibility affects only the perspective of the trier(s) of fact, affecting the way in which the fact finder(s) view the witness, such scathing cross-examination should be held in abeyance for the time and the place when the fact-determining process is underway.

That does not at all mean that the advocate conducting the deposition cannot elicit background information from the witness that may later be developed more fully before the fact finders. Indeed, you should. The inquiry into peripheral matters will be far more objectionable at a deposition, however, than at a trial. Therefore, the inquiry into tangential matters must in some fashion be connected to the litigation rather than brought up purely for purposes of credibility or your adversary is going to object most strongly.

DEVELOP YOUR TRIAL THEME NOW

In the next chapter I speak in more detail about the fact that you must develop a theory and theme for the litigation. In short, after having interviewed the witnesses, after having unearthed the facts as best you could so far, after researching the law, you must home in on the theory, the theme, of your litigation, the banner that you are going to carry during the trial. In other words, plaintiff's advocates, what is your theory of the case? Defense advocates, what is your theory of defense?

Depending on what you determine, so goes the balance of the case. In other words, you can't just sit on the fence, blowing hot or cold in any direction that the wind takes you. You must develop a theory, a theme, and then mold the fabric of the case around that theory.

DEPOSITIONS CAN HELP DEVELOP THE THEME

It may be somewhat premature to develop full-blown theories of the case before you complete the depositions.

You must ever keep in mind, however, that you must develop your theory, your theme, your posture for the case, and the depositions may help you frame that theme.

You may, if you wish, refrain from committing yourself wholesale to the theory until the completion of all depositions and discovery, using the information developed to flesh out all the facets of the case so that when finally completed you will have the entire mass of legal matter with which to formulate the final theory of your presentation.

PREPARE YOUR WITNESSES FOR THE DEPOSITION

The deposition is the first opportunity that your adversary has to have a "go" at your client or your witnesses. By the same token, it will be the first time that your client or witness stands up to fire. Just as in those chapters on direct and on cross-examination, I advise you here that you cannot permit your client/witness to face a deposition without prior preparation.

Further into this book, I indicate that Courts often speak of the foolishness of an attorney who puts a witness on the stand without knowing what that witness is going to say, without knowing what the testimony will be.

It is anticipated, yea, it is your responsibility to know what your witness is going to say and to prepare that witness for the ordeal. This does not mean that you manufacture the witness's testimony. Far from it. You never, never get involved in manufacturing anything! An advocate's responsibility is to bring out the facts, not to make the facts. However, the witness is a layperson and must be prepared and educated in what to expect.

ANSWER ONLY THE QUESTION ASKED

One of the most significant pieces of information that you can impart to your witness who is going to be deposed is that he or she should answer ONLY the question asked. This may seem simplistic. It is not, however.

Testimony is not social conversation. And your witness, unless he is a person with substantial other testimonial experience, is accustomed to speaking, to responding to questions in a social atmosphere. Thus, if it were a beautiful day, bright sun shining, blue, cloudless skies, and someone were to ask the witness if it were raining, the witness might socially respond, "No, it's a beautiful, sunny day." If, for another example, your witness were driving a blue car and were asked if he were driving a red car, he might respond, "No, the car I was driving is blue."

Those answers are perfectly fine—for social conversation. Not for litigation.

The question, is it raining out should be answered: "No." The question, were you driving a red car should also be answered: "No."

TEACH YOUR WITNESS TESTIMONIAL JUJITSU

In the martial art of jujitsu, the person attacked uses and continues the energy of the attacker against the attacker himself. Thus, the person attacked does not try to repel backward, but tries to combine his or her energy with the energy of the attacker, to throw the attacker off balance.

In testifying, and this concept will be repeated during the chapters on direct and cross-examination, you must teach your witness NOT to lend energy to the adversary, thus supplementing the strength of the adversary.

The best method for your witness not to aid the adversary is not to lend energy to the adversary. This is done by answering ONLY the question asked and by not providing any additional energy (read, gratuitous remarks).

To answer the example questions by the gratuitous information that it is a nice sunny day, or that the car was blue, is to lend energy, to GIVE the adversary information rather than require the adversary to develop the information him- or herself.

Therefore, your witness must be schooled that the only proper way to answer a question is to answer that question ONLY, and not to supply other information.

YOU CAN BRING OUT ADDITIONAL INFORMATION

Often, witnesses add additional information in the answers given to questions propounded by your adversary in the mistaken notion that they have to get every bit of information out in the open every time a question is asked.

That is because they do not understand the procedures.

And their failure to understand the procedures is your fault. Yes, it is. You should have advised them that there are two separate methods for answering questions. The first is that they answer your questions with full information. The second, when the witness is being interrogated by your adversary, is the "answer to the question ONLY" method.

You must make the difference crystal clear to your witnesses. Let them know unquestionably that if you want to bring something out, you will. But! But! when your adversary asks a question, that is not necessarily the time to give all the information in the witnesses' head.

THE TIME TO GIVE FULL INFORMATION

Advise the client that there are, however, certain areas in which fulsome answers are perfectly fine. For example, when the adversary in a negligence case wants to know the extent of the plaintiff's injury, tell the plaintiff that he or she can go on forever about aches and complaints.

THERE ARE NO PLAINTIFF HEROES

In ordinary everyday life, complaining is not admired. However, an action brought to obtain compensation for injury is not everyday life. Therefore, a witness must articulate the full extent of the injuries, the pain and suffering, without keeping a stiff upper lip.

A stiff upper lip is counterproductive to a plaintiff's case. And a plaintiff should know that. And you have to tell him or her so.

NEVER CLOSE THE DOOR TO THE PHYSICAL CONDITION

A person being deposed must never close the door to the details that he or she may be supplying concerning their physical condition. This is not the same rule for testifying during a trial. More, anon.

EXAMPLE:

Q. Was there anything else that the doctor did at that time?

A. There may have been, I can't recall at this time.

Q. Is there anything else that was bothering you, physically, after the accident?

A. That's all that I can think of right now. There may have been more. I just can't recall right now.

The reason why is obvious, of course. You don't close the door in the event that indeed there *are* other things that your client hasn't mentioned.

THE DOCTOR ALWAYS EXAMINES THE PATIENT

Oftentimes, the defense advocate tries to limit the amount of examination and treatment given by a doctor and therefore tries to limit the seriousness of a claimed injury. Plaintiff's advocates will do well by their clients to explain that the doctor is always examining the patient, even when the doctor is sitting and talking to the patient. Examination is not restricted to listening through a stethoscope, or X-raying the patient's body.

THERE ALWAYS MAY BE OTHER THINGS

As part of not closing the door, have your witness prepared to testify that there may have been other examinations, other visits to the doctor, other prescriptions or treatments, but he or she can't remember right there and then. This keeps the door from closing on the evidence that you might be able to present at trial.

This is not being evasive or dishonest. This is keeping your options open.

THE OPEN-DOOR POLICY GOES FOR ALL DEPOSITIONS

The methodology of answering questions as set forth here is not limited just to negligence cases. It is the proper manner of answering questions in any deposition, whether the subject matter of the litigation is contracts, torts, or admiralty.

DEPOSITION TESTIMONY IS NOT TRIAL TESTIMONY

Although the testimony given at a deposition is cast in stone and is very difficult to circumvent at trial (see use of prior inconsistent statements under oath in the chapter on cross-examination), testimony NOT given, specifically not remembered and left open by the open-ended answer is still available at trial.

> **Q.** Didn't you testify at your deposition that those were all the things you remembered?
>
> **A.** No, I said there might have been more that I didn't remember then.
>
> **Q.** And have you had a sudden recollection just in time for this litigation?
>
> **A.** Not just in time for, just because of this litigation. Thinking about coming here, I was thinking about the case, and then I remembered that there was more.

The witness cannot not remember facts at trial, however, because this is the end of the road, this is all there is, there isn't any more. There is no more time to go home and remember, which is specifically how depositions differ from trials and why the open door policy relates only to depositions.

INTERROGATORIES

Rather than a deposition where oral questions and answers are posed and responded to, you, the advocate, may opt for written interrogatories.

This device is sometimes used in place of deposition—you cannot have both. You may choose between having a deposition and having interrogatories. Where it is inconvenient to conduct a deposition, where you have only certain information you want from the witness, or just where you feel it more appropriate, you can write out your questions and submit them to your adversary, asking, in turn, that the witness for whom they are intended submit written answers to the posed questions.

These answers to interrogatories are then signed, sworn to, and returned to the adversary demanding the interrogatories and can be used in basically the same way as if you had a deposition in hand. That is, these are the sworn statements of the person who has supplied the answers to the interrogatories.

Interrogatories are often used where there are long distances between the individuals, between the advocate and the adversary's witnesses involved in the litigation. Oftentimes, the written interrogatory serves as well as a deposition does and saves a great deal of time and travel.

LETTERS ROGATORY

Letters rogatory are a discovery device very similar to the written interrogatories mentioned here, except that letters rogatory are usually used interjurisdictionally, between states, often between foreign countries.

The questions are written out in much the same form as interogatories and submitted, but they must then be handled in accordance with the laws of the foreign jurisdiction in which the witness resides or is presently abiding.

ROGATORY COMMISSION

Rogatory comission is yet another item on the discovery menu. This is where both advocates commission someone, often a magistrate of a foreign jurisdiction, to undertake an inquiry of a witness who is presently or permanently out of the jurisdiction of litigation.

These are conducted according to the law of that foreign jurisdiction and may not end up as questions and answers in written or transcript form. It may very well be an inquiry by a magistrate who then writes out his or her notes or impressions of what occurred, rather than submit a verbatim record.

The adversary against whom this sort of discovery is used during litigation back in his or her own backyard may complain that such inquiry should not be permitted as it is not in acceptable form. But he or she may find him- or herself in for a surprise. If the commision passes muster in the jurisdiction where it was undertaken, it may very well pass muster in the Court in which the result is being presented.

Thus, get a good line on what is going to occur in the foreign jurisdiction before consenting to the commission.

NOTICE TO ADMIT

This is yet another discovery device. The Notice to Admit is used to obtain admission of specific information that the advocate believes is irrefutable, unquestionable, indisputable.

This is similar to a judicial notice by a judge, except that it is from your adversary that you are requesting acknowledgment or admission.

For example, you may ask that your adversary admit the existence of an event, a document, or a state of facts.

Where you get into facts that are questionable, naturally you are not going to get an Admission. Remember, I indicated that it had to be in connection with something that was fairly indisputable.

If, however, it is a statement of facts that are certainly and clearly correct, if there is the existence of a document and a signature on the document, you can send out a Notice to Admit.

Naturally, the purpose of the Notice to Admit is to save you the necessity of presenting a witness for a fact or circumstance that is readily ascertainable and admitable by your adversary.

The interesting thing about Notices to Admit is that often your adversary just ignores them and decides to tell you, inferentially, to go fly a kite. As a result, the item you demanded BECOMES DEEMED ADMITTED by tacit admission.

And, ordinarily, no amount of lamentation or protestation erases the "admission" made when your adversary told you to fly a kite.

Protective orders

In connection with all the above discovery devices, if you feel that your adversary's demand, request, notice and the materials requested therein are far too broad, irrelevant, protected, or whatever, if you do not think your adversary should have the same, you cannot just ignore the demand/notice. You cannot tell your adversary to fly a kite. You cannot send the document back.

You must enlist the aid of the Court.

You must seek a protective order, one that will protect you from such events as tacit admissions that result from your failure to provide the material requested, your failure to produce.

Seek the aid of the Court. Make a motion. Schedule a conference to discuss the propriety of the demand/notice.

Don't ignore a legally served document. Even if you think it was illegally served, seek the aid of the Court. Just as testimony is not social conversation, so, too, litigation is not a tennis match. It is a strictly controlled event, the rules of which must be honored at all times.

Self-help has never been a rule of procedure in any jurisdiction.

10

THE THEME'S THE THING

You are about to begin to address, to speak to the fact finder(s) about the case, whether the fact finder(s) are a jury or a judge at a bench trial, whether you are in a jurisdiction where the advocates select the jury or where the court selects the jury.

Therefore, this is the right place to advise you that you must begin now, and never stop until the trial is over, to expound the theme of the litigation, to set the tone you have determined is best to develop the issues, the facts, the evidence that you intend to present in this case.

IT'S NOT A SENTENCE; IT'S A THEME

Some lecturers on trial advocacy suggest that the first words, the first sentence that is said to the jury cast an almost uneradicable hue to the case.

That's true.

And so do the rest of the words that you speak to the fact finder(s) throughout the trial.

If a well-developed first sentence—or even a theme—spoken by either side to the jury carried the day on every occasion, the defense bar in every case would be totally lost except on the happenstance that the plaintiff's advocate says the wrong first sentence, picks the wrong theme.

Indeed, it is true that setting the right theme is essential, right from the get-go. But the war is not necessarily won or lost based on who speaks the first sentence to the fact finder(s). Since there are so many words spoken to a jury, in so many orders, it is difficult to determine which are the very first words that will remain with the jury.

For example, the first sentence about the case may be spoken by the judge when he or she makes a preliminary statement about the case just before jury selection. This is particularly true at a criminal trial. After that, in many jurisdictions, the judge picks the jury. Or, in those jurisdictions where the advocates select the jury, the plaintiff/prosecutor addresses the jury and makes another preliminary statement at the beginning of selecting the jury.

Thus, if you are the defense advocate at a criminal trial, you will NEVER get to speak first, to say the first words to the jury. Yet no one can say that there are never defendant's verdicts in criminal cases because the plaintiff's advocate/prosecutor spoke the first words to the fact finder(s).

The same is true in a civil trial. The defense addresses the jury second, both at the *voir dire* and at the opening. And no one would dream that there are defense verdicts only where the plaintiff's advocate chooses the wrong first sentence because of the order of addressing the jury.

The first words that the plaintiff's attorney says to the jury are important.

No less important are the first words spoken by the defense.

For the jury's point of view is framed based upon these statements. The first words begin to set the tone, the theme of your presentation; they cause a first impression. Thereafter, everything you do in presenting your case, your client, or yourself to the jury either is in keeping with your chosen theme or unravels that theme, changes the theme you have undertaken to present.

THE FIRST IMPRESSION IS SIGNIFICANT

The fact finder(s), whether jury or bench, do have a tendency to absorb their first impression and retain it throughout the trial.

Sometimes it is called "primacy" and "recency." Primacy is the listener's tendency to recollect the first, the prime impression and recency being the listener's tendency to remember the last of the *first* impressions. In short, listeners of any stripe, including the court and jury, tend to subliminally retain their first and last impressions of a subject.

With this in mind, begin right and be consistent throughout the trial, ever vigilant that everything you say and do in the courtroom either supports your chosen theme or works against the theme of your adversary.

THE HONEST SLOB VERSUS THE CREEP

An apt illustration of the primacy/recency theory is to describe a person as being *honest, sloppy, stingy, hard working*. Primacy attaches with the word honest; recency with hard working: the first and last words heard about the person. Sure, there are some negative aspects of the person in between, but the totality of the first and last impression that the listeners retain is "honest" and "hard working." The prime and most recent adjectives are far more likely to remain than are the intermediate aspects of being sloppy and stingy.

When the listener is asked for his impression of the person here described, the answer is likely to be favorable: a decent enough person, has some faults, but in the main, is upstanding, honest, decent, an honest slob.

Turn that around, describe the person as sloppy, honest, hard working, stingy, and more than likely, the impression generated is negative, unwholesome: a creep.

And that impression is likely to remain throughout the trial.

THE THEME CAN OVERCOME THE FIRST IMPRESSION

Fortunately, there's more to a trial than the first impression. That's only the beginning. That first impression that you may strive to create in the collective mind of the fact finder(s) must, thereafter and throughout the trial, be consistently presented to the jury.

The use of certain words, certain phrases, certain characterizations, all supporting your "theme," must be continually built in a crescendo of orchestrated presentation to the fact finder(s).

IT'S NOT WHO'S FIRST; IT'S WHO SELECTS BEST

In those jurisdictions where the court selects the jury, such as in the federal court, the court is the first person to speak to the fact finder(s) about the case.

Fortunately, however, judges have a tendency to be rather nonpartisan and evenhanded in their description of the case when they familiarize the prospective jurors with the type of case that is upcoming. Thus, despite the fact that the judge may speak first to the jurors, may have the first word, the first "go" at the jurors, it is still left to the advocates for both sides to be partisan, to describe the case as it is viewed from opposite sides of the counsel table.

Therefore, when you have the opportunity to be partisan, to give the trier(s) of fact the primary partisan view of the case and your client, be sure that the view is properly focused for your side, that the opening's primary salvo is telling, and that the message it conveys is the one that you want the jury to retain for the balance of the trial.

YOU HAVE TO LIVE WITH YOUR FIRST WORDS

It isn't likely to escape anyone reading this section that the first words spoken to the trier(s) of fact on your client's behalf may haunt you throughout the trial. As the initial mind-set of the fact finder(s) will be the filter through which every word of testimony and every exhibit in the upcoming evidence will flow, it is essential that in the first moments—seconds, no more than a minute—you set the positive "prime" tone for your case and your client.

And then retain that tone for the rest of the trial.

Now, of course, it is obvious that advocates for both sides speak a first sentence to the jury, each describing the theme of the case from his or her own point of view. The jury then selects which impression more aptly sets the tone of the trial.

It may be different for the various jurors.

So the real challenge is for you, as advocate for either plaintiff or defense, to select the tone, the theme, that will be more forceful, more compelling than that of your adversary. Your presentation must negate the first impression that your adversary has or shall try to set in the mind of the fact finder(s).

WORK ON THE OPENING SENTENCE

Don't worry about the totality of the voir dire or the Opening statement. Work on the Opening sentence. It's going to set the tone for the rest of the trial.

And work from there. Every sentence, every word, one after the other, maintains the tone, maintains the theme.

Sure, other evidence can persuade, can change the mind-set of the fact finder(s). But if the prime impression is negative, you're working uphill, against the tide. The evidence that comes later, that may turn the jurors around to your way of thinking, would be like an overwhelming conflagratory blast in your favor had the jurors' mind-set been primarily positive.

Therefore, don't let the evidence have to work to turn around a negative impression the fact finder(s) has in his or her mind. Have the mind-set tuned in your direction from the outset. Use the subsequent evidence to reinforce, to lock in the positive impressions you've already conveyed.

Thus, it is essential that you work on the first sentence you speak to the fact finder(s). It should incorporate your theme for the rest of the case.

Then let your second, third, and all the other sentences that follow support that theme.

Your subsequent questioning during the voir dire, your subsequent description in the Opening about what the upcoming evidence will show—should—must—fall into a lockstep of consistency behind the prime theme.

Think about what impression you want the jury to carry around with them throughout the trial. Is your client going to be the "honest slob" or just some creep who may have some good qualities that the jurors can't remember. Get that first impression into the fact finder(s) mind right from the opening gate.

Plaintiff's First Statement (Theme)

> This is a case about a little girl walking across the street on a summer afternoon to get an ice-cream cone, and about her being mowed down by a music-blaring car, driven by yackety-yacking teenagers. Mowed down, never to walk without a leg brace for the rest of her life.

Defendant's First Statement (Theme)

> This is a case about every driver's nightmare: a jaywalking child coming out from between parked cars.

Prosecutor's Theme

> This is a case about sleeping in your home and being suddenly attacked out of the darkness by a frightening, heartless shadow who turns out to be this defendant.

Defense Theme

> The crime described by the prosecutor may certainly have occurred. But the defendant was simply nowhere near the scene of the crime at the time it occurred.

Are you getting the idea? Don't waste the first words on hackneyed legalese. Get right to it. Let fact finders get the right, the dramatic prime impression, the one that they are likely going to carry in their heads for the rest of the trial.

Plaintiffs/prosecutors, set up a really compelling theme that comes out in the first sentence. You can capture them right there and then, in the first sentence. Gain the initiative, use that momentum to carry you through the rest of the trial.

Keep it that way, and you'll win.

Defense advocates, try to set up the counter theme, to negate the primary theme set up by the plaintiff. It is entirely sufficient just to neutralize the impression of the case that the plaintiff/prosecutor has tried to make upon the fact finder(s). If the jury is neutralized, if it is not captured into the plaintiff's camp but stands outside both camps, not knowing which camp to join, you have been successful in neutralizing the plaintiff's Opening foray.

Keep it that way and you'll win.

Wait a minute! They both can't win. True. The one who wins is the one who can erect the compelling theme and maintain it throughout. And, remember, your adversary is always looking to trip your theme, make it fall flat on its face. So you have to be vigilant throughout.

ALWAYS FORTIFY THE INITIAL IMPRESSION

If you picked the jury and gave the initial affirmative impression, reaffirm that impression in your Opening.

Throughout the trial, you must be carrying a theme, the theme you've decided as the vehicle to carry your case. You began to impress the jury with that theme with the first words you spoke at the voir dire. Now you fortify that prime impression in your Opening. You do not have to use the same words, of course. You may use the same words, if you wish. But the concept must be the same. The essence of your case is the concept. Give it to the fact finder(s) again in your opening, again through your presentation of evidence, your cross-examination, and in your Summation.

THE THEME'S THE THING TRIALS ARE MADE OF.

11

JURY SELECTION

JURY OR NON-JURY

You're ready for trial. You're ready to prove your case or parry the evidentiary thrusts of your adversary. Since either side, except the prosecutor in a criminal case, has a choice of whether or not a jury is desired, before plans are laid as to what kind of a jury is wanted and how to select that jury, first decide whether or not you want a jury at all.

THE PURPOSE OF A JURY

A trial is a fact-finding exercise. The jury, or a judge at a bench trial, is the finder of facts, the exclusive judge of the facts. When litigation begins, a plaintiff, civil or criminal, charges that a defendant did some act that should not have occurred. The defendant, joining the issues, denies having done something that should not have been done. The trier of the facts, then, must determine just what was done and if, indeed, it should or should not have happened.

If there are no arguments or disputes about the facts, there is no need for a trial. Judgments, whether money judgments or penal sentences, are simple enough for a judge to render or impose once that judge has facts that have been determined by the trier of facts.

Since we do not as yet have magic computers that can electronically sort out which witnesses tell the truth, and where the facts truly lie, the finder(s) of fact, jury or judge at a bench trial, must make factual determinations, must sift and sort evidence, and must make a factual determination as to what actually occurred.

No factual issue, no jury

Occasionally, there are no disputes about the facts, merely about the interpretation of those facts according to the law. For example, a contract exists, indicating that a certain amount per cubic yard is to be paid to an excavator-plaintiff. The defendant does not dispute the written terms of the contract or the amount of material the plaintiff excavated. The plaintiff has contended, however, that the wording of the contract provides for payment of 50 cents extra per load at night. The defendant contends that the very same wording provides for 50 cents extra per load at night only on weekends.

There is no factual dispute in this situation. It is merely the legal import of words that both sides agree are in the contract. They dispute only the legal interpretation of the words. Thus, they have no factual dispute. A jury is unnecessary to decide this case. A judge is necessary to interpret the law. This case readily lends itself, therefore, to a Motion for Summary Judgment or a Court determination upon an agreed statement of facts, which, put down on paper and signed by both parties, can be presented to a judge who then makes a legal determination based on the predetermined facts.

Thus, the jury's function is solely to decide facts. If there are no facts to decide, there is no need for a jury. If parties can stipulate to the facts, there is no need for a jury.

Who has the choice

In a civil case, the plaintiff's attorney is bringing the action on behalf of his or her client. Clearly, the defense attorney would not be at all unhappy if the case were never put on the calendar, if the case were to wither and die on the vine. Thus, the plaintiff ordinarily puts the case on the calendar. At the point of submitting papers that place the matter on the court's trial calendar, the plaintiff has the first option as to whether or not a jury is desired. If the plaintiff determines that a jury is desired, the Defense cannot eradicate that choice and opt for a bench trial.

If the plaintiff were to indicate at the initial filing of the calendar papers that a jury is NOT desired, however, the defendant has the option to indicate that a jury IS desired, and the plaintiff cannot eradicate the defendant's choice and return to bench trial status.

In a criminal case, the prosecutor CANNOT waive a jury trial, as it is the defendant's absolute right (except for some minor charges like traffic summonses) to have trial by a jury of citizens (peers is not in the constitution).

In some states there are certain crimes for the trial of which a defendant CANNOT waive a jury. These are ordinarily capital cases. Other than in such cases, under certain conditions a defendant is permitted to waive a jury and opt for a bench trial.

Under the federal rules of criminal procedure, the United States attorney must consent to the jury waiver of a defendant. Thus, while a defendant can waive a jury, it is only with the consent (whim) of the prosecutor in the federal courts.

In other jurisdictions, waiver of a jury is conditioned upon the approval of the judge, who must satisfy himself/herself that the defendant is not waiving a jury for some tactical advantage.

In both the foregoing instances, the federal prosecutor's approval of a bench trial, or the court's satisfying itself that there is no tactical advantage in having same, runs the good-guy paranoia concerned limiting the bad-guy's (criminal defendant's) capacity to get away with something. Apparently, somehow, the very legislators who wrote these laws permitting waiver of a jury in a criminal case didn't trust that judges could give society a fair shake during a bench trial. Or, perhaps the philosophy is that anything defendants voluntarily choose can't be poisonous enough, so don't let them have it. No amount of dialogue will ever make some people believe that defendants going to trial are citizens accused of crime and are presumed innocent; they are not criminals already convicted of crime.

WHEN TO OPT FOR A JURY

Each case must be decided, as we all know, on its own merits. There are specific factors peculiar to each case that lend themselves to jury determination or not. And these, of course, vary, depending on which side of the counsel table a party sits.

For example, there are situations where an infant has very disfiguring injuries, which necessarily will create strong sympathy in the minds of jurors. This, of course, is not advantageous to the defendant. In these circumstances, a defendant might very well opt for a bench trial. Of course, the advocate representing the infant/plaintiff certainly wants a jury, wants all that sympathy for his infant/plaintiff.

Thus, the determination of who wants a jury depends on the side each advocate represents. Which brings to mind an axiom spoken by a former chief judge of the Federal District Court of the Eastern District of New York: "Where you stand, depends on where you sit."

In a criminal case, on the other hand, there might be a most severe criminal act charged, say the setting of a fire that resulted in the deaths of many people in a social club. Here, sympathy runs to the victims, and the defendant is going to be hard pressed to get a jury that can divorce itself from sympathy or identification with the innocent victims. In this situation, a defendant might well opt for a bench trial where a judge is far less likely to respond to sympathy, and is far more likely because of everyday experience in the court to be able to view the evidence with an eye to the elements of the crime and not to emotion.

The choice also hinges, however, upon the particular judge in front of whom the case is to be tried. As in all of life, judges, who are, it is said, human beings, have personal idiosyncrasies and personal tastes, and they have tendencies which over a period of time of presiding at trials have manifested themselves. A judge may be a plaintiff's lawyer, defense-oriented, a hard-nosed law-and-order person, or a bleeding liberal. You may not have anything against bench trials in general, but the judge in front of whom you have to try a particular case may be a disaster vis-à-vis the facts of the case. Under such circumstances, don't waive a jury.

On the other hand, the judge in front of whom you are scheduled to try a case is erratic, pushy, intolerant. In front of a jury, however, that judge curbs her harsh ways, not wanting to appear to the jury to be exactly what she is. Don't waive a jury.

It should be fairly obvious, then, that you have to determine when to waive a jury on a case-by-case basis, depending specifically on the particular facts of your case and the circumstances of the court and the attitude of the judge.

THE VOIR DIRE

In a trial, there are two instances of use of voir dire, which literally means to see to hear, basically an opportunity to inquire. One instance is what we are about to discuss, the selection of a jury. The other is, during the midst of trial, to inquire about the bona fides of physical or documentary evidence being offered by your adversary. More about this latter voir dire infra in the chapter on documentary evidence.

The purpose of the voir dire to select a jury is to inquire about the personal and educational background of prospective jurors to determine if those jurors are qualified to sit on the particular case about to be tried.

The overriding qualification of jurors to sit at a trial is that they be fair and impartial to both sides. Fairness is the polestar toward which both sides and the court set their course in the selection of a jury.

A particular juror may have the educational background, the temperament, in short, the surface credentials to be a fair and impartial juror. Some experience that the juror may have had in his or her life, however, may color his or her outlook. For example, he may have been involved in an accident and may believe that the insurance company was unfair and arbitrary in dealing with his personal settlement. This prospective juror might not be qualified to sit on the jury in an accident case because he may be prejudiced against the defendant (insurance carrier).

On the other hand, in a criminal case, the relative or friend of a juror may have been arrested, and the juror may have some tendencies for or against the prosecution, for or against a defendant in a criminal case as a result of that experience. This prospective juror might be fine to judge the facts in the aforementioned accident case, but not to judge the criminal case. And the opposite also applies. The juror who had a bad experience connected with an insurance claim might be perfectly neutral to sit and decide a criminal case fairly and impartially.

Perhaps, in a civil case, a prospective juror may be married to, related to, or may be someone who is herself somehow affiliated with a casualty insurance company. This might very well cause the plaintiff's attorney to seek to disqualify that prospective juror. Similarly, in a criminal case, a prospective juror may be married to, related to, or may be himself somehow affiliated with the local police department. This factor might cause defense counsel to opt to excuse the juror. It might very well be that the insurance-related person would be acceptable in the criminal case and that the police-oriented person would be acceptable in the accident case.

To discover the facets of the jurors's backgrounds to give you a better insight in order to challenge the jurors' qualifications, then, is the purpose of the voir dire.

WHO QUESTIONS THE PROSPECTIVE JURORS

In the federal system, the judge questions the jurors during the voir dire, with some help or suggestions as to questions to be asked from the attorneys. Counsel for the parties then assert challenges for cause as well as exercise peremptory challenges for their respective sides, all based upon the probing accomplished by the judge.

Some federal judges do permit some participation by counsel in the questioning process. This practice is individual with different judges. In the main, however, a federal judge does the questioning of the prospective jurors, in open court, in the presence of the advocates for both sides; input from counsel for the parties is minimal.

Many state legislators have proposed that state systems that permit questioning of the jury by counsel for the parties be revised to mandate questioning by the court, as in the federal system, in order to speed up the selection process and therefore save judicial time. Many state systems, however, maintain the process in which counsel for each side questions the prospective jurors directly.

Obviously, if you are appearing in a federal court or in a state system where the judge does the questioning of the prospective jurors, your task is mainly to suggest areas of questioning for the judge, to listen to the answers of the jurors, and to raise challenges for cause or peremptory challenges.

In those state systems that permit advocates to question the jurors, you must be prepared to go forward with the voir dire yourself. And that's what this chapter is about.

CHALLENGE FOR CAUSE

In all jurisdictions, the qualifications for jurors are set out by statute. In the main, the qualifications are that a juror not be related to a party, either by blood or sympathy, that the prospective juror be physically and mentally able to participate in a trial, and that, basically, there be no impediment that would cause that person not to be able to function fairly and impartially to both sides.

If, indeed, during the questioning either by the court or by the advocates factors surface that, in the mind of one or the other of the advocates, cause that juror not to be qualified to act as a juror, that juror should be challenged for cause.

A challenge for cause is just as it sounds: a challenge directed toward the qualifications of the juror based on a specific set of articulable circumstances or factors.

Oftentimes, the disqualification of the juror is such that both sides recognize it immediately and simultaneously. For example, the juror cannot hear sufficiently well to even answer the questions posed. Or the juror is not sufficiently conversant in the English language to follow the flow of the testimony. Or the juror cannot see well enough to observe the witnesses or view the evidence presented. These disqualifications are obvious, and if both sides agree and the judge approves, the juror may be excused.

Notice, even if both sides agree, the judge need not necessarily disqualify the juror. A challenge for cause is an application to the Court, that is decided at the Court's discretion. If the Court disagrees, even though both counsel join in the application, the Court may still refuse to disqualify the juror.

In most instances, however, where both sides agree, the Court usually sees the same impediment to the prospective juror and approves the challenge.

Some challenges for cause may not be so obvious, nor may they be agreed upon by both sides. For example, in a criminal case, a prospective juror is connected with some governmental body, particularly one involved with police work, or with the processing of prisoners (probation, corrections, and so forth). In addition, the particular prospective juror indicates that as a result of such experience, she has seen hordes of people accused of crime, including a great many who are not very truthful, honest, or decent. The concern of the defense is, naturally, whether such a point of view spills over into the prospective juror's view of *this* defendant. If the defense believes that this person could not be fair and impartial to the defendant, the defense challenges this prospective juror for cause.

On the other hand, the prosecutor wants the Court to determine if the juror, notwithstanding her experience, would be fair and impartial to both sides. The prosecutor feels that a person with such skepticism might be a good juror for the prosecution.

> ***NOTE:*** *If the judge does not disqualify a juror that you believe to be unqualified, you must make a record and preserve the issue for appellate review. Sure, you can later peremptorily challenge that juror, but then you are using a peremptory that you might sorely need for another and different prospective juror in the case; you will be without a peremptory because the Court may have erred. This situation, then, may impact on your case later, and the issue should be preserved now.*
>
> ***ANOTHER NOTE:*** *Oftentimes, jurors want to serve on a jury. When asked if they could be fair and impartial to both sides, it is simple enough for the juror to say "yes." In such a situation, you will be hard-pressed to have that anxious-to-serve juror say "no, I can or will not be fair and impartial." Thus, some skepticism may remain in the mind of one or the other advocate concerning a dubious-back-grounded prospective juror, even after a prospective juror says that he/she will be fair and impartial.*
>
> *When such doubt remains and the Court does not sustain the challenge for cause, there is always a peremptory challenge.*

PEREMPTORY CHALLENGE

The peremptory challenge is a challenge to the juror's qualifications based not upon cause, not upon a qualification basis that can be articulated, but rather upon the discretion of one or the other advocate.

In other words, you challenged a prospective juror for cause; the other side opposed your application, and the judge denied the challenge. You still can eliminate the unwanted prospective juror with a peremptory challenge—if you exercised your peremptories judiciously and you still have one remaining to you, that is.

Peremptory challenges are specifically limited in number. In each type of case, there are just so many peremptory challenges available to each side. In many civil cases, there are six peremptory challenges to each side. That means that each advocate can challenge six prospective jurors for other than cause. In a criminal case, depending on the charge against the defendant, there may be as many as fifteen peremptory challenges for each side. Usually, this high number of challenges is available only for the most serious of charges, for example, murder.

> ***NOTE:*** *If there is more than one defendant, the number of challenges for each side normally remains the same. Thus, if there are four defendants in a homicide case, the number of peremptory challenges remains the same, to be agreed upon or doled out amongst the defense advocates.*
>
> *In a situation where there are antagonistic defenses or where there are split interests amongst the parties on one side of a cause, a request can be made to the presiding trial judge to permit additional peremptories because of the diversity of claims or defenses. The judge has the discretion to permit additional peremptories and may do so. But, don't expect more than one or two additional challenges.*
>
> ***ANOTHER NOTE:*** *Within recent time, objections have been made to the peremptory challenges of either prosecutor or defense counsel where it was perceived by the other side that the adversary was systematically eliminating people based on race, creed, or some other arbitrary basis, for example, wanting to eliminate all the white or all the black jurors. Several Courts have condemned such use of peremptory challenges. However, where an advocate can articulate a nonracially-biased reason, even a very personal one, not rising to a challenge-for-cause basis for the use of such peremptory challenge, the same may be used as the advocate desires.*

THE BASIS FOR THE PEREMPTORY

In all of life we exercise judgments based upon what impinges on our senses. Go to a cocktail party; you see a person you find pleasant, attractive. There is something about the person that is agreeable, based upon some criteria long ago set up in your mind, whether you are conscious of the particular basis or not.

This is how the peremptory challenges work. Remember what was said earlier in this book: A trial is like a novel, a play, being presented to an audience (the jury) to persuade them of the rightness of your cause. Now you have come to realize through your life experience that the instant you meet them, there are people whom you can or cannot get along with, whom you would never talk to at a cocktail party. This may not be an infallible radar system,. but it works. From experience you know it works, because this or that type of person you always have difficulty with, you can't bear or can't tolerate, whatever. It is a very personal, but a very real thing.

Well, in questioning, listening to the answers of a prospective juror, you find that the juror is just not going to be one who responds to you or your message very well. Since a trial is a presentation that you must make, if there's a person in the jury that is just not going to respond to you—for reasons that are known way inside your head—you're going to have a difficult time with your presentation. That juror is just not going to respond. Why even have the possibility of such a juror in the midst of the others? Such a juror could be an impediment to a verdict, and could be the mainstay of an adverse verdict.

Let's face it, the selection of a jury is not an experiment in chemical science. We are all human, yes, even your adversary and the judge. And the selection of the jury is not different from selecting people to talk to at a cocktail party or selecting people to have dinner with on a sea voyage. If someone strikes you as wrong, as not suited to the presentation that you are going to make, then peremptorily challenge him or her. That's what the peremptories are for.

It isn't only *you* personally that may rub against the grain of the prospective juror, or vice versa. It may also be the particular case, facts, or the circumstances of your case that you *feel* the juror will not be able to view with the eqanimity required of a fair and impartial juror.

For example, in a particularly violent and bloody crime, where the victim (particularly if the victim was a woman) was tortured or molested, you might not want a shy, retiring, elderly, single woman who might be horrified by the details of the case, might hate your client for even being thought capable of such activity, who shuts her mind down and would be a hostile juror throughout the case.

In a particular civil case, brought by a black plaintiff, who is alleging racial discrimination against a corporation in the hiring/firing of the plaintiff, you might, as defense counsel, find some difficulty with a black juror who you perceive would be sympathetic to the plaintiff regardless of the evidence. On the other hand, there might be a black accountant, articulate and thoughtful, whose everyday function is to make two plus two add up to four. You might want that latter prospective juror on your jury, both because he is black and because he is an accountant. On the other hand, you might not want the former, whose background and mind-set would be against you and would not be fair or impartial to both, or either, side. Challenge the first and accept the second of those prospective jurors.

When you can articulate a basis to exclude a prospective juror from your jury, even if it is a very personal, but a very real basis—not merely for the purpose of depriving a party of a jury of individuals who might be receptive to the opposite cause—then whether the juror be black, white, Asiatic, or whatever, go ahead and challenge him or her.

LET YOUR CLIENT PARTICIPATE

Your client's cause is the cause you are trying. He may or may not sit with you at counsel table. Nonetheless, the jury will be hearing your client's case, looking at your client, and listening to your client if he testifies. The prospective juror may "love" you but "hate" your client. Your case is still undermined by unfairness and partiality of the juror against your client.

Your client can—and should—be consulted to determine if the juror is the sort of person your client would enjoy or hate at first glance at that cocktail party we talked about previously.

If the jury or one or more of the prospective jurors do not like or wouldn't strike up a conversation with your client at a cocktail party, or vice versa, your cause suffers. Thus, ask you client to look over the prospective jurors. Does he "hate" any of them? Do any of them "hate" him? If so, challenge them peremptorily.

> ***CAUTION:*** *Your client doesn't know much about picking juries. Thus, do not accept as gospel each word your client speaks about a juror. Listen to the client and then make your decision. Even if your client doesn't like a particular juror, you may have a reason to want that juror. You may perceive that the shy, retiring woman mentioned earlier has a professional background that is needed in the case. Suppose you're defending a doctor in a malpractice case, and the woman happens to be a nurse, or has some experience with the medical world. You might want such a person on your jury because this prospective juror would be better able to gauge the fallacy of the plaintiff's case from her experience.*

Thus, there are more factors to weigh in exercising your peremptory challenge than just whether you like the juror as if he or she were a personal friend. The factors of the jury's background blended with the facts of the case is the matrix upon which you make your peremptory decisons.

THE SELECTION PROCESS

In civil cases the selection process is often conducted in a separate area of the Courthouse by a clerk of jurors and the advocates for all parties—not necessarily in a courtroom—while the judge attends to other business. The judge participates only if there are difficulties in the selection process, if, for example, one of the advocates is asking questions to which the other objects. Then, the judge is consulted to resolve the objections. In the event that there are no objections, the jury is selected by the advocates, who then report to the assigned trial judge's courtroom for the trial.

Ordinarily, in criminal cases, the voir dire is conducted right in the courtroom assigned for the trial, with the trial judge presiding. The judge gives the jury a preliminary statement of the case and of the law in general and then may ask general questions that can be directed uniformly to the entire panel. Thereafter, in those jurisdictions where the advocates conduct the voir dire, the advocates are permitted to question the prospective jurors and select the jury.

In federal Courts, in both civil as well as criminal cases, since the judge selects the jury, the voir dire is usually in the courtroom and is, naturally, presided over by the judge.

In some federal Courts, as well as in other jurisdictions, several juries are selected at the beginning of the term (month) for several cases to be tried during the ensuing term. For this purpose, an entire array (panel) of jurors are assembled at the courthouse at the beginning of the term. Some may be selected for one jury, others for a different jury. When the various jury selections have been completed, the jurors are directed to return to their homes and their regular activities until notified by the jury clerk that the trial for which they have been selected will begin in two or three days. On that given day, the jurors report to the courthouse, and the trial begins. The voir dire and the questioning under such a pre-trial system, obviously, is exactly the same as when the jurors are selected immediately before trial.

KEEP A CHART

Regardless of who conducts the voir dire, judge or advocates, the advocate must keep a chart of the jurors on which to record information about each juror and his or her background in order later to consider the prospective jurors' qualifications and determine to accept or to challenge them.

Ordinarily, I have a jury selection chart in my Trial Book. The chart is divided into 14 or 16 small side-by-side rectangles lengthwise on a page. On this chart, I write the names of the prospective jurors in the same order as they are sitting in the jury box or in the chairs assigned, along with the individual information obtained from each juror, whether in response to the judge's questions, my adversary's questions, or my own questions. Later, when making the determination about whether or not to accept or challenge the particular juror, I can consult my chart, where I have the necessary information about each juror to review and compare in making my final selection.

Obviously, you are keeping this chart for the purpose of keeping track of the particular backgrounds and personal facts of many new people in a very short period of time. It is most difficult to keep track of all that information without recording the jurors' names and their personal information on the chart in the same order as those jurors are sitting in the jury box or chairs for the voir dire. Afterward, when it comes time to make decisions as to keeping or excusing jurors, the chart is a minipicture of the jury, in the exact order that the jurors are seated, and the task of selection is simplified.

Ordinarily, at the outset of selection, the clerk of jurors or courtroom clerk draws the names of prospective jurors to be interrogated from printed jury slips mixed in a revolving drum. Then the clerk either hands the slips to the judge or announces the names of the jurors and advises them in which chairs to sit. It is at this time that the names of the prospective jurors are added to your chart.

Thereafter, as the Court elicits information, as your adversary elicits information, as you inquire directly, you add the information you feel significant to the individual boxes on your chart.

PRELIMINARY GENERAL QUESTIONS

> ***REMEMBER!*** *Before you even start questioning the first juror, you want to set the tone, you want the first things you say to the jury to have impact, to strike a telling note. As I've indicated before, the first impression has a tendency to be a lasting message. Therefore, in any preliminary statement focus the jury, set the tone, and let them hear what this case is about in such a fashion as to impress them favorably.*

There is an entire chapter, supra, devoted to the setting of tone, to getting the prime message to the jury the moment you begin to address them, whether it be at the voir dire or the opening statement. Don't select a jury without reading that chapter.

SECOND PRELIMINARY NOTE: *Obviously, if the Court picks the jury in your jurisdiction, it is most difficult to get the first word in, to be the first one to address the jury. Fine. When you get your opportunity, be sure to set the tone at that time, to bend every word that you say into the shape that you calculate will properly influence the jury, to win them to your side.*

Whether asked by the Court or by the advocates, general questions can be asked of the entire panel in the box, asking those prospective jurors to whom the questions apply to raise their hands so that further questions may be asked of them directly.

In both the federal jury-selection process and in some state Court proceedings, the judge may either have questionnaires passed out or may orally ask all the jurors to answer certain general questions.

In those jurisdictions where the jury selection, particularly in a civil case, is handled by the advocates themselves, then the plaintiff's attorney will ordinarily pose the following preliminary questions:

name;

occupation;

educational background;

marriage status;

prior jury service, if any

(after introducing the parties by name or identification)
Does anyone know any of the parties to this litigation?

(after identifying counsel for all parties)
Does anyone know any of the attorneys for the parties or had any dealing with them or heard of them?

(after reading a list of the anticipated witnesses)
Does anyone know or has had any dealings with any of the anticipated witnesses?

SECONDARY GENERAL QUESTIONS

Where the advocates are conducting the voir dire, after the preliminary information is obtained—and written on your chart—the next questions to be asked are also general questions, that is, asked of the entire panel in the jury box.

> *NOTE: The prospective jurors should be advised that if there are any answers that they would prefer to discuss privately, not in the hearing of the other jurors, that they may so indicate, and then some provisions should be made to have the individual prospective juror come out of the jury box and discuss the matter privately with the Court or with the advocates.*

The secondary general questions may be as follows:

> a) Has any juror, or any close friends or relatives of any juror, ever been involved in any litigation, whether as a witness or as a party?

If any prospective jurors raise their hand on this question, further inquiry should be made of those jurors as to what their role in the litigation was, and whether anything in connnection with that experience has caused them to form any opinions, one way or the other, that would favor either party and would cause the juror not to be fair and impartial to both sides in this litigation.

By asking this question in very broad strokes, you permit a juror who may have been a defendant in a criminal case, or who may have been the victim of an unpleasant crime, or who may have been a defendant in a civil lawsuit that reveals something too personal to be discussed in front of the other prospective jurors, to raise his or her hand, come to the side bar, and, in private, tell what his or her prior legal involvement was without everyone in the jury knowing that person's business.

The jurors appreciate this privacy and will give you more candid answers than they would within the hearing of the other prospective jurors.

Next secondary general question:

> b) Does any juror have any friends or relatives who either are lawyers or who are involved in investigations or law enforcement?

This question is intended to obtain information from a juror who has a very good friend or who has someone in his or her family who has a very good friend who is a lawyer. It isn't so much that the friend is a lawyer but, rather, that you want to know if the lawyer-friend practices in the field of law involved in the case at Bar, and if the prospective juror discusses the lawyer's cases or experience with that lawyer. You may not want a prospective juror to come into the jury box with preconceived notions about the law of the case you are about to try, notions which that juror has obtained ex parte from another lawyer.

In addition, in both the civil and the crimilar case, this question serves the purpose of determining if any prospective juror is so close to law enforcement personnel as to cause that juror to tend to give more credibility and more attention and belief to police personnel or law enforcement witnesses who may testify or to be more aligned with the prosecution than with the defense.

Another general question, which may be used at this time and which also has a secondary purpose is:

c) Does any juror have friends or relatives who work with an insurance company?

Now, jurors are not supposed to be told or advised that there is an insurance carrier involved in the defense of a negligence case. But the question, which may uncover any leaning on the part of any juror who works for an insurance company or who has friends who work for, own, or deal with insurance companies, also indirectly alerts the rest of the jurors that insurance is involved in the case.

As you have seen earlier, in connection with the rules of evidence where there is both a proscribed basis (hearsay) and a second legitimate purpose (merely to affect credibility) for something introduced in the trial, the legitimate basis oftentimes negates the proscription. Since it is legitimate to know if anyone in the jury has a tendency to favor a defendant's case because of association with insurance companies, the question becomes valid, despite the fact that some noodling suspicion about the existence of insurance coverage may become apparent to the prospective jurors.

Next general question, which is asked mainly in criminal cases:

d) Has any prospective juror or close personal friend or relative of a juror ever been the victim of a crime?

What a sad comment on our society, at least in some locations, when a myriad of hands are raised in the jury box on this question.

Naturally, the purpose of the question is to determine if there are those amongst the prospective jurors who have had such a negative experience that they might identify with one side or the other. It is not only that a person may have had a nightmarish experience at the hand of a perpetrator and may thus lean toward the prosecution. The victim might be unhappy with the activity of the prosecutor or the police in his or her own case and might have a tendency to vent his or her displeasure by leaning toward the defense. Thus, this question is intended to find a person who might favor one side or the other unfairly or with partiality.

FOLLOW-UP QUESTIONS

Ordinarily, a judge picking the jury will ask the prospective jurors at this point whether there is anything that they know of that might cause them not to be fair and impartial to either side. Asked as a general question to the jurors at large, the answer tends to be an anonymous, pat, simple no. The judge, satisfied by this answer, is sure that the jury is fair and impartial and concludes the voir dire.

In a desire to obtain a jury in the least amount of time and therefore to get right to the trial of the matter, legislators and judges in various jurisdictions laud the clean, swift jury selection conducted by judges rather than what they consider to be the unnecessarily long voir dire conducted by advocates.

The fact of the matter is that although it may take a few minutes longer, there are few, if any, studies that determine that the advocate-conducted voir dire takes substantially longer than a Court-conducted voir dire.

And it isn't that the continued voir dire takes that much longer. Indeed, more often now, judges in non-federal settings permit each advocate no more than 15 minutes per round to inquire of the prospective jurors.

How long can a voir dire continue when each advocate is restricted to 15 minutes per round for the first two rounds, and less for the third or fourth round, if there are such?

It might be asked, then, what's the difference, if it takes so little extra time, what great result or change can be effected in such a short period of time? One often encounters, when questioning continues after the pat, general question asked at a court-conducted voir dire, a very different picture from the plain-vanilla lick and a promise by the Court.

Often, there are substantial differences, as we shall see. If the additional expenditure in time isn't great and some trial benefit for each side can be accomplished, if deeper insight can be obtained of each of the prospective jurors, thus insuring a better balanced jury for each side by giving each advocate more information with which to make judgments on their peremptory challenges, why shouldn't no more than one (1) additional hour be spent as an investment in a fair trial?

An illustration: Many years ago I was picking a jury in a homicide case. A prospective juror seemed ideal from the defense side of the case. Not to give a signal to the prosecutor that this juror was well-liked by the defense, questioning continued with random questions intended to give the impression to the prosecutor that the prospective juror was still an undecided commodity. Often, if this is not done, your adversary, out of sheer perversity or a fear that you know something that he or she doesn't, will tend to reject a juror that you have revealed you like, by exercising a peremptory challenge.

During the camouflage questioning of the said desired juror, that juror came up with an answer to a question that was surprisingly narrow, prejudiced, and bigoted and which earned that juror a resounding defense peremptory challenge when the time came.

The continued questioning by the advocates can unearth responses and positions that are not even touched by the general, plain-vanilla interrogation of a judge. Thus, a few minutes of personal questioning of the jurors serves two purposes. It digs a bit deeper on a one-to-one basis into the juror's background, and it gives the parties a better view one-on-one experience with the prospective juror, thus permitting a more judicious exercise of their peremptory challenges.

I suppose you want to know some of the questions to ask when you continue questioning the jurors. Okay, fair enough. But before I explore this area of the voir dire with you, I should suggest that there is a secondary purpose fulfilled in continued questioning of the jury. That purpose is to educate and precondition the jury.

Now there's the rub, isn't it? There's the reason that the legislators and judges object to the advocate-conducted voir dire: the lawyers brainwash the jury.

But, since both advocates have an equal opportunity, the "conditioning" from each side results in an education for the jurors. And, anyone who says that a better-educated, better-informed jury is not desired, is an enemy of fair trial. Moreover, neither your adversary nor the judge is going to permit anyone to misstate the law or to state the wrong law to the jury. Nor is your adversary or judge going to permit you to minicharge the jury. If the questions that you ask properly inquire into the jurors' capacity to follow the law or the judge's charge, so long as your questions do not become a lecture or a minicharge, there should be nothing whatever objectionable.

Indeed, if such questioning evokes candid, open responses to questions that are right at the heart of the trial at hand, it seems that they are much more efficacious in selecting a fair and impartial panel that the plain-vanilla "do you know of any reason why you can't be fair and impartial to either side" asked by the judge of a group of jurors sitting in unified anonymity.

LET THEM KNOW THE AWFUL TRUTH

The voir dire is not only the opportunity for you to get to know the prospective jurors, but also to let the jurors get to know about your case, particularly the more damaging aspects of the case. Might as well. If there are any skeletons in your client's closet, the jurors are going to hear about them anyway. Your adversary will be delighted to bring this information to their attention. And, if this information is going to turn the prospective jurors off and traumatize them into being less than fair and impartial jurors, then it's far better to turn them off now—during voir dire—than later, when it's too late, during the trial. At least now you can challenge those jurors who would be too distracted by the damaging information to be fair and impartial to your client.

(e) What do you do when there will be some evidence that the defendant is or was a narcotics addict at the time of the commission of this crime?

Let it all hang out now. Hiding from it won't make that Achilles heel go away. And since your adversary is going to attack what he or she thinks is a vulnerable area during the trial (wouldn't you?), bring out the information yourself, right now, and get rid of those jurors who would weigh against you because of that debility. As a result of this tactic, you're pulling the teeth of the beast that would attack you before the attack even begins.

But give the prospective jurors a chance to see the light before you drop the trapdoor from under them. This not only brings out the true qualities of the single prospective juror you question, but educates the balance of the jury at the same time.

Q. Now, Mr. Annobil (prospective juror), no one is about to tell you that addiction to drugs is commendable or exemplary. But as Her Honor has indicated, this case concerns whether or not the prosecutor has sufficient evidence to show that Mr. Defendant committed murder. The defendant is not charged here with any crime having to do with narcotics. This case, and the prosecutor will agree with me, I am sure, is not at all a prosecution about narcotics. And I am sure the prosecutor will also agree . . .

Adversary: Your Honor, I object to counsel telling the jury about all the things I'm going to agree about. I can speak for myself.

The Court: That's true. Just speak for yourself, counsellor.

Advocate: Very well, Your Honor. I was about to say, prospective jurors, that *I* am interested in jurors who would be able to fairly and impartially decide the real issues in this case and not be distracted by a nonissue, the fact that the defendant is or was a user of drugs. It's going to come out. I can't hide from it. At one time in my client's life, it was a reality. But that was then. And that fact has nothing whatever to do with the occurrence in this case.

You know I do not speak for my adversary, only for myself. The judge, our entire system of justice desires a fair, impartial jury that can well and truly weigh the issues, and only the issues, the real issues in this case. No one wants, is looking for an unfair edge, a thumb on the scale of justice. So, Mr. Annobil, my question is, would you be able to function, for the time that you are here as a juror, if selected, without sympathy or emotion, without preconceived notions about the defendant, or the fact that he once used drugs, just weighing the evidence put on the scale by the prosecutor, however much or however little evidence there is? Or would you, because of some drugs in the defendant's past, be unable to sit here, listen to the evidence, and render a fair and true verdict concerning a homicide?

A. I think I'd be fair.

Q. Is there a doubt in your mind about your capacity to cast aside anything that might come out about drugs—which doesn't have anything to do with this case—and act fairly and impartially to both sides in this case based solely on the evidence?

A. No. I can do it.

One of the things you've done is made the entire panel of jurors face a problem that you know is going to come up. But when it does come up during the trial, the jurors will have already heard about it. It's old news. They've already said they'll work around that past problem. After all, it isn't a factor in the case. You've already said so. Your adversary has acquiesced. The judge has too. Now how many of the jurors are going to steadfastly insist that all druggies, living or dead, are capable of committing any and all crimes?

A few, you say. Probably true. But, amazingly, many of those will tell that to you or the prosecutor or the judge and be excused. As for the others, they'll have a tough time selling that to the other jurors who have already been preconditioned to the fact that the taking of drugs has nothing to do with the case at hand.

Let's get back to Mr. Annobil. For some reason deep in your head, you already doubt that you will keep Mr. Annobil as a juror. Maybe he's just not the guy you'd like to get stuck in conversation with at a cocktail party. So you know you're going to peremptorily challenge him when you get the chance. All right. You can't, however, just dump him in mid-questioning.

Remember when I spoke about not showing your hand concerning a juror whom you know you want because otherwise you might cause your adversary to exercise a peremptory? Well, you can't just abruptly dump a juror whom you know you are going to peremptorily challenge. Why?

Callous treatment of a juror might just cause resentment in other jurors. So you continue to ask that juror a few more questions just so it appears that you are giving evenhanded treatment to all.

As long as you're at it, then, use that prospective juror as a stalking horse, to cover subjects and to get answers that impart desired information to other prospective jurors.

> **Q.** Let me put it another way, Mr. Annobil. Do you truly believe that you can disregard the fact that the defendant here once took drugs, in evaluating the evidence in this case, or do you think that a person who took drugs has more of a tendency to commit a crime, any kind of a crime?

Of course, this material is loaded with information that may be damaging to your case. Your adversary knows about this damaging information and can't wait to drop it on your client's head during the trial. It's going to be worse when your adversary drops this addiction bomb on the jury during the trial. Do it now. Do it yourself. Defuse it or get rid of the jurors who can't live with it.

> **A.** I think I could listen and make a decision based on the evidence.
>
> **Q.** Can you accept as a possibility that a person may be able to afford to buy narcotics, and although a drug user, might not commit other unlawful activity?
>
> **A.** I guess if a person can afford to buy drugs, I guess he wouldn't be necessarily getting involved in other crimes.
>
> **Q.** In other words, Mr. Annobil, can you accept the proposition that the need for funds to buy drugs, not the drugs themselves, might cause a person to become involved in other unlawful activity?
>
> **A.** I never thought about it like that. I guess it's the money, when a person needs a fix. If he's got money to buy, I guess that is different.
>
> **Q.** How about you, Ms. Gildersleeve, do you come here to become a part of this jury with the idea fixed in your mind that any person who once used drugs must necessarily commit other crimes?

Comment: Ms. Gildersleeve has already been educated by listening to your inquiry of the previous juror.

> **A.** I guess it depends on the circumstances.
>
> **Q.** Do you understand, Ms. Gildersleeve, I am not trying to con you into believing that drugs or drug addiction is wonderful. I

am only trying to find jurors—as is my adversary, although I'm not speaking for him—who can impartially weigh the evidence in this case. This defendant is not charged with drugs or drug addiction. The charge here is murder. Would the fact that he might have used drugs—whenever it was—cause you necessarily to believe that he probably, more likely, committed the crime charged, or would you be able to say to yourself, the fact that he used drugs is not part of the case, I have to listen to the rest of the evidence if that's what the judge says I should do?

A. I'll listen to the evidence.

Q. How about you, Mr. Gilette, can you weigh the evidence here fairly, impartially, or does the fact that the defendant has a drug background, personal drug use that is, cause you to have a tendency to think that he might have or is more than likely a person who would have committed this crime.

A. I've had some bad experiences. I don't know if I could put it out of my mind.

The Court: Ms. Advocate is right. This defendant is not charged with any crime related to drugs. He is charged with murder. Drugs are not an issue in this case. Mr. Gilette, is it your perception that you could not put aside, that a person who uses—or used—drugs personally is likely to commit other crimes, and that your view of the evidence would be colored by that perception. In other words, it might interfere in your being able to weigh the evidence fairly and without preconceived notions.

A. I think it might interfere, Your Honor.

The Court: Very well, I'll excuse you, Mr. Gilette, with our thanks for your candor and honesty. You see, Ladies and Gentlemen, we want only people who can weigh the evidence fairly and impartially. That's how the system works. Mr. Clerk, fill Mr. Gillette's seat.

Comment: When Mr. Gilette's seat is filled with a new prospective juror from the audience, one who has, we hope, been listening all the time to the questions asked of the other prospective jurors, go directly to that juror.

Q. Ms. Quigley, have you heard all the questions that have been asked of the prospective jurors in the box?

A. Yes, I have.

Q. And as a result, is there any information that you feel should be brought to the Court's attention, anything that would make you feel partial to one side or the other here?

A. No, not at all.

Q. Would you be able to sit and decide, fairly and impartially, whether the defendant committed this crime, despite the fact that it may be brought out that he once used drugs, understanding that this is not a drug case?

A. A lot of people have taken drugs.

Q. Yes, ma'am. But could you decide this case, just on the evidence and not on the question of the drug culture in this country, in the world?

A. Yes, sir, I could, if that's what the judge will tell me.

The Court: Fair and impartial, is exactly what I'll tell you, Madame Prospective Juror.

A. I could do that, judge.

The introduction of a new subject:

Q. Mr. Cole (next propspective juror), you've heard the judge indicate that the defendant, as he sits here in this courtroom, is presumed to be innocent of the charges, have you not?

A. Yes.

Q. As innocent as anyone in this courtroom, as innocent as the prosecutor, the other jurors, the judge himself?

A. Yes.

Q. Have you also heard the judge indicate that the prosecutor has the entire burden of proof here, that the prosecutor has to prove the defendant's guilt beyond a reasonable doubt?

A. Yes.

Q. You understand that under our system of justice, the defendant need do nothing, say nothing, that unless the prosecutor brings in enough evidence to dispel reasonable doubt, brings in enough evidence to leave you beyond a reasonable doubt, as the judge will define reasonable doubt for you, you must, under your oath as a juror, acquit the defendant?

A. (the juror hesitates, a mite confused)

Remember: All the jurors are listening to this dialogue, and are equally absorbing the material you are dispensing.

Q. Let me put it this way: if by some happenstance, at this very minute, you were transported with your fellow jurors into the jury room and asked to make a determination as to the guilt or lack of guilt of this defendant, what would your verdict be?

A. I don't really know.

Q. Remember, the defendant is presumed to be innocent as he sits here. And the Court has told you the prosecutor must prove the defendant's guilt beyond a reasonable doubt. Without a shred of evidence being presented, your verdict under the law, at this point in the proceedings, would have to be not guilty, do you understand that?

A. Oh, yes, I understand.

To the next juror:

Q. Do you understand under our law that is the verdict you would have to render at this point, sir?

A. Yes, I haven't heard any evidence.

Q. Do you have any difficulty with that proposition, or those propositions of law, that is, that the defendant is presumed innocent and that the prosecutor must bring in enough evidence to prove the defendant guilty beyond a reasonable doubt?

A. None at all.

Switch to other jurors on the same proposition.

Q. How about you, Miss Bagley, do you understand that if you were to go into the jury room right now and be asked for a verdict that your verdict would have to be not guilty?

A. Yes.

Q. And, Miss Gildersleeve, can you accept the judge's direction that the prosecutor must prove with evidence beyond a reasonable doubt, that the defendant is guilty?

A. If that's the law, yes, I can accept it.

Q. Does anyone have any difficulty accepting the propositions of law, as the judge has stated them, that the defendant is presumed innocent, and the prosecution must prove the case to you with evidence beyond a reasonable doubt?

A. (All jurors respond by nods and shakes of their heads.)

Comment: All the law you are quoting to the jurors, the judge should have already given in a preliminary statement. If that has not occurred, carefully work the propositions of law into your questions. Be sure that the propositions of law that you give are simple, basic, and correct, so that your adversary does not, cannot oppose or object to them.

> **Q.** We've been, I've been talking about a fair and impartial jury, one that can fairly and impartially weigh the evidence—and only the evidence—and give a reading, an evaluation, without sympathy or emotion for either side. It's almost as if, during your service as a juror, you are asked to become part of a mechanical scale that will weigh the evidence and indicate as precisely as possible the weight of that evidence. Miss Bagley, would you have any difficulty, if selected as a juror in this case, acting as part of a mechanical scale, set at zero right now, weighing the evidence as best you can and calling out the result—in your verdict—exactly as your conscience sees it?
>
> **A.** No.
>
> **Q.** How about you, Miss Gildersleeve?
>
> **A.** No.
>
> **Q.** Mr. Poston?
>
> **A.** No.
>
> **Q.** Anyone have difficulty with that proposition?
>
> **A.** (All jurors, as you look each of them in the eye, shake their head.)
>
> **Q.** And, Miss Bagley, do you also understand that the Court is going to, in her charge, describe what reasonable doubt is, she's going to give you a definition, indicate how much evidence the prosecutor has to put on this scale before you can change your current verdict from not guilty to guilty? Can you accept the fact that the judge is the exclusive judge of the law in this case and that what Her Honor says is the weight of evidence that you must accept and utilize?
>
> **A.** Yes.
>
> **Q.** Any difficulty rendering a verdict, calling it right down the middle, whether it favors the prosecutor or the defense, according to how much or how little evidence the prosecutor puts on this mechanical scale called the jury?
>
> **A.** None.
>
> **Q.** Any of you have any difficulty calling it right down the middle, no matter whom such verdict favors, whether the defendant or the prosecutor?
>
> **A.** (The jurors nod their heads.)

Q. Mr. Rocco, any difficulty saying not enough, not sufficient, not guilty, if indeed, your conscience tells you that the prosecutor hasn't presented enough evidence according to Her Honor's instructions?

A. If the judge defines it that way, I have no difficulty with it.

Q. To use a homely analogy, guilty is like pregnancy. Either you're pregnant or you're not. Either there's enough evidence on which to render a guilty verdict or there's not. Anything short of actual pregnancy is not pregnant, no matter what symptoms there are. Anything short of guilty is not guilty. You understand that, Miss Bagley?

A. Yes.

Q. Mr. Poston?

A. Yes.

Q. Miss Gildersleeve?

A. Yes.

The Court: Counsellor, your time is about up.

Advocate: Yes, Your Honor. I have about one more minute.

The Court: That's exactly right, Counsellor.

Q. One further thing, no question about it, this case will involve some evidence against the defendant. The prosecutor didn't bring this case because he had nothing else to do. The question you will have to decide, if selected as jurors, is if there is enough, sufficient evidence against the defendant according to the measure the judge will describe to you. Do you understand, Mr. Cole, at the end of the case, you may not be convinced of the defendant's innocence beyond a reasonable doubt? But that isn't the measure. Not innocence beyond a reasonable doubt, but guilt. Anything short of what the judge instructs you is not enough, not sufficient, not guilty. Would you be able to do that?

A. Yes, sir.

Q. And this is the last question, for all of you. Think, now, deep into your heart's heart. Nobody says this will be easy, and no one wants you to do anything except what is fair and impartial. Even if there is some evidence against the defendant, but not the amount that the judge will describe as necessary for you to say guilty, would you all be able to do that, vote your conscience, say not enough, regardless of sympathy, emotion, call it right down the middle?

A. Yes.

Q. And, of course, if there is enough, to say that too, right down the middle, fair and impartial, exactly as you see it?

A. Exactly as I see it.

Q. How about you, Ms. Gildersleeve?

A. Yes, as the judge tells me, fair and impartial.

Q. Any problem with calling it as you see it, as you read the scale, Mr. Drogan, regardless of who it favors, the people or the defendant?

A. None.

Look into the eyes of each of the jurors. Ask each of them:

Q. Any difficulty calling it right down the middle, sir?

A. None.

Q. Despite the fact that the defendant might not be, at the end of the case, innocent beyond a reasonable doubt, ma'am?

A. None.

Q. Ms. Bentley?

A. None.

Q. Mr. Babbitt?

A. None.

Advocate: I have no further questions at this time, Your Honor.

STEP-BY-STEP SELECTION PROCESS

Comment: During the selection of the jury, always speak loudly enough for those prospective jurors not currently in the jury box to hear so that if and when they replace any of the prospective jurors currently in the box, you can ask them questions as if they'd been sitting in the box all along.

Indeed, advise the prospective panel in the audience that you are speaking as loudly as you are so that they will pay attention, hear, and be able to come forward and tell if any of the questions so far asked has caused them to realize whether or not they could be fair and impartial to both sides in the case.

Now that you know what sort of challenges there are, what sort of questions to ask, you might as well know how the voir dire is conducted and how you exercise your challenges.

THE PANEL

A panel is the total number of prospective jurors out of which, it is hoped, you and your adversary shall be able to select the jury.

The jury clerk assembles the panel and brings them to the designated place in which the voir dire will be conducted. There may be 40, 50, 75, 100 prospective jurors in the panel, depending on the kind of case, the number of jurors you will be selecting, the attendant publicity, if any, concerning the case, which would make selection of the fair and impartial jury somewhat more difficult and would therefore require more jurors.

THE ROUNDS

The voir dire is conducted in rounds, with a specific number of prospective jurors seated in an actual jury box or in designated seats, separate from the other prospective jurors in the panel.

ROUND #1

The first round begins with the plaintiff's advocate opening up the questioning. Usually, in order to set the stage for the questioning, the plaintiff's advocate gives the prospective jurors—loudly enough for those in the box as well as those in the audience—a short, thumbnail sketch of the upcoming controversy so that they will know the kind of case it is and may know some of the aspects that the plaintiff's advocate thinks of as important.

THE INTRODUCTORY STATEMENT

The nuts and bolts of the jury-selection process has been explained here. Now you're going to stand on your feet and begin to put those nuts and bolts in place to build a structure, or more aptly, to select a jury.

It is now that you have to make an introductory statement to the jury in order that you, and later your adversary, shall be able to formulate meaningful voir dire questions in quest of fairness and impartiality.

As I have already discussed, the jury is now going to get their first impression of your case. Work on the first words, the first statement that you are going to make to the jury about the case. The first impression, the prime impression, is ordinarily a long one; one that if it is going to have to be changed, is going to be hard to change, is going to take a great deal of energy to change. Why have to use all the time and energy to change something that you can set in place properly to begin with?

Set the right tone. In this respect, you can also refer to the beginning of Chapter 10, infra, which has to do with exactly this subject, the setting of the tone of the trial, the giving of the correct prime impression, which you must carry throughout the trial.

In both the preliminary statement to the jury during voir dire and in the actual opening to the jury, there is a need to set the right tone, to get the jury's mindset properly focused on what your case is about.

THE TIME FOR CHALLENGE

If, during Round #1—whether during the plaintiff's or the defense's inquiry—there are jurors who express some reservations or doubts as to their ability to sit fairly and impartially, and if you and your adversary as well as the judge (if the judge is present during the voir dire) can agree, that prospective juror may be excused from the jury box during the round and replaced by the clerk with a new prospective juror.

If you and your adversary cannot agree as to the dismissal of the prospective juror, then that juror shall remain until time for challenges, which will be at the end of Round #1.

THE SECOND INTRODUCTORY STATEMENT

When the plaintiff's advocate finishes his or her Round #1 questioning, the defense advocate continues the questioning on behalf of the defense. If there is need for a further introductory statement on behalf of the defense, it is given now. The necessity of a further statement is governed by whether the jurors have sufficient facts that the defense deems necessary to fully question the jurors. If the defense advocate feels that plaintiff's advocate may have glossed over some salient point that should be brought out in order to question the jurors, then, by all means, add that or those circumstances.

Remember, this is not an opening statement or a summation. At the same time, however, be mindful that it is the beginning of the trial, the beginning of your sphere of influence with the jury, so you can and should begin to influence and sway the jury.

After a further statement to the jury, the defense advocate questions the jurors for whatever period is permitted or necessary to formulate an opinion concerning the qualifications of the jurors.

EXERCISING THE CHALLENGES

At the end of the questioning by the defense, the respective advocates proceed to the side bar (or the corner of a room in some less luxurious facilities) where they exercise any challenge for cause relative to the prospective jurors sitting in the box.

If a judge is present, the judge decides the challenge, sustaining or denying the challenge. If a judge is not present, the advocates and the clerk attempt to resolve the challenge. If there is no resolution, the clerk, accompanied by the advocates, shall proceed either to the judge designated to preside over the trial or to the miscellaneous judge in the courthouse designated to resolve miscellaneous matters, ex parte matters for the day or the week.

In the federal jurisdiction, as well as in jurisdictions where cases are assigned exclusively to one judge from the outset of the case, that judge will ordinarily be available, and the challenge for cause shall be decided on the spot.

On your chart, mark in the small box you've made for each juror which jurors have been challenged and which jurors have been removed from the box.

When the challenges for cause are resolved for both sides, the plaintiff's attorney and then the defense attorney are asked if they have any peremptory challenges. Ordinarily, at the end of Round #1, the plaintiff's advocate first indicates which, if any, of the jurors he or she wishes to excuse peremptorily.

On your chart, separately record the number of peremptory challenges you and your adversary exercise.

When the challenges for cause have been resolved and the peremptory challenges have been exercised at the end of Round #1, the clerk, en masse, reads out the names of the jurors who have been challenged, without indicating which have been challenged for cause, which challenged peremptorily, or by whom.

The jurors who have been excused leave the jury box. Their seats are filled with prospective jurors from the panel, who have been sitting in the audience of the courtroom or nearby, listening to the proceedings.

Out of the original twelve (or six) prospective jurors in the box, you may be left with, for example, four agreed-upon or selected jurors.

This is the end of Round #1.

ROUND #2

At this point, if Round #2 is going to be long, or if the number of jurors yet to be selected are many, the judge may have the selected jurors sworn, then excused to go to the jury room to relax, read, or attend to personal matters while the advocates go through Round #2. If the time or the number to be selected is short or small, the judge may have the selected jurors remain in the box, while the other juror or jurors are selected.

However many seats in the jury were emptied by challenges at the end of Round #1, is how many are now to be filled from the remaining prospective jurors.

Round #2 begins. It is conducted in the same fashion as Round #1 was, except, of course, that a preliminary statement is unnecessary as both advocates had been speaking loudly enough for the entire panel to hear the proceedings.

The voir dire, the challenges for cause, and the peremptory challenges are exercised in the same fashion as in Round #1.

Some judges may require the defense advocate to exercise the peremptories first in Round #2; some require the same rotation in each round. It matters little, except that it is always preferable to exercise last so as to know if your adversary would use one of his or her peremptories on the prospective juror you wish to challenge. This way, you'd save a peremptory.

If necessary, there may be a Round #3, a Round #4, and so on until an entire jury is selected.

ANOTHER PANEL

If the challenges have been particularly numerous, there may not be enough prospective jurors left in the remaining panel to complete the jury or the selection of the alternates. In this event, the Court will send for an additional panel—perhaps not as large as the first—to complete the selection process.

In the event that there is a new panel, then the entire procedure is repeated, including the introductory statements by each side and the regular selection process here described until the jury is completed.

THE ALTERNATES

When the entire number of jurors to be selected for the jury is obtained, the Court may decide that you should select some alternate jurors. The alternates are selected in the same fashion and from the same panel of waiting prospective jurors who have been attending the entire voir dire.

The only difference in the process is the peremptory challenges relative to the alternates. The number of peremptory challenges available to any side for the selection of a jury does NOT include challenges for the alternates. Thus, when the judge decides that there is to be a continued selection process for the purpose of having alternates, each side ordinarily has two challenges per alternate seat. These are exercised at the end of the questioning, first by the plaintiff's attorney, then by the defense attorney.

NOTE: Ordinarily, peremptory challenges unused by either side at the end of the selection of the jury (the first six or twelve) cannot be exercised retrospectively against the jurors that have already been selected. That is, once you fail to peremptorily challenge a particular juror and proceed to the next round, you cannot go back and utilize one of your peremptories that might still be available.

Of course, a judge is free to conduct his or her Court in the fashion he or she sees fit, and occasionally, jurors may be selected but not sworn until the entire panel is selected. In such a situation, the judge may allow retrospective exercise of the challenges.

PEREMPTORIES FOR THE ALTERNATES

In exercising peremptories during the selection of alternates, the peremptories do not accumulate, so that if you don't use the two challenges available for seat 1, you cannot accumulate them for seat 2. Once an alternate seat is selected, you pass on to the selection of alternate #2, and the number of challenges will be two, regardless of whether you excercised any challenges during the selection of alternate #1.

EXERCISE PEREMPTORIES CAREFULLY

Always exercise peremptories carefully; don't squander them. Always keep your eye on what's still remaining in the prospective pool. You may peremptorily challenge a so-so juror, only to find yourself out of challenges and King Kong sitting in the jury box.

NOW YOU HAVE YOUR JURY

Now you have your jury. You must be ready at this point to make your opening statement. Often, there is a hiatus between the completion of the jury selection and the opening, but that is not necessary. Indeed, the energetic judge is going to go right into the opening statements or the first witness immediately upon jury selection. So be prepared. And good luck.

Of course, you will often find that the harder you work, the luckier you'll be.

12

OPENING STATEMENTS

PURPOSE

An opening statement is just that, an opening, a beginning. In jurisdictions where the Court selects the jury, the Opening is the first taste of the actual trial prepared by the advocates and served up to the jurors. It is the first time that the advocates address the jurors on the subject of the trial.

REMEMBER THE THEME

Just as was indicated in the section in Chapter 9, supra, don't forget that the fact finder(s), whether jury or bench, are humans, humans who have a tendency to absorb their first impression and retain it.

WORK ON THE OPENING SENTENCE

Also remember what was said previously: Work on the Opening sentence. It's going to set the tone. Sure, other evidence can persuade, can change the mind-set of the fact finder(s). But if the prime impression is negative, you're working uphill, against the tide.

IT IS NOT EVIDENCE

An Opening statement is not, however, evidence. It is merely each advocate's preview, overview of what the evidence during the forthcoming trial shall be, so that the jurors, the fact finders, shall be better able to follow the presentation of evidence. Never forget, the only evidence in the case comes from the mouths of witnesses who take the stand, or is introduced by stipulation or by judicial notice. Nothing that either advocate or judge says, in an Opening, or at any time, unless they are sworn as witnesses, is evidence.

> ***NOTE:** Whether the trial is before a jury or it is a bench trial, the judge may, or may not, want an Opening Statement. Thus, just because it is a bench trial, the Opening is not necessarily waived. And at the same time, merely because it is a jury trial doesn't necessitate an Opening.*

DON'T PROMISE THEM TOO MUCH

It may be that you occasionally say something in your Opening that later you cannot produce: a witness becomes unavailable, some physical evidence just doesn't materialize. That's okay, if essentially you've been straightforward and haven't blown yourself out of the case with promises you can't fulfill.

An overblown Opening can be turned around on you by an adversary who knows that you've overstated your case and tells the jury to listen to the evidence and see if everything that you, his or her adversary, has described is real, true, actually supported by the evidence.

Economy is preferable to indiscriminate spending. Get the first impression right and describe what's going to come up during the trial, so the fact finder(s) can better follow the flow, and then sit down.

YOU MAY WANT THEM TO KNOW THAT WHAT YOUR ADVERSARY SAID IS NOT THE EVIDENCE

If your adversary makes an impressive Opening, you may partially defuse that Opening by reminding the jury, candidly and openly, that nothing that your adversary has said is evidence. Indeed, you may also remind them, to show that you are fair and evenhanded, that nothing you say is evidence either. Thus, if anything in your adversary's Opening is stinging or harmful, you take away the sting with the dismissing but factual revelation that NOTHING that your adversary says is evidence.

Notice, right from the get-go you must work *your* case. You must be ever alert and vigilant and must make each part of the case, even that which is *not* evidence, work for you.

WHEN TO MAKE AN OPENING STATEMENT

You might ask at this point that if an Opening is not evidence, if it is not proof of anything, if it is merely a preview, then why bother at all. Go directly to the evidence and let the jury begin to get into the case. The fact is that some judges, at least in civil cases, do just that, direct the advocates to go directly to the evidence and not bother with an Opening.

In criminal cases, however, there are statutory requirements that the plaintiff's advocate (read prosecutor) *must* make an Opening statement. In such circumstance, of course, there must be an opening at least on the part of the plaintiff.

As plaintiff/prosecutor must prove the case and has the burden of bringing forth sufficient evidence to convince the jury to the measure required by either the civil or penal law, plaintiff's Opening statement is made right at the beginning of the trial, the first thing that the plaintiff's attorney does.

As to the defense, an Opening can be waived. Since defendants need prove nothing, indeed since defendant's purpose is not to prove a case, but to disprove, dilute, and minimize the plaintiff's case, defendants need not make an Opening statement.

There are some defense advocates who opt to reserve their Opening statement until the defense case begins. I do not think that reserving the Opening is a very sound maneuver.

The primacy/recency theory spoken of in Chapter 9 shows you that to permit your adversary to make a presentation and for you to remain totally silent is to permit the jury to retain your adversary's view of the case, which causes you to continually be shovelling against a silent, negative tide that you permitted to flow against you in your adversary's unanswered Opening.

If you permit plaintiff's advocate to spread the entire fabric of the plaintiff's allegations—even though not in evidentiary form—before the jury without neutralization, you have helped create a formidable bulwark against yourself and your client that you now have to tear down during the trial. You would have been far better off not to permit your adversary to have built that bulwark in the first place. You would have been far better off to destroy that "prime" impression that your adversary put before the trier(s) of fact.

During an effective plaintiff's Opening, the plaintiff's advocate may cause a tilt in the mind-set of some of the jurors, may cause them to anticipate and later view the ensuing evidence with the perspective set by the plaintiff's Opening. This would unnecessarily make the defense advocate work harder to realign the jurors' perspective.

To avoid the necessity of working from a negative position, defense counsel should attempt to neutralize the plaintiff's opening with a vigorous defense counter-Opening, leaving the jury totally familiar with what the case is going to be about, but unsure of who is going to prove what.

Although the plaintiff's advocate wants to sway the jury totally with his or her Opening, the defense should be delighted with a jury that has a state of mind that is unsure where the evidence is going and awaits the evidence to know who was correct. This is not a harmful jury.

From the plaintiff's point of view, however, the neutral Opening is not harmful, just neutral.

THE EVIDENCE WILL SHOW

The Evidence Will Show is the magic phrase of the Opening statement, that should be served more by your recollecting the concept in your head as you Open than in continually repeating the phrase to the jury.

Since the Opening statement is not evidence that can in any fashion be considered by the jury in its deliberations, the advocate should take measures to advise the jury that the factual recitation that the advocate is describing is not evidence. This is ordinarily accomplished in a variety of statements that let the jury know specifically that what is being described in the Opening is merely a preview of the evidence that will be presented.

> The evidence will show;
>
> Witnesses will be called who will testify that;
>
> It will be proven that;

are all phrases that signal the jury that the statement the advocate is making is not intended to be evidence, but is only to outline, to preview.

It is not necessary to punctuate your Opening with such phrases. It is sufficient that you tell the jurors in the beginning that what you are about to tell them is a preview, a bird's-eye view of what is about to come.

There are points in an Opening, however, where you may be presenting something really heavy, perhaps dynamic, dramatic, and you can underscore this presentation, as well as defuse your adversary's objection, by presenting that particular portion with a cautionary emphasis:

> *And, the evidence is also going to show that at the time of this event the light was red against the plaintiff.*
>
> *Yes, the evidence is going to show that the plaintiff was the one who drove through the traffic signal and caused the accident that resulted in his own injury.*

KEEP PUNCHING

Merely because what you are doing in your Opening is giving the jurors a preview of what is about to come, even though what you tell the jury is not evidence, you are not restricted from bombarding the jury with an overwhelming factual presentation of your case.

In other words, the Opening need not be, nay, should not be a dry, boring recitation of a witness list or evidentiary list that they are about to hear. It should be a dramatic presentation filled with impact and punch—so long as you initially, and intermittently thereafter, remind the jury that "the evidence will show" or "witnesses will be presented to prove."

> ***CAUTION:*** *As I indicated before, don't bombard the jury with misinformation, or with promises that you can't fulfill. The Opening is a promissory note. You're going to owe the jury what you describe. While the Opening is an opportunity to set the tone for the rest of the trial, it is not an opportunity to "snow" the jury. Remember, you have to face that same jury again at the Summation.*

In short, make as many points as you can in the Opening. Don't fritter any opportunities away. And conversely, whittle away, neutralize any points that your adversary may make.

WHITTLING AWAY YOUR ADVERSARY'S CASE

Whether you be the advocate for the plaintiff or of the defense, whether you Open to the jury first or last, prospectively or retrospectively, whittle away the case of your adversary. Don't let your adversary build a fortification that you later have to storm; don't permit your adversary to erect a fortification that you have to unbuild. Always try to prevent your adversary from building in the first place. And this caution includes the Opening.

Although neither the Opening for the plaintiff nor for the defense is evidence, as said before, it sets a tone, it frames what is to come. Let your plaintiff adversary frame out a preview of an overwhelming case against you, and the jury is impressed (primacy) and may get a tilt toward the plaintiff. Don't let that happen. Knock it down. Neutralize it.

On the other hand, as a defense counsel, whether your adversary makes a compelling Opening or not, don't miss the opportunity to make a big Opening, to set the tone of the case, to put in place what you consider the case to be. And, indeed, if your adversary has made a big Opening, as I've said before, knock it down, neutralize it.

If, at the end of the Opening statements, the jury knows quite well what the case is about but doesn't really know who was at fault and who was not, the Openings have been successful, for both sides.

Plaintiff's Opening Statement—Criminal

Ladies and gentlemen of the jury, this part of the case is called the Opening. It is the first opportunity that I, as representative of the people, have to address you. It is my opportunity to give you a preview of what this case is about, what is about to come. I sometimes liken the Opening to a description by a tour guide describing a trip that you are about to take, so that you can anticipate, be aware of what there will be, so that you will know what to look for on your trip.

Now, nothing that I say during this Opening, during this entire trial, by the way, and nothing that my adversary will say, indeed, nothing that the judge will say, is evidence.

The only evidence there is in this case will come from the mouths of witnesses who take the witness chair, or will be physical or documentary evidence introduced through the witnesses.

At the end of the presentation of evidence, I will have a second and last opportunity to speak with you. That will be called the Summation. At that time, I will be able to discuss with you the evidence that has been introduced, discuss with you the trip that you have already taken.

Now, what is the evidence that you are about to hear? What is this trip upon which you are about to embark?

In a nutshell, the indictment, that the judge has already mentioned to you, that is also not evidence, charges this defendant with the crime of receiving stolen property in the second degree.

There will be witnesses called, executives of the Rolex Company, who will tell you about certain watches that had been taken from the Rolex Company without permission of Rolex.

Other witnesses will testify, former employees of Rolex, that they, the witnesses, actually stole these watches from their employer. The stolen watches, the testimony will show, were worth wholesale about $5,000 each.

Now, when these watches were disappearing, the witnesses will testify, investigations were undertaken within the Rolex Company to determine where and how the watches were disappearing. And the Rolex executives will testify that after this investigation, it was determined that certain employees were stealing these watches. And the testimony will show that these particular employees were confronted by detectives hired by the Rolex Company.

As I've already said, some of the witnesses will be the former employees of Rolex who will admit that while they were employees of Rolex, during the course of their employment there, they began to steal watches.

You will hear James Smith testify that he was an employee of Rolex, that he worked there for almost a year. That while working at Rolex he stole several watches and brought them to Gem Jewelers of 100 Fifth Avenue, New York City. There, Mr. Smith will testify, he sold the watches to Robert Roe and John Doe, the defendants in this case. Mr. Smith will identify Mr. Roe and Mr. Doe as the persons to whom he sold several watches, one for $4,500, and another for $1,900.

Mr. Smith will also describe to you how he spoke to a fellow Rolex employee named Casey Jones, told him of his larcenous activities and told him where he was going to *fence* the hot watches, whom he was selling them to. And Smith will testify that he told Jones to see the defendants in this case, Mr. Roe and Mr. Doe, if he wanted to move *hot* watches.

You will also hear Mr. Jones testify. Mr. Jones will tell you that he, too, began to steal watches from Rolex. He will tell you how he stole these watches, at first without anyone at Rolex knowing that the watches were stolen, and selling to the folks at Gem Jewelers. Jones will also testify about how he was caught, about a confrontation, or several confrontations and conversations he had with detectives and officials of the Rolex Company.

Mr. Jones will also testify that later he identified to the officials of Rolex where he had sold the watches and how much he had obtained for them.

Both Smith and Jones will also testify that they were arrested for their larcenies; that they pleaded guilty to certain crimes; that they await sentence for these crimes; that they agreed to testify and tell a jury about their crimes and about how they sold the watches they had stolen from Rolex to Roe and Doe, the defendants in this case; and about a cooperation agreement that they entered into with the District attorney's office, whereby in exchange for their testimony, their sentencing judge would be advised of their cooperation, which cooperation could be taken into consideration by that judge when he sentences Smith and Jones. Both Smith and Jones will also testify that they received no other promises for their cooperation from anyone.

In addition, you will hear from Hiram Walker, who works for a private detective agency in New York. Mr. Walker will testify that while acting as an undercover agent, working in cooperation with the police and the Rolex Company, he went to Gem Jewelers at 100 Fifth Avenue on the 15th of April 1989 with a Rolex watch that had been obtained from the Rolex Company.

Mr. Walker, at the time he went to Gem Jewelers, was wearing a recording device, one that would record the conversations that he had there with Mr. Roe and Mr. Doe.

You will hear with your own ears the conversation that Hiram Walker had with Mr. Roe and Mr. Doe, a conversation in which Mr. Walker specifically told Mr. Roe and Mr. Doe, with whom he was negotiating, that the watch he was selling was stolen.

Mr. Walker will testify that he told the defendants that the watch he was selling was stolen. You will hear that recorded conversation, in which Mr. Walker tells the defendants specifically that the watch was stolen. And after being told that the watch was stolen, the defendants counted out $1,900 to pay for the watch that they had just been told was stolen.

That, in a nutshell, is the evidence that you will hear in this case. It's a rather simple, straightforward case, in which you will hear the larcenous Rolex employees, with your own ears, tell you of their thefts. You will even hear these defendants, with their own voices recorded on tape, committing the crimes charged.

After you hear that evidence, you will also hear the charge or instruction of the judge on the law, what the elements of the crimes charged in the indictment are, what intent the defendants need, what knowledge they must have, how you are to gauge their actions.

And, as I said, I will have the opportunity again to talk to you at the end of the evidence I have described, and when I do, I am going to ask you to convict the defendants of all the crimes that have been charged in the Indictment in this case.

Thank you.

Opening Statement: Defendant—Civil

Ladies and gentlemen of the jury, on behalf of the defendant in this case, this is my opportunity to make an Opening statement. As my adversary has advised you, this is like a preview, a bird's-eye view of what the evidence in the case will be.

And of course, it is true, that whatever I say is not evidence. It is only a guide, so that you will have an idea of what the case ahead is going to be, and, more important, what it is not going to be.

The evidence, however much or however little of it, will come only from the witness chair, or from physical evidence introduced through witnesses who take the witness chair. And it will be your function to weigh the evidence, and just the evidence, to determine if, indeed, the plaintiff has met the burden of proof required of him by the law and by the judge's instructions on the law.

Now the plaintiff's attorney has told you that the plaintiff will show that the incident in this case occurred because the defendant, my client, was negligent on the twentieth of November 1989. The plaintiff has told you that the evidence will show that while the plaintiff was driving a vehicle on behalf of the police department, in an emergency situation, the defendant was negligent in failing to stop his vehicle, causing the collision that undoubtedly occurred.

The fact is, however, that the evidence will actually show that that is *not* what occurred on the day in question.

That's right. The evidence will show that what the plaintiff described to you is not the way in which the accident here occurred.

The evidence will show that the police vehicle, driven by the plaintiff, was driving westbound on Canal Street, true.

And the evidence will show that the police had sent plaintiff and his partner, Sergeant Ryan, to find the girlfriend of a man who had perpetrated a bank robbery and was then and there holding hostages inside a bank in lower Manhattan. All that, the evidence will, in fact, show.

But! But! The evidence is going to show that the defendant, on his part, was driving carefully and lawfully on Seventh Avenue, or Varick Street—at some point the avenue name changes; I'm not sure exactly where Seventh Avenue becomes Varick Street—and the evidence will show that the defendant was driving within the speed limit;

the evidence will show that the defendant was driving with the other traffic;

the evidence will show that the defendant had the green light in his favor;

yes, that's right, the evidence will show that the defendant had the green light in his favor;

and the evidence will show that in the midst of the beginning of the evening's rush-hour traffic going into the Holland Tunnel, a mass of thousands of cars, in this melange of traffic, suddenly appears the plaintiff in an unmarked police car.

The plaintiff has mentioned—barely mentioned—that this police car was unmarked. The evidence will show that this police car unquestionably was a Plymouth, a black, unmarked, plain, everyday Plymouth, driving, as the evidence will show, in the midst of hundreds of other black, and blue, and dark-colored Plymouths and Chevvies trying to get into the tunnel that night.

And the evidence will show that under the conditions created by the plaintiff—although on police duty—the evidence will show that the conditions created by the plaintiff and his vehicle were dangerous conditions, that plaintiff created an emergency situation to which defendant had to react instantly.

Indeed, the evidence will show that there were two emergencies that night. That's right, two emergencies.

As the plaintiff has indicated, the first emergency was the police emergency, the hostage situation.

The evidence will show that the second emergency on November 20, 1989, was at the intersection of Canal and Varick Streets; that second emergency was the emergency created by a dark, unmarked Plymouth—even though it was driven by the police for good purposes—careening through the intersection against the light, in the midst of evening rush hour traffic.

Now the evidence is not going to show that the police were goofing off, going out for coffee. The evidence will show that they were about some very serious, very grim business. Under extreme conditions. And in those extreme conditions, the police unfortunately but unquestionably created another grim situation, one that is known in the law as an emergency situation.

Later, the judge is going to explain the law to you. As we've already talked about, you are the exclusive judges of the facts; His Honor, the exclusive judge of the law. And there will come a time, at the end of the trial, when the judge will instruct you on the law. And part of the judge's instruction will be an instruction on the law of emergency.

Now I'm not talking about what you and I think of as an emergency. I'm talking about the fact that the judge will charge you that the law imposes on people in emergency situations certain responsibilities, things that they should do, to be reasonable men or women, to be without fault.

I won't in any fashion intrude upon the judge's exclusive province of the law. I only ask you to await any judgment on the facts, keep an open mind concerning the facts, until such time as you have the other side of the coin, an instruction on the law.

The evidence will show that the defendant here did absolutely everything that a reasonable man should have, could have done under the emergency circumstances created by the police action the evening of November 20, 1989.

The evidence will show that the incident, the accident, the injuries that resulted—and by the way, there is no question that there were injuries here sustained by the plaintiff—that the cause of those injuries were precipitated by—the evidence will show, solely and wholly—by the action of the police, or rather by the police action taken by the plaintiff himself.

The evidence will show that the defendant did absolutely nothing that he should not have done. That he did everything that he could have done.

And that, under the law, as the judge will instruct you, the evidence will show that the defendant is not at all responsible for the injuries sustained in this case.

I will have another opportunity to address you at the end of the case. I only ask you to keep your eyes and ears open, not to form any judgment until the end of the case, and when you do, based on the evidence and the law, as the judge gives you the law, you will find that the evidence will show that the defendant did nothing that any reasonable person would not have done, could have done under the situation created by the police.

In short, the evidence will show that the defendant is not responsible for the injuries to the plaintiff.

At the end of the case, I'm going to ask you to fulfill your oath, your responsibility, without sympathy, without emotion, deciding only the fault, the cause of the injuries. But this must await the evidence.

I will speak to you again, at the end of the case. Thank you.

OPENING STATEMENTS APPENDIX

To really get the true flavor of Opening statements, I include herewith the actual Opening statement of James LaRossa, one of the leading trial lawyers of New York.

The example Opening is from a criminal case in which Mr. LaRossa's client, a prominent negligence trial lawyer, was charged with attempted grand larceny in allegedly concocting a phony negligence claim on behalf of the wife, six children, and estate of a deceased man who met his death in an elevator shaft that had been horribly maintained by the City of New York.

Mr. LaRossa's Opening was the initial volley in a case that resulted in the total acquittal of Mr. LaRossa's client.

MR. LAROSSA: May it please the Court, Mr. Moskow, Mr. Miller, ladies and gentlemen of the jury. Mr. Moskow told you that this is an attempt to steal \$7,000,000 from the City. This case has its roots in a tragedy that occurred 10 years ago on April 4, 1979. It occurred in a building that was owned by the City of New York. It occurred because a man by the name of Aaron Krieger opened an elevator door believing an elevator to be there, walked into a darkened shaft, fell to the bottom of the shaft, broke up his body in so many pieces that for 25 days they kept him alive, and then he died.

This case is about shattered dreams and shattered families and about the defendant's involvement on behalf of that estate. This case is about a building that the City of New York owned at 291 in the Bowery, a building that was a slum by any other description. It had an elevator that didn't work. It had doors that were beat up. It had safety mechanisms that didn't work and nobody cared.

We're going to prove to you that the City knew about it. We're going to prove to you that the City rejected to repair this elevator. We are going to prove to you that nobody really cared about Aaron Krieger and his six children other than the defendant. We are going to prove to you that nobody even bothered for six months to fix this elevator that the City owned. We're going to prove to you that nobody even notified the elevator repair people for three months, for 90 days.

We're not talking about stealing \$7,000,000 or attempting to steal anything. When you see the pictures that are introduced in this case, the same pictures that were introduced to a civil jury in 1985 you will see a slum; forget what people tell you, you're going to see pictures of the bottom of a shaft with two feet of garbage. You're going to see pictures of an elevator door so smashed up that it couldn't close properly. You're going to see a mechanism that didn't work. And you're going to hear an assistant corporation counsel by the name of Laura Shapiro, who walked into a courtroom in 1985 to mislead and to deceive 12 jurors. She chose to stand before a jury and mislead the jury about what really occurred, who chose to deceive a jury in that case. Who chose purposely to lie to a jury in that case.

I'm going to tell you and prove to you that Laura Shapiro disregarded all of the facts that were before her. For example, the elevator door had a metal door. Someone many years ago took a drill and drilled a hole into it. The only way to open that door was to take an old spoon or an old knife to open it. And that's what the people from Stanton Trading had been doing for years. I'm going to prove to you that she ignored a lady by the name of Wilamena Oliver, an employee of the City, who testified that three times a week she went to 291 Bowery, three times a week, and yet she argued to that jury that no one in the City knew that this slum building even existed.

But, ladies and gentlemen, that was a different case. This is a criminal case. The defendant here is my client. I'm proud and pleased to represent him in this, the most important event that ever occurred in his life.

The prosecutor spent 20 minutes reading an indictment off to you. You should understand that those words mean nothing. You heard judge Aiello tell you that. They are merely a charge. They are words to apprise a defendant of what the charges are. In our society, we require that somebody should write words on a piece of paper that says, this is what the charge is.

When the defendant walked in here and said, not guilty, that the People here must prove, beyond a reasonable doubt that the defendant violated each and every aspect of each count, as judge Aiello will give it to you at the end of the trial or you must, must, find him Not Guilty.

Author's Note: The advocate introduces an admirable picture of his client early on to positively place the jurors mind-set about his client.

You will learn that the defendant is now 57 years old. He is married. His wife is a lawyer and happens to sit as a Justice of the Supreme Court in this County. He has two daughters. He came from humble beginnings in this City. He was educated in the public school system, was a good enough student to be accepted at Harvard Law School, went to Harvard Law School and has for 30-some-odd years been representing people like the estate of Aaron Krieger, like the wife and six children, to sue institutions like the City of New York for what they are entitled to, in this case for what the City permitted to occur.

In this case, for the pain of Aaron Krieger after being immobilized at the bottom of this pit and lying in a hospital for 24 days; for the fact that his wife would have no further husband and his children would grow up fatherless, all six of them. That is what he undertook some years ago.

You will find that Aaron Krieger had a brother, also an attorney, who, after this regrettable event occurred, took this to a law firm to handle it for him, and when he took it to that law firm he found the defendant as a partner in that law firm.

You're going to find it was a reasonably large law firm. One well-known in our legal profession for handling these kinds of lawsuits.

You are going to find that the defendant, from 1979 when this accident occurred—by the way, I am also going to prove to you the City has never given Mrs. Krieger or the children one cent, now going on its tenth year—you will find that this law firm had other lawyers and that when the estate went to that law firm, other lawyers prepared, handled, and shepherded this case until 1985, when it hit the courtroom and the defendant was assigned the responsibility of trying that case.

You will find that that law firm before the defendant ever joined it used an investigator by the name of Goldman, the same man as Mr. Moskow is talking about. You will find that when the defendant joined that law firm, he inherited Mr. Goldman. But you will also find that Mr. Goldman had a unique understanding with respect to lawyers and had a reputation amongst lawyers for someone who knew what he was doing and that it is the way the defendant found him in 1985.

You're going to find that other lawyers thought he was an expert on elevator accident cases. You're going to find that other lawyers thought he was an honest, sincere, good investigator.

Author's Note: Mr. LaRossa has begun to alert the jury to the weakness of the prosecution's prospective evidence.

You're going to hear two witnesses that John Moskow calls to the stand to testify to this. You're going to hear that people regarded Elliot Goldman as what they call a hands-on investigator, someone whom you give a case to when it occurs, who goes out and investigates it, gets all the material necessary, speaks to witnesses, determines how accidents occur, takes pictures of scenes. In some cases, determines what the theory of liability should be. And that's the package that the defendant got in 1985 when he entered the Supreme Court of this County, just down the street, a building or two, at 60 Centre Street to try this case. That is the backdrop of it.

Now, I am going to prove to you that notwithstanding everything that Laura Shapiro knew about this case, when she opened to that jury, notwithstanding the fact that she saw pictures of what I described as a slum—and you will see and have the opportunity to decide that—notwithstanding the fact that she knew there were many, many incidents of problems with this elevator, she knew that the City had an absolute liability to Aaron Krieger and his family. She prepared a memorandum to her respective superiors at the Corporation Counsel's office, and that memorandum spoke to what she knew about this slum, what she knew the City's responsibility was to the people who use this building; and she spoke to what she believed the Krieger's family was entitled to get from a jury.

So now let's talk about an attempt to commit grand larceny. Laura Shapiro stated in that memorandum that she believed the sustainable value that the defendant was trying to get for the Krieger family at that point was somewhere between $3.6 million and $5 million. Those were her numbers that she put down, what she believed the sustainable value of Aaron Krieger's life was worth to his family, and pain and suffering. The City paid nothing.

Laura Shapiro got up, and you will see her on the stand, and attempted to fool a jury. She did it in every sentence and every paragraph that she opened to that jury. She did it because she didn't want the city to pay one cent to Aaron Krieger's family, because she didn't want the city to pay one cent to the wife, children, and estate of Aaron Krieger.

Now, let me get back to Elliot Goldman, if I may. He is the investigator. If you notice, most of the clauses that John Mosckow read to you in the indictment, that is the charge, referred to Elliot Goldman speaking to someone. I think you're going to hear the tapes of Elliot Goldman, particularly a tape with Mr. Cohen, and I think it will be clear that Elliot Goldman stepped over the line. I think it will be clear that, for whatever reason, he not only stepped over the line, but the things he did were unethical. It will become clear that Mr. Goldman attempted to have witnesses say things that were either exaggerated or not true.

But Mr. Goldman is not here. I don't represent Mr. Goldman. I am not here to try him, defend him, or bury him. That has nothing to do with what is going on here. The issue here is what did the defendant do.

So along comes this witness, Mr. Cohen, and you're going to find him a very interesting man, Michael Cohen. An employee of Stanton Trading where Aaron Krieger worked. One of the first people to find the shattered body at the bottom of the shaft. After he received a phone call from Elliot Goldman, where he contends that Elliot Goldman said, "We want to control you or I want to control you," he runs to Laura Shapiro and Laura Shapiro takes this and uses it as you will see, to stop this lawsuit. She takes him upstairs to what is called the Inspector General's office of the Corporation Counsel, City of New York. They call in people from the Department of Investigation.

As a matter of fact, the very man who will be sitting at this prosecution table, Mr. Hynes, and other men from the Inspector General's office, police officers assigned to the Department of Investigation, they all get into a car with

> Mr. Cohen and they drive to Mr. Cohen's house and they wire Mr. Cohen, put a wire on him and they tell Mr. Cohen what they want him to do.
>
> And Mr. Cohen waits for Goldman, and Mr. Goldman comes in; he has a short conversation with Mr. Cohen and then starts to leave. But he hasn't done anything wrong yet. So Cohen says, "Wait a minute!" And he is going to testify here and admit he said I couldn't let Goldman leave. He hadn't done anything wrong yet. I was there to catch him. He was Laura Shapiro's bait to get out of this lawsuit. So they taped Goldman, and you will hear it, and Goldman certainly goes over the edge.
>
> But after that, what happens? We know they didn't go, after hearing that tape, before the judge in that civil lawsuit the next day to tell him something happened. They didn't do that. The City doesn't do that. The Inspector General of the Corporation Counsel doesn't do that. The Department of Investigation doesn't do that. They say, "Let's go a step further. Let's see if we can get plaintiff's lawyer, the defendant here, to bite. Let's see if we can get him."
>
> So Cohen starts to call the defendant, who is in the middle of another civil trial. He doesn't even return the calls. This happens once, twice; finally, he returns the phone call. Cohen says, "I have to see you." That's when that meeting in the coffee shop occurs. You're going to hear a tape of that meeting.

Author's Note: It is always "you are going to hear" what will come up in evidence. Mr. LaRossa never forgets this is an Opening, not Summation. But yet he is able to hammer hard on the prosecution's Opening.

> You are also going to hear what Cohen had to say about that tape. Cohen is going to tell you that the defendant never asked him to lie on the stand. Cohen is going to tell you that the defendant never asked him to perjure himself. That is what Mr. Moskow just told you. What I am telling you—and hold me to it—that Michael Cohen is going to tell you on the witness stand, notwithstanding the fact that he is the protagonist in this case, the main actor in this drama, notwithstanding the fact he is going to tell you he considers John Moskow his close friend, notwithstanding the fact he is going to tell you he has told other people go up and see John Moskow, mention my name—he still is going to swear under oath that the defendant did not ask him to say anything untrue on the witness stand. Did not offer him any money and did not attempt to get him to lie.
>
> Matter of fact, no one will testify that the defendant did any of those things. This is an attempt to get you riled up with respect to Goldman and hope you make the jump from Goldman to the defendant.
>
> You're going to hear what Michael Cohen told people outside the room in the District attorney's office without John Moskow being able to protect him.

When he was trying to tell the truth. When he didn't know people were listening as intently as they were, you're going to hear that he said "The defendant never asked me to lie; the defendant never asked me to perjure myself; the defendant never asked me to do anything wrong the defendant never asked me to do anything inappropriate." This is Michael Cohen.

I am also going to prove to you, ladies and gentlemen, that Michael Cohen has lied under oath at a prior occasion. What did he lie about? He lied about whether the Department of Investigation, Pat Hynes, and a police officer by the name of Marinez gave him instructions on what to say when he wore these tapes. And this perjury, ladies and gentlemen, occurred over a year ago, and no one has ever corrected it until today. No one has ever gone to Judge Aiello or any other judge in this building and told them, "Michael Cohen perjured himself under oath." But I am going to prove it to you! You're going to be able to judge what you believe and what you don't believe with respect to Michael Cohen.

Now, there was a meeting with Michael Cohen and the defendant in a coffee shop early one morning. The defendant on the way to work, Cohen badgering him to meet him after the Elliot Goldman meeting. And he meets him, and they do have a discussion, and Cohen says, "You know, Elliot Goldman talked to me about paying me." And the defendant says, "We are not going to pay you! We will give you some money if you lost wages; we will help you make that up. But don't talk about paying." And then the two of them have a conversation about deceiving Laura Shapiro, the same Laura Shapiro who lied to a jury, the same Laura Shapiro who refused to do what was appropriate, failed to get up in front of a jury and say, look, I represent the City, and I live in the City, and I am part of the City, and I apologize for what the City did in this case. Why don't you all figure out how much money we owe this wife and six children? She didn't do that. Yes, the defendant asked Mr. Cohen, go back and deceive Laura Shapiro. He used words like mitzvah, told us this is a mitzvah, a gift. Get her to put you on the stand.

What Michael Cohen will tell you is that the defendant never asked him to perjure himself or lie under oath. That interpretation, ladies and gentlemen, will only come from John Moskow.

Now, what happens after that? They now have the defendant on tape and it goes back to the Department of Investigation. police officers take it back. They make what we call a transcript of the tape, which means someone listens to it and writes out the words and it is typed. They now get a chance to review it. They now get a chance to hear what the defendant said to Michael Cohen.

Well, you've got to say to yourself, did they arrest him that day? Did they take the defendant in custody that day? No! What they do is get Michael Cohen to go back and try to get him again. And you're going to hear the whole background, you're going to hear about phone calls that are made. This is into December 1985, right in the middle of this civil trial.

By the way, Mrs. Krieger is sitting right here in the front row of this trial.

They make the decision, they being the Corporation Counsel, Laura Shapiro and all the other inspectors, that they're going to create a fictitious report, and they do. They take an old retired police officer who happened to come to the scene of the accident in 1979 and found Aaron Krieger in the bottom of the shaft. They take him, and they create a false statement. They get a statement allegedly from him that's fictitious and made up, no truth to it, and they walk into court, right in the middle of the civil trial with Mrs. Krieger sitting in the front row and hand it to the defendant and the other lawyers as if it's the product of a witness who's about to take the stand. Even though they knew that it was untrue and a fraud. And you're going to hear how they knew, because Laura Shapiro, with the help of the Department of Investigation, hooks up a wire to her phone and calls this retired police officer, now living in Pennsylvania, who's physically infirm, who can't even come to New York; they tape him, like he had something to do with this. They find out on that tape that this man knows nothing about what happened. He responded to three of these a week and has no recollection of which one this is. So they create this false and phony report after taping this innocent retired police officer and hand it to the defendant in a courtroom much like this to see if the defendant would take another bite.

I'm going to prove to you that that was long after he speaks to Cohen, where they tape him, long after Cohen calls him a multitude of times and tapes him. No arrests. No arrests. No decision to arrest him at that time. They wanted to go one step further, so they create this phony report.

And then, the defendant, for the first time, is put smack into the middle of the bait and, you know what, he doesn't buy the bait. He doesn't offer the retired policeman any money. He doesn't attempt to get the retired policeman to change his testimony. The bait didn't work. But Mrs. Krieger still sits in the front row and for 30 more days this farce trial goes on.

Why do I say a farce trial? Because everybody knew at that point, except for the defendant, that this was going to be a mistrial. So they played the little game for 30 days. Mr. Hynes is at the root of it. And you know what, it works. There was a mistrial. That was in January 1986. The trial ends. Do they arrest the defendant? No! Why? They wait for the defendant to try the Krieger case again. They wait until Miriam Krieger sits in another courtroom in the front row. They wait until the defendant begins to make a presentation to 12 more people like you. That's when they arrest him. That trial has to be a mistrial. Go home, Mrs. Krieger, your day will come but it hasn't come yet.

Now what about this man, Michael Cohen, this Samaritan of a witness who was one of the first people to find Aaron Krieger at the bottom of the shaft?

> Well, he's going to testify, and I'm going to prove to you that Michael Cohen didn't like him. He didn't like Aaron Krieger. You know why? Because Aaron Krieger made a mess after he cleaned up. And he said, "I will damn well let him know." And when he went to the Department of Investigation, on this great adventure of his, when they were going to hook up the wire to him, he testified under oath "I am not sympathetic to this family." And you are going to hear that he told people that he spoke to about what a great adventure this was, going to the defendant with a tape on. How exciting the confrontation was. He loves to testify and be cross-examined. How much he enjoys it. How well John Moskow treats him. What a close friend he is of John Moskow's. "Mention my name," says Michael Cohen, "that will get you in the door."

Author's Note: Mr. LaRossa anticipates calling a witness to the stand who previously gave false testimony at the civil trial. Anticipating the cross-examination by the prosecution, tearing into that witness by using the prior inconsistent statement under oath, Mr. LaRossa decides to beard the lion in his own den, to spring the prosecutor's trap, thereby defusing, neutralizing the sting that he knows will come.

> Now, let me cover one thing, and that is Ailets' testimony at that trial. Let me make it easy for John Moskow. Mr. Ailets testified falsely. He testified falsely about whether he received a suit. He testified falsely about whether he was compensated for his testimony, and he testified falsely about transportation back and forth to the courtroom.
>
> Don't even bother thinking about it. I'm telling you straight out that that was false testimony.
>
> I'll tell you another thing. The defendant sat in the courtroom and heard it and knew it was false. Okay. I'm going to make it easy for John Moskow. But now let me tell you what really occurred. Ailets was an old man. An employee of Stanton. These issues were what lawyers call, and you're going to hear testimony about it, collateral matters. Mr. Friedman did talk to Mr. Chase, who was sitting next to him, about it, and Mr. Chase will tell you "I don't think he should have done anything about it. He should have just left it alone."
>
> The defendant spoke to another associate in his office, a man by the name of Eisenstein. Eisenstein said, "I think you have a problem. Maybe you have to do something about it."
>
> I'm telling you that people will testify, experienced trial lawyers, that this is an enigma that trial lawyers are placed in. He didn't put this false testimony into Ailets' mouth. That was the fourth day of testimony and it was on recross-examination. He sits there with a duty to his client. You are going to hear people testify that he had a duty to his client and that duty was

superior to any duty to report the false testimony, right or wrong. Maybe he was wrong. That's not the issue here.

The issue here is, did the defendant commit a crime? We're not talking about whether that was a good decision or a bad decision. We're talking about whether someday you can go back in that room and decide did the People prove this case beyond a reasonable doubt that he is a criminal.

You're going to hear he's a fierce advocate, as well he should be. You're going to see what he had to fight against Laura Shapiro and the City. You're going to see that he was tireless. You're going to see a number of things. You're going to see memoranda from his files by the bushel load. You're going to hear his very thoughts and very private notes about this case. You know why you're going to be able to read and hear them? Because he chose to keep them sacred, and when the District Attorney subpoenaed them, he said "Come on in. Go through them. Keep what you want."

I'm not talking about any D.A., I'm talking about John Moskow. You copy what you want and take it.

When they told him they were thinking about an indictment, he waived immunity. Namely when you go before a Grand Jury, you are immunized from prosecution. He said "I'll waive," and he walked into the Grand Jury room with no protection—his lawyer couldn't even object to anything at that point—and sat and John Moskow asked him questions for two days.

And you heard that whole indictment. You didn't hear anyone count in that indictment about perjury before that Grand Jury. And I'll also prove to you there are no perjury counts ever charging the defendant with perjury in front of that Grand Jury.

Now advocacy is not what this is all about. You're going to make a decision in a couple of weeks whether to stamp the defendant a felon, and you're going to make that decision based on what you see here, what you hear here, what your analysis of the tapes is, and you're going to go back and look at why they had to create this Seaburg [phonetic] report, the end of 1985.

And the woman involved in disrupting this trial, because Laura Shapiro is an advocate too, a good advocate, she hasn't paid one penny. And let me tell you something else about Laura Shapiro. I'm going to prove to you that she's been under investigation for the last year. By whom? The Department of Investigation of the City of New York. Same people. Patrick Hynes, right in the middle here. If he finds she's committed a crime, it's passed from the Department of Investigation to John Moskow. So in judging Laura Shapiro's belief and honesty, I'm going to prove to you that she's under the hammer right now, and the people who are going to make a decision whether she is under the hammer are the Department of Investigation and John Moskow and the District attorney's office. We'll get to that.

Author's Note: Mr. LaRossa here gives them a thumbnail sketch of the law.

> You know, ladies and gentlemen, the law is such, particularly in this state, that the defendant need prove nothing to you. If you listened to Judge Aiello carefully he said the defense, if they wish, may open to you. I have no requirement to present evidence to you. I have no requirement, so says the law, to prove the defendant innocent. That's not where we are. John Moskow has to prove the defendant's guilt beyond a reasonable doubt to each and every essential element of every count. That's what the law says.
>
> Now, what do I expect from you as jurors? I asked you a lot of questions at the beginning to decide basically whether you could be fair, whether you'd be honest, whether you would be interested enough in what goes on here so you pay attention, because the defendant is entitled to that. And you all agreed you would. You all agreed you would have an open mind. You all agreed you would pay attention. You all agreed that you would follow the law as Judge Aiello tells you the law is, and that's all I want.
>
> When I say "I" you understand that I'm standing in the defendant's shoes. I speak for him much like he spoke for Aaron Krieger, but I speak for him and I've taken on that responsibility. You have taken on a responsibility to him, as well; that is, you've agreed to be openminded, honest, and sincere; and I think you all are. What that means is you don't talk about this case, because you haven't heard a word yet, not a word. You haven't heard what the case is all about, other than what John Moskow said and I said. And remember what Judge Aiello said, in this Opening statement we're not giving you evidence. We're giving you theories. We're giving you what we expect to prove even though I don't have to prove anything.
>
> I will prove to you beyond any shadow of a doubt that the defendant was an honest, deliberate advocate in that courtroom trying to represent these seven people because they had lost husband and father. And the defendant violated no law, did nothing improper. I ask you for two things, an open mind and a hundred cents on the dollar in terms of attention, because if you give me those things then you will see through the Michael Cohens and the Laura Shapiros and the sting operation that went on here and the phoney legal proceedings that occurred, and you won't find the defendant guilty of anything. You will have to, if you follow the oath, say it loud enough so we can all hear it, but I have the feeling three weeks from now you are going to want to scream it out, scream it out that the defendant violated no law because I'll prove to you he didn't.
>
> Thank you for your attention.

13

DOCUMENTARY AND PHYSICAL EVIDENCE

WHAT IT IS

In the Opening, you've seen the advocates tell the jury that what each adversary says throughout the trial and what the judge says is not evidence. Evidence is only that which is spoken by witnesses under oath while on the witness chair, OR it is documentary or physical evidence introduced through an actual witness.

BE MOST CAREFULLY ADVISED, however, that not a single piece of physical or documentary evidence, unless there is a stipulation or the Court takes judicial notice thereof, may be presented to a jury EXCEPT if it is introduced through a live witness who takes the stand and testifies about that particular piece of physical evidence.

Every piece of physical or documentary evidence must be determined first as a matter of law by the judge, as being relevant, significant, a part of the evidence. In order to do this, the judge must hear a proper foundation established through a live witness. That witness, in short, must be led by the advocate who proffers the witness through testimony, establishing the proper foundation for the admission of the physical item or document into evidence.

PROPER FOUNDATION

Since the taking of testimony is shortly to begin and you are soon to present witnesses, you'd better know what a proper foundation to introduce physical or documentary evidence is and what it is not.

Each piece of evidence may be different. But the proper foundation for evidence is fairly much the same for each. Once you learn what a proper foundation is, like riding a bicycle, you will never forget it, nor will you have difficulty understanding what it is that you need to do before introducing any piece of evidence, no matter how large or how small.

RELIABILITY: ESSENCE OF THE FOUNDATION

The rules of evidence, the rules that govern the submission and admission of physical or documentary evidence, are all designed to protect the integrity of the trial evidence, to ensure that not a wit of evidence is presented unless it has been fully and well-tested for reliability.

Reliability means that the evidence is fairly presented to the jury, subject to scrutiny by both the advocate introducing the same and the adversary by cross-examination.

That doesn't mean that you can cross-examine a document or a piece of physical evidence. But you must be able to probe and test the person who is the conduit for the introduction of that physical evidence.

In other words, as I've said previously, not a wit of evidence is admitted into any trial except that a live witness testifies to the proper foundation thereof, and is subject to cross-examination as to that document or physical evidence.

An advocate cannot just take a document or a piece of evidence and say, Your Honor, I offer *this* in evidence, and that object is admitted in evidence.

Rather, there must be a live witness who can testify to the origin, the source of a piece of evidence, the chain of custody, the "pedigree" or background of that evidence before it can be admitted into the body of the case.

If a proper foundation is not submitted, the Court shall reject the offer as a matter of law, and no matter how significant you believe the evidence to be, it will not be admitted.

Thus, when you know you have a document or a physical object that has to be admitted at your upcoming trial, you'd better start thinking immediately, how am I going to get this into evidence, through whom can it be introduced. If you can't find an answer to those questions, you are not going to get that item into evidence.

THE FOUNDATION

The foundation necessary to admit any document or physical object into evidence is pretty much the same regardless of what the item is.

For example, in a criminal case, you might want to introduce a weapon, a pistol found at the scene of the occurrence. You would initiate the introduction as follows:

Advocate: Your Honor, I'd like to have this marked People's Exhibit 1 for identification.

The Court: Very well, Mr. Reporter, mark it for identification, People's Exhibit 1 for identification.

Explanation: The advocate introducing the item cannot even testify as to what the item is. Therefore, he or she doesn't say, I show you this weapon, this pistol. Rather, the advocate indicates, I show you "this," leaving the identification or explanation of whatever the object is to the witness.

However, for appellate purposes—if such become necessary—for preserving the Record, the item is marked for identification, identifying the item for later review or discussion in the event that the item is NOT admitted into evidence. This, or course, is done for the reason that it is very difficult, to say the least, for appellate courts to know what "this" is without some further identification.

Q. Now Officer Conroy, I show you what has now been marked People's Exhibit 1 for identification and ask you if you recognize what this is?

A. Yes, I do.

Q. And what do you recognize People's 1 for identification to be?

A. This is a pistol that I found on the floor of apartment 53F at 41 West 86th street when I responded to a radio run on April 15th 1986.

Explanation: Now the witness has identified the exhibit that has been marked for identification and has testified why or how he can identify the same. But this is not yet enough for introduction into evidence. As the purpose of the foundation is to ensure that the item is precisely identified and connected to the case in a direct way, further questions of identification and relevance are necessary.

Q. And how is it that you recognize this to be the same weapon as you saw that day?

A. I scratched my initials onto the trigger guard with the tip of a small penknife that I always carry.

Q. And do you see your initials on People's Exhibit 1 for identification?

A. I do.

Q. Where are they?

A. Right here (indicating), on the bottom surface of the trigger guard.

Advocate: (Indicating a place at the bottom of the trigger guard, on the bottom of the trigger guard, close to where that trigger guard meets the handle of the weapon).

The Court: Does that seem appropriate, Mr. Adversary?

Adversary: Yes, Your Honor, he described the location of some sort of initials properly.

Note: The place where a witness describes his initials to appear, or where something appears in a photograph, or the location of anything in or on any piece of evidence is not apparent to an appellate court, or to you, dear reader, merely by the words written on paper: here it is, here they are.

It is the responsibility of the advocates, therefore, to describe where the witness has indicated or placed or located or estimated in or on the particular piece of physical evidence.

This is done by saying, aloud in the Record: "Indicating," and then describing the location, size, or setting described by the witness.

Q. Is there any other way that you can identify People's Exhibit 1 for identification?

A. Yes. I also took down the serial number that was on the weapon when I vouchered the weapon.

Q. What does that mean, voucher the weapon?

A. The police department has a procedure where evidence is taken, put in sealed envelopes, turned into the property clerk's office, where it is preserved and stored until the time of trial, or until it's needed for some other purpose. Each voucher envelope has a number printed on it that is used for that envelope and that vouchered item only.

Q. And what do you do when you voucher an item?

A. Put it in the numbered envelope, fill out a sheet of paper with the same number, turn the sealed envelope to the property clerk. I keep one copy of the voucher receipt, one goes in the file, one goes to the property clerk.

Q. And was there a voucher number issued for this piece of evidence?

A. Yes. Number 16784.

Q. Do you have the voucher document with you?

A. Yes. Here it is.

Advocate: Your Honor, may we have the voucher document marked People's Exhibit 1-A for identification?

The Court: Mark it.

Q. Officer, does the voucher number appear on that voucher receipt document, People's Exhibit 1-A that you are holding?

A. Yes, number 16784.

Q. And what is the item or evidence vouchered under voucher #16784?

A. A Smith and Wesson .38 caliber revolver.

Q. And on that voucher receipt is there a serial number for a weapon written down?

A. Yes, .38 Caliber, Smith and Wesson, serial number 3423685.

Q. And what is the serial number of the weapon that you have there on the counter before you, the one that is marked People's Exhibit 1 for identification?

A. Serial number 3423685.

Advocate: At this time, Your Honor, I offer People's Exhibit 1 and People's Exhibit 1-A, now marked only for identification, into evidence.

The Court: Show them to your adversary.

The foregoing is the basic formula or foundation for introducing any item into evidence. The evidence must be identified, its connection to the case must be clearly established, its chain of custody must be clearly defined, and there must be a witness available and on the stand to be cross-examined about the evidence.

There is virtually no difference in the foundation necessary for introduction of a document or a piece of physical evidence, regardless of what the item or document is.

Another example: You are trying a contract dispute, and you have called to the stand the president of your client corporation, one of the signatories to the contract.

Note: Exhibits can be premarked for identification by yourself in any sequence that you wish, or they can be marked for identification in open Court at the moment that you are dealing with the particular item. To save time, to have a smoother flow to your presentation, it is far better to premark items. Most stationery and law office supply companies carry exhibit stickers for plaintiff and defendant.

You can put any numbers or letters on the item as you wish, as the aim and purpose is to "identify" the item. So long as the marking or letter is specific and unique to the particular exhibit, it is acceptable.

Special Note: Plaintiffs' attorneys (prosecutors) always use numbers to identify their exhibits. Defendants' attorneys always use letters of the alphabet.

Although this doesn't affect plaintiffs, when a defendant goes through the alphabet once, exhibits are then marked with double letters, and, if necessary, triple letters, Exhibit BB, Exhibit WWW, and so forth.

Q. Mr. Witness, I show you plaintiff's Exhibit 5 for identification and ask you if you recognize this.

A. Yes, this is the contract that we, when I say we, I mean Considine Corporation, that we signed with Cherrybrook Corporation.

Q. And how do you recognize it as such?

A. Our attorneys drew the agreement. I went over it many times before it was executed. And, in addition, where handwritten corrections were made at the time of execution, my initials and Tony Sargeant's initials, Cherrybrook's president, are written in the margin, and my signature appears at the bottom of the contract.

Q. Can you point out your signature on plaintiff's Exhibit 5 for identification?

A. Yes, this is my signature (indicating).

Advocate: For the record, indicating the bottom of page 5 of plaintiff's Exhibit 5 for identification.

Q. And do you see your initials on the Exhibit 5 for identification?

A. Yes, right here (indicating).

Advocate: Indicating on page 2 in the left bottom margin, and page 3 in the right margin in the middle of the page, of plaintiff's Exhibit 5 for identification.

Q. Is there any doubt in your mind that this is the final version of the contract that was executed by your company with Cherrybrook on the fifteenth of April 1992?

A. None at all.

Advocate: Your Honor, I offer plaintiff's Exhibit 5 for identification into evidence.

The Court: Show it to your adversary. Any objection?

Adversary: No objection.

The Court: Received.

Notice that the foundation for the introduction of a weapon in the criminal case and the contract in the contract case were basically the same. And so it is with every item of physical evidence or document that you will ever introduce into evidence.

Therefore, study the foregoing and following examples carefully and get the formula down precisely. The more specific identifying aspects of the exhibit that you can point out to the Court, the more likely it is that the exhibit will be received in evidence.

RECEPTION IN EVIDENCE IS NOT AUTOMATIC

Advocate: Your Honor, may I have these items collectively marked People's Exhibit 3 for identification?

The Court: Yes, so mark them.

Q. I show you what has been marked People's Exhibit 3 for identification and ask you if you recognize what these are.

A. Yes, these are shell casings that were found at the scene of the crime.

Q. And when you say shell casings, what do you mean?

A. A cartridge, commonly known as a bullet is made up of two things, three things: a casing, which is the container that holds the charge or powder; the powder, which is the explosive material; and the projectile, usually a soft metal substance, which, when the weapon is fired, is forced through the barrel and becomes a projectile. The casing is that part that holds the explosive charge and remains behind in the weapon, or is ejected from the weapon at the time of firing.

Q. And when you say the casings that form part of Exhibit 3 for identification were found at the scene of the crime, to what do you refer?

A. The homicide that occurred the morning of April 15, 1989, in apartment 2 of 2133 Walton Avenue, Bronx County.

Q. Were these found by yourself?

A. No, by my partner.

Q. And is there anything about these items that cause you to recognize them?

A. I believe my partner put his initials on the casings.

Q. Do you see his initials on People's Exhibit 3 for identification?

A. These are his initials.

Advocate: Indicating at the rim or closed end of each casing, the initials CMB. Your Honor, I offer People's Exhibit 3 for identification in evidence.

The Court: Show it to your adversary. Any objection?

Adversary: Yes, Your Honor, there hasn't been a proper foundation laid for the introduction of this exhibit. This is not the officer who found the items, nor marked them, nor can he differentiate these items from any other similar items. I object.

The Court: Yes, I agree. I don't think that this witness has sufficiently identified the exhibit or laid a proper foundation. I'm going to sustain the objection at this time, without prejudice to renewing the offer of the exhibit with a proper foundation.

Voir Dire

Remember the voir dire we discussed during the selection of the jury? It meant, in effect, to inquire into the credentials and qualifications of the jurors. Remember also that at that time I told you that there was one other occasion during a trial that you conduct a voir dire, and that is to inquire into the *bona fides* of an offered piece of evidence.

When your adversary offers something into evidence, you are, as we have seen here, in a position to object to the offer on the basis of a failure of proper foundation—or any other basis that may be applicable: lack of relevance, improperly or unnecessarily prejudicial, and so forth.

If you are not sure, however, that you have sufficient basis for your objection because you do not have all the facts in connection with the specific piece of evidence being offered, then you are entitled to ask the judge if you may inquire on a voir dire of the witness through whom the item is being offered in order to develop the objection.

> *NOTE: An evidentiary voir dire concerning a piece of evidence is a very specific device. It is not intended as a mini cross-examination into the substance of the witness's testimony in chief. It is merely intended to permit you to develop sufficient information* only *about the piece of proposed evidence in order to determine whether or not to proffer an objection.*

Sample Voir Dire

Adversary: Your Honor, I'd like to have this marked plaintiff's Exhibit 4 for identification.

The Court: Mark it.

Q. Mr. Witness, I show you plaintiff's Exhibit 4 for identification and ask you if you recognize what it is.

A. Yes, I do.

Q. What do you recognize it to be?

A. This appears to be the headlight that I picked up from the street just after the accident occurred.

Q. What were the circumstances of your picking up that headlight?

A. I heard the noise of a crash, as I said. I was just in front of my store. I turned around, and there were the two cars, all crashed into each other. This headlight was on the ground, right near my curb, right in front of my store, so I picked it up.

Q. What did you do with it after that?

A. I had it in my hand, and I was walking over to see if I could help anyone in the accident.

Q. What, if anything, else occurred?

A. The driver of the blue car, I guess that's the defendant, Mr. Smith, said that the damn thing wasn't working anyway, it wasn't worth a damn.

Q. What if anything did you do with the headlight after that?

A. When an investigator from your office came to ask me some questions, last year, I gave it to him.

Q. Is there any doubt in your mind that that's the headlight that you saw just after the accident?

A. It appears to be the same.

Adversary: I offer plaintiff's Exhibit 4 for identification into evidence.

The Court: Show it to defense counsel.

Note: At this point you have an objection to the offer. However, there hasn't been sufficient antifoundation developed on the record for you to properly articulate your objection.

Advocate: Your Honor, may I have some questions on the voir dire?

The Court: You may.

Advocate: Mr. Witness, when was the last time you saw the headlight that you found in the street in front of your store?

A. About a year, year and a half ago.

Q. That was when you gave it to the investigator from Mr. Adversary's office?

A. That's right.

Q. Did you in any way mark that headlight that you had in your possession, put your initials on it, take down a serial number, anything like that?

A. No.

Q. Is there anything particular or different about that headlight, plaintiff's Exhibit 4 for identification, that makes you recognize it as the same one you found in the street just after the accident?

A. Well, it looks like the one, same shape, same everything.

Q. Is there anything on this Exhibit 4 for identification that makes it different, that you can identify it from any other headlight made for an automobile that you can buy in an auto parts store?

A. Well, its, . . . no, there's nothing particular about it. It's a regular headlight from a car.

Q. Similar to millions of headlights?

A. I guess.

Q. Can you say, from looking at Exhibit 4 for identification, other than the fact that Mr. Adversary handed that headlight to you, that that's the same one that you had originally found and then gave to the investigator?

A. It looks like it.

Q. Other than it looks like it in general?

A. Not really.

Advocate: Your Honor, I object to the introduction of this item. There is insufficient foundation to indicate that this is indeed the same headlight that was found by this witness at the time of the accident.

The Court: At this time, I have to agree with Mr. Advocate. Perhaps if you have another witness later, you may introduce it. But at this time, I'm going to sustain the objection.

CHECKLIST

As the introduction of all physical or documentary evidence requires fairly similar foundation, the following checklist should be sunk so deep in your memory that it becomes as a second nature in your trial work.

(a) Premark or have the item marked as an exhibit for identification;

(b) show the item to the witness for his or her recognition;

(c) have the witness identify the item;

(d) have the witness describe the circumstances of his or her identification of the item;

(e) have the witness describe on the record the particular identifying marks or aspects of the item;

(f) offer the item into evidence.

With that checklist in memory, you should fairly well be able to put into evidence any type of physical or documentary evidence, from an ambulance report to a xylophone (it should be spelled with a "z" if you ask me).

AMBULANCE REPORT

Q. I show you defendant's Exhibit C for identification and ask you if you recognize the same.

A. Yes, this is the ambulance report that I made out in connection with Alphonse D'Artagnon on the morning of April 15, 1990.

Q. How do you recognize defendant's Exhibit C for identification to be that same ambulance report?

A. I wrote it out. It's in my handwriting. It's on the usual form that I use when making out ambulance reports. It's dated April 15, 1990. The name of the patient is Alphonse D'Artagnon.

Q. I guess there isn't any doubt that this is the ambulance report, then, relating to Mr. D'Artagnon?

Adversary: Objection to the leading, to the form of the question, Your Honor.

Advocate: I'll withdraw it, Your Honor, and rephrase it.

Q. Is there any doubt in your mind what defendant's Exhibit C is?

A. None at all. It's the ambulance report relating to one Alphonse D'Artagnon made out by me on April 15, 1990, at or about 4:30 A.M.

Advocate: I offer it in evidence, Your Honor.

The Court: Show it to your adversary. Any objection?

XYLOPHONE

Q. I show you what has been marked plaintiff's Exhibit 4 for identification. Can you tell the Court and jury if you recognize what plaintiff's Exhibit 4 for identification is?

A. Yes, it's a xylophone.

Q. A xylophone is a musical instrument, is it not?

A. Yes, it is.

Q. And do you recognize this xylophone to be any particular musical instrument?

A. It appears to be one that was stolen from the music room of Carnegie Hall on the evening of April 15, 1990.

Note: The foundation can be interspersed with other, nonfoundation questions.

Q. What is your connection with Carnegie Hall?

A. I am the custodian in charge of the physical plant, which, of course, includes the music room.

Q. And did anything occur on the 15th of April 1990 in connection with the music room?

A. Yes, there was a theft there.

Q. And when you say a theft, what occurred?

A. Several musical instruments were stolen, including a xylophone that belonged to the Philadelphia Orchestra.

Q. Do you know when the xylophone in question was put in the music room at Carnegie Hall?

A. I was told . . .

Adversary: Your Honor, I object to the answer as far as it's gone. It is unquestionably hearsay.

The Court: Yes, strike it out.

Now for a Foundation Within a Foundation

Q. I show you plaintiff's Exhibit 6 for identification and ask you if you recognize what this is.

A. Yes, I do.

Q. And what is it?

A. Its the inventory of instruments that were in the music room on the evening of the 14th of April 1990. We make such an inventory every evening before the music room is locked for the night.

Q. And was this inventory prepared under your direction in connection with the regular and ordinary business of Carnegie Hall.

A. Yes, it was.

Q. And when was this particular report made?

A. On the evening of April 14, 1990, as I said.

Q. And thereafter what happened with this document, plaintiff's Exhibit 6 for identification?

A. It is kept in a book in my office, or at least a copy of it is. Another copy is kept in the music room itself. And there is another copy in the director's office.

Q. Is that the director of the orchestra in question?

A. No, the director of Carnegie Hall.

Q. And are you the custodian of these records for Carnegie Hall?

A. Yes.

Q. And did you bring this document to Court subject to a subpoena duces tecum for its prodouction?

A. Yes.

Q. And on the list or inventory of the music room from the evening of April 14, 1990, is there a xylophone, or xylophones listed?

A. There are two.

Q. Are there any identifying marks or descriptions contained on the list for the xylophones?

A. Yes, there are the manufacturer's name and serial number of the instrument.

Q. And can you tell us what the description of the xylophones that were in the Carnegie Hall music room on April 14, 1990?

A. Yes, there's an Alpha number 12547 and an Omega 678954.

Q. I ask you, madam, to look at the instrument that was first presented to you as plaintiff's Exhibit 5 for identification and ask you if there is any brand name and serial number contained anywhere thereon?

A. Certainly. This is Omega brand number 678954.

Q. And what do you recognize plaintiff's Exhibit 5 for identification to be?

A. The instrument that was stolen from the music room of Carnegie Hall on the fourteenth of April 1990.

Advocate: At this time, Your Honor, plaintiff offers plaintiff's Exhibit 5 and 6, both for identification, into evidence.

The Court: Show them to your adversary. Mr. Adversary, you can come up and identify the xylophone; it's a little difficult for the Court officer to bring the same to the counsel table. Any objection?

ZYMOSCOPE

(Don't tell me I don't know z is the last letter of the alphabet.)

Q. I show you defendant's Exhibit 4 for identification and ask you if you recognize what it is?

A. Yes, this is a zymoscope.

Q. And precisely what is a zymoscope?

A. It is an apparatus, a mechanism used to determine the fermentation of yeast.

Q. How does it work?

A. It measures the carbon dioxide that evolves from, is given off from, a quantity of sugar.

Q. And do you recognize this to be a zymoscope manufactured by the Zeta Zymoscope Corp.?

A. It was made to look like one, but it is not a true Zeta zymoscope.

Q. What is the basis for your opinion? In other words, on what do you base your opinion that this is not a Zeta Zymoscope?

A. First, it is not the right color. Ours are made of copper. This one is some base white metal that was painted to look like copper. See here where paint is chipping off.

Advocate: (Indicating an area at the base of the apparatus where there are some paint chips missing.)

A. (continuing) And it is longer than ours. As you can see from Exhibit 3, which is one of our zymoscopes, this one is 6 inches longer. And ours has our name and a serial number embossed under the cover. This one has no serial number, no name.

Q. Is there any doubt whatever that this zymoscope is not one manufactured by the Zeta company under license to Mr. Zyzmore, the inventor and patent holder?

A. None at all.

Advocate: Your Honor, I offer this exhibit in evidence. Your Honor?

The Court: I'm awake. I was just reading from my law journal.

Advocate: I offer this exhibit in evidence, Your Honor.

The Court: Show it to your adversary. Any objection?

A SECOND BITE AT THE APPLES

Remember that earlier the advocate tried to introduce a headlight, but the witness could not differentiate the headlight from any other headlight manufactured by the same manufacturer? The judge refused to admit the exhibit.

If your purpose in introducing the item is not something particular to that item, but your purpose is to have a physical exhibit that you can use as an example of the type and shape of the headlight in question, you might have the same introduced as follows:

Advocate: Your Honor, may I have a couple of additional questions in reference to the exhibit?

The Court: Of course.

Q. You've indicated that there are no identifying marks or anything on this exhibit that make it stand out in your mind as the specific headlight that you found at the curb that morning, is that correct?

A. It looks like it, but no, there are no marks or numbers that I remember, if that's what you mean.

Q. I ask you to look at the exhibit again. Does this exhibit—although it may not be the very one that you found at the curbside that morning—does this exhibit fairly and accurately resemble the one that you found?

A. I think it's the same one.

Q. Does it look exactly like the one you found the morning of the accident?

A. That's what I'm saying. It's exactly the same.

Advocate: Your Honor. With the modification that this may not be the exact one that was found, I offer this exhibit as a headlight that fairly and accurately resembles the one that was found by the witness on the morning of the accident.

The Court: Well, for whatever it's worth, as long as the jury understands that this is not being offered as the exact headlight that was found the morning of the accident, but one that looks very much like, is identical to it, without being the very one found, I think we can permit it. Any objections?

Adversary: Yes, Your Honor. It's not the headlight that the witness found. He can't identify it.

The Court: That's what I said. This is not the headlight. It is one that looks like it. Received.

Another example:

Q. Officer, I show you plaintiff's Exhibit 2 for identification and ask you if you recognize it?

A. Yes, this is a picture of the intersection of Smith and Barney streets.

Q. And how do you recognize it as such?

A. I walked that beat every day of my life for 10 years. I know what the street looks like.

Q. Is there any doubt in your mind that this is the intersection of Smith and Barney streets?

A. None at all.

Advocate: I offer plaintiff's Exhibit 2 for identification.

The Court: Any objection?

Adversary: May I have some questions on the voir dire, Your Honor?

The Court: Certainly.

Adversary: Did you take these pictures, officer?

A. Me? No.

Q. Do you know who did?

A. No.

Q. Do you know when these pictures were taken?

A. No.

Adversary: I object to this exhibit, Your Honor; improper foundation.

Advocate: May I, Your Honor?

The Court: Go ahead.

Q. Officer, looking at plaintiff's Exhibit 2 for identification, does this fairly and accurately depict the intersection of Smith and Barney streets as they were on the morning of the incident?

A. Yes, sir.

Q. Is there anything in this photograph that is not a fair and accurate representation or depiction of the intersection on that morning?

A. It looks exactly the same in the picture as it was.

Advocate: Your Honor, I renew my offer of the exhibit as a fair and accurate depiction of what the intersection looked like on the morning of the incident.

The Court: Any objection?

Advocate: No, Your Honor.

With the knowledge of a proper foundation in hand, or at least in mind, let's proceed toward the next step just before the taking of testimony.

14

TRIAL MOTIONS

WHAT IS A TRIAL MOTION?

Bear with me if I cover material that may seem obvious. Perhaps it is not obvious to some. Perhaps, too, what may seem obvious to you is because you have it wrong. In any event, motions are necessary, before and after trial, and very significantly, during trial. For that reason, just before we begin to take testimony, this subject needs be covered.

A trial motion is an application to a judge related to the pending trial seeking resolution of a disputed legal issue.

A trial motion can be oral or in writing. It might be made at any time during the trial.

ORAL MOTIONS

It is easier to understand motions by beginning with the oral motion.

During a trial, oral motions are ordinarily made. There are oral motions made other than at trial, as well, of course. But every oral motion is made when you appear before a judge.

During trial, each time that you object to a question asked by your adversary and the judge sustains or overrules your objection, you have made a motion and the Court has made a decision on that motion.

If your adversary asks one of your witnesses, on cross-examination, to tell the jury what she heard another witness say, you stand and object.

You say aloud only "OBJECTION." You don't necessarily have to say "on the ground of hearsay," unless the Court asks the basis of your objection.

But what you are actually saying is: *I move that the Court disallow the question asked on the ground that the question is legally improper, calling, as it does, for hearsay.* The Court then considers your applications and sustains your motion, disallowing the question, or overrules your motion, permitting the question to be answered.

Each time during a trial that you ask the Court to take judicial Notice of some item of information or evidence, you are making a motion. Indeed, each time, during the course of a trial, that you ask the Court for any recognition, direction, ruling, or permission, you are making an "oral" motion.

Of course, during the preliminary stages or conferences with the Court, each time that you ask the Court for some ruling, direction, permission, for some additional discovery material, or for items by way of additional "particulars," you are also making an oral motion.

Upon such motion, your adversary may object or consent to your application, and the judge may make a decision granting or denying your application. Or, the Court may ask that you make the application in writing.

THE MOTION PRESERVES ITSELF

Years back, there was a time when, if you received an adverse ruling during trial, you had to take an exception to the Court's ruling in order to preserve the issue for appeal.

This necessity has been eliminated. Now, the very motion itself, having been made and ruled upon, is sufficiently in the record, preserved for review on appeal merely because it was made, because it is there in the record.

Thus, you need not do or say anything after the Court rules in order to preserve your position concerning any matter on which the judge rules.

The only place in the trial where an exception is necessary, that is, the word *exception* must be specifically articulated, is, in some jurisdictions, during the Court's charge. Here, if asked by the Court whether you have any exceptions to the charge or any further requests to charge and you articulate either a request for further instruction or an exception to an instruction already given, if the Court rules against you, you must say exception.

ARGUMENT ON THE ORAL MOTION

I indicated earlier that it is easier to discuss motions by beginning with oral motions. This is because when you stand before the judge and make an application, you buttress that application with logic, reasons why the motion should be granted, supplementing the argument with legal citation, precedent, and the like.

Written motions bore

Strangely, although a written motion should be much the same, or at least could be much the same, written motions are often stilted, prolix, suffused with "legalese" language, going on and on with boiler plate that bores and disinterests a judge or his law clerks when they read it.

Remember, yours is not the only motion that the judge has to read. The judge may have 20, 50, 100 motions to decide. And each lawyer, if writing the same legal, boiler-plate motion, is adding to the boredom of the judge and doing a disservice to the client.

Therefore, rather than die from boredom reading each of these motions that looks and sounds so much like the ones before it, and although the prayer for relief may be completely different, the judge and the law clerks begin to skim the material in the written motions.

It's not that the judge is not doing his or her job. You would do the same if the material with which you were presented were exactly the same, repeating by rote, almost in the same stilted lawyer's language, the history of the case and the arcane reasons why such relief should be granted.

Conversely, on one's feet in front of the judge, an advocate would argue succinctly, to the point, and not talk in a stilted language or with clichéd phrases. But as soon as that same application is reduced to writing, it becomes stiff, prolix, and rambling.

Orally, you would try to get to the point directly, convincingly, with logical impact and citation. Try putting your thoughts together on paper in the same fashion.

Prepare skim-proof written motions

I've already indicated that there is a tendency in judge's chambers, and elsewhere—you may even do it yourself when receiving opposition papers in your office—to skim through the preliminary, the boiler plate, the background material to get to the heart of the matter.

Okay. You know it's going to happen to your written motion. Write them, therefore, with the skim in mind. Write short, succinct paragraphs, the first sentence of which carries the message of the rest of the paragraph. If the judge is interested in the thoughts, he or she will read the rest of the paragraph. If not, he or she will skim to the next short, succinct paragraph that carries its message in the first sentence.

Give yourself a break by giving the judge a break. Don't bore him or her to death. In your so doing, the judge is going to pay more attention to and understand your motion the more easily and will grant or deny your motion on its merits, not out of boredom.

THE MIRROR TEST

If you don't believe that you have a completely different method of presenting your motions orally and in writing, then stand facing an imaginary judge and try to spout out the long, dreary paragraphs, word for word, that you have filled those written motions with. You will find that you wouldn't do it. You'll start boring yourself to death reciting all the "legalese" that you've packed into those written motions.

If your own motions bore you to death, what do you think they do to the judge who isn't involved in your case, who gets hundreds of similar boiler-plate motions every month? If you wouldn't orally mount the argument that you have put into the written motion, then tear that dreary pap out of the written motion yourself before submitting it. Try to get the snap, the directness of oral motions into your written motions. You'll find them far more effective.

WRITTEN TRIAL MOTIONS

This subject is easy, right? A written trial motion is where you ask a Court for any recognition, direction, ruling, or permission during trial, in writing.

It isn't very often that the Court asks you to put your trial motion in writing. There should have been time enough for that pretrial. Occasionally, however, when the relief requested calls for something more complex than the common evidentiary ruling at trial, and also if the Court feels that there is enough time for you to make the motion without unnecessarily delaying any proceedings, he or she may ask you to submit it in writing with appropriate citations. This is because the subject you have broached is not usual, somewhat involved and tricky, and the Court needs more time and stare decisis in order to make a ruling.

The Court may not even halt the proceedings, but may require you or your adversary to prepare such motion in writing after hours, to be presented and considered while the trial continues. So not only do you have to continue with the trial, but afterward you have to get back to the office and get the motion made. And it has to be completed in time so that the presentation or striking of evidence that you have requested is still a viable issue. In other words, you have to get it completed before the moment is lost, before it is too late to use the evidence or too late to stop your adversary from using the same.

Often, when the Court refuses to entertain an oral motion, insisting on the motion being submitted in written form, it is because the Court wants the opportunity to know and to study the full range of your application, together with the supporting law on the subject. It may also be that such a motion, according to the rules or statutes in your jurisdiction, must be made in writing.

It may also be, however, that the judge knows that there are many lazy advocates who will abandon a motion rather than reduce the oral application to writing. Thus, by indicating that the motion should be in writing, the judge may effectively remove an evidentiary weight from his or her shoulders. As incredible as this seems, there are many advocates who refuse to write, who are more interested in prancing what they consider "their stuff" before the jury than they are in writing and briefing a point. Thus, when the judge requires the motion in writing, he or she may be counting on the fact that considerable numbers of advocates cannot try a case and draw up motion papers at the same time. The judge is counting on the lethargy of those advocates who are willing to let the motion die aborning rather than to go to the trouble of putting it in writing.

Don't be in that category of advocates who talk a good game, but who, when called upon to submit something in writing, fall by the wayside.

PRETRIAL MOTIONS

Pretrial motions, obviously, are motions the purpose of which is to prepare the road for the trial, to obtain amplification or explanation of the charges in the complaint, to obtain discovery of facts and information upon which the opposition relies to prove their case, to correct, to dismiss, to protect, to require compliance with notices or requests.

All these motions are intended to pave a smoother way during the trial. One of the motions mentioned and available pretrial is a motion to dismiss portions of the complaint or indictment as being unsupported by the facts or, assuming all of the facts as true, insufficient to form a complaint under the law of the particular jurisdiction in which the action has been brought.

Naturally, if you are able to dismiss the entire charging instrument, you have no further lawsuit to fight. Even if you are not successful in dismissing the entire charging instrument, if you are able to eliminate some of the causes of action, some of the counts of the indictment, the more you can concentrate on what remains, the less of a fight you have to mount. Therefore, move against a complaint or an indictment if it will nip the litigation in the bud.

Remember, the main purpose of litigation is to protect your client's interests, not to do battle for it's own sake.

DON'T MAKE MOTIONS THAT MERELY EDUCATE YOUR ADVERSARY

Oftentimes, a motion to dismiss the complaint or accusatory instrument by a defense advocate will result in nothing more than a dismissal and the filing of recast or alternative allegations that have been immeasurably improved as a result of the education you have provided your adversary by way of your motion, the law you have submitted to the Court, and the decision of the Court.

In other words, there are situations where a defense advocate may see a defect in a pleading that is lying dormant, waiting to be corrected. At that point, you have to think about this: If your adversary, the attorney for the complainant, thought there was such a gaping defect in his or her pleadings, she would have alleged it differently in the first place. Your adversary is apparently not aware of such defect, or she has very thin material to work with and has done the best she could have with the material on hand.

The decision the defense advocate has to make is whether to move to dismiss or not.

That depends.

Depends on what, you ask. It depends on whether or not the motion that you might make will be effective, and will cut down on the litigation, or will merely point out the defect and permit your adversary to recomplain, this time remedying the insufficiency thanks to your pointing the same out, and educating the adversary by the law that you have submitted to the Court in support of your motion.

> ***REMEMBER:*** *If the statute of limitations has not run and there be a dismissal not on the merits, your adversary may very well have the opportunity to replead, to initiate another and new cause of action against your client, this time armed with the education you have provided and the better, stronger complaint you have helped forge.*

In such a situation, you have to decide if the pretrial motion is going to be more effective on behalf of your client at that point or would be better made at some later stage of the proceedings.

For example, if you are moving against a complaint or indictment that you deem defective, but which may very well be remedied by repleading, you may be better off doing the research that makes the deficiency apparent, keeping it in a handy place in your file, and at the end of the plaintiff's (prosecutor's) case, move to dismiss on the ground that proofs submitted are insufficient to support a charge cognizable under the laws of your jurisdiction.

Because you are at the postevidentiary stage rather than at the pretrial stage, the failure may be fatal to the cause of action. If the judge happens to agree, the motion is the more effective because you have waited for the propitious moment to make it. The judge is hardly going to permit a repleading, and the matter is now dismissed on the merits.

This same tactic also applies against counterclaims as well as defenses interposed by defense counsel. The same logic applies to that situation as well. Therefore, there are times when despite the fact that you have a solid motion to dismiss available, you hold such motion in abeyance, moving only after the plaintiff/prosecution case is presented, or in the case of a counterclaim, after the defense has presented the same, and then for failure to prove a prima facie case. At that point, the die is cast and the Court will ordinarily not permit your adversary to reopen his or her case at that point.

Naturally, if by making the motion you will eliminate entirely the necessity for going to trial, you must make the motion pretrial. As I've indicated, whether or not you make such a motion pretrial depends.

POSTTRIAL MOTIONS

Of course, if you've been successful during trial there are few circumstances that would require you to make a posttrial motion.

If the trial didn't go as well as you might have wanted, however, then you might make some posttrial motions, to set aside the verdict, to vacate judgment, or to effect various other motions that might undo the negative results of the trial.

All these have to do with motion practice, and this is a book on trial practice. The admonition about dry, boring, unimaginative motions set forth here is applicable to these, however, as well as to all written trial motions.

15

The Record

Protect the Record with Your Life

Throughout the trial, it is essential to "make a record" of all that transpires so that, in the event that the trial or some portion thereof does not go as you expect it to, you will be able to perfect the issue on appeal.

Remember, the record does not make itself. True, the reporter, or the audio- or video-recording machines will take down what occurs in the courtroom. But, unless you or your adversary make a point of preserving an issue for the record by articulating the point, by saying something concerning the point to the judge, pointing the issue out to the Court, if it is not spread upon the record in all of its glorious details, the point shall equally NOT be there for appellate purposes.

Therefore, you must make a record.

I'm going to repeat that: Make a record.

And once again: IT IS ABSOLUTELY ESSENTIAL THAT YOU MAKE A RECORD.

Why?

Why have I repeated that message, with increasing intensity? Because I don't want you to forget it; because too many advocates think that the record will be there, with no effort on their own part. It won't.

THE RECORD IS OF PRIME IMPORTANCE

As you are going through the trial, you may find that the Court denies your effort to introduce some piece of evidence, to ask some line of questions, to bring forward a theory you believe to be perfectly proper, essential to your position, or all of the above.

But the Court runs the show, and you have been precluded from pursuing what you consider essential. The first thing you must do to remedy this situation is to *Make the record.*

The second thing you can do is to try some alternate way to get the matter before the trier(s) of fact. If you want my opinion as to which of the two alternatives is the more important (actually, do both), I'd say, making the record is the more important.

Without the one issue or question, your trial is limping, true. But the Court has made up her mind. You may change that mind with research, you may get the point across with the alternate approach. But then again, you may not. Without having preserved the issue on the record, in either the first or the second instance, all is lost, evaporated into evanescence, without recourse, without hope.

Therefore, the first thing to do is to preserve you point on the record; then, have a go at the alternative method. And if that fails, don't forget to make a sufficient record on the alternate position as well.

THE RECORD DOES NOT MAKE ITSELF

At this juncture, I think it important that you realize what the record really is.

Of course, it is the record of the proceedings that occur. I'm not talking only about the stenographic or mechanical recording of what occurs. I'm talking of the record as the memorialization of what you want to bring to the attention of the appellate Court. In other words, part of the record may be what isn't in the trial, what the Court refused to permit you to bring out, what the Court denied you.

Occasionally, the Court may not only thwart your effort to pursue an issue or a line of questions, but may even thwart your effort to preserve such issue on the record for appellate review. Aye, there's the rub. The Court is thwarting you from making what you consider is the proper record.

Now what do you do?

MAKE THE RECORD ANYWAY!

How?

Q. And thus, Mr. Witness, at the time that you say you were having this conversation with the defendant, you were somewhat inebriated, correct?

Adversary: Objection.

The Court: Sustained.

Advocate: Your Honor, I'd like to pursue this area. I believe it is important.

The Court: Go to your next question.

Advocate: May I approach the side bar with my adversary, Your Honor?

The Court: You may not! Ask your next question or I will have the witness step down from the witness chair.

Advocate: But, Your Honor, I believe . . .

The Court: Step down from the witness chair, Mr. Witness. Do you have another witness, counsellor?

Advocate: Your Honor, I'd like to make an offer of proof on this issue.

The Court: And I'd like you to call your next witness, if you have one.

Advocate: Is Your Honor precluding me from making a record on this issue?

The Court: I'm directing you to call your next witness unless you don't have any other witnesses, or unless you've decided to rest.

Advocate: I do have other witnesses, Your Honor. I'm merely asking if you are precluding me from making a record.

The Court: Call your next witness or rest.

Advocate: Very well, and very reluctantly, Your Honor. I call Mr. Moriarty.

You've made the record. Even when the Court doesn't permit you to make a record, so long as you register your objection to the Court's proceeding without the particular point that you wish to make, without permitting you to articulate at the side bar what issue you wish to preserve, you have made a record of the fact of what the Court has not permitted.

In other words, what you have preserved is the Court's adamant refusal to permit a fair trial, even to the point of refusing you to articulate the point for the record.

On appeal, you will be able to bring out the point that you wished to bring out on the record during the trial, the one that the Court refused to permit you to even mention at the side bar. It may even have been as important as you thought it was.

The appellate court may agree that you should have been able to bring the point out during trial. The appellate court, on the other hand, may also agree with the judge after reviewing the record. But at least you've preserved your opportunity to bring the point before the appellate Court because you preserved the record even when the judge didn't want to permit you to do the same.

In the face of some adversity from the Court, think what would have happened if you had stood there, wordless, without insisting, without developing some dialogue. The record would be barren. And, in the cool atmosphere of the appellate court, on the state of the record—or lack of it—your appellate adversary may very well argue that you abandoned your point, that it wasn't preserved for review. And he'd not be far wrong.

Why? Because you failed to make the record.

OTHER HOLES IN THE RECORD

When you fail always to keep in mind that the record is merely a mirror of what you say or do in the courtroom, another, if somewhat less dramatic, example of the muteness of the record is the following:

> **Q.** And how big was the hole in the sidewalk in which you saw the plaintiff's foot get caught?
>
> **A.** I'd say about this wide (indicating) and about this deep (indicating).
>
> **Q.** And had you ever seen that hole in that sidewalk before the day plaintiff's foot was caught in that hole?
>
> **A.** Absolutely. It was there for several weeks.

Okay, how large was the hole in the sidewalk?

What? You say you don't know. Why don't you know? You have as much before you as the appellate court is going to have in front of it on the state of the record that was made. And it was you who left the record in that sorry state. How did you expect the appellate court to figure out the size of the hole from this barren, mute record?

> **Q.** How long was the knife you say was in the hand of the defendant?
>
> **A.** It was about this long (indicating).
>
> **Q.** Is there any question that the defendant is the person who was holding that knife?
>
> **A.** None at all.

Okay, how large was the knife?

Again, you can't say, nor could the appellate court on appeal, because the record is not complete, because you permitted the record to make itself, which is something everyone knows doesn't happen.

Q. Mr. Witness, I show you this and ask you if you recognize what this is.

Adversary: Your Honor, I object.

The Court: Sustained.

Advocate: Your Honor, may I have a side bar in connection with this line of questioning?

The Court: You may proceed. Do you have any other questions?

Advocate: Very well, Your Honor, I have no further questions.

Okay, what was *this*, the object to which there was an objection, which the Court sustained?

I don't know either. Because you failed to preserve it for review. Now the record is mute, and it is YOUR FAULT. Oh, yes it is. You should have made it specifically clear for the record just what "this" was.

For, if the matter must be appealed, the appellate judges won't have any more idea what "this" was than you do right at this moment. You will hardly be in a position to ask for review of the Court's refusal to permit "this" into evidence. No one knows what "this" was. And it is impermissible to go dehors the record to explain "this." The appellate record speaks for itself or, as in this case, fails to speak for itself.

How, you ask, can the above holes in the record have been avoided?

Very simple. Let's go back.

COMPLETING THE RECORD

Q. And how big was the hole in the sidewalk that you caught your foot in?

A. About this big.

Advocate: The witness is indicating with her index fingers, held parallel to each other, approximately 9 inches, if it please the Court.

Adversary: It looks more like 6 inches, Your Honor.

The Court: Let's agree on 8 inches.

Advocate: Very well, Your Honor.

Now when I ask you how big was the hole in the sidewalk, can you answer me? Of course.

Why? Because someone knew that the record didn't speak for itself; someone knew that unless you make sure that the record is preserved, it won't be.

> ***CAUTION:*** *Wishing doesn't make it so. You can't think that you want to preserve the record. You must actually say the words. Say the words, and the record will be preserved. Merely think the words, and there is no record.*

Let's go back again.

Q. How long was the knife you saw in the defendant's hand?

A. About this long.

Advocate: May the record reflect that the witness is holding her two palms, parallel with each other, approximately 10 inches apart.

The Court: That seems about right. You agree, Ms. Adversary?

Adversary: That seems correct, Your Honor.

And now you and the record know how long the knife was.

Advocate: May I have this marked plaintiff's Exhibit 4 for identification?

The Court: Have it marked.
(At this point, the object is marked by the reporter plaintiff's Exhibit 4 for identification.)

Q. Mr. Witness, I show you plaintiff's Exhibit 4 for identification and ask you if you recognize what it is.

Adversary: Your Honor, I object.

The Court: Sustained.

Advocate: May I have a side bar in connection with this Exhibit, Your Honor.

The Court: You may proceed. Do you have any further questions?

Advocate: Is Your Honor indicating that I can't make a record?

The Court: I'm indicating that you should proceed with your questioning if you have any further questions.

Advocate: Based on Your Honor's ruling, I cannot proceed. I have no further questions.

Now you have a record. And you have an exhibit that is clearly identifiable, so that on appeal that object, that Exhibit—as marked for identification by the reporter—can be included in your appeal, can be brought to the attention of the appellate Court, and you do not have to ask any favors of your adversary, do not have to ask anyone to guess what the object was. The object was made part of the record, even though the Court did not permit the same to be used at trial. Indeed, the very essence of your complaint is that the Court was wrong in refusing to permit you to use the object, to pursue a line of questioning.

NOTE: *In the last exchange, you have doubly preserved the record—as much as could have been done—by highlighting the Court's refusal to permit you to inquire about the object and, thereby, curtailing your line of questions. Moreover, you offered to approach at the side bar to make an offer of proof, which the Court refused. You went even further; you asked the Court to make a record—knowing, of course, that the Court was not going to answer that question in the affirmative—and then you hammered the record shut with the fact that you could not proceed based on the Court's rulings.*

SECOND NOTE: *You may not run into a judge as irascible as the Court illustrated here. Your judge may be erudite, calm, evenhanded. In that case, you won't have a problem. You don't even have to gird your loins to deal with a reasonable Court.*

Prepare for the worst, however, and you'll be prepared for everything. And hope for the best.

And all this, because you said a few words ON THE RECORD.

16

DIRECT EVIDENCE

DEFINITION

Direct evidence, very simply, is evidence brought forward by parties, whether plaintiff or defendant, on their own cases, on their own behalf, through their own witnesses, to support their own theory of the case.

In short, it is the evidence brought out by a party in an attempt to prove his or her own side of the issues. Direct testimonial evidence is that which shall then be subject to cross-examination by the adversary representing the other side.

TESTIMONY IS NOT SOCIAL CONVERSATION; PREPARE YOUR WITNESSES

When you read decisions of appellate courts, you often come across phrases that indicate, in sum or substance, that it is foolish for a lawyer to put on the stand a witness with whose testimony the advocate is unfamiliar.

It is, therefore, not only perfectly proper for an attorney who anticipates calling a witness on his or her "direct case" to discuss that testimony which the witness shall give at trial, it is expected that the advocate shall prepare the witness for the ordeal.

And it is an ordeal.

Being a trial witness may not be the experience to end all experiences, but it is different, particularly for a layperson who has not often, or ever, been in court before.

This "differentness" of experience is particularly borne out when your adversary stands and begins to cross-examine your witness concerning the direct testimony. After all, it isn't at every cocktail party that a person has his or her comments subjected to the purposeful scrutiny and attack of a professional interrogator, conducted under very stringent rules of permissible responses, under the supervision and with the approval of an all-powerful arbiter (the judge), before the eyes of an impassive audience (the jury).

Talk about being different!

And if your witness is intimidated, shy, annoyed, or anything but cool, calm, and confident, the jury may misinterpret that for evasiveness, unsureness, confusion, or whatever, which will serve only to undermine your case.

Therefore, when you have a witness who is going to testify on your case, be absolutely sure that you sit down with that witness, go over his or her testimony, explain the procedures that the witness will encounter in court, and in various ways ease that person into being a "witness."

SHAKY WITNESS: SHAKY CASE

Remember that I mentioned previously that you have to set the tone in a case right from the moment that you begin to address the prospective jurors at the voir dire. Well, that tone must be continued throughout the case, particularly throughout the direct evidence. If you present witnesses who *appear* to be unsure, vacillating, having difficulty with their recollection, the jurors may understandably get the impression that your case is unsure, vacillating, and difficult.

This impression may be totally incorrect, but the jurors don't know that, the jurors don't know your witness, don't know his or her particular personality, idiosyncrasy, intellect, or knowledge. The juror gets to know only what they know about your case through the testimony and the demeanor of the witnesses on the stand during the trial.

Therefore, you must take steps to ensure that your witnesses are sharp, precise, truthful, and armed with full knowledge of what they speak—or as relatively close thereto as you can manage.

How do you accomplish this? Prepare the witnesses.

HOW TO PREPARE THE WITNESS

First of all, you must prepare the witness well in advance of the anticipated trial. In fact, it may be necessary to have more than one session during which you prepare the witness, which is the reason you have to begin well in advance.

The first session with your witness may be no more than preliminary initiation and familiarization with the basic court procedure. During that first session, you should give the witness an explanation of the basic events that the witness can expect during the trial. In addition, you should definitely have a discussion and a preliminary go-through of the anticipated testimony.

Then permit the prospective witness to go home, to think about the discussion, the facts of the case that you have just discussed, and the anticipated procedures that you have outlined.

At the second or subsequent sessions, you will ordinarily find that the information and lesson from the first session has seeped into the witness's mind. What actually occurs is that the witness thinks about the case, the testimony, and your admonitions in the context of your previous discussion, and this process has recurred over and over inside his or her head. The witness should now be far more in tune with you and with the process and the material that you have to go over.

The Three Areas of Preparation

There are three basic areas of preparation for a witness whom an advocate intends to present for direct examination:

(a) the procedures ahead;

(b) the direct evidence; and,

(c) the cross-examination.

Each of these areas must be totally and thoroughly explained to the witness in order that the witness is familiar with what is about to happen, so that the witness will appear natural, relaxed, and, therefore, truthful to the jurors.

I didn't say that your witness was untruthful. Nor did I say that you should create evidence or testimony to accommodate your side of the case. I just said that the witness must *appear* to be truthful.

It is not enough that the witness is truthful. The witness will be in the presence of the individual jurors for the first time in their lives, and his or her only contact with the jurors is those few moments, the brief period that the witness is on the stand. Therefore, in those few moments the witness has the only opportunity to convey to the jurors who and what the witness is all about. Thus, your witness must not only be truthful, but must appear to be truthful, sincere, and credible.

THE PROCEDURES AHEAD

You must describe and explain to your witness the basic procedures that lie ahead and even describe the physical layout of a courtroom. What does that mean, you say. Well, the average person has spent very little, if any, time in a courtroom. He doesn't know what it is like—the layout, the code of conduct—he knows nothing. He doesn't even know where the judge's bench is, in relation to the witness chair, or the jury box. I know, I know, he's seen television. But the average layperson doesn't know if what he has seen on television is real or not. In truth, most of the courtroom scenes and dramatized testimony that a person sees on television are major distortions of reality made suitable for the dramatic ending anticipated by the writer.

Thus, start with the basics. Tell your prospective witness about the physical layout of the courtroom, where the judge's bench is, where the witness sits, who the reporter is and where he or she sits, where the jurors sit, and where the advocates sit. And, most important, where you will sit and that you will be there at every moment to protect and champion his every move. Although this may seem like an exercise in simplicity, your explanation and assurance gives the witness knowledge and confidence that he is not walking into a total unknown when he steps through the door into the courtroom.

Remember, even though you may do this every day of your life, the witness does not. The witness has to be told everything that is going to happen, including that he has to walk up to the witness chair, face the clerk or judge, and be sworn. Then he sits in the witness chair and waits.

To the witness who has never been in a courtroom, this foreknowledge relieves a lot of questions in his or her mind, like, what do I do, stand around like an oaf? Will I look foolish? After you bring him through the whole physical procedure, he feels more comfortable. He knows what to expect and what to do when what is expected occurs.

Explain that he will be called to the stand, that he will sit next to the judge, that there will be a stenographer or mechanical recording device taking down his testimony. that the jury will be sitting off to his side, that he will be sworn in, and that the procedure is rather formal but simple enough.

Try to make the witness familiar with the anticipated flow of testimony: that you will ask questions first, that your adversary may object to some procedures, that the judge may make rulings. And you must drill into the witness's head that while the judge is considering her or his ruling, he must wait for the ruling before giving an answer, and that the judge may ask questions.

Very important: make clear to the witness that during his testimony he must speak to the jury, not to you, not to your adversary, not to the judge, but to the jury. Even if the Court asks a question from behind or to the side of the witness, the juror may turn around to look at the judge for a moment, but should then look back to speak his testimony *toward the jurors*.

THE DIRECT TESTIMONY

Next, you must explain to the witness that because the witness is one that you are presenting on your case, you are not permitted to ask leading or suggestive questions. Indeed, you should advise the witness that you prefer that he be prepared to be asked the following two questions and be ready to give his entire testimony in response.

> **Q.** Do you recall the night of the fifteenth of April 1990?
>
> **A.** I do.
>
> **Q.** Will you tell the Court and jury what you recall about that night. Please speak slowly and loudly enough for the last juror sitting in the jury box to hear everything you are saying.
>
> **A.** Very well. . . .

With only those questions asked, the witness should be prepared to give the entirety of his testimony in narrative form.

Surely you can, and probably will, stop the witness occasionally to emphasize a point of his testimony, but, in the main, he should be prepared to give a flowing narrative of his entire testimony.

> **Q.** Let me stop you there for a moment. You say you walked along Nineteenth Street toward Third Avenue. About what time was it when you were approaching Third Avenue?
>
> **A.** I'd say it was about 7:30.
>
> **Q.** In the evening?
>
> **A.** Yes.
>
> **Q.** Very well. Please proceed.
>
> **A.** As I reached . . .

WHAT IS LEADING?

Basically, because the witness is your witness, and you have had an opportunity to prepare, to know in advance the witness's testimony, because the witness is anticipated to be friendly to your position in the trial—otherwise you wouldn't present the witness in the first place—you are not permitted to suggest in your question the answer to the witness or supply in the wording of your question any information with which to formulate the answer.

In order not to lead, therefore, you ordinarily just ask questions that call for a narrative and, thereafter, some plain-vanilla questions that call for some more focused explanation of a particular point you wish to emphasize. Then you should merely tell the witness "to continue."

Some of the questions that are acceptable and not considered leading are the following:

Q. What, if anything, then occurred?

Q. Did anything else occur?

Q. Was anything said thereafter?

Q. What, if anything, did you do then?

Q. Did you go anywhere after that?

In none of these questions do you supply any information whatever to the witness. Indeed, you do not even suggest the direction of a response.

These following questions, on the other hand, are leading because you are supplying information or a direction to the witness.

Q. Then what happened?

Q. Where did you go after that?

Both of these questions, though seemingly simple, imply that something did happen: what was it, the witness did go somewhere, where was it?.

Q. What did you say to him, what did he say to you?

Q. What did he say, after you said that to him?

Again, you are assuming something. It would be better to ask these questions in a more neutral way.

Q. Did anything happen after that?

A. Yes.

Q. Please tell the Court and jury what next occurred.

A. We had a conversation.

Q. What, if anything, did you say to him, what did he say to you?

Of course, it may seem that there is hardly any difference in these questions, but in the former questions, some information or direction is being given to the witness; in the latter, the question is not leading, does not assume or contain affirmative information in its formulation.

As long as you are not supposed to lead, don't! Be precise and correct, and hold your adversary to the same standard when he or she is working on the case.

Samples

Q. Do your recall the 15th of April 1990.

A. Yes, I do.

Q. Please tell the Court and jury what occurred on that day?

A. I was driving my car south on Seventh Avenue. Traffic was kind of heavy.

Q. Let me stop you for a moment. What was the weather condition at the time?

A. The weather was clear, dry. A fine evening.

Q. And the natural light, what was the natural light at the time?

A. It was bright, very bright evening, still very light.

Q. Please continue.

A. As I got to the intersection of Canal Street, the light was green in my favor, so I proceeded through the intersection. Just then, a car came from my left, against the red light holding westbound traffic. I put on my brakes as fast as I could, as hard as I could, I tried to steer away from the car. But it just drove right in front of me, and there was a collision.

Q. Were your windows opened or closed at the time?

A. Open. It was a nice spring evening, and the windows were open.

Q. By the way, do you have any physical disabilities?

A. None.

Q. Specifically, do you have any vision or hearing impairments?

A. None at all.

Q. Did there come a time that you discovered the identity of the driver of the other car?

A. Yes.

Q. And who was that?

A. It was Sergeant McDonald of the New York Police Department.

Q. Was the car that Sergeant McDonald was driving a regular police car or was it an unmarked police car?

A. It was a black Chevrolet. No markings whatever.

Q. Did you ever hear a siren, see flashing lights, coming from that unmarked police car?

A. Never.

Q. Did you try and avoid the collision?

A. I did everything I could. As I said, I tried to steer away from the collision, I tried to brake. They just drove right in front of me. There was nothing I could do.

Advocate: Your witness, Sir.

WHY IT IS ESSENTIAL, WHEN PREPARING WITNESSES FOR DIRECT, THAT YOU ALSO PREPARE THEM FOR CROSS

When you are preparing the witness for direct examination, one of the most important areas for which you must, I repeat, *must* prepare your prospective witness is cross-examination. While that statement may seem somewhat incongruous, considering the fact that you are preparing your witness for direct examination, it is not.

Perhaps it would be better for you to think of the preparation of your witness not as a preparation for direct testimony, but as a preparation of your witness to testify.

There are, of course, two aspects of testifying: direct testimony and cross-examined testimony. These are two sides of the same coin; there is no cross-examination without direct testimony, and there is no efficacy, no significance to direct testimony unless it has been exposed and chastened, or at least made available to cross-examination.

Thus, in order for you to prepare your witness to be presented to testify, you must prepare him to be chastened to be exposed to the cleansing fire of the cross-examination that is as sure to follow your direct as the night follows the day.

It would be totally foolish if you were to prepare your witness to give the narrative recitation of his version of the events, without a thought to the cross-examination that is to follow. Ruefully, you might find that this calm, practiced witness who has given the jury a concise, precise narrative on direct is confronted by a low-down, mean, ornery cross-examiner who doesn't have your kid-glove approach, and your witness—*and your case*—are turned into a sorry lump of confusion.

If that happens, you didn't do your job!

After all, the witness didn't know what to expect, what was coming.

But you did!

You were aware of what was to happen during the proceedings. Cross-examination was inevitable, was part of your witness's testimony. The direct and the cross *together* make up your witness's testimony. Therefore, if you only prepared your witness for direct, you didn't prepare your witness for testimony, and you didn't do your job properly.

PREPARATION FOR THE CROSS

The first thing to tell your witness about cross-examination is that it is not direct examination.

Not much of a revelation, you say. Well, in fact, it is. Because your witness doesn't know what real testimony is, except what he has seen in the movies or on television. And the movies and television aren't real. Movies and television are make-believe versions of procedures, written by laypeople to work for the dramatic effect of the production.

For direct examination, you've prepared your witness to give an open, fulsome narrative of everything that happened on the day and time in question.

On cross-examination, you MUST tell your witness that he must do two very different things from what you told him to do on direct.

To begin with, tell your witness that on cross-examination, he must:

(a) answer only the question asked;

(b) respond in as few words as possible.

These two directives are intended to curtail and frustrate your adversary by requiring your adversary to use his or her own energy rather than to syphon the energy of your witness.

In the art of jujitsu, the one attacked uses the movement, motion, momentum, and energy of the attacker by continuing the flow of action in the direction initiated by the attacker.

In a cross-examination, a witness assists the cross-examiner whenever that witness gratuitously gives, volunteers, the energy of extra words and gratuitous explanations that are not truly responsive to the questions.

Thus, the two directives I've suggested you give the witness whom you are preparing for the cross-examination side of his testimony are intended to curtail the energy flow *to* your adversary, therefore requiring the adversary to use his or her own energy.

THE QUESTION THAT IS ALWAYS ASKED

Cross-examiners invariably ask witnesses at some point of the cross-examination whether or not they discussed their testimony with their lawyer, with the lawyer who presented the witness to the jury.

And, amazingly, witnesses are very often stumped by this question. The witness doesn't know what to answer. Should they answer yes? Wouldn't that mean that they were coached, that their testimony is not spontaneous? Should they lie and say no?

You can actually see the unprepared witness thinking and squirming for an answer on the stand. And, if that happens, again, you didn't do your job properly.

The answer to the question, did you discuss your testimony with your lawyer, is a resounding "YES, of course I did."

Remember what was said at the beginning of this chapter. Courts look upon an advocate who presents a witness without knowing what that witness is going to say as a very foolish advocate. Of course you are expected to talk to your witnesses about their testimony. And they are expected to talk to you.

Q. Let me ask you this, did you discuss your testimony with your lawyer?

A. Of course.

NOTE: As you will see in another few paragraphs, your witness is not to supply gratuitous remarks to your adversary. The short, succinct answer is best.

Q. And did your lawyer tell you what to say when you testified?

A. Certainly not.

Q. What did you and your lawyer discuss when you discussed your testimony?

A. She asked me what happened on the day in question. I told her.

Q. What else did she tell you?

A. She told me just to tell the truth. That all I had to do is tell the jury the truth and they'd give me a verdict because our cause was just.

Adversary: I object to that answer, Your Honor.

The Court: Oh no. You asked the question, that's the answer you got. Next question.

FURTHER PREPARATION FOR CROSS-EXAMINATION

> **Q.** Was the weather sunny on the day in question?
>
> **A.** No, it was kind of cloudy.

That is an improper answer to the cross-examiner's question. Use this example with the witness you are preparing, Tell him that the cross-examiner's question was, "Was the weather sunny?" on a particular occasion. The answer is either yes or no. PERIOD.

The response that it was kind of cloudy is gratuitous, nonresponsive, and is a cancer that you must eradicate from your witness's response mechanism because it gives energy (read information or direction, to wit, cloudy) to the adversary. While cloudy may not be important, if the witness were being asked about lighting conditions, you can more readily see that gratuitous remarks are directly counterproductive to your cause.

> **Q.** Was it dark on the occasion that you first saw the defendant?
>
> **A.** It was kind of dark.
>
> **Q.** So it was not completely dark, was it?
>
> **A.** I said it was kind of dark.
>
> **Q.** But not completely dark, was it?
>
> **A.** No, not completely.
>
> **Q.** The fact is, you could see fairly well, right?
>
> **A.** Not really.
>
> **Q.** Well, it wasn't really very dark, was it?
>
> **A.** Yes, it was.
>
> **Q.** Didn't you just a moment ago tell the jury that when you were asked if it was dark, that it was kind of dark? Weren't those your exact words?

Don't you see what's happening to your witness that you didn't properly prepare for cross-examination? He is getting beaten up. The area might not be the essence of the case—perhaps it is—but the continual hitting will eventually take its toll. The witness is going to get tired, give up. Think about a prize fighter in the ring with an opponent who continually flicks out jabs that hit your fighter in the nose. Flick; flick; flick. Not one of the blows is enough to take your fighter down. But after a while, that nose is going to bleed. And meanwhile, while your fighter is being flicked to death, he isn't touching his opponent. He is constantly trying to stay away from the jabs, the flicks.

Now, wouldn't it have been easier and quite truthful and direct for your witness to have answered the above questions as follows:

> **Q.** Was it dark on the occasion that you first saw the defendant?
>
> **A.** No.

NOTE: That answer is as exact as the first—it was kind of dark. If it was kind of dark, it was not totally dark. But the difference is that the cross-examiner now has to guess what that answer means. Guess or probe. And that guessing or probing absorbs your adversary's energy, not your witness's. Better that your adversary is getting flicked to death, has to work extra, rather than your witness.

> **Q.** Was the car that you saw coming down the street that day, black?
>
> **A.** No.
>
> **Q.** Was it blue?
>
> **A.** No.

Notice, the cross-examiner has to work. The car was really white. Your witness is frustrating the cross-examiner, making her work, tiring her. That is exactly what your witness is supposed to do. It isn't hard to explain to your witness the correct method of answering the cross-examiner. But it is essential that you do explain the difference between answering questions on direct, and answering questions on cross. Explain it to your prospective witness in general terms and then delve into it in depth in connection with the information concerning your case.

Your adversary continues:

> **Q.** Was the car red?
>
> **A.** No.
>
> **Q.** (Sarcastically) Surely, this car must have had a color?
>
> **Advocate:** Objection, Your Honor. Argumentative.
>
> **The Court:** Sustained.
>
> **Q.** Did the car have a color?
>
> **A.** Yes.

You see, even with the last answer, your witness is flicking his protective jab in the nose of the cross-examiner, holding the cross-examiner at bay, frustrating the cross-examiner. Your witness could easily have responded to any one of the questions asked by volunteering the color. But that answer would *not be responsive* to the question asked, and, worst of all, it would have been assisting, hence, supplying energy to your adversary.

Q. (Frustrated) What color was the car?

A. White.

Q. Couldn't you have told us that before?

A. I've been trying just to answer the questions you've been asking, just as the judge told me to.

In order for you to prepare your witness properly for cross-examination, however, you must think properly yourself. Think in cross-examination responses when you are explaining to your witness just how he is to respond to cross-examination questions.

***NOTE:** As was indicated earlier, trial testimony is not social conversation. It has its own rules, its own rhythm. This is what you must impart to your witness. Direct examination has one rhythm; cross-examination has its own, different rhythm. It is your job to help your witness understand this, to know this.*

EXPLAIN RE-DIRECT EXAMINATION AS WELL

Sometimes, the difficulty a witness has in handling cross-examination is the false impression he gets that perhaps he is not testifying to all the information that should be in the case, that things are going badly, that there's a necessity for him to supply additional information to the jury.

Make sure your witness knows that if you wish to get more information into the record, you can bring it out on re-direct. By explaining the protocol of testimony, the witness will not think that he has to make up for what he thinks is a deficiency in the testimony. Do not let your witness run the show, or even his own testimony. If there is something that must be brought out, you bring it out. Do not let your witness volunteer it, unless you want that to happen, unless it is part of your plan.

More Samples

Q. Was the light red as you approached the intersection?

A. No.

Q. Did there come a time as you approached the intersection that the light changed?

A. No.

Q. Is it your testimony that the light was green during the entire time, up to the time of the impact?

A. No.

Q. Was there a time that the light changed?

A. Yes.

Q. When was that?

A. After I was already in the intersection, the light changed.

NOTE: *If this were tennis instead of trial, the last question would indicate that the witness has broken the cross-examiner's serve on this subject, causing your adversary to resort to asking the witness for any answer that the witness wants to give. This, of course, indicates that your adversary has lost control of his or her cross-examination. See the chapter on cross-examination, infra.*

There is another effect of your witness answering questions in the manner described here. It slows the pace, doesn't permit your adversary to get a driving rhythm going, and doesn't permit your adversary to use your witness as a foil to bring out your adversary's case.

This slowness of pace, as I've already said, frustrates the cross-examiner and basically interferes with his or her game plan.

Perfect! That's exactly the effect you wanted your witness to achieve on cross-examination.

REPRISE

Prepare your witnesses fully for direct by being sure they are familiar with direct and cross-examination, as well as re-direct and re-cross-examination. Indeed, go through some cross-examination, hit them with devil's advocate cross-examination questions. See if they're ready. Get them ready.

If they're ready, you're ready.

If they're not ready, you're nowhere.

17

CROSS-EXAMINATION

Cross-examination is the single most effective and significant weapon of a trial advocate. It is the cleansing fire of the judicial system.

Through cross-examination, the trial advocate whittles down your adversary's direct evidence, hones down the pieces of the case against your client, takes testimony and exhibits intended by the adversary to damage your client and neutralizes or dilutes them substantially.

NO HARM: NO CROSS-EXAMINATION

When your adversary puts a witness on the stand whose testimony does no harm whatever to your client, there is normally no need to cross-examine that witness as there is nothing you have to overcome, nothing that needs whittling down.

Remember, your aim as trial advocate is to protect your client's interests, not sharpen the cutting edge of your cross-examiner's blade. Thus, the first tenet of the cross-examiner's creed is that a witness whose evidence is either favorable, neutral, or that fits comfortably into your own overview of the ultimate mosaic of your case should not ordinarily be questioned.

CURTAIL THE EVIDENCE AGAINST YOU

The next best thing to having no adverse evidence admitted is to permit as little harmful evidence as possible to be introduced against your client.

The cross-examiner can be instrumental in accomplishing just this by initially curtailing the introductory flow of an adversary's evidence.

Where you have the opportunity to curtail adverse evidence by objecting to its admissibility, you would indeed be very foolish to be magnanimous, to be silent, to tacitly permit your adversary to build a fortress you must ultimately storm.

THE CARDINAL TARGET AREAS

As stated previously, cross-examination is the trial advocate's tool with which to subject the testimony of an adverse witness to searing heat, to hone that testimony down to unadorned, unflowered fact. To do this, the cross-examiner attacks testimony in three cardinal target areas:

1. the general capacity of the witness;
2. the witness's specific knowledge of the particular event; and
3. the witness's personal character and integrity.

GENERAL CAPACITY OF THE WITNESS

The general capacity of the witness refers to the witness's capacity to know, to understand, to observe, to remember; that is, the witness's general capacity to be a recording and recounting agent. This capacity is revealed during even the most fundamental questioning, through the witness's capacity to hear and understand your questions, to respond with basic common intelligence thereto, with his or her capacity to describe events, to gauge distances, to be consistent.

A jury can observe the witness's demeanor on the stand, his or her basic reliability, at the same time as you are inquiring into other matters. In other words, you do not have to devise an I.Q. test as preliminary cross-examination to permit the jury a view of the witness's general intelligence.

While you are examining a witness, either on preliminary matters or on essential facts, you should, at the same time, be drawing the witness out in the area of his or her general intelligence. If the jury sees and hears a witness whose story about an event is perfectly and consistently recited time after time, yet, in every other area except the story of the actual event in issue, the witness is floundering, confused, incapable of speaking with accuracy or intelligence, that jury will get the idea that the witness has merely been rehearsed, but is generally a person they—the jury—would never rely upon even for common traffic directions. Therefore, try to draw the witness out; make him or her think and speak for the jury; pose questions that require actual thought in order to respond to your questions, instead of triggered responses to anticipated inquiries.

SPECIFIC KNOWLEDGE OF THE EVENT

In addition to drawing out the general intelligence of the witness, the specifics of the event or the occurrence about which the witness is testifying must be probed.

Despite the fact that the witness may have superior intelligence and retentive capacity, if the witness was not in a position to see or hear what he or she has described, if the witness could not possibly have been able to perceive the events described, then all the intelligence and wisdom in the world should not permit the witness to withdraw from the witness stand unscathed.

Your cross-examination may be long or short, depending on the particular case and witness. Where there is a gross and glaring error or inconsistency, which would, by itself, render the witness's testimony ludicrous and patently false, then to bring this error or inconsistency to the jury's attention would be all that the cross-examiner need do to discredit the witness totally.

ORDINARILY, THERE IS NO BIG KILL

I quickly suggest here that, ordinarily, cross-examination is not so dramatic or absolute as to result in what I call the "big kill." Where the witness's story is inconsistent and inaccurate in more subtle ways, cross-examination will obviously have to be longer and more subtle, setting factual traps into which the witness, it is hoped, will fall. The ultimate result should be a display of inaccuracy, inconsistency, and unreliability that prevents the jury from totally accepting the witness's version of what occurred. A chink in every witness's armor reduces your adversary's army to a disarmed mob.

PERSONAL CHARACTER AND INTEGRITY OF WITNESS

Even though a witness is intelligent and was potentially in the perfect position to have seen or heard what has been described, he or she may be discredited as a person of questionable character or an interested witness, one who has an ulterior motive to effect a result favorable to the party on whose behalf he or she has testified. This does not mean that a mere attack upon a witness because he or she may be living in unsolemnized union, or because the witness once was convicted of a crime or once had a disagreement with the party against whom the witness testifies shall, *ipso facto*, totally discount the witness's testimony in the eyes of the jury. Indeed, such fact might accomplish precisely that. On the other hand, even a prostitute, a criminal, a drunk, a person who delves in any sort of behavior that might be considered antisocial, could have a truthful or lucid moment, which, if believed by a jury, could be your unstringing.

Thus, your cross-examination must be channeled toward meaningful, telling targets that are relevant, material, and significant to the issue on trial, and are not merely an abstract exercise in cross-examination.

CROSS EXAMINER, CONTROL IS THE KEY

Control! Control! Control! That is the beginning, the middle, and the end of cross-examination.

After all the materials that you will employ in your cross-examination have been analyzed, after the cross-examination script has been prepared in the calm, cool atmosphere of your office or library, you rise to your feet in court and face the adverse witness. Your task is simple. You must control everything like a Renaissance prince, which, for the moment, you are. Control the witness, control the question, control the flow, control the subject matter.

But, most of all, and most important, you must control yourself.

THE QUESTION IS THE KEY TO CONTROL

Newton's theory that for every action there is an equal and opposite reaction is applicable to cross-examination.

Your question, and your question alone, directly controls the answers and responses of the witness. In order, therefore, to control that witness, to contain the hurt he or she may do your case and your client, to compel him or her to answer questions in a manner you desire, you must ask very measured and calculated questions.

I repeat, for indeed this is the essence of cross-examination. In order to control the witness, to contain the hurt he may do your case and your client, you must ask very measured and calculated questions.

This does not mean that every time you ask a question in a certain, carefully couched way, the witness will respond with the desired answer. But, without doubt, in the first instance, your questions give direction and substance to the examination. Ask the witness about rain, and the witness will speak about rain; ask about automobiles, he or she will speak about automobiles; ask about lighting conditions, and the witness speaks about lighting conditions. Thus, it is your choice to ask questions about the subject matter you wish to ask and have the witness restricted to that subject.

NOT ONLY WHAT YOU ASK, BUT THE WAY YOU ASK

The method for your asking questions about the particular subject results in particular answers on the subject.

Not only must you control the subject matter you wish to probe, however, you must also limit the boundaries of the corral in which you permit the adverse witness to roam with his answer.

For instance, if you had a horse in a 3-acre field, the horse might stay within the boundaries you selected for him and yet elude being caught for a substantial period of time. If you place the same horse in a 12' x 12' stall, you have permitted him very little room in which to elude you at the moment you wish to put a halter and lead line on him. In both locations, the horse is free to move about comfortably and safely, but in the latter situation, you have far more substantially controlled the horse; there is no way you're going to permit him to elude you in the smaller area you've permitted him.

The same applies to the witness you cross-examine. Not only must you limit the subject matter, but additionally, you must inquire concerning that subject matter in such a limited fashion and select your questions with such restricted wording that the witness can move comfortably but is quite restricted in the answers he or she may give.

For example: If you ask the witness to tell the jury about the weather on January 5, 1990, the witness is free to tell that jury anything about any aspect of the weather: He or she could testify about the bitter cold, the wet, or the wind, and describe it in any fashion he or she pleases. It was you who opened the door to any sort of answer concerning the weather on January 5, 1990, by couching the question as you did. You might better have asked questions concerning that day's weather as follows:

Q. On the evening of January 5, 1990, it was raining, was it not?

A. Yes.

Q. In addition, it was cold?

A. Yes, it was.

Q. The streets were not covered with snow though, were they?

A. No.

Q. Nor were they covered with ice?

A. No.

Q. Now the rain, by the time you were driving east across Houston Street, had pretty much stopped, hadn't it?

A. Yes.

Q. In fact, it was only a drizzle at the time you were going east on Houston Street, isn't that right?

A. I guess so.

Q. Please don't guess, Mr. Witness, just tell the court and jury whether it's a fact that it was just drizzling when you were driving east on Houston Street on the evening of January 5, 1990.

A. It was drizzling.

The preceding example contains a number of questions, all of which were purposely chosen to point out the kind of limited questions you might ask about the weather of January fifth. The example also points out the fact that, often, to better restrict the witness's answers, it may take many small questions to get to the point you wish to arrive at. By so doing, however, at least you arrive at your destination by means of transportation you choose, not that which the witness chooses.

A cross-examiner can't be lazy. In order to get where you're going, ask the questions that will result in answers that are not going to blow you out of the water. If it is too much trouble to ask all the questions necessary, then the subject matter about which you are asking must not be significant enough to warrant the effort. Don't ask about it at all. If the question is worth asking, however, then it is worth asking correctly.

REDUCE THE SUBJECT TO BASIC INGREDIENTS

To be sure that you are not going to be given an answer that you do not want, break the subject of inquiry down into basic ingredients and ask only as much of the subject in one question that can be answered in a simple and direct answer. IF YOU WANT TO CONTROL THE ANSWER, YOU MUST FIRST CONTROL THE QUESTION.

For instance, you can ask the witness to describe an individual he says he saw on a particular occasion as follows:

Q. Mr. Witness, please describe the man you say you saw on the morning of March fifteenth.

A. He was kind of tall, about six feet, and had blond hair and looked very much like your client there. In fact, he had the same bushy eyebrows your client has. That's why I've said your client is the man I saw.

Since you asked that blanket question, you are entitled to be inundated with that blanket answer. The way to have avoided the witness's giving you the unwanted answer was to have controlled the space in which he could have meandered with his answer. This should have been done by strict attention to, and control of, your questions.

For instance, if you want to explore the description given by a witness, you might do it as follows:

Q. Now you described this person you saw as being of medium height, is that correct?

A. Yes.

Q. What would you consider medium height? My size?

A. Just about, maybe a little taller.

Q. When you say a little taller, do you mean an inch or so?

A. Yes.

Cross-examiner: May the record show, Your Honor, that my height is 5 feet, 10 inches.

The Court: Very well.

Q. And you also described this person as having blond hair, is that correct?

A. Yes.

Q. In fact, you described that blond hair as short and curly; almost kinky, isn't that correct?

A. I don't remember that.

Author's Note: Your client here does NOT have blond kinky hair.

Q. You remember being interviewed by a police officer after the incident occurred, do you not?

A. Yes.

Q. And that police officer asked you questions, did he not?

A. Yes.

Q. And you responded to those questions?

A. Yes.

Q. And at the time you told the police officer, whatever you told him, you were describing what you had seen that very night, were you not?

A. Yes.

Q. And the reason you were describing what you had seen was to give the police officer accurate information so that he might investigate that incident, isn't that correct?

A. Yes.

> **Q.** And isn't it a fact that you told the police officer at that time that the person who was involved in this incident had blond hair; very short, curly, very kinky hair?
>
> **A.** I don't believe I did.

In the preceding example you have attempted to control the witness's description of the alleged perpetrator without permitting the witness to make gratuitous remarks or to add unwanted information. Additionally, the last part of the cross-examination, as to a prior statement made to a police officer, is the requisite method to laying the foundation needed to ultimately call the police officer to testify that the witness did, in fact, make a prior inconsistent statement, in which the witness described the perpetrator as having short, blond, kinky hair.

A few more examples of controlling the witness's answers by controlling your own questions are here appropriate.

For instance, you could ask a witness to describe an incident that occurred, or you could describe the incident yourself in your question, requiring the witness only to affirm or negate your description.

THE WRONG METHOD

> **Q.** What occurred when you were attacked?
>
> **A.** I was walking toward the door of the bar. I was just reaching for the handle of the door when I felt a tremendous blow on the back of my head. I turned and your client, the defendant, was behind me, with two other men, and a pool cue in his hand. I fell to the floor unconscious. I woke up in the hospital.

In the preceding example, the witness repeated the same story he told on direct testimony. And you've just helped him to sink his hook further into your client.

A witness should rarely be asked to repeat his or her direct testimony. Rather, the witness's testimony should be attacked in piecemeal fashion, with questions that do not permit the witness to empty his guns at your client.

The preceding examination should have been conducted as follows:

> **Q.** Now you say that just before you were struck in the head with this terrible blow, you were walking toward the door of the bar, is that correct?
>
> **A.** Yes.
>
> **Q.** In fact, you had reached the door just before you were hit?

A. That's right. That's right.

Q. You were just reaching for the doorknob, is that correct?

A. Yes.

Q. Now up to this point you hadn't seen the defendant behind you?

Your Adversary: Objection, Your Honor, at what point?

The Court: Yes, sustained as to form.

Q. Up to the point that you reached the door and were reaching for the door handle, you hadn't seen the defendant behind you?

A. I saw him as soon as I was hit. I turned around.

Q. The question is: before you were hit, you didn't see anyone, did you?

A. No.

Q. You saw someone behind you, whoever it was, *only after* you received the blow on the head, isn't that correct?

A. Yes.

Q. In fact, before you received this blow, you were facing toward the street, weren't you?

A. Well, sort of facing the street, sort of facing in, you know.

Q. You weren't walking sideways, were you?

A. No.

Q. So you were still facing the door normally while you were walking normally toward the door, weren't you?

A. Yes.

Q. And you were still facing the door when you reached for the doorknob, weren't you?

A. Yes.

Q. And it was then that you received this blow, isn't that correct?

A. Yes.

Q. The very first thing you even knew about an attack that night was when you were hit on the head, correct?

A. Yes.

Q. And this blow was a terrible blow, wasn't it?

A. Well . . .

Q. Haven't you described this very blow to the jury and previously to the police officer as being a terrible blow on the back of your head?

A. Yes.

Q. And it was that, wasn't it, a terrible blow on your head?

A. Yes.

Basically, in both of these examinations, you have asked the witness for the same information; that is, what he saw at the time of the alleged attack. Yet there is a substantial difference in the way the jury hears those two versions of the incident: One is in the witness's own words, whatever words the witness chooses; the second version is in your words, whatever words you have chosen for your questions, permitting the witness only enough room to affirm or deny. And, whether the witness affirms or denies your questions, he should not be able to damage you so severely that you cannot keep going and still emerge in a strong position.

For example, let me change a significant answer that the witness gave in the preceding example. Suppose, for instance, that he answered as follows:

Q. You saw someone behind you, whoever it was, only after you received the blow on the head, isn't that correct?

A. At the same time as I got hit, I saw him (pointing to your defendant). At the same time.

Remember, an adverse witness is there to hurt your client, and sometimes witnesses go to extremes to do that. Be prepared for just such an eventuality. You unflinchingly continue the examination as follows:

Q. At the time you were walking up to the door, you hadn't already been hit, had you?

A. No.

Q. Anybody curse at you, spit at you?

A. No.

Q. Anybody threaten to beat you up, tell you to get the hell out of the bar?

A. No.

Q. So as you were walking up to the front door, you were doing so only because you wanted to, not because anyone made you?

A. Right.

Q. And you weren't suspicious of anything that had happened up to that point, because nothing had happened, right?

A. Right.

Q. And when you got to the door, you reached for the doorknob to go out, right?

A. Yes.

Q. And at that point, when you were reaching for the doorknob to go out, you were facing the door, weren't you?

A. Maybe not facing the door completely.

Q. You weren't standing facing the bar, reaching backwards over your shoulder to open this door, were you?

A. No.

Q. You were going out of a bar normally, opening the door in a normal fashion, weren't you?

A. Yes.

Notice that the witness is not voluntarily being cooperative, he is looking for an opportunity to hurt you, and you must contain that desire by the questions you allow him to answer.

If you had permitted the witness to give his answer in one narrative, you would be arguing with him about whether or not he really meant what he said. By breaking the questions up into palatable pieces, you can control the direction in which to take the next questions and answers; you can lead him back carefully over material; you can even abandon a fruitless line of small inquiries without giving up the ship. In the event that you permit the long narrative, you cannot abandon the cross-examination without abandoning your client.

The difference between the preceding sample examinations, relative to the happening of the incident in the bar, is twofold:

(1) Where you ask blanket questions, you receive any answer that the witness wants to give you. Naturally, if that witness is testifying against you, the answer that he is going to give you is not going to be beneficial if he can help it.

(2) Although the second examination is direct and to the point and does not permit the witness to answer anything that he pleases, it is also much longer and much more detailed.

Therefore, if you want to be effective as a cross-examiner, you must get into the habit of breaking the subject matter down into bits and pieces that can be answered with direct, simple answers. The lazy man's approach, the question that asks for blanket answers because the fragmented bits-and-pieces examination is too long or too tedious, will result in your being inundated by answers that you do not appreciate or desire, which are not helpful to your client's cause. If you are too lazy to ask all the questions necessary to control the witness, if it is too much trouble to break the questions down into palatable pieces, don't bother to cross-examine; pack up your bag, go home, and handle real estate closings.

REQUIRE YES OR NO ANSWERS

The best method of all to control the adverse witness is to pose questions that require either a yes or a no answer.

In this way, the cross-examiner supplies all the information the witness and the jury hears, permitting the witness to answer only in the affirmative or in the negative. Thus it is the cross-examiner who is totally controlling the information that is put forth before the jury, and no misinformation or damaging information that is unnecessary and undesirable can be blurted out or gratuitously supplied by the witness.

There are two steps to take in order to obtain the desired yes or no answers. The first is to ask simple questions that can, in fact, be answered yes or no. The second is to advise the witness that he should tell you when he cannot answer the questions in this way, and you will rephrase the question. Do not permit the witness to answer the question if he says it cannot be answered yes or no.

YOUR ADVERSARY IS GOING TO OBJECT

Almost automatically, when you tell the witness you want yes or no answers, your adversary or the court may attempt to curtail your demand for such answers. This is the result of scads of poor cross-examiners in the past who have asked questions that have not lent themselves to yes or no answers. Courts have come to regard suspiciously the demand for merely affirming or negating information supplied in a question.

Therefore, the cross-examiner now must be careful with his or her questions, and must persuade the Court, by proper questions, that the demand for yes or no answers is quite sound and appropriate. Your adversary's motives for not wanting to permit you to compel yes or no answers from the witness are another story. Your adversary doesn't want you to supply all the information that the jury hears, thus eliminating the witness's opportunity to purposely damage your case by blurting out information before the jury, or to eliminate the witness's opportunity to repeat, time and time again, your adversary's version of the case.

In an attempt to stop your demand for yes or no answers, your adversary may advise the Court that not all questions can be answered yes or no and that the witness is not able to answer questions in such limited fashion and so must give answers with further explanation.

It is quite reasonable for a court to permit the witness an opportunity to give a full answer to your question. Thus, your best efforts to curtail and control the witness will be subverted, and you shall be inundated with whatever answer your adversary has rehearsed the witness to give under such circumstances, unless you are alert and react properly under these conditions.

What to do?

First, it is arrant nonsense that you should not be permitted, under any circumstances, to compel witnesses to give yes or no answers. The difficulty is that most cross-examiners do not pose proper questions and that the questions they ask cannot, in fact, be answered in a yes or no fashion. The first discipline to be mastered by the cross-examiner desiring yes or no answers, therefore, is to ask questions that strictly lend themselves to such answers.

The solution to this dilemma, which has long plagued cross-examiners, is not simple. But the unquestionable first step on the road to compelling the witness to the yes or no answer is to ask the question that is answerable in the yes or no form.

In other words, as previously stated, it is you, the cross-examiner, who is totally responsible for the questioning of the witness, the area of questioning, the actual wording of the question, and every other aspect of what questions are asked of the witness. If you ask a question that has a very limited scope and that can, in fact, be answered yes or no, there is no basis for your adversary to claim that such a question cannot be answered in a yes or no fashion.

The greatest number of problems in this area arise when the cross-examiner asks a question that he ardently desires to have answered yes or no, which question, however, has not been asked in simple enough form. At the end of this nonsimple question, when the witness attempts to give a full answer, the cross-examiner demands that the witness answer yes or no. To this the adversary objects, the court sustains, and the witness gets an opportunity to give a full and complete answer.

The fault is not with the adversary, the court, or the witness. It is with you! You have asked the question that cannot be answered yes or no. And, thereafter, you are not justified in your demand that the question be answered in such fashion.

The best thing for you to do is to rephrase your questions and to ask proper questions.

For example:

Q. At the time of the accident, the traffic was rather light, wasn't it?

A. Not really.

Cross-examiner: Your Honor, I'll ask the court to direct the witness to answer that question yes or no.

Your Adversary: Objection, Your Honor, not every question can be answered yes or no. Certainly not that one. The witness should be permitted to give a full answer.

The Court: Ms. Witness, if you can answer that question yes or no, please do so. If you feel that you cannot, then you may explain fully.

Author's Note: Is there any doubt what the next words of the witness will be?

A. I cannot answer that yes or no. The traffic wasn't bumper to bumper, but there were a number of cars on the road. Particularly, there was a car in front of me that blocked my view of the road for a moment. But that car moved over and then I was in a position to observe your client's car very clearly, directly in front of me. Three car lengths ahead of me.

It might seem that the question *at the time of the accident, the traffic on the road was light* is simple. However, that which followed by your adversary and the court was not unreasonable. And, you have given the adverse witness an opportunity to bury you a little deeper. The information might better have been elicited in the following fashion, with a more beneficial result:

Q. At the time that you observed the vehicles, particularly that of my client, were there other vehicles on the road?

A. Yes.

Q. This was and is a public highway in the State of New York, correct?

A. Yes.

Q. And there were various lanes of traffic going in each direction, weren't there?

A. Yes.

Q. And at the time of the accident, there were other vehicles on the road besides yours and my client's?

A. Yes.

Q. And some of these other cars were traveling in the same direction as yourself and my client?

A. Yes.

Q. At the time just prior to the observations that you say you've made, were there vehicles behind your car?

A. Yes.

Q. You noticed these, did you not?

A. Yes.

Q. Did you observe them through your rearview mirror, or had you turned around in order to see them?

A. I observed them through the rearview mirror.

Q. So that you were driving carefully, observing what was ahead of you and behind you on this occasion, is that correct?

A. Yes.

Q. And at the time just prior to the observation that you said you made, there were vehicles ahead of you on the road, in addition to the car of my client?

A. Well, there were other vehicles but . . .

Cross-examiner: Your Honor, I object to the answer going any further and ask that Your Honor direct the witness to answer only the question asked and not to give gratuitous remarks.

Your Adversary: Your Honor, I object; not every question can be answered yes or no, and I think that the witness should be provided an opportunity to give full and complete answers.

Cross-examiner: Your Honor, the question was simply whether there were vehicles other than the defendant's and witness's vehicle. This question is subject to a yes or no answer. If my adversary wishes the witness to answer other questions and give further information, he can have a re-direct examination on this subject.

The Court: While not every question can be answered yes or no, I think that question can be. The cross-examiner has asked merely whether or not there were other vehicles on the road ahead of this witness's vehicle, other than the defendant's. Answer that just yes or no. You can inquire, Mr. Adversary, on re-direct examination, if there is further information you wish the witness to bring out.

Q. Were there other vehicles on the road ahead of yourself, other than the vehicle of my client, prior to your making the observations.

A. Yes.

Naturally, some people reading the preceding example can think that the court could just as easily have permitted the witness to give a full and complete answer at that point, and that is true. I cannot specify simply, and in every case, a situation where the court will not react adversely to your contention that a question can be answered yes or no. I can assure you, however, that the simpler question, the one that does not permit a wide range of possibilities for answers, is the one that will more than likely pass muster on the yes/no test.

The secret of containing the witness is simply that you must not try to travel by yards, asking questions that move quickly past the information, for these are the questions that will be susceptible to answers of equal measures.

You must be prepared to move slowly, in measured cadence, which does not require more of an answer than you are willing to have the witness make.

ASK THE WITNESS TO ADVISE YOU IF HE OR SHE CANNOT ANSWER YES OR NO

At the outset of your cross-examination, alert the court and the witness that you intend to ask questions which can be answered in a yes or no fashion, as follows:

Cross-examiner: Ms. Witness, I am about to ask you various questions which you will be able to answer yes or no. In the event that you cannot answer these questions yes or no, please advise me of that, and I will rephrase the question. All right?

A. Yes.

Now you have laid a foundation properly for asking questions that can be answered in a yes or no fashion, and in the event that the witness believes a question cannot be answered in a yes or no fashion, the witness should be properly restrained from giving a full-out, burying kind of answer. Rather, the witness should advise you of the fact that the question cannot be answered in a yes or no fashion, and you then should ask another question that can be answered this way.

> ***CAUTION:*** *Do not permit your cross-examination to become sloppy, casual, or without discipline. The instant the witness advises you that the question cannot be answered yes or no, ask another question. Do not lose the initiative. Do not let the witness select the question to answer, nor your adversary, nor the judge. Ask another question that you feel can be answered yes or no. Keep at it. It's hard work, but it's worth it.*

Q. Were you alone on the stairway at that time?

A. I cannot answer that question yes or no.

Q. Very well. When you first entered the stairwell, did anyone else enter with you?

A. No.

Q. And there were several flights of steps going down, correct?

A. Yes.

Q. You were on the fourth floor?

A. Yes.

Q. As you were walking down, was there anyone walking on the same flight as you?

A. No.

Or perhaps you might have asked:

Q. Was the work on the computer machine done by anyone other than yourself?

A. I can't answer that yes or no.

Q. There were several different functions and tasks that could be done on that computer, correct?

A. Yes.

Q. And you accomplished one of them?

A. Yes.

Q. Other people may have used the same computer for different functions or for different clients, correct?

A. Right.

Q. Were you the only one who did your particular computer specialty for this particular client?

A. Yes, I was the only one.

Thus, the two steps necessary in attempting to contain the witness, in order to curtail her answers to yes or no:

(a) ask the simple question that can be answered yes or no; and

(b) where the question cannot be so answered, have the witness advise you of that and then ask a question that can be answered yes or no.

OLD CHESTNUTS DIE HARD

To prove that all questions cannot be answered yes or no, the old chestnut that is constantly thrown at you in a courtroom, or in other treatises, is the question "Have you stopped beating your wife?" The classic objection is that neither a yes nor a no answer could fully explain to the jury that the man is not married and thus has never beaten his wife.

Under those circumstances, naturally, the judge must permit the witness to fully answer the loaded question, which does not lend itself to a yes or no answer.

The obvious fault in the classic question is not with the witness, your adversary, or the judge. It is with the question. That question, "Have you stopped beating your wife?" does, in fact presume two circumstances that may or may not be in evidence: (a) that the man is married, and (b) that he had, in the past, beaten his wife. If you artlessly ask a question of that sort, then you deserve to be inundated. Perhaps, as an example, the cross-examiner might have better asked:

> **Q.** Are you married?
>
> **A.** Yes.
>
> **Q.** And have you ever beaten your wife?
>
> **A.** I can't answer that yes or no.

Actually, the witness could answer yes or no.

> **Q.** Well, have you ever struck her, or hit her in the face, or about the body, with your hands or any object, for any reason whatever?
>
> **A.** Yes.
>
> **Q.** Have you struck your wife in such fashion within the last two months?
>
> **A.** Yes.
>
> **Q.** So this is an activity that has continued right into the recent past, isn't it?
>
> **A.** Yes.

In the preceding example, you have obtained all the information that was required from the original question, "Have you stopped beating your wife?" The only difference is that, in order to be answered, the question had to be broken down into pieces that could properly be answered by a yes or no.

NEVER ASK A QUESTION UNLESS YOU KNOW THE ANSWER

All cross-examiners, neophytes as well as seasoned veterans, have heard this bromide: never ask a question unless you know the answer. And having heard such, you've probably wondered, as I did, what does that statement actually mean? Or, if it literally means what it sounds like, how can you possibly know in advance answers to questions you haven't even asked? Or, how can you possibly know the testimony of the adverse witness unless you first ask the questions and wait for the answers?

Simply put, the solution—as is most everything connected with cross-examination—is in strict discipline. As I hope I have hammered home in preceding passages, strictly disciplined interrogation is the key to effective, aggressive cross-examination. If your question is properly put and is one in which you supply all the information the jury hears, permitting the witness, therefore, only the very limited function of affirming or denying your posed question, you are automatically to the point where you already know what the witness can or will answer. You've reduced the possible answers to two: the affirmative yes or the negative no.

Think about that!

If you ask sloppy, random questions, which permit the witness to answer in any rambling fashion he or she chooses, how can you possibly know what the witness will say?

You can't!

When cross-examination is a sloppy, random thing, going in any direction the witness's answers may buffet you, like a ship without a rudder at sea during a storm, there cannot possibly be direction to your cross-examination—no true and right course. The witness is taking you anywhere he or she wishes, and you calmly, coolly, and with equanimity are having your brains kicked in.

If you employ strict discipline, as outlined in previous chapters, to manage the witness, to contain the witness, to make the witness only affirm or deny the information you pose in your questions, however, you are obviously substantially closer to your goal of knowing what the answer to your question will be—even before you ask it.

THIS IS NOT THE END OF YOUR TASK

While reducing the potential answers to either yes or no is certainly some progress toward the goal of knowing what the answers to your questions are before you ask them, it is not the end of the line by any means. In fact, it is just the beginning.

The next step in predicting the witness's answers to your questions is to formulate questions that can be answered only in a fashion you already know, based upon information already supplied by the direct examination, by the pretrial or on-trial discovery, which have been uncovered in some prior statement, inconsistent or otherwise.

Many Paths Lead to the Center of the Circle

Your aim in cross-examination, as mentioned more times than it should have been, is to make progress toward neutralizing the harmful effect or credibility of the adverse witness in the eyes of the trier of the fact.

This can be done in several ways: by undermining the accuracy of the witness's account of the event; by casting doubt on the credibility or moral character of the witness; or by bringing to the jury's attention the fact that the witness has an interest in seeing the adverse party successful. With some witnesses, all of these can be accomplished; with others, perhaps only some of them. Your aim is to inject as many of the neutralizing elements as you are able, to undermine the jury's confidence in the witness.

In doing so, however, you must not shoot from the hip with questions that might, you hope, bring out some factor you wish the jury to hear, if only the witness would give the desired answer.

The witness may be able to shoot from the hip right back. True, an occasional hip shot may hit its mark. But that is a matter of luck. And, what you are desirous of developing is a method that can permit you to be a successful, effective marksman on all occasions, not a potluck hip-shooter who occasionally may do an effective job.

Therefore, in analyzing your approach to the witness, in preparing your cross-examination script and your line of attack, review the information on hand, and, utilizing that, develop the lines of questions that you intend to use. Do not dive into a pond you do not know, and the bottom of which you cannot see. If you know the witness has a background that has some antisocial history, use it; if there is a criminal record, use it; if the direct testimony is illogical and inaccurate, attack it; if the witness has given prior statements that are inconsistent with the trial testimony, spread them before the jury.

By formulating questions based on information you already know, you naturally already know the answers to the questions, and your task is merely to orchestrate that information in such fashion as to bring out the effect that is most damaging to the adverse witness.

In utilizing prior inconsistent statements, you should lead the witness into the trap of repeating the inconsistency: You must concretize the inconsistency for the jury. If the witness gave information to the police at the time of the incident, for instance, where she indicated she could not identify your client, then lead the witness into that area. If the witness now says (on trial) that your client is, in fact, the person she saw at the incident, take out your inconsistent statement and, laying the proper foundation (see sections on this subject, infra), destroy the witness's credibility based upon the prior inconsistency.

Even though you may not know with total certitude whether the witness will or will not identify your client in the preceding example, you do know that the witness will answer only one way or the other, and you are prepared for either answer. If the witness answers in a fashion helpful to your cause, fine. If it is harmful, you are prepared to destroy the witness's answer. Thus, by formulating a question, the only possible answer to which you already know and are prepared for, you have arrived at the cross-examiner's Valhalla—total control.

In all situations where you cross-examine, then, you should have information already on hand before you formulate your questions. Have a police report, a medical history from the hospital, the doctor's report, a prior statement, the testimony given at an EBT, a Grand Jury appearance, testimony from a prior trial, or merely the exactly recorded direct testimony. Based solely on known information, you then mount your attack. It is ludicrous to mount an attack with unknowns, without information, groping like a blind person in the dark into areas that are totally foreign to you. You may be destroyed with the same question that you hope brings victory. Since your goal is not to exercise your vocal cords, but to get to the center of the circle, and since there are 360 paths to that center, you should not haphazardly strike off on any path, regardless of whether you know the way along that path or not. Try a path that you know, for which you have some information, instructions, or prior knowledge.

Therefore, the old chestnut about never asking a question the answer to which you do not already know can be somewhat modified to read: Never ask a question the answer to which you do not know may be given and which you are not prepared to handle.

You Can Win a Battle Only Once

It is never necessary to beat a dead horse, or a witness, and it is never necessary to show the jury how marvelously clever you are. Trick shots are not necessary. A straightforward demolition in front of the jury is satisfactory and, once done, is enough. Do not tempt the fates by trying to kill a witness twice; you may not be so successful the second time, and you may, in the bargain, resuscitate the drowned adversary. Leave well enough alone and sit quietly, silently, privately pleased with your success—even if it is not *yet* apparent to the jury.

Even if the known information available for cross-examination is not sufficient for the big kill, or is not as dramatically damaging as you might like, it is still a known quantity; you must use it, and it alone. Think about this! The big kill that you imagine may lie in the unknown, may not. Worse, that may be your destruction, rather than the witness's, lurking beneath the surface. Satisfy your urge to attack the unknown with the adage: That which lies beyond what is, is not.

YOUR MANNER OF INQUIRY IS EQUALLY IMPORTANT

Incidentally, there are ways of utilizing material that, when asked correctly, dramatically, and effectively, can be far more beneficial than if it were piddled away with some whimpering inquiry. You'll get more mileage from a correctly asked question based on known information than you will from some hesitant, doubtful beating around the bush with the same information.

Thus, not only must you ask questions to which you already know the answers, utilizing information at hand, you must ask those questions in a fashion that is going to bring out the most damaging, most harmful answers from the witness. More about this anon.

YOU CAN'T ATTACK WHAT YOU CAN'T REMEMBER

At this point, it would be helpful for the prospective cross-examiner to know how to systematically record, totally and exactly, the adverse witness's direct testimony, to thereafter prepare a script for cross-examination, and, in general, to prepare to attack the adverse witness and the adversary's case.

MAKING NOTES IS ESSENTIAL

First of all, in order to cross-examine, you must be able to recall the direct testimony exactly, verbatim. This does not mean that you have to be a stenographer or have an photographic memory to cross-examine; nor does it mean that you have to hide a tape recorder on your person. It does mean, however, that you must train yourself to capture the testifying witness's exact words in writing, so that you will be able to refer back to that testimony for cross-examination purposes, at any time later in the trial, and again at summation.

Such training is not really as hard as it sounds on first reading. You do not have to record every word the witness utters. What you must do is capture *the essence of every answer* the witness utters and record it in your notes. The italicized words in the preceding sentence are the essence of being able to recall the direct examination exactly. First, you must record the true essence of every answer fully. General impressions of the direct examination, succinct abbreviations, random phrases, won't do. Every answer must be noted. And, every answer must be noted in writing.

HOW TO RECORD THE TESTIMONY

The following is an excerpt of direct examination of a police detective in a homicide case.

Direct:

Q. Now, Detective, will you tell this court and jury what, if anything, you said to the defendant at that point, and what, if anything, he said to you?

A. Yes, sir. I said to the defendant: "Now, calm down. Sit down, sit down. Calm down. Relax. You want to tell me what happened today? You want to tell me the truth?" And he said "Yes."

Q. All right. You said, "You want to tell me the truth?" Please proceed.

A. And he said that he opened the window, but he couldn't get into the apartment because the gate that was on the inside of the window was locked. Then he said he came back up the fire escape. And that he and his partner started to lift the TV set over the roof when he heard a noise on the fire escape. And he walked over to the edge of the roof, and he looked down the fire escape. And he saw a police officer coming up the fire escape. And he said to his partner, "la jara, la jara." I asked him what that meant. He said, "the cops, the cops." Then I said, "Then what happened?" He said he hid and crouched down behind the stairway wall, and he saw the cop go by him, and he had his gun in his hand, and he was pointing it at his partner. And he said that he was afraid; he saw the gun. At that point, the defendant put his hands over his face, and he said "Mi Dios; Mi Dios! I did it! I did it!"

And I said, "What did you do?" He said, "I shot the officer. I shot him in the back."

Had you been trial counsel to the defendant, there, at the very moment that the detective testified, you should have made notes of his testimony, so that you would be able to mount the attack that should follow on cross-examination. My notes would have been read as follows:

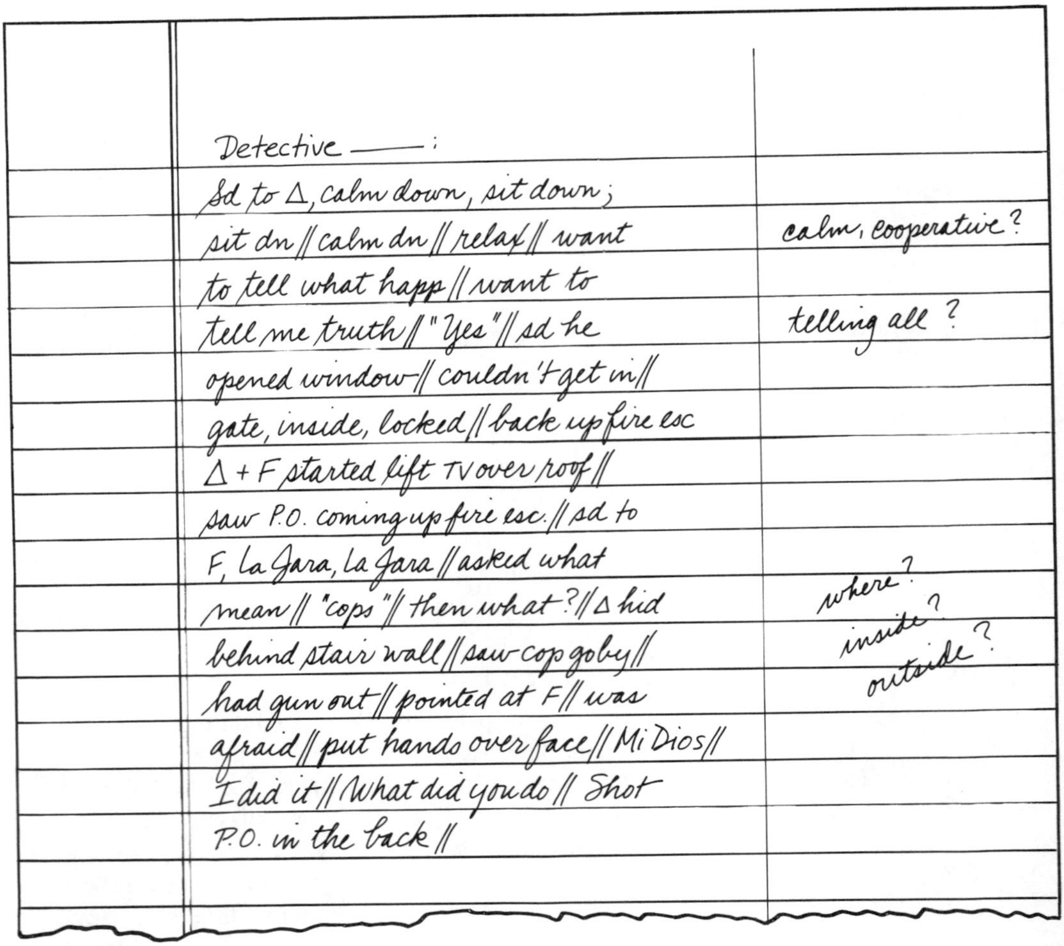

Notice that, while I have not recorded each and every word of the detective's direct testimony, I have actually captured enough so that I could, days or weeks later, practically verbatim, read back to the court, my adversary, or to myself, the entire testimony of that witness. Notice that there are no questions recorded; only testimony. As indicated previously, that's all you'll need. But you shall need every word of it, and you should not be so foolhardy as to presume that you can remember it without recording it in writing. Even if you could perform such a feat of cerebral legerdemain, you would be wasting valuable energy remembering something that an inanimate piece of paper uses no effort whatever to preserve precisely.

Preparation Permits Smoothness and Flow

All of the smooth, easy flow of a good cross-examination does not come from the seat of the pants. It comes from careful preparation, note-taking, cross-checking and cross-referencing, preparation of a cross-examination script, and even a careful stacking of referenced, needed material, near where you will stand to cross-examine, so that you will have the time and the confidence to make it look as if you just stood up from the table and were able to easily trap a witness who was obviously trying to fool the jury.

If it appears that you have to work too hard at tearing apart the witness, if you have to hurriedly flip through pages of testimony while the witness, the court, and the jury idly watch you—which makes you more nervous and the witness more confident and calm—the jury may get an impression that the witness is a lot tougher than he or she really is and that the necessity of your effort underscores the truth and veracity of the witness's testimony. A little preparation will help you make the witness look like a pussycat.

An Actual Script

When the direct testimony of each witness is completed, theoretically at least, you shall have an opportunity to prepare your cross-examination of the witness. Ideally, you will be able to do so at your leisure overnight, so that when you proceed to court the next morning, you will have a carefully orchestrated, cross-referenced cross-examination script with which to work.

As hinted at earlier, the opportunity to prepare your cross-examination script slowly, overnight, with plenty of time to consider and reconsider your approach, to form, and reform and revise questions, even whole areas of questioning, is the ideal.

Unfortunately, you may often not be afforded so luxurious an amount of time in which to prepare for the assault. Sometimes the witness, even if formidable in terms of substance of testimony or hurt inflicted, has testified for only a few minutes; the court, measuring the time necessary to prepare your cross-examination by the amount of time the witness has testified, may permit you only a few minutes to formulate your attack.

Other times, even if the direct testimony of the witness took a substantial part of the morning session, there is still the entire afternoon session for you to cross-examine. Thus, regardless of how devoutly you wish for an overnight recess to prepare yourself, the court has an obligation to keep the trial moving briskly. In such case, you might have to make do with a luncheon recess in order to prepare for your cross-examination. With a bit of practice, however, a luncheon recess will become ample time for the preparation of at least enough cross-examination to carry you through the afternoon session, so that, if necessary, you can then prepare the remainder of your cross-examination in the evening and continue in the morning.

THE BETTER PREPARED—THE LESS TIME REQUIRED

As outlined previously, if you have prepared for the trial thoroughly, it should not be necessary to take very long to be ready to cross-examine any witness. Remember, you have already studied all the prior statements, testimony, and EBTs of the witness and are mentally prepared to collate all that material with the direct testimony that you have just recorded in your notes. With time and experience, you will be able to put together an effective cross-examination rapidly.

Incidentally, as you cross-examine on your feet, even if you have a full-blown cross-examination script in hand, you are not hidebound by that script, but are continually revising and adjusting the cross-examination to accommodate the twists and turns that inevitably arise as the witness twists and turns to elude the thrusts of your questions; therefore, that capacity and flexibility to improvise and formulate cross-examination quickly, while on your feet, is the same capacity which permits you to formulate your attack well, quickly, and professionally, despite the shortness of preparation time.

CROSS-EXAMINATION IS NOT A LIVING EXPERIENCE

While you may occasionally be required to get up on your feet without the ideal, carefully created cross-examination script, and while you may occasionally be required to improvise while on your feet in certain areas of your attack, cross-examination is not something that is done willy-nilly, just by standing up and attacking headlong with any question that first pops into your mind. The headlong attack is one that is obvious; it is also obviously open to counterattack, obviously the area that must be defended. Thus, this is also the area that the witness will be best prepared to defend. A direct, immediate, headlong attack at the obvious target might be so well-rebuffed, that you might find yourself sitting vanquished back at the counsel table, without so much as a by-your-leave.

Thus, when it is suggested that, with time and experience, you may be able to do a creditable job just standing up and attacking carefully, despite the fact that you haven't had a great deal of time for preparation, that does not mean that it is easy, that does not mean that you haven't prepared in advance, that doesn't mean it doesn't take practice and that anyone with a law degree can do it the minute he or she stands up. In fact, most lawyers cannot do it, ever. However, with practice and careful attention to this book, you are going to be able to do it.

With time, after preparing many cross-examinations in full detail, and with full scripts, you may be able to quickly home in on the subtle approach, the right tack to use to begin to unravel the adverse witness's testimony. When you have developed that capacity, then, even if the judge gives you very little time to prepare, you can begin a proper cross-examination. Then, during recesses, luncheons, and so forth, you will be able to plan your continuing attack sufficiently enough, say, to carry you to the next recess when you can breathe a little easier and plan for the ultimate moment of truth.

> ***REMEMBER:*** *Most of the basic pattern for your cross-examination should already be in your head; all the digesting of the prior, pretrial and on-trial information accomplished, waiting only for the Direct to be completed so that you may collate all the material. You may even have a basic idea where you want to begin your cross the moment the direct testimony ends. You might even have your first assault planned. Fine, but that doesn't mean you do not prepare—even if only for a few minutes—a careful, final battle plan. A crafty cross-examiner, having analyzed the opponent's case, already knowing what ground the proffered witness would attempt to cover, and even without having heard the direct, knowing in broad terms what the witness will testify, can plan basic countermoves in advance, waiting only to hear the direct testimony to know if your educated guess was correct. If it was, you are far ahead on the road of preparedness.*

THE SCRIPT ITSELF

Let's take a sample of direct testimony, make the notes therefrom, and then formulate a proper script from which to cross-examine. As a test, while reading the following, make up your own notes on the direct.

The testimony is in a homicide case; the witness is a girlfriend of an alleged accomplice in the homicide. She testified that on the evening of the crime, three conspirators, including her now-cooperating boyfriend, came to her apartment to talk over the crime that was going to be committed. She testified on direct as follows:

Q. Mrs. Witness, how long have you lived at 743 East 86th Street, Brooklyn?

A. Since June of 1989.

Q. And where do you live in this said building?

A. I have an apartment in the basement.

Q. And with whom do you live?

A. My son; he is three years old.

Q. Does anybody else live in the building?

A. On the first floor, Roger, my boyfriend, my boyfriend's grandmother and aunt. And, on the second floor, his mother and father.

Q. How old are you, Mrs. Witness?

A. Twenty-three years old.

Q. And did you know Stanley A. Victim?

A. Yes, he was my uncle.

Q. Now on April 15, 1990, were you living at the same address?

A. Yes.

Q. Now can you tell what, if anything, happened on that evening?

A. Well, I had been in my apartment and I left and went up to the second floor, and I was there with Roger.

Q. Can you describe the apartment you were in?

A. Well, there is a main door that leads into a kitchen, where I was.

Q. And who else was up there at that time, besides yourself and Roger?

A. My son was asleep downstairs, but I think that Roger's mother was at home watching TV in her bedroom.

Q. And what else occurred, if anything?

A. About 8:30 or a little after, somebody came to the door downstairs. They came in and said, "Louie sent us here."

Q. Do you know who let them into the building?

A. No.

Q. Go ahead.

A. Anyway there were two men; I didn't know them. And they said Louie sent us here.

Q. Where were they when they said this?

A. In the foyer on the second floor.

Q. And do you see anybody in this courtroom who resembles the individuals that you saw that evening?

A. The two men sitting there at that table.

Prosecutor: Indicating the defendants, Your Honor.

The Court: Let the record show that the witness has indicated the two defendants.

Q. Is there any doubt in your mind that these are the men that came into the house that evening?

A. No.

Q. What happened after that, if anything?

A. I saw the two men walk into the kitchen and introduce themselves as Ken and Andy. I don't remember if each introduced himself or if one just said we're Ken and Andy. Anyway, they said that they had passed by the house a few times and it was dark there, and that they were going to go back in a while.

Q. Did you have a good opportunity to observe these individuals on that occasion?

A. Sure. We were sitting at the kitchen table.

Q. And who was doing the speaking, describing what had happened?

A. Ken did most of the talking. And Andy was very quiet.

Q. Did the defendants look the same as they do now here in the courtroom?

A. Well, Ken was wearing glasses. Andy looks the same, but Ken had glasses.

Q. Now, did they indicate whose house they had been to where the lights were out?

A. I don't remember if they said which house, but I was sure it was my uncle's.

Q. And when you say your uncle, you mean Stanley A. Victim?

A. Yes.

Q. Do you remember if anything else might have been said on that occasion?

A. No, I can't remember anything else.

Q. How far away from you were these people while all this conversation was going on?

A. Approximately five to six feet away.

Q. And you say that there was no further conversation?

A. Well, there was other conversation, but I didn't hear it.

Your notes, relative to the record of that direct testimony would look something like the following.

Joan Richards // 125 E. 15th St. //
6/25/79 same address // lived in basmt. 3 1/2 yrs.
with son 4 yrs. old // 1st fl. Grand. + Aunt //
2nd fl., moth. + fath. // 23 yrs. old // deceas. uncle
day in ques. left bas. to 2nd fl // with Roger //
stairs lead to foyer and door // son was asleep
down st. // thinks Roger's moth. at home, watch TV //
about 8^{30} - little after // someone came to door //
doesn't know who let in // 2 men // didn't know //
said Louie sent them // said in 2nd fl. foyer //
(points out 2 Δs) // no doubt about it // walked
into kitchen // introd. as Andy and Ken //
doesn't remember if ea. introd. himself // saw
both Δs clearly // said passed by house a
few times // dark there // go back in a while
Ken was quiet // only spoke to Andy //
Andy did most of talking // Andy wore glasses //
and mustache // doesn't remember if they said
which house // (Sure was uncle's) // doesn't
remember anything else they said // they
were 5 or 6 ft. away - maybe closer // was
other conversation betw 2 // didn't hear //

legitimate? married? Roger's son?

mustache??

guessing

do anything

call uncle? PD?

never said were committing crime

Based upon your careful study, you already know that the witness made three prior oral statements, which have been recorded in writing, the first by a police detective, the second by an Assistant District Attorney on the same day as the one of the detective, and the third by another Assistant D. A. sometime while the case was pending. Additionally, you know that the witness testified under oath in front of the Grand Jury. Thus, you have three prior statements reduced to writing and one prior statement made under oath to collate and use in cross-examination.

> ***NOTE:*** *When there are multiple prior statements (whether under oath or reduced to writing), a good practice is to analyze each of them in writing, side by side on a page, just as you would with direct testimony.*

Thus, in connection with the four prior statements of the foregoing witness, I commit them to paper as follows. Being now familiar with the recording method, see if you can read what the actual statements were.

A	B
DETECTIVE 3/23	ASST D.A. 3/23
Louie said he'd set it up[1]//send	Louie, few weeks before, at Marina,
2 guys//wanted to get into	sitting on boat,[3] talked of ripping off uncle,[3]
uncle's house//2 men arrived//	had to get others to help[5]//Roger in on
6/25, little after 8[2]//stayed 20	conv.//Roger spoke to Louie after that[6]//
mins//3 went to door//witness	on 6/25 Roger spoke to Louie at Louie's
went down to own apt//45	house[6]//on 6/25, 8 or a little after, 2 men
mins later, Roger came back alone//	came to house[7]//no one else present//
while in kitch, Andy said no	Louie sent us//Andy said it[7]//drove
one at home[2]//no cars//go back	around uncle's - no one there// Andy
before we go in to burgl[2]//	said it//all dark there//no one home//
all had been whisp[2]//	wait//then go back[8]//they got up + left[8]//
	Ken head down during conv// they spoke
	among themselves[8]//didn't hear all//said
	pass by again//other guy didn't say
	anything//Roger agreed[8]//Roger told
	witness about burg[9]//they were there
	15-20 mins[9]//left 8:25, 8:30//1/2 hr - 45 min
	Roger returned//said not much
	happened//about 11, 11:30, bro. came,
	talk about uncle dead[9]//went to
	mother's.

C ASST D.A.	D GRAND JURY
Saw Louie at Marina[4] // he	2 people came to home in evening[14]
knew uncle[4] // told about burg[9]	never saw before[14] //
6/25, 2 men came to house - Louie	came into house[15] // someone[15] else let in
sent us[12] // Roger opened door[40]	came upstairs[14] // not much conv.[20]
drove past uncle's // everything	talking in foyer[20] // they said Louie sent us[22]
dark // go back soon // Roger knew	passed uncle's a few times // ready to
uncle // called uncle Frank[39] //	go out[22] // that's all[23] // ready to go
whispered among themselves // only	back[24] // no one answered //
said hello to them // Roger said	whispered among themselves // that's all
nothing // 2 +[13] Roger left / there	ever saw of them[26] // introduced as
15 minutes[41] // arrived 8^{30}-8^{45} //	Andy + Ken only[33] // found out Ken's
Roger returned // she had gone	name (last) after arrest[44] //
downstairs // Later Louie came	Andy had a thick mustache //
over + Roger left with Louie	
again[14] //	

Now, fully armed, I prepare my cross-examination script as shown.

	Richards
	Richards not maiden name // what is
	when married - divorced?
	living with Roger - 3½ yrs
	not married to Rog / son, 4 yrs
	R not father // mother let stay in bastmt
	Employed? not since child - 4 yrs.
	Roger supports / sole support? / welfare
	advise welf., common law relation
	looking for work?
	who else lives at house
	home on 6/25 - had been out
	with R. and his mother
	see anyone in street
	in parked car - double parked car
	went up to 2nd fl.
	later 2 men to door
	Louie sent them
	testimony - you do not know who said that
B-7	actually, Andy said
	Andy did most of talking
C-39	whispering together
	never saw before - never spoke before to Ken
	only knew as Andy - Ken - no last names

Andy had southern accent
men in court here - same men as 6/25
able to recognize from then
the way these men look - the same as the men 6/25
actually difficult because man had thick mustache
D45 Louie sent them - knew Louie
met several weeks before - not with Andy or Ken
met at Marina - on boat
didn't see again before 6/28
expecting them
if no - didn't know why there at first
if yes - {had had prev. conversations with Louie about uncle rip-off
Deceased was uncle - blood uncle
mothers' brother
families close - ~~go to his home~~ he came to yours
went to his house once - (12-13 yrs. old)
show photo of scene → recognize picture - except for body - uncle's house
ever talk - ever in life - about ripping someone off
A-1 with Louie - just started talking about uncles
B-3 after convers - call uncle - mother - P.D.
no one?
You testified - knew talking about uncle's home
weren't horrified - didn't scream for P.D.
nothing?

The script appears at this point in the book merely as an example of the physical layout of a script, not necessarily for its completeness. There are many more things that are illustrated in ensuing sections and with which you must become familiar before you can put together detailed, complete, cross-examination scripts. Therefore, merely view the script here for its form, not its substance.

Notice that the cross-examination script is a unilateral document. It contains only your questions. Notice, too, that it begins the attack slowly, subtly, inquiring into the marital status (for those jurors offended by a married woman with child living in a flagrant, meretricious relationship, we offer them something to think about), and then it slowly develops the witness's relationship with the deceased, her blood uncle (for jurors offended by a young woman helping to plan, or at least knowing in advance, that her mother's brother was going to be the victim of a crime, we offer them something else to think about). You develop the cross-examination subtly, leaving no gaping holes in the direct testimony, but only chinks, clouds, and nagging doubts.

WHAT IF THERE ARE NO PRIOR INCONSISTENCIES?

It may well be that, in a particular case, there are no prior inconsistent statements that you have been able to uncover. That does not mean that you can't cross-examine the witness, or that you don't prepare a script. It merely means that you have to pursue other methods to make the witness look bad, to make the jury realize that the witness is not a reliable, credible person.

For instance, inconsistencies may exist in the direct testimony itself; conflict between this witness's direct and the testimony of other witnesses; other evidence already introduced; physical impossibilities; or all sorts of other discrepancies may exist and may be attacked. And when you put your script together, when you orchestrate the dismembering of the witness, the full, dramatic, factual impact of all these discrepancies is revealed full-blown to the jury.

YOU MUST BE ABLE TO VARY THE SCRIPT

While you have spent considerable time on your preparation, on your line of attack, don't anticipate that it is a set speech or is carved in stone, or that you must follow it to the letter. You set up the script as a guide that you follow carefully, unless some brilliant new idea or gaping new target appears on the scene. You may, based on an answer, go off on a tangent for a while, asking questions prompted by the witness's answers, and then return to the script. You may abandon a particular tack you set up in the script that, because of the answers received, is no longer applicable or viable. You should, however, follow the script unless something significant arises to cause you to vary therefrom.

PREPARATION IS ALWAYS NECESSARY

As aforesaid, the preparation for cross-examination is always the same; only the time in which you prepare varies. If the court permits you time to leisurely prepare yourself, you should do neater—not better—work, with more details, more cross-references, and so forth. After some experience, you should be able, only if necessary, to put together a decent cross-examination script or a substantial part thereof in a scant few minutes. Perhaps the judge gives you ten minutes after the direct to gather your thoughts, your notes, and so forth. Use that time to put together the first part of the examination.

In that time, with your pretrial and on-trial investigation, you can put together a good, basic start on the cross-examination. If the witness is only a peripheral witness with not much direct testimony, you can probably put together the entire cross-examination script in a few minutes. If the witness is one you intend to have on the stand for hours or days, you can work your script together at different times. Work the first part of a long script together in the few minutes the obstinate judge gives you after the direct. That should carry you to lunch break or to the end of the day. If it carries you to the end of the day, then you are home free and can prepare the rest of your script that night. If it carries you only to lunch break, during that lunch break you prepare enough script to carry you to the end of the day.

THE PRELIMINARY BREATHER TECHNIQUE

Oftentimes, if you have a witness who has given direct testimony near the end of the trial day, you can put together enough of a nonessential cross-examination to carry you to the end of the day so that you can then prepare your heavy barrage overnight.

When you have an important witness you intend to have on the stand for a long time, always try to angle for the sidelines, for the lunch break, for the overnight, so you can properly prepare a full-blown script. You can sometimes get such breathing room by undertaking to first examine the witness as to personal background, education, where he or she has lived throughout his or her life, where he or she has worked, and so on, and so on. You can usually gain about 45 minutes with this type of examination, at the end of which, depending on the time, you might indicate to the court:

Cross-examiner: Your Honor, the next part of my examination is going to be quite lengthy. I wonder if this might be an appropriate time to take a break (adjourn for the day) so that the jury can hear all the cross-examination at one time rather than it being disjointed.

The Court: Very well, ladies and gentlemen of the jury, we'll recess a little early today, and we'll begin a little earlier tomorrow morning to make up for it. Good night, and do not discuss this case amongst yourselves or with anyone else.

PRIOR STATEMENT UNDER OATH DEFINED

A prior statement made under oath may be testimony from a prior trial; or it may be testimony taken during an examination before trial, at a preliminary hearing; or it may have been before a Grand Jury or during some official proceeding, at which the witness, under oath, made statements that run, at least in part, full tilt afoul of the testimony given at the trial. Statements made under oath need not be handwritten or signed by the witness in order to be used during cross-examination. The reliability of the statement rises from the strength of the oath and the sanction of perjury.

ESTABLISHING THE PRIOR STATEMENT

In order to confront the witness with a prior inconsistency under oath, the cross-examiner must establish that:

(a) there has been a previous statement made under oath,

(b) the time,

(c) the place,

(d) the occasion of such previous testimony, and then proceed with the cross-examination to establish the inconsistency.

The following extract, taken directly from an actual criminal prosecution for attempted murder, tried in the Supreme Court, New York County, points out the proper method of utilizing a prior inconsistent statement made under oath.

(a) Background. Your client, a man approximately 45 years of age, with graying hair, is on trial for attempted murder. Two others not on trial and your client are accused of having beaten the complaining victim with a pool cue in a barroom. The victim has just testified that he had been in the bar many times and knew your client to be the regular bartender. He identified him as one of the men who struck him a terrible blow on the back of the head just as he was reaching for the door handle to leave the bar. The victim testified that he turned at the moment of impact and clearly saw your client with a

pool cue in his hand. The witness testifies that he then fell and awoke in the hospital.

(b) The Previous Statement Under Oath. At the conclusion of the witness's testimony, your adversary hands you several pages of the witness's sworn Grand Jury testimony taken several weeks after the incident. The D. A. also gives you a copy of a police report made out by a police detective who visited the witness. This is a prior inconsistent statement made to a third party, reduced to writing by the third party, and is handled in a manner different from a statement made under oath.

The Grand Jury minutes you have just been given contain, *inter alia*, the following:

Q. Do you remember the seventeenth of August and being in the Tipple Inn in New York County?

A. Yes, that's the day they beat me.

Q. Will you tell the Grand Jury what happened to you on that occasion?

A. I was there having a few beers, you know. And then I got up to leave. I walked to the door. As I reached for the door, they were behind me.

Q. Who was behind you?

A. Three of them. A fat guy with blond hair, a skinny guy with black hair, and a guy with white hair.

Q. How were they standing?

A. Behind me.

Q. In what order were they standing, all together, single file?

A. The skinny guy and the blond guy were more or less side by side. The guy with the white hair was right there with them, maybe a little behind.

Q. And then what happened when you reached the door?

A. I reached for the door, you know. And then I caught this terrible shot on the head with something very hard. You know, it wasn't a fist or something. It was a hard object. I spun and saw them standing there. And this one guy had a pool cue in his hand.

Q. Which one had the pool cue in his hand?

A. The guy with the black hair.

Q. What happened after that?

A. After that, they started to beat me all over. I was on the ground. I woke up in the hospital.

Naturally, the adverse witness's trial testimony is gravely inconsistent with his Grand Jury testimony, attributing the actual weapon to a completely different person (your client is not "the guy with the black hair").

USING THE INCONSISTENCY UNDER OATH

Now it is your function to take this Grand Jury testimony, which conflicts dramatically and significantly with the witness's trial testimony, and utilize it to hone the trial testimony, to get it right down to the shape of the truth—in this case, that your client was not the one who hit the victim with the pool cue.

You might wonder, why bother? Perhaps it's just a slight mistake as to who wielded the pool cue; there's no question that the witness was beaten. True. But by whom is the relevant question. The essence of the charge against your client is this witness's identification, and if you can show it is an erroneous identification, that the main witness is lying, mistaken, or confused, you are well on your way to neutralizing his testimony.

Before you begin to question the witness about his Grand Jury testimony, however, you should first reinforce his trial testimony about the man with the white hair wielding the pool cue; sink it into the jurors' minds so that the witness cannot deviate from it.

Previously, I suggested that normally it is counterproductive to cause a witness to repeat his direct testimony. Such repetition only assists your adversary, reinforcing the direct case. However, there are exceptions, as in our current example, when you want to reinforce certain portions of the witness's direct testimony to make sure it is clear and unequivocal, all for the purpose of making his unhorsing the more dramatic.

> ***NOTE:*** *The examination should be subtle, the salient questions smoothly blended in a flow of other questions so as not to tip off the direction or aim of your examination to the witness. In the testimony following, the real meat questions relative to the prior inconsistent statement are marked with an asterisk.*

CROSS-EXAMINATION

Q. Mr. Witness, you say there were three men behind you when you went to reach for the door. Is that right?

A. Yes

Q. One was fat and blond, correct?

A. Yes.

Q. And one was skinny, with black hair?

A. Yes.

Q. The third person had the white hair, an older man?

A. That's right.

***Q.** This is the man with the white hair here, isn't it? (You point to your own client.)

A. Yes.

***Q.** And according to your testimony, it was this man with the white hair who had the pool cue in his hand. Is that right?

A. He's the one.

Q. Before you started to leave the bar did anyone hit you, kick you, punch you, anything like that?

A. No. Only after I got to the door, then they hit me. He hit me (pointing) . . .

Cross-examiner: Your Honor, I ask that the answer be stricken as not responsive and ask you to direct the witness to answer only the question asked and not make gratuitous remarks.

The Court: Yes, stricken. Mr. Witness, you must answer only the questions asked.

Q. Before you reached for the door, did you get punched, hit, kicked, or anything like that?

A. No.

Q. Before you reached for the door, did anyone curse you, say nasty things to you, insult you?

A. No.

Q. So that before you reached for the door, say as you were walking toward the door, there was nothing that had happened to you that was unusual, part of an assault or altercation or any sort. Is that correct?

A. Yes.

Q. It was just an ordinary leaving of a bar, correct?

A. Yes.

Q. And there was no cause for you to be particularly suspicious of anyone in the bar, right?

A. Not until I got to the door.

Q. And then you reached for the doorknob, and only then, for the first time, felt this terrible blow, right?

A. Yes, he hit me with the pool cue. (The witness points to your client.)

Cross-examiner: Your Honor, I ask that this answer be stricken, and I again ask Your Honor to direct the witness to answer only the questions asked.

The Court: Mr. Witness, answer only questions. Don't make gratuitous remarks.

Q. Now, when you were at the door, ready to go out, and you reached for the doorknob, the men were behind you, right?

A. Right behind me.

***Q.** And when you were at the door, ready to go out, reaching for the doorknob, which way were you facing?

A. I was reaching for the door, but I saw them.

***Q.** The question is, when you were at the door, before ever being hit, without any suspicion, and you reached for the doorknob to go out, which way were you facing?

A. I was facing the door, but then I turned and saw him.

***Q.** Before you were hit, then, you were facing the door, weren't you?

A. Yes, but I turned fast.

***Q.** You didn't see anything behind you before you turned to look, did you?

A. I saw him, I saw him hit me.

Q. By the way, was it a hard blow on the head?

A. It was a terrible blow; very hard.

Q. Did it hurt?

A. You get hit on the head with a pool cue and see if it hurts.

Q. Did it knock you down?

A. Not right away. I went down though.

***Q.** How many men had pool cues?

A. Only one—him (pointing to the defendant, your client).

You realize, of course, that this witness is trying very hard to make sure the jury knows who he is identifying. This overkill identification works in your favor, as the jury realizes the extra effort of the witness.

***Q.** And this man is not the fat blond man, is he?

A. No.

***Q.** And he's not the skinny man with the black hair?

A. Right.

Q. You're sure about that?

A. You look at him. He's got blond hair.

Now for the previous statement under oath.

***Q.** Do you remember testifying in front of the Grand Jury in this case, on October 2, 1990? (You now start thumbing through to the page you've previously marked.)

A. Yes.

***Q.** You remember that, at that time, you were sworn to tell the truth, just as you were today?

A. I remember.

Q. And that was about six weeks after this assault took place, Right?

A. Right.

***Q.** By the way, was your memory of the event better six weeks after the incident took place, or today, eleven months later?

A. It was better then, I guess.

***Q.** Do you remember being asked these questions at the Grand Jury, and giving these answers? And please wait until I read both the question and the answer to you, and then tell the court and jury if you remember being asked these questions and giving these answers. On page 16 (you advise the judge and prosecutor) . . .

> **G.J. question:** And what happened when you reached the door?
>
> **G.J. Answer:** I reached for the door, you know, and then I caught this awful shot on the head with something very hard. You know, it wasn't a fist or something. It was a hard object. I spun and saw them standing there. And this one guy had a pool cue in his hand.
>
> **G.J. Question:** Which one had the pool cue in his hands?
>
> **G.J. Answer:** The one with the black hair.

Q. Mr. Witness, do you remember those questions being asked in the Grand Jury and your telling the Grand Jury the man with the black hair had the pool cue?

A. That's not the way it happened.

Cross-examiner: Your Honor, I object to the answer as unresponsive and again ask the court to direct the witness to answer.

The Court: Strike it. Answer the question. Read it back for him, Mr. Reporter.

Q. I'll rephrase it, Your Honor. Do you remember being asked those questions and giving those answers when you were under oath in front of the Grand Jury?

A. It's there, I said it, but it's not the way it happened.

Cross-examiner: Your Honor, will the District Attorney concede that I have read the portions of the Grand Jury testimony of this witness correctly, and exactly as they appear on the pages the District Attorney supplied?

District Attorey: Mr. Cross-Examiner has read the minutes correctly, your Honor.

Q. Was what you swore under oath in the Grand Jury true?

A. I don't remember saying that.

Q. Whether you remember or not, was what I read from the Grand Jury proceedings, six weeks after the assault, an accurate description of the event?

A. That's not the way it happened.

You have now gained about as much as can be gained from the prior inconsistency. It's not necessary to beat the point to death. The jury sees the point, sees the inaccuracy and confusion of the witness; you've brought it squarely and firmly to their attention. Now, continue with other segments of your examination.

Civil or Criminal, the Use of the Oath Prior Inconsistency Is the Same

The use of prior inconsistency under oath is exactly the same, whether the trial issue is civil or criminal. In fact, both the subject of the trial and the source of the prior inconsistent statement is immaterial (examination before trial, preliminary hearing, prior trial, and so forth) as long as the inconsistent statement was under oath and was about the subject matter of the present testimony.

Sink Your Hook Deep in Front of the Jury

You would be serving your client well never to forget that it is not enough merely to establish that the witness made a prior statement under oath concerning the subject matter at hand, or even that such prior statement is inconsistent with the present testimony. You must bring this point home effectively to the jury to have fulfilled your functions. I've said here that you shouldn't try to stretch your cross-examination needlessly, trying for the big kill. On the other hand, it is not enough to merely drag the point into the courtroom, placing it dormant before the jury, without vitality, with only you, the judge, and your adversary knowing its potential explosiveness.

Explode it!

The jurors are not lawyers. They may not realize the legal nuances of an undeveloped destruction. Make sure the jury sees it, knows what the significance is: impale the witness (if you can) on the horns of inconsistency.

WHAT NOT TO DO

The following excerpt of testimony will illustrate how a good piece of evidence can be frittered away, left unexploded. This is what you should not do with a glaring inconsistency given under oath on a prior occasion:

Q. You say the light was green in your favor when you were approaching the intersection of Main Street and Tenth Avenue?

A. That's right.

Q. You're sure of that?

A. Yes.

Q. Do you remember testifying under oath at an examination before trial on September 12, 1976?

A. Yes.

Q. Your Honor, I'd like these minutes marked for identification.

The Court: Very well, mark them.

Q. Read page 35 of these minutes to yourself, Mr. Witness, and when you finish, I'll ask you other questions (hands the EBT to the witness).

A. I've read it.

Q. Did you give those answers to those questions?

A. Yes, I guess I did.

Q. I offer the page in evidence, Your Honor.

The Court: No objection? Received in evidence.

At this point, the cross-examiner sits, prepared to read those minutes to the jury during summation; and you, the reader, have witnessed a total foul-up of good cross-examiner's material. The jury doesn't know the significance of what occurred any more than you, the reader, do right now. By the time summation comes along, they may have already forgotten that meaningless cross-examination.

NOTE: Remember what we said much earlier about always maintaining a tone, a theme for your trial? If the jury had heard the inconsistency, their point of view concerning this witness, the case, and your client might have been entirely different for the rest of the trial. You may find that the Summation is far too late to change their minds.

The able cross-examiner would have ripped into the witness and brought any inconsistency to the jury's attention, focusing the time picture for jury scrutiny. It is very important that the opinion of the jury, as it hears the unfolding evidence, be properly formed. To attempt to withhold good ammunition from the jury until Summation is to run the risk that the juror may make up their minds (although they're not supposed to) before you feed them what you think is salient information.

Get the pieces of the mosaic formed out in the open, in front of the jury; let them see and hear it happen. Summation is a recapitulation of what occurred during the trial, not a one-armed paperhanger's show.

THE PROPER USE

The far better approach for the cross-examiner in the last example would be the following:

Q. You say the light was green in your favor when you were approaching the intersection of Main Street and Tenth Avenue?

A. That's right.

Q. You're sure about that?

A. Yes.

***Q.** Do you remember testifying under oath at an examination before trial on September 12, 1976?

A. Yes.

***Q.** Do you remember these questions being asked and giving these answers; please wait until I read both the questions and the answers, and then I'll ask you another question. (You now read aloud:)

> **EBT Question:** What street were you driving on?
>
> **EBT Answer:** Main Street, approaching Tenth Avenue.
>
> **EBT Question:** Was there a traffic light you could see at that point?
>
> **EBT Answer:** I couldn't see it. A tree blocked my view.
>
> **EBT Question:** When you couldn't see the traffic light, did you slow down?
>
> **EBT Answer:** No.

> **EBT Question:** Did you ever see the traffic light before you reached the intersection?
>
> **EBT Answer:** Yes, just before I reached it.
>
> **EBT Question:** What color was the light when you first saw it?
>
> **EBT Answer:** It just turned red.

Q. Do you remember, Mr. Witness, being asked those questions and giving those answers?

A. It must have been green before it turned red, right?

Q. Do you remember swearing under oath that you either didn't see the light or, when you did—before the intersection—it turned red?

A. Yes.

Q. Was that accurate?

A. (Long pause—no answer.)

Q. I have no further questions.

Now the jury is focused. It can listen to the rest of the case more intelligently; the witness stands in a far different light now from the way he did after the previous example of his cross-examination.

Do not think the illustration of what not to do is naive or insulting. In the midst of battle, while on your feet, you can easily think you did something effectively, but your cerebration was not put into words or action before the jury. It is still inside your head. Neither wishing nor thinking something makes it so. Discipline yourself to actually, and mechanically, like a pilot, use a checklist to be sure you did everything you should have.

CHECKLIST FOR PRIOR OATH INCONSISTENCY

(a) Prior statement under oath;

(b) inconsistent with present testimony;

(c) mark for identification.

(d) Inquire as to recollection of prior testimony under oath

  (i) as to date

  ii) as to place or occasion.

(e) Read both question(s) and answer(s) to witness.

(f) Inquire whether witness recalls being asked such questions and giving such answers.

(g) Inquire whether facts of prior statement are correct . . .

(h) . . . And present testimony in error

(i) if memory of events was better then than it is now.

(j) Inquire—through court—whether adversary concedes you read the transcript exactly as it appears.

PRIOR INCONSISTENCY IN THE HANDWRITING OR BEARING THE SIGNATURE OF THE WITNESS

A prior inconsistent statement not made under oath can still be used directly on cross-examination if, in fact, the prior statement was signed by the witness; or, if not signed, was at least made out in the witness's own handwriting.

Naturally, as with any prior inconsistent statement, the quintessential ingredient before a cross-examination based on the prior statement may be undertaken is that the statement must actually be inconsistent with, or contradictory to, the present trial testimony.

HOW TO USE SUCH PRIOR WRITTEN INCONSISTENCY

Once you've determined that the inconsistency exists, you must then establish the authenticity of the prior document by having the witness identify his or her signature or handwriting. Thereafter, you establish whether the witness recalls writing or signing such statement on the particular occasion it was made, for example immediately after the incident, or at the police station, or when an investigator interviewed him at home two months later; that the reason the information was written or signed was to record the fact of the event for the future; that when the statement was given, it was given truthfully; that (if only signed) the witness read the statement before signing it; the statement the witness made at that time (spell out specific prior inconsistency); and, that the present testimony is not as accurate as the prior statement.

ESTABLISHING THE WRITING

In order to use a prior inconsistent statement in the handwriting of, or signed by the witness, obviously, the *sine qua non* is to establish the fact that the document is, in fact, in the handwriting of, or signed by the witness.

Without that single ingredient being established, you have a document that cannot be used to cross-examine the witness.

The following are examples of preliminary examinations to establish the authenticity of a prior inconsistent statement; either (a) in the witness's handwriting, although it contains no signature, or (b) only signed by the testifying witness.

(After marking the document for identification:)

Q. I show you this document, defendant's Exhibit B for identification, and ask you if this is written in your handwriting.

A. (The witness begins to read the document.)

Q. It's not necessary for you to read the document at this time. The question is, is that written in your handwriting?

A. Yes.

If the document is not made out in the handwriting of the witness, but rather in the handwriting of an investigator, a police officer, or someone else; or if it is typewritten, but contains what purports to be the witness's signature, then you inquire as follows:

Q. I show you this document, defendant's Exhibit B for identification, and ask you if that is your signature which appears at the bottom.

A. I didn't write this out.

Q. Do you know who did?

A. Not off the top of my head.

Q. In any event, do you recognize the signature at the bottom as your own?

A. Yeah, that's my signature.

Now you are in a position to begin to utilize the prior inconsistent statement to discredit the witness.

USING THE WRITTEN OR SIGNED INCONSISTENCY

On direct testimony, the witness testified that he saw the defendant, on a ladder, cause certain canned goods to fall on the plaintiff's head. You now cross-examine:

Q. Who was present when you saw the shelf of canned goods fall on the plaintiff's head?

A. I heard the noise, turned, and saw the plaintiff just as he was hit with the cans and John Smith, defendant, was on the ladder right next to him.

Q. You saw John Smith right as you turned after hearing the noise?

A. Absolutely.

Cross-examiner: Your Honor, I'd like to have this document marked for identification.

The Court: Very well, mark it.

Q. Mr. Witness, do you recognize this document, defendant's Exhibit B for identification?

A. It's got my signature on the bottom.

Q. That is your signature?

A. Yes.

Q. You remember an investigator talking to you on April 15, 1991, at your home, about this case, and writing down what you said?

A. Yes.

Q. And when you signed this document, what is written on the pages before you was already there?

A. Yes.

Q. And you read what the investigator wrote down before you signed your name on the bottom of the page?

A. Yes.

Q. In fact, there were some mistakes made by the investigator that were crossed out, and you put your initials next to the crossed-out parts; isn't that correct?

A. Yes, those are my initials.

Q. Who wrote the initials that appear on this document?

A. I did.

Q. And when you read it, signed it, and initialed it, what you signed was an accurate account of what had occurred, wasn't it?

A. Yes.

Q. You weren't telling the investigator a phony story, were you?

A. No.

Q. And this statement was signed one week after the accident?

A. Yes.

Q. Was your memory of what occurred the day of the accident better one week after the accident or today, two years after the accident?

A. Better then, I'd say.

Q. May I have that document back, please. Do you recall that you told the investigator that, when you turned, you only saw plaintiff on the floor, and in your fright and concern you did not notice anyone else?

A. That's not correct. I did see [the defendant].

Q. Would you read the second paragraph of this document? (You hand the document back to the witness).

Your Adversary: Your Honor, I object to Mr. Cross-examiner reading from a document not in evidence. Let Mr. Cross-examiner introduce the entire document in evidence.

Cross-examiner: Your Honor, this document deals with many other matters I do not believe are relevant at this time. I do not offer the document in evidence. I merely wish to use it as a prior inconsistent statement. The witness has already identified the signature as his own.

The Court: Mr. Adversary, the document need not be introduced in evidence. You can introduce it on your own case if you see fit.

Q. Have you read the document?

A. Yes.

Q. And didn't you previously say that, in your fright and concern for the plaintiff, you did not pay attention to anyone else?

A. Yes.

Q. That you rushed over to help the plaintiff, and Mr. Smith, the defendant, came over and was also helping?

A. Yes.

Q. And isn't that the way it actually happened?

A. That's not the way I recall it happening.

Q. Your memory of this was better, though, on April 15, 1991?

A. I guess it was.

SIGNIFICANTLY DIFFERENT FROM USE OF A STATEMENT UNDER OATH

Notice that, while still dealing with prior inconsistent statements, the use of a statement made under oath is vastly different from one written or signed by the witness. In the oath statement, you ordinarily have questions and answers that must be read to the witness and he must then be asked if he recalls the questions being asked and recalls giving the answers.

In the written or signed statement by the witness, there are no questions or answers, but rather an entire statement. You must either let the witness first read the prior statement, and then question the witness as to its contents, or you must introduce the statement in evidence and read it—with the inconsistency it contains—to the injury.

INTRODUCING THE PRIOR STATEMENT INTO EVIDENCE

As outlined in the preceding excerpted sample cross-examination, the prior inconsistent statement need not be introduced in evidence in order to be utilized on cross-examination. This holds true for both a prior statement under oath as well as a statement written or signed by the witness. Oftentimes, the statement contains matters in addition to the prior inconsistency that would be improper for the jury to see. This does not mean, however, that there are not times when you do wish the document to be before the jury *in toto*. If the document is strongly in your favor, or if the witness denies the inconsistency, it is essential that you have the document introduced in evidence for later reference, or for tangible evidence of the inconsistency.

INTRODUCING THE PRIOR INCONSISTENT DOCUMENT INTO EVIDENCE

Having had the witness identify the handwriting or the signature as his own, you then establish the time, place, and occasion when such statement was made. You may then introduce the document into evidence. It is advisable not to coldly read a document to the jury, but rather to establish its significance with preliminary questions so that the inconsistency has some meaning.

For Example: You have a witness on the stand who has testified that she saw your client on a fire escape leading away from the scene of a crime. You have in your hand a statement made to an investigator that the witness could not identify the man on the fire escape because she did not have a chance to see the man's face. You should inquire as follows:

Q. Ms. Witness, you say that Mr. Defendant is the man that you saw on the fire escape on the occasion in question?

A. Yes.

Q. Do you remember an investigator coming to your house to interview you on the fifteenth of April 1991?

A. Yes, I remember.

Q. And do you remember that at that time the investigator asked you certain questions about what you saw on the day in question?

A. Yes.

Cross-examiner: Your Honor, I would like this document marked for identification.

The Court: Mark it defendant's Exhibit B for identification.

Q. I show you defendant's Exhibit B for identification and ask you if you recognize the signature on the bottom of it?

A. It's my signature.

Q. In fact, there are various mistakes made in the writing of the document, and there are initials next to the mistakes and the crossings out. Who wrote those initials?

A. I did.

Q. And, on the bottom, is that your handwriting, which indicates that the preceding statement is true to the best of your knowledge?

A. Yes, I wrote that.

Q. And that was true, at the time you wrote it, wasn't it?

A. Yes.

Q. And didn't you say at that time, and isn't it contained in that document, that you could not identify the man on the fire escape because you never had a chance to see the man's face?

A. Did I say that?

Q. That's the question. Perhaps the document, if you read it to yourself, will refresh your memory.

A. (She reads) That's what it says.

Cross-examiner: Your Honor, I offer the document in evidence.

The Court: Show it to Mr. Adversary. Any objection?

Adversary: I do object, Your Honor, as being improper use of a prior statement.

The Court: No, I think it's proper. The witness has identified the signature as her own. Received.

Cross-examiner: Your Honor, at this time, I'd like to read part of this document to the jury.

Adversary: Your Honor, if Mr. Cross-examiner is going to read from the Exhibit, he should read all of it.

The Court: It's actually not necessary to read any of it to the jury. The document is in evidence. If there's a portion, however, that Mr. Cross-examiner doesn't read, and you want it read, I'll permit you to read it to the jury. Proceed.

Cross-examiner: I'm reading from defendant's Exhibit B, now in evidence, which reads, in part, "I was in my apartment. I heard a noise on the fire escape. When I looked out the window, I saw a man going up to the next floor. I didn't get to see what he looked like, because he was already higher than my window."

Q. (to the witness) You did say that to the investigator on April 15, 1991, didn't you?

A. I guess I did.

Cross-examiner: I have no further questions, Your Honor.

REMINDERS CONCERNING INTRODUCING A DOCUMENT IN EVIDENCE

(a) The document that you wish to use, as a prior inconsistent statement, to cross-examine a witness, whether that document be a prior statement under oath, a prior handwritten document, or one that has been merely subscribed by the witness, need not be introduced in evidence in order to use the same for cross-examination.

(b) If you do wish to introduce the document in evidence, you need not read it to the jury at the time of introduction. However, I strongly recommend that you do. If it's significant enough to be introduced in evidence, it's significant enough for you to read to the jury and hammer home the point.

(c) When you do read from the document, you do not have to read the entire document. You can read as much of it as you desire. Your adversary may object. The court may require you to read the entire document. But, properly, you could read any, all, or none of the document to the jury.

(d) Your adversary can read the rest, any, all, or none of the rest of the document to the jury.

ONLY A PORTION OF THE DOCUMENT NEED BE INTRODUCED

As indicated, there are times when a document contains not only an inconsistency that you wish to have before the jury, but other extraneous, even damaging, material that would not properly be introduced into evidence.

In this situation, you can request of the court that your introduction be limited to the particular portion of the prior statement. This is quite proper, as the document is not even evidence in the case; remember, even if introduced, it is only proof of the inconsistency and the tendency of that prior inconsistency to affect the credibility of the witness. The document is not evidence-in-chief.

Ordinarily, there is no difficulty eliminating extraneous material in the statement, as you can use blank paper to form a mask over the unwanted portion of the statement, admitting only the wanted portions of the document, and the excised version can then be introduced in evidence in place and instead of the original. The original should be marked as court's exhibit for preservation in the event of an appeal.

When the Witness Denies the Writing Is Hers

It is conceivable that the witness may deny that the signature on the document is her own, or deny that the handwriting that made out the document is her own. This can be a very serious problem, for, as indicated here, the identification of the writing is essential to an examination based upon a prior inconsistent statement allegedly written, or at least signed, in the handwriting of the witness.

Where the document was made out by a third person, that is, an investigator, and only signed by the witness, and where the witness denies that the signature is her own, you may treat the document as a prior inconsistent statement made to a third person (see infra) and proceed to an examination of the witness, laying the foundation to bring in the third person to testify that the witness did indeed make such statement, exactly as it appears on the document.

Where the document contains a typewritten or handwritten statement allegedly made out by the witness, however, and the witness has denied signing the statement or has denied the handwriting in which the statement is written, you have a very serious problem that must first be resolved by other proofs before you can further cross-examine the witness based on that statement.

Prior Inconsistent Statements Made to Third Parties Recorded

Another form of inconsistent statement that can be utilized on cross-examination is a prior inconsistency that was made orally to a third person, and which that third person thereafter reduced to writing.

These inconsistencies may take the form of an oral statement made to a policeman at the scene of an accident, thereafter incorporated in the policeman's written official report; or a statement made to a hospital attendant or nurse, thereafter incorporated into the hospital record; or a statement made to an employer concerning the happening of an industrial accident, again being made part of a report by the employer; or any similar situation of a statement being made to any third person, who thereafter reduces said statement to writing.

Completely different from oath or handwritten inconsistency

While prior inconsistencies made orally to a third person are indeed prior inconsistencies, they are completely different from both a prior inconsistency made under oath or one made in the handwriting of the testifying witness. The method of using such third party statement on cross-examination is completely different from the method of using other inconsistencies.

The basic difference is that the statement previously made to a third person cannot be used directly to confront the testifying witness who has denied having made such prior statement. Of course, if the witness admits that he or she has made such prior inconsistent statement, you have accomplished as much as you could accomplish with that portion of your cross-examination. For the most part, however, witnesses on the stand are reluctant to admit that their present testimony is erroneous, or at least inconsistent with prior versions of the same event.

It is actually hearsay

If the witness denies having made a prior inconsistent statement to a third person, or having signed a statement prepared by a third person, you may not directly confront or cross-examine the testifying witness with the fact that a third person attributes a prior, different, and inconsistent statement to the witness. You may establish only that the witness denies the statement.

Without the stamp of authenticity of oath or acknowledgment of the witness's own handwriting, a statement made to a third person, even where that third person had reduced the same to writing, runs full afoul of the hearsay rule. Simply put, the writing of the third person, wherein it is indicated that the testifying witness made a prior inconsistent statement, is not the writing, or, actually, the statement of the testifying witness at all. It is the statement of the third person. And the testifying witness cannot be cross-examined about the statement that some other person has made.

Simply put, a witness to an accident has told the policeman who responded that she, the witness, did not see the accident happen. The policeman writes such statement in his police report, properly and clearly attributing the statement to the witness. On the stand, the witness to the event testifies on direct as an actual eyewitness. When you, on cross-examination, confront the witness with questions as to whether or not, on prior occasions, the witness made inconsistent, contradictory statements concerning her view of the accident, the witness denies having made such prior statement.

Thus, the present testimony of the witness is an actual eyewitness account of the event and a denial of ever having made a prior inconsistent statement. The conflicting written report of the police officer is hearsay to the testifying witness, for it is the writing and the statement of the police officer, a third person, not the testifying witness, even though the police officer's report attributes the prior statement to the testifying witness. You cannot directly confront the witness with the police officer's report; you cannot do anything more than ask the witness if she made such a statement to the police officer.

A denial then requires you to lay a proper foundation for calling the third person to the stand for that third person's version of the taking of the oral statement from the testifying eyewitness.

Thus, unlike the other inconsistent statements previously covered, where you could directly ask the witness about the prior inconsistency, the inconsistency made to a third person requires a far different approach and method to use.

THE WRITTEN STATEMENT OF THE THIRD PERSON CAN BE INTRODUCED INTO EVIDENCE THROUGH THE THIRD PERSON

While you cannot use the oral statement made to a third person to cross-examine the testifying, denying witness, there is a method of utilizing such prior statement if the proper foundation is laid to later call that third person to the stand to testify about the taking of the prior statement.

BACKGROUND FOR LAYING THE FOUNDATION

An example of the method of using a prior, inconsistent oral statement to a third person, which statement was reduced to writing by the third person, is in order.

A. Background

This is an excerpt from a homicide trial in New York County Supreme Court. On the stand was a witness who had made many prior statements to police officers who the witness thought were violating their duty by accepting bribes to cover up the witness's illegal activities.

Actually, the police officers were making reports of every conversation they had with the witness, and these reports were turned over to defense counsel for cross-examination purposes after the witness's direct testimony. Amongst the statements turned over was a report in which the witness had described to the two police officers how he, the witness, had murdered someone (not the subject of the prosecution in the case on trial) in Florida. This example examination not only exposes a prior inconsistent statement of the testifying witness, but at the same time serves to further undercut the reliability of the witness by showing a propensity to vicious and criminal acts and an immoral character, which is a subject we shall explore in more depth infra.

B. The Police Report

Clark met with us in the Two Steps Down Inn on the evening of April 15, 1991, at or about 8 P.M. It was a meeting to collect the money for the week. He invited us to have drinks with him, which we did. While speaking generally, the witness related to us how he had murdered a person known as John Smith, in Florida, in 1971. Clark told us that John Smith was involved in a scheme to bankrupt a chewing-gum business with Clark, but that since the police were then investigating the business, Smith was very nervous and refused to lie to the police if they questioned him.

Clark told us how he lured Smith to Florida on a fishing trip. That, when out of sight of land (Key Largo) on the boat, he shot Smith in the chest with a .38 caliber revolver. He shot twice. When he went to grab Smith by the arm to lift him over the side, Smith grabbed Clark. At that point, Clark took a fishing knife—one used to clean fish—and stabbed Smith repeatedly in the chest until the knife broke in Smith's chest. He then picked up a gasoline can and beat Smith over the head with the can. Afterward, Jones, who had also come from New York to Florida with Clark and Smith, and who had been steering the boat, took a .22 caliber rifle and shot Smith in the head. The two of them then, with handcuffs, tied Smith to a heavy weight on the boat and threw Smith overboard.

Clark said that the water was so clear that he could see Smith on the bottom, after he was thrown overboard, with his eyes still open. He also said that he thereafter had nightmares for months thinking about Smith in the water.

I questioned Clark as much as I could, but could get no better location for Smith's dumping site than somewhere off Key Largo. We indicated that we thought he was making the entire story about Smith up, but he swore it was true.

Further investigation from official police files reveal that one John Smith of the address given by Clark reportedly left for Washington in 1971 and has not been seen or heard from since.

Det. M. Johnson
Counter-Signed: Lt. John Official

You can rely on one thing for certain. The witness is not going to admit to you or the jury, on the stand, that he is guilty of murder. If he does, of course, you have him admitting heinous crimes. On the other hand, if he does not admit such crime, you should question him in depth about the statement and the murder. Force him into continual denial, laying a solid foundation to use the prior inconsistency that shall establish the witness's unreliability, as well the witness's immoral, unreliable character.

Another thing that you, as cross-examiner, can rely on is that the disinterested police officer who made the foregoing official report in fulfillment of his official duties, who signed the same and had it countersigned by his superior, is not going to testify that the report is inaccurate, untruthful, or in any fashion a deviation from actual events. It stands to reason that the officer would be jeopardizing not only his credibility, but his job, by testifying that he made out the official report with less than absolute rectitude.

Now, although you have substantial ammunition in your hand to show that the witness made a prior statement inconsistent with his trial denial of being a murderer and that he is a highly immoral character as well as a liar, all to be buttressed by the rectitude and authority of the police department through the person of the detective who made the report, you must still lay a proper foundation or the judge will not permit you later to call the detective to the stand to testify about the prior statement.

Therefore, in laying the foundation, you must give the witness sufficient information to refresh his recollection; to call his mind to the time, the place, and the person to whom the alleged statement was made; and you must also refresh his recollection as to the alleged statement.

If you do not do all of this in a specified fashion, you have not laid a proper foundation. If you do ask the witness the proper questions, however, fully giving him an opportunity to remember and agree or deny that he made such prior statement, and he denies having made the statement, then you can later call the third person to the stand to testify about the prior statement.

AN EXAMPLE OF LAYING THE FOUNDATION

Q. Did you ever meet with Detective Johnson at the Two Steps Down Inn?

A. Many times.

Q. Do you recall meeting with him on the fifteenth of April 1991?

A. I might have.

Q. Did you ever tell Detective Johnson, at that time and place, that you had participated in the murder of an individual named Smith?

A. No.

Right at this point, you know you have him!

Q. Did you tell Detective Johnson, at that time and place, that you had had a scheme with Smith to bankrupt a chewing-gum firm?

A. No.

Q. Did you tell Detective Johnson, at the Two Steps Down Inn, on April 15, 1991, that Smith told you he was going to tell the police everything he knew when they questioned him?

A. No.

Q. Did you tell Detective Johnson, at that time and place, that you lured Smith to Florida on a fishing trip?

A. I never did, no.

NOTE: *You cannot be asking the witness these questions by reading from the statement of Detective Johnson, for that would be reading from something not in evidence. Thus, you have to remember the things that Detective Johnson's statement contains and ask the questions without reading from the statement. You could, surely, from time to time, check your notes, in which you would have Johnson's statement; but you cannot read from it in front of the jury.*

Each denial by the witness, eo instanti, creates another area to attack with the prior inconsistent statement, which conflicts with the horrendous statement to which the police detective will have to testify to if called to the stand. This is the reason to go through the statements specifically.

Q. Did you tell Detective Johnson, and assume that all these questions relate to the same time and place, did you tell Detective Johnson that you shot Smith with a .38 caliber revolver in the chest?

A. Absolutely not.

Q. Did you tell Detective Johnson that thereafter, in attempting to throw Smith overboard, Smith grabbed your hand?

A. No.

Q. Did you tell Detective Johnson that you panicked and grabbed a scaling knife and began stabbing Smith in the chest many times?

A. No.

Q. Did you tell Detective Johnson that the knife broke in Smith's chest?

A. No.

Q. Did you tell Detective Johnson in the Two Steps Inn on April 15, 1991, that you then began to hit Smith in the head with a gasoline can?

A. No.

Q. Did you then tell Detective Johnson that you then handcuffed Smith to a barbell and threw him overboard?

A. No.

Q. Did you then tell Detective Johnson that you had nightmares for months because you could see Smith looking up through the water with his eyes open?

A. No.

Now you have set the stage, have nailed down the witness's position firmly for the jury. As indicated at the outset of this book, a trial is like assembling a mosaic, the ultimate aim being the overall view of the evidence that you present to the jury at summation. The entire picture need not be put together in one continuous movement. So, in the case of the witness who has just now denied both the murder and having spoken to the police officer about it, the witness steps down from stand. Your adversary continues with his evidence-in-chief. You bide your time until it is your turn to introduce evidence.

If there are any steps that must be taken to ensure the appearance of the third person at the trial, such as a subpoena, you should undertake them immediately. When the appropriate moment arrives, you put the third person (here, the detective) on the stand.

THE THIRD-PERSON INQUIRY

Q. Detective Johnson, by whom are you employed?

A. The Police Department, City of New York.

Q. And your assignment?

A. Vice Squad.

Q. How long have you been a detective?

A. Eleven years.

Q. And in 1991, did you know a person by the name of Harold Clark?

A. Yes.

Q. In reference to an official investigation?

A. Yes.

Q. Can you tell us about the investigation?

A. We were investigating prostitution, and we had reason to believe that Mr. Clark was involved. We questioned him. He suggested that he could make it worth my while if I cooperated with him. I indicated to him that I would think about it. I reported the same to my superiors, and they indicated that I should make it appear that I was going along with him so that I could get further information which might otherwise be unavailable.

Q. And did you work with Clark?

A. I made it appear that way.

Q. Did you take money from him?

A. I did; and then I vouchered it, and made a report each time that I did.

Q. So that you were just pretending to be taking a bribe from Clark?

A. That's right, sir.

Q. And did you meet with Clark on April 15, 1991?

A. I believe I did, sir.

Q. I show you this, which I have had marked defendant's Exhibit B for identification. I ask you if you know what this is?

A. It's a copy of a DD5, a report which I turned in concerning Clark.

Q. Is your signature on the bottom of this document?

A. It is.

Q. And was this document, your report, also countersigned by someone?

A. It was. By Lieutenant John Official.

Q. And was this report turned in as an official report in compliance with your official duties as a detective on the police force?

A. It was.

Q. And when you made the same out, you were making it out carefully and as accurately as you could, knowing that it was an official report?

A. Yes, sir.

Q. On April 15, 1991, did Clark tell you that Smith had said he was going to tell all he knew to the police, if and when questioned?

A. He did.

Q. Did Clark tell you that he lured Smith to Key Largo, Florida, for a fishing trip?

A. I believe he did.

Q. Is there any doubt about the fact that he said that?

A. I'm not too sure about each thing he said. We met and spoke many times.

Q. Look at your report, Detective, and see if, after reading it, your memory is refreshed on that point.

A. (After reading) He did say that.

Q. Did he also say, on that occasion, Clark, that is, say that when out of sight of land, he shot Smith with a .38 caliber pistol?

A. He did.

Q. Did he say, when attempting to throw Smith overboard, that Smith grabbed his hand?

A. He did sir.

Q. Did he tell you that he then started to stab Smith in the chest with a scaling knife?

A. A fishing knife; yes, sir.

Q. Did Clark also say that the knife broke in Smith's chest?

A. Yes, sir.

Q. Did he tell you that he then started hitting him on the head with a gasoline can?

A. Yes.

Q. Did Clark also tell you that another person named Jones, on the boat, also from New York, shot Smith with a .22 caliber rifle?

A. Yes, I believe he did.

Q. Is there a question about that in your mind, officer?

A. No, not really.

Q. Did he say they threw Smith overboard and that he was attached to a weight by handcuffs?

A. Yes, sir.

Q. Did he say he had nightmares for months after that, thinking about Smith with his eyes open on the bottom of the sea?

A. Yes, sir.

Q. Did Clark swear to you that the things he told you were true?

A. I'm not sure about that.

Q. Would you read your report and see if that refreshes your memory?

A. (After reading) I told him I didn't believe him and he swore that it was true; yes, sir.

You have now completed all the steps in the use of prior inconsistent statements, and the credibility and reliability of the witness is squarely before the jury for its determination.

CHECKLIST

A. You must apprise the witness on the stand:

i. where

ii. when, and

iii. to whom a statement had previously been made.

B. You must inquire specifically of the witness if he or she had ever said (whatever was said) to such a person, at such a time, and so forth, thus establishing the trial testimonial position.

C. You must call the third person to the witness stand to testify to the actual, original, inconsistent statement.

PRIOR ORAL STATEMENT MADE TO A THIRD PERSON NOT RECORDED

Another variation of a prior inconsistent statement is one that may take the form of an oral statement made to a police officer at the scene of an accident, to a hospital attendant, or doctor, or to any third person on any prior occasion, which has never been memorialized in writing or a report of any sort.

DIFFERENT AGAIN

Again, these prior inconsistent oral statements must be treated by the cross-examiner in different fashion from prior inconsistent statements under oath, or in the witness's writing, or even prior inconsistencies made to third persons that were thereafter memorialized. The reason, of course, is that these inconsistencies have neither the authenticity attached to a handwritten or sworn statement under oath, nor the memorialization of a prior oral statement that the third person reduced to writing. In short, this type of prior inconsistency is the most unstable and volatile of all the prior inconsistencies.

THESE CANNOT BE USED FOR DIRECT CONFRONTATION

As with the prior oral inconsistency that was reduced to writing by the third person, these oral inconsistencies that were not memorialized cannot be used to directly confront the witness as you might do with a prior inconsistency made under oath or made in the handwriting of the witness.

When you are aware of a prior oral inconsistency, all that can be done is to ask the witness whether on the day, at a particular place, to a particular person, he or she said whatever it is that comprises the inconsistency. If the witness admits the prior inconsistency, of course, then you have effectively brought out before the jury the possible unreliability of the witness. If, on the other hand, the witness denies making such prior oral statement, you must then bring forward the third person to testify as to the prior oral statement.

The reason that you may not directly confront the witness with the third person's version of what was said on a prior occasion is, obviously, that the witness on the stand has testified such oral statement was never made. As to the witness, the declaration of the third person is hearsay; the witness cannot be cross-examined about what someone else says the witness said. The only one who can introduce the oral statement into evidence is the third person who alleges that the statement was made.

STATEMENTS TO THIRD PERSONS ARE VOLATILE

A word of caution: cross-examination based on unmemorialized, prior, inconsistent oral statements is more difficult and possibly more dangerous than other types of prior inconsistencies, because of the fact that the inconsistency has not been memorialized and is not, therefore, as unchanging as a statement recorded, sworn, or signed. This type of oral inconsistency is subject to the frailties of all verbal communication, including forgetfulness, variation, haziness, and even denial by the third person that such a statement was ever made.

Therefore, you must be aware that the statement you are now dealing with is as volatile and unstable as nitroglycerine. Be sure of your third person and of what he or she will testify before you get yourself totally committed to this line of cross-examination. Once sure, however, this method can be as effective a method of utilizing a prior inconsistent statement as any of the others already discussed.

LAYING THE FOUNDATION FOR THE ORAL INCONSISTENCY

The method of laying a foundation for cross-examination based on an unmemorialized oral inconsistency is similar to the foundation needed for the inconsistencies to third persons that were memorialized (supra). But these again differ from the foundation required for inconsistency made under oath or in the handwriting of the third person.

When you are aware that the testifying witness made a prior oral statement to a third person, which is directly contradictory to the testimony you have just heard from the witness's own mouth, in order to use such prior oral inconsistency, you must:

(a) remind the witness of the time, place, and person to whom something inconsistent to the trial testimony was said;

(b) ask the witness whether he or she made such inconsistent statement, specifying the actual inconsistency; and

(c) produce the third person who heard such inconsistency to testify.

EXAMPLES OF FOUNDATION

An example of the foundation that must be laid in order to use such prior inconsistent oral statement made to a third person is as follows:

Background: The issue at hand is an accident where an eyewitness told a storekeeper at or near the scene of the accident something different from the direct trial testimony of the eyewitness.

Q. You've testified that you saw the vehicle of the defendant go through the stop sign and crash directly into the side of the plaintiff's vehicle, isn't that right?

A. That's right.

Q. Do you recall, just after the accident, that you spoke to Mr. Mint, the owner of the hardware store in front of which the accident occurred?

A. I'm not sure if he is the owner.

Q. Whether he is the owner or not, you do recall speaking, just after the accident, to the man who worked in the hardware store, don't you?

A. Yes. He came out to see what happened, and we were talking while we waited for the police and the ambulance to arrive.

Q. So there's no question that you do remember the man, whether he owned the hardware store or not, who was working in the hardware store at the time of the accident.

A. No question.

Q. You discussed the accident with him, didn't you?

A. I don't know if we discussed it. We spoke about it, mentioned it. I mean, it was right there in front of the two of us.

Q. At that time and at that place, did you say to the man from the hardware store that you had been looking in the window of the store at the tools and heard a big crash behind you, and you turned to see the cars for the first time?

A. Did I say that?

Q. That's the question; do you remember ever saying, immediately after the accident, to the man from the hardware store, that you were looking in the store window when the crash occurred?

A. I never said that.

NOW—THE THIRD-PARTY EXAMINATION

Having completed the preceding foundation for the use of prior, inconsistent oral statement made to a third person—in this case, the owner or worker from the hardware store—you must now produce the third person for testimony. If your adversary does not call that third-person witness to the stand, then on your case, or on your rebuttal, call that third-person witness to the stand solely for the purpose of affecting the credibility of the testifying eyewitness.

When you have that third-person witness on the stand, your examination should be as follows:

Q. Sir, do you own the hardware store located at 54 Main Street?

A. Yes.

Q. And were you at your place of business on the thirty-first of May 1980?

A. I was.

Q. And did an accident occur on that day, in the street in front of your store?

A. It did. Two cars crashed in the street right in front of my store.

Q. Did you see the accident yourself?

A. No, I didn't.

Q. Did you go out of your store at any time after the accident?

A. Sure. Right after the accident.

Q. By the way, do you know Mr. Eyewitness?

A. Yes. I know him from around town. I've seen him many times around town.

Q. Did you see him on the day of the accident?

A. When I went outside, he was standing right in front of my store.

Q. Did you have a conversation with him?

A. Not much. I asked him what happened.

Q. Did Mr. Eyewitness say anything?

A. Said he didn't know exactly. He said he was looking at the shovels in my window; it was springtime, you know; and he heard a crash behind him. When he looked, the cars had already crashed.

Q. This is what Mr. Eyewitness said to you?

A. Yes.

Q. Is there any question about that in your mind?

A. Of course not, why should there be?

This examination is an example of the mosaic art of cross-examination, for when the actual eyewitness finished testifying, he denied wholly that he had ever said his back was to the accident when it happened. He got off the stand with those words ringing in the jurors' ears.

Now, much later, on your own case, you have put a witness on the stand who refutes the eyewitness account. You did not give the big kill, or instantly shove the big lie down the witness's throat. Yet, for the purposes of your client's case, you have effectively, ultimately, neutralized the eyewitness. Now, at Summation, you will put all the pieces together for the jury. As said before, however, all the pieces must be there in order to put them together for the Summation; so keep in mind where you're going and make sure you touch all the bases on the way.

BE SURE OF THE THIRD PERSON'S TESTIMONY

In this type of examination, it is essential that you first investigate and ferret out the prior statements of the witness. When you have carefully done this, and have found that the witness has made a prior inconsistent statement to a third person, you then should interview that third person to get a feel for her capacity to remember the prior statement, her capacity to testify, her capacity for truthfulness, and so forth.

In other words, don't put a witness on the stand cold, one to whom you have never spoken, or whose testimony remains a mystery to you. You could be very rudely surprised.

In fact, the best practice is always to take a written statement from a prospective witness, even a negative statement, so that the witness cannot have her memory suddenly refreshed by an eager adversary. If you have a written statement from the third person, that does not take the place of a memorialization of the original prior inconsistency of the testifying witness, of course; but at least it gives you some strength in your cross-examination, knowing that the third party will not suffer amnesia or change of testimony after you put her on the stand.

Thus, be sure of the testimony of the third person and try to have it nailed down before you put her on the stand to bolster your case. You want the third party's testimony to be a boost, not a knock on your case.

CHECKLIST

(a) Investigate and discover the prior inconsistency.

(b) Be sure to interview the third person.

(c) When the original witness is on the stand, you must establish whether he recalls making a statement at

i. the time,

ii. the place,

iii. on the date,

iv. and to the third person (named or identified).

(d) Ask the witness if the following specific statement was made on that occasion to the specified third person. Then specify the statement.

(e) Upon a denial that such statement was made, you have completed phase 1 of the interrogatory. Later, on your own case, you must produce the third person to testify.

REFRESHING RECOLLECTION

When a witness on the stand testifies that he cannot recall a certain fact or event, his recollection may be refreshed by the use of any extrinsic object that refreshes that witness's recollection.

You, as cross-examiner, may show the witness a menu from a restaurant that in no other fashion is relevant to the case; or a newspaper, a piece of wood, a bumper from a car; in short, anything that may, in some fashion, jar the memory of the witness. The essential prerequisites that must be present to refresh the recollection by the use of such extrinsic objects are

(a) the memory of the witness must first be exhausted before you can resort to refreshing; and

(b) the object used must, in some fashion, tend to refresh or remind the witness of what he originally knew.

REFRESHING IS NOT A SUBSTITUTE FOR THE WITNESS'S KNOWLEDGE

The use of extrinsic objects in order to refresh the recollection of the witness is just that: a refreshment of a memory or a knowledge that was originally there. In order for you to be permitted to refresh that memory, the witness had to have known the information originally and now have no recollection of the fact or the event. The use of the extrinsic object is not, therefore, intended to permit the witness to read a document or see an exhibit that, in some fashion, will give the witness an answer, or make obvious the fact about which you want the witness to testify. Such an attempt shall immediately call for an objection by your adversary and an adverse ruling from the court.

Laying the Foundation

The foundation for refreshing recollection is rather simple compared to some of the other formulae that have preceded this section. All that is necessary—but it is essential—is that the witness indicate that he cannot remember, that he has no recollection of the fact sought by the questioner. But that point must be reached before the questioner proffers the extrinsic object intended to refresh.

Thus, in a civil case, where the condition of the roadway and the weather are significant to show that the plaintiff was not acting prudently under the conditions then and there existing, you might ask an independent witness the following:

Q. And what were the weather conditions on the early morning of April 15, 1980?

A. I know it was nice later in the day. I'm not really sure about the early morning.

Q. You were awake in the early morning, were you not?

A. Oh, I was awake all right. I just don't, to tell you the truth, remember the weather early in the morning.

Q. I show you this and ask you whether this, in any fashion, refreshes your recollection of the weather on that day?

(You hand the witness a copy of that day's newspaper.)

The Court: Don't say anything, just look at that silently, and then say just, "Yes it does," or "No it does not refresh my recollection."

A. Yes, it does.

Q. And do you now recall what the weather conditions were on the early morning of April 15, 1980?

A. There was a sudden, kind of flash storm, with lightning and thunder. And a pretty heavy wind, now that I recollect.

You might just as easily have handed the witness a copy of the weather bureau report of April 15th, or an insurance policy, or a piece of siding from a barn—anything that might have refreshed the witness's past recollection of the event. In other words, the purpose of the extrinsic object is to jar the witness's recall. It is totally unimportant what it is that helps the witness to recollect. The extrinsic object is not, in any fashion, intended to give the witness the information about which to testify; it is merely to trigger his past recollection.

DON'T BE PREMATURE

If the witness is not in such situation where his present memory and recollection of the event are exhausted, you may not resort to an attempt to refresh the witness's memory with extrinsic objects. For instance:

Q. What color was the car that you saw that day?

A. It was either blue or dark gray; dark blue or dark gray.

Q. I show you this photograph and ask you whether this refreshes your recollection as to the actual color of the car you saw.

Your Adversary: Objection, Your Honor, the witness hasn't indicated anything that suggests that his memory needs refreshment.

The Court: Quite correct. You haven't laid the proper foundation as yet, Mr. Cross-examiner.

Q. Did you get a good look at the car?

A. Actually, I didn't. I didn't really know what color it was.

Q. I now show you this photograph and ask you whether this refreshes your recollection as to the color of the car you saw that day.

Your Adversary: Objection, Your Honor, the witness has testified he doesn't know. There is no refreshing necessary here. This is leading.

The Court: Quite correct. You haven't laid the proper foundation, Mr. Cross-examiner.

This flurry of questions all resulting in your being set down by the judge is not helping you in front of the jury. Don't strain the situation where it is not called for; don't attempt to use a piece of evidence improperly, or to conduct an improper examination of the witness. It could backfire by turning the judge or the jury against you.

In the preceding situation, however, if you had brought the witness to the following point, you would then have been permitted to refresh his recollection as to the color of the car:

Q. When you say the car was either blue or dark gray, you're saying for sure that it wasn't yellow, red, or brown?

A. No, it was either dark gray or blue, dark blue.

Q. And in order to give that answer, you have a picture in your mind, a recollection of what that car looked like, however vague the picture you recall?

A. Oh, I have a picture in my mind, all right. It was either dark gray or dark blue.

Q. Can you try to concentrate and bring that memory into sharper focus and see if you can recollect whether it was the blue or gray you have testified about?

A. (The witness concentrates silently, then shakes his head.) No, I can't tell you, to tell the truth.

Q. I show you this photograph and ask you whether or not this refreshes your recollection.

A. (He studies the photograph.) No, it doesn't.

NOTE: Once the witness tells you whether or not the photograph refreshes his recollection, he is then back in the present memory, and his testimony is of the present recollection. In other words, the refreshment is intended only to bring his present memory up to date, to refresh it. But the testimony that you elicit is from the present memory. Thus, the examination might proceed as follows:

Q. I show you this photograph and ask you whether or not it refreshes your recollection as to the color of the car you saw that day.

A. (He studies the photograph.) It does.

Q. And now that you've had the opportunity to refresh your recollection, what color was the car you saw?

A. Dark gray Oldsmobile.

YOU ARE BOUND BY THE WITNESS'S ANSWER AS TO WHETHER OR NOT IT REFRESHES

Once you show the object to the witness, the witness decides, subjectively, unilaterally, whether or not the object in any fashion refreshes his recollection. This is, of course, as it must be, for there is no expert, no mechanism in the world that can be put before the jury to convince the jury that when the witness said that his memory was not refreshed, it actually was, and that the witness was fabricating his testimony. Only the witness knows if his memory is refreshed. And if he says it was NOT, then you are bound by such answer and must proceed onto some other method of cross-examination. You will see in a section following shortly that misusing a piece of evidence to refresh recollection can, in effect, also kill that piece of evidence for other use. Thus, be sure you are not using valuable cross-examination material wastefully.

DO NOT WASTE A PRIOR INCONSISTENT STATEMENT TO REFRESH RECOLLECTION

Oftentimes, a cross-examiner has in hand a document that indicates that the witness's prior version of the facts in the case was other than the present, on-trial testimony. But the cross-examiner totally misuses the document by using it to refresh the witness's recollection. For example, the cross-examiner has in his hand a prior inconsistent statement, signed by the witness, in which the witness indicated that the car he saw on the day of the accident was actually a rust-colored car. The examination proceeds as follows:

Q. What color was the car that you saw that day?

A. It was either blue or dark gray. Dark blue or dark gray.

Q. When you say the car was either blue or dark gray, you're saying for sure that it wasn't yellow, or red, or brown?

A. No, it was either dark gray or dark blue.

Q. And in order to give that answer, you have a picture in your mind, a recollection of what that car looked like, however vague the picture you recall.

A. Oh, I have a picture in my mind, all right. It was either dark gray or dark blue.

Q. Can you try and concentrate and bring that memory into sharper focus, and see if you can recollect whether it was the blue or gray you have testified about?

A. (The witness concentrates, then shakes his head.) No, I can't tell you, to tell the truth.

Q. I show you this document and ask you whether or not it refreshes your recollection of what you actually saw that day.

The Court: Read that to yourself, Mr. Witness, and then just indicate whether or not it refreshes your recollection.

A. (After reading) It doesn't.

Q. You say that document does not refresh your recollection as to the color of the car you saw that day.

A. No, it doesn't.

You have now practically ruined a perfectly fine cross-examination weapon by showing it to the witness with the hope that he will kindly recollect what he has no obligation to recollect. Remember, whatever he says as to whether or not his memory is refreshed cannot be changed by argument or other contradiction. It would have been far better to use that document as a prior inconsistent statement and then cross-examine accordingly (see supra).

NOTE: Even though the cross-examiner may continue to utilize—now as a prior inconsistent statement—that very same document with which he attempted to refresh the witness's recollection, it has lost a great deal of its impact in front of the jury and psychologically, it hasn't the same dramatic punch as if it had originally been used as follows:

Q. In order to give the answer you've just given, you have a picture in your mind, a recollection of what that car looked like, however vague the picture you recall.

A. Oh, I have a picture in my mind all right. It was either dark gray or dark blue.

Q. Do you recall that after the accident happened, the police arrived?

A. Yes, about ten minutes later.

Q. And were you still at the scene?

A. Sure.

Q. Did the police ask you any questions?

A. I believe they did.

Q. Your Honor, I'd like to have this document marked for identification.

The Court: Mark it.

Q. Will you look at this document, Mr. Witness, and tell me whether or not that's your signature which appears at the bottom thereof?

A. (The witness begins to read the contents of the document.)

The reason the witness wants to read the document is that the witness wants to know what it is and where you're going with it. That's why you try to stop the reading for the moment.

Q. Don't read the document; just tell the court and jury if that's your signature on the bottom.

A. It is.

Q. (Taking the document back from the witness) And you signed this document for the police, didn't you?

A. I didn't read it. If you let me read it, I'll tell you the answer.

Q. Regardless of what the document says for the moment, there's no question that that's your signature on the bottom, is there?

A. No question.

Q. I offer this document into evidence, Your Honor.

The Court: Show it to your adversary.

Adversary: (Reads it, twice, then:) I object, Your Honor.

The Court: No, I'll receive it. The witness has identified his own signature on it.

Q. And when you spoke to the police officer that day, (now reading from the document in evidence) didn't you tell the police that the car you saw was rust-colored?

Adversary: Your Honor, the document speaks for itself. Counsel can read it to the jury if he wishes.

The Court: He can, or he can read any portion of it, or refer to it in any way. If you want to read the rest of it to the jury, or whatever counsel leaves out, you certainly may do that.

Q. Can you answer the question?

A. What was the question again?

Q. May the reporter read the question to the witness, Your Honor?

The Court: Yes, read it. (Reporter reads question.)

Q. Having heard the stenographer read the question, can you tell the jury whether you told the police that the car was rust-colored?

A. If it says it there, that's what I must have said.

Q. And when you said that to the police, you were telling what you had just seen, weren't you?

A. I don't know what I told them. I don't remember much about the accident now.

Q. You must have remembered more about it then, ten minutes after the accident?

A. I guess so.

Q. And when you said it was a rust-colored car that caused the accident, that must have been the truth?

A. I guess so.

Thus, you have used a document that might have either refreshed the witness's recollection or might have been used as a prior inconsistent statement. Unquestionably, driving a spike into the witness's testimony by using the document as a prior inconsistent statement is far more effective than using the same document as a memory stimulant—particularly where you run the risk that the witness can scuttle your boat by indicating that it does NOT refresh his recollection. This possibility, however, doesn't eliminate the use of refreshing recollection in other situations where the witness's memory has actually failed.

PRIOR IMMORAL, ILLEGAL, BAD ACTS

In addition to other material available to the cross-examiner, an advocate may use any antisocial acts of the adverse witness to attack that witness's credibility. These acts can be criminal, immoral, loathsome, or be any act that, in some fashion, shows the adverse witness to be unreliable, unworthy of belief, capable of deceit, distortion, and so forth.

Basically, the use of these antisocial acts on cross-examination is to permit the jury to obtain a full view of the witness, to be better able to evaluate the testimony in its true light.

Needless to say, despite antisocial acts, whether criminal or otherwise, a jury is still free to believe that the witness, despite his or her background or habits, is worthy of belief, at least in this one instance. Therefore, in the ordinary situation, having information that the witness has done some antisocial act is not the beginning and end of your cross-examination; it is not the material of which the "big kill" is made. It can help, of course; it can be damaging. But it can also be something that the jury can determine is insignificant, or is unimportant in the context of the testimony.

For example, many times co-defendants in criminal cases cooperate with the prosecution and testify against their "alleged" accomplices, with the hope of gaining favor on their own behalf from the court which passes judgment on them. These witnesses may not only have horrendous backgrounds, perhaps the worst you ever heard of—they may have been guilty of murders and swindling, going back years and years more—but they may also have a self-serving purpose in testifying in a fashion acceptable to the prosecutor. Yet, for the purpose of convicting the defendant against whom the witnesses testify, the jury often finds them sufficiently credible.

How can that be? How can the jury accept the word of a con man, a thief, a cheat, a person who lies to serve his or her own interests? I don't know. If presented with such a person in their ordinary business dealings, I assume the individual jurors would run as if they were being drawn into the jaws of death. But in innumerable criminal cases, you'll find the jury accepting just such persons in order to convict the defendant on trial.

In the ordinary civil cases, the cross-examiner does not run into anything quite so dramatic. But you may run into witnesses who have unsavory aspects to their background. You can utilize such material, whether in a criminal or civil case; but remember, it is only another piece of the mosaic, and it should be used as such—something that adds to the weight of your cross-examination, but which can hardly carry that cross-examination all by itself.

ILLEGAL ACTS

When you become aware of the prior criminal history of an adverse witness, whether supplied by your adversary or discovered by your own investigation, you are not bound to cross-examine merely about the convictions that the witness has suffered. You are able to utilize not only convictions, but the underlying facts of any illegal or immoral act of the past, regardless of conviction. There are different methods, however, of using the different materials.

CONVICTIONS

If the witness has been convicted of a crime previously, you are able to ask the witness about that conviction and the underlying circumstances thereof; for example

Q. Mr. Witness, on July 6, 1965, were you convicted of the crime of felonious assault in New York County?

A. Yes, I was.

Q. You were guilty of attacking someone physically?

A. I guess you could say that.

Q. And were you also, on September 12, 1967, convicted of the crime of impersonating a police officer?

A. Yes, I was.

Q. You posed as someone you were not?

A. Right, right.

Q. In order to do this, you had to lie, to say things that were not true?

A. Right, right.

Q. And were you also, in July 1968, convicted of the crime of murder?

A. Yes. And I did my time.

Q. How much time? When were you released from prison?

A. 1980. July 1980.

Q. Just six months ago?

A. Right.

Q. And in that crime of murder that you said you were convicted of, was a woman, an 80-year-old woman, murdered?

A. Yes, but I didn't do it.

Q. Was this woman victim that you had nothing to do with beaten to death with some blunt instrument?

A. Yes, but I didn't do it.

You have used the material as much as the law allows. Would the jury, doing some business or having some dealings with this person, accept anything that he says, knowing now what they know about him? It is doubtful. Will they accept such testimony to injure your client? Perhaps. But you have sown serious seeds for thought and doubt.

NONCONVICTIONS

In addition to criminal acts of which the witness has been convicted, you are also permitted, under certain conditions, to ask about the underlying facts of other criminal acts that the witness committed, of which, however, he has not been convicted. You cannot ask about arrests. And, you must know exactly how to pose these questions, or you will be cut short rather rudely by the court.

You are not permitted to ask the witness if he had been arrested for a particular act, and rightly so, because, in our system of justice, the mere fact that a person has been arrested for (accused of) a crime is not sufficient for such fact to be used against that witness. The witness may have been totally without guilt of such charges; our system's method for determining legal guilt is by adversarial legal proceedings. Therefore, when the adverse witness was arrested but not convicted of a criminal charge, you cannot inquire about the arrest.

You are permitted, nonetheless, to ask questions as to whether or not the witness actually committed the immoral acts underlying the criminal charge. But you are bound by the witness's answer. In the event that you receive a negative answer, you are bound thereby.

For instance, you find that the witness was arrested in 1985 for felonious assault and in 1987 for grand larceny. As a result of the witness's having retained a superb cross-examining lawyer, there are no convictions. You are permitted to ask the following:

Q. Did you, on July 19, 1985, assault a person named Hector Rogers with a baseball bat?

A. No, I didn't.

Q. And did you, on February 11, 1987, steal several cars in the 48th Precinct in The Bronx, New York?

A. No, I didn't.

You can ask those questions, and you are bound by those answers. Are they worth it? Well, ordinarily, they certainly can't hurt, and when laced with enough factual content, as evidenced here, can give a jury pause.

OBJECTIONS

Oftentimes, you will have objection by your adversary to your use of non-conviction material as indicated here. And often, the judge may agree with your adversary. The fact is, however, that you are permitted to inquire as to any illegal, immoral, or illicit act in the adverse witness's past, regardless of whether or not a conviction resulted.

As aforesaid, you cannot ask if he was arrested for such act if there was no conviction. But you certainly can ask if he committed, perpetrated, or did such a thing on a certain date, regardless of criminal legal proceedings. Surely the jury can catch the drift that you are not asking the witness questions out of the blue about an event that occurred in a certain month, certain year, or even on a certain day, in a certain place.

When the witness denies the same—as, ordinarily, he will—it is difficult to assess the damage, if any, done to the witness's credibility by the question and by the negative answer, particularly when the judge may very well admonish the jury that the question is not evidence, that only the answer is. Not being able to assess, one way or the other, whether such information is going to impress the jury, you might as well use the same except when you know full well that using such information is most likely going to backfire on you and injure your presentation. This can happen when the witness may have done an antisocial act 40 years before and since then has led an exemplary life, has done great deeds for the community at large, is generous, honest, upstanding, and so forth. Asking such a witness questions about an event that may have been committed when he was 16 years old may very well antagonize the jury against you and your cause.

Inasmuch as the damage that you could do your own cause could be substantial, it is hard to discern what the benefit might be in pursuing such inquiry. Each situation and each witness stands alone, however, and must be evaluated by you under all the attendant circumstances. If you decide that the use of such material shall be beneficial to your cause, then by all means, you should use the material. Just remember, you cannot ask about arrests. You can ask about the underlying facts, regardless of whether or not an arrest resulted in no conviction.

GOOD FAITH ESSENTIAL

In order to pursue a line of inquiry as to immoral or illicit events, even those underlying arrests that did not blossom into convictions, you must have a "good-faith" basis for the inquiry. You may not be able to—may not be permitted to—prove those underlying events. But that does not mean that you may, in bad faith, ask questions not based on fact, questions that are total figments of imagination. You may hear an objection from your adversary, and the court may ask you the basis for your questions. If you are unable to give the court a "good-faith" basis for your questions, you may be in deep, hot water. Such behavior is censurable and perhaps contumacious and should never be indulged in by a trial attorney of integrity.

EVEN ACQUITTAL DOES NOT STOP THE INQUIRY

Indeed, even if the witness had been acquitted of a crime with which he was charged, you may still ask whether or not he, in fact, committed such an act. An acquittal, a verdict of not guilty based on some technical ground or lack of evidence, does not mean that the witness was totally innocent (as opposed to not guilty under the law) of the charged act, that he did not actually commit the act. He still might have committed the act, and you are permitted to ask whether or not he did. You are, of course, still bound by the witness's answer, and you still cannot ask if he was arrested, though later acquitted.

An example of such follows:

Q. Mr. Witness, on June 6, 1973, did you assault a woman with a bottle in New York County?

A. I was accused of it, but I was acquitted.

Cross-examiner: I object, Your Honor, to the witness giving gratuitous remarks in front of the jury, and I ask that you instruct the witness to refrain from such and to only answer the question asked. I also ask that the answer be stricken.

The Court: Yes, strike the answer. The jury will disregard the answer. Just answer the questions asked, Mr. Witness.

Now, after the witness has foiled your thrust so well with his gratuitous remarks, it is hardly likely that questions about the underlying facts can be of much significance in front of the jury, but they may be. You continue:

> **Q.** Did you, in fact, assault a woman with a bottle on June 6, 1973?
>
> **A.** I already told you.
>
> **Q.** No, you said what happened in court. I'm asking you if you, in fact, did hit a woman with a bottle on June 6, 1973?
>
> **A.** No.

Although you are getting negative answers, the witness may also be transmitting hostile, negative vibrations to the jury, which will cause them to distrust or disbelieve the witness. Thus, you accomplish something with your questioning, even where the witness doesn't openly admit his unreliability.

Immoral and Illicit Acts

Any acts that are antisocial, that are immoral, illicit, or loathsome, and that basically have a tendency to give the jury a better insight into the witness's character are grist for the cross-examiner's mill. But again, you are bound by the witness's answer. The reason you are so bound is because the issues of the trial at hand are the issues to be adjudicated. Whether or not a witness did or did not, in fact, commit an immoral or illicit act at another time are collateral matters and cannot be substituted or added to the issues to be decided.

Thus, if you ask the witness whether or not he beat his wife, and he says he did not, you cannot bring in the wife who shall testify that, indeed, he did beat her. For then the issue of the trial at bar becomes clouded with the question of the mini-issue: whether the witness actually beat his wife. Such is impermissible. You are certainly permitted to ask about illicit acts, and unless they are substantiated by conclusive facts, such as convictions, and so forth, you are not permitted to pursue them beyond the witness's answer.

The foregoing does not preclude your use of illicit acts for cross-examination in an attempt to impeach the witness's credibility with the use thereof. You merely must accept the answers given to your questions. Even negative answers may have an effect on the jury, however, because, as indicated, the witness may be saying no, but the jury, seeing the witness's discomfort at the questions, amd observing the witness's demeanor may disbelieve his answer and may be so appalled by his shady background as to disbelieve his testimony and discredit it. For example:

Q. Mr. Witness, do you have a drinking problem?

A. I have no problem with drinking, no.

Q. What I'm asking, Mr. Witness, is, have you been under the influence of alcohol to such an extent that your senses were unable to function properly?

A. Maybe a couple of times in my life, when I was a kid.

Q. Would it be more like several times a week, right now?

A. No.

Q. Have you such a problem with alcohol that you have to seek medical aid?

A. No.

Q. Have you been hospitalized on several occasions as a result of such drinking?

A. No.

Your Adversary: Your Honor, I object and request that advocate and myself be permitted to approach at the side bar.

The Court: Very well.

Your Adversary: (At the side bar): Your Honor, these questions are improper and asked in bad faith. Counsel should know better than to ask such questions. I ask for some offer of proof as to good faith, or ask, in the alternative, that the court instruct the jury to disregard this line of questioning completely.

The Court: Mr. Cross-examiner?

Cross-examiner: Your Honor, I have proof that the witness has been hospitalized several times for chronic alcoholism. I intend to introduce such evidence.

Your Adversary: That is totally collateral, even if true, Your Honor.

Cross-examiner: The witness is now perjuring himself in front of the jury, Your Honor. I should be permitted to show that. I am not now talking about his alcoholism. I'm talking about his untruthfulness right now, in front of the jury.

The Court: I'll permit it.

Thus, although you are stuck with the witness's answers in reference to illicit or immoral acts, you can show the jury that the witness is perjuring himself, or is, at the very least, unreliable, by introducing proof of his hospitalization; by proof, in other words, that the witness's version of actual factual circumstances is erroneous and unreliable.

Credibility is Always in Issue

The statement that appears here, that credibility is always in issue, may help to resolve any contradictions that might seem to appear in foregoing paragraphs as to whether or not you would be permitted to inquire into denials of illegal, immoral, or illicit acts.

A witness's credibility is never collateral. A witness's credibility is always in issue. Thus, if the witness testifies he did not commit an act, you are bound by the answer. However, if the witness, as in the preceding example, testifies that he was not hospitalized and you have documentary proof that he was, in fact, hospitalized for his alcoholism, you would be permitted to bring that out in front of the jury. But then, hospitalization is not an act, illicit, immoral, or otherwise; it is a factual circumstance to which the witness has testified falsely. And the erroneous, unreliable quality of testimony is always in issue.

Thus, the rule of thumb might be that you are not able to probe beyond the witness's answer into the immoral act or whether or not the same was, or was not, committed by the witness. But, if you can twist the cross-examination to factual circumstances that accompany an act, you may be permitted to show that the witness's factual recitation is wholly fabricated or erroneous.

Checklist

(a) You may inquire into illegal acts either when

i. the witness has been convicted of a crime, or

ii. the witness has actually committed an illegal act, regardless of arrest, conviction, or acquittal.

(b) You may ask about the underlying facts of a criminal act, regardless of any arrest or prosecution procedures.

(c) You may not allude to arrest, but rather, just to the commission of the act.

(d) You may inquire about immoral or illicit acts at any time, but you are bound by the witness's answer.

(e) You are able to show that the witness is unreliable by showing misstatements of fact—not as to immorality, and so forth, but as to events about which the witness has testified erroneously, falsely, or unreliably.

Learn the Language of the Expert

In order to best cross-examine the expert, familiarize yourself with the area of his expertise, or at least the area about which you know he must testify, relative to the issues or trial. You shall, as you research, *ipso facto*, familiarize yourself with the words or phrases that the expert may use. Amazingly enough, once you are familiar with the subject matter, the expert is no longer talking a foreign language; the expert now talks a language you understand, and the validity of her testimony, or lack of it, the logic, or lack of it, become immediately apparent to you.

Translate for the Jury

Oftentimes, experts attempt to expand the importance and significance of their field of expertise by using a language mere mortals do not ordinarily use (lawyers and judges do the same); they also hide behind a smoke screen of arcane words, saying something rather ordinary in nonordinary terms. Thus, a doctor might, for the jury, describe a sprained ankle as a subluxation of the peroneal tendon. That condition can be translated into lay terms, and it is your job as cross-examiner to do so. After all, the expert witness is there only to help the jury understand a special subject. An expert is not called to explain to the jury what it means to walk up to a door and knock on it. An expert isn't called to describe the sensation of walking along a sidewalk to a movie house. These are common experiences. The expert's function is to help the jury understand a subject they may not have in common experience. The expert's opinion—as the judge will charge the jury—is not a substitute for the jury's thinking and deliberation. The expert is to help the jury understand.

But the jury can't understand unless the expert's terms of art, the specialized words, are broken down for them and reduced to lay person's language, so that the jury can digest and weigh the expert's opinion in its true perspective.

For example of such *reductio ad* lay person's language, I offer the following excerpt of the cross-examination of a doctor in a criminal case, where one of the witnesses was a recovered chronic alcoholic who gave crucial testimony that the defendant admitted to him, the witness, that he had murdered the deceased:

> **Q.** Have you, Doctor, in your experience with chronic alcoholism, come across individuals who have hallucinations or delusions as to what has occurred in the past?
>
> **A.** Yes, I have.

Q. If a person, Doctor, who is no longer hallucinating, no longer a chronic alcoholic, refers back to events when he was hallucinating, could that person, in the present, believe a hallucination to have actually happened?

A. There are variations on that. In most instances, the individual recognizes the abnormalities of the hallucinatory or delusional experience.

Q. Doctor, this would be, am I correct, a person who has had the delirium tremens, or the DTs, and who thought he saw pink elephants. When he recovers, he realizes that, in fact, he didn't see pink elephants; is that correct?

A. Generally that is correct; yes.

Q. Doctor, a person who had hallucinations as a chronic alcoholic may recall a conversation that actually existed, and he may also recall a conversion that did not actually exist; isn't that correct?

A. That's correct.

Q. And when a person recognizes what he recalls was actually a hallucination, he recognizes in logic that he couldn't have seen a flying building or pink elephants or anything of that sort; is that correct?

Your Adversary: Objection.

The Court: Sustained.

Q. Can you always recognize, Doctor, when a person describes a hallucinatory experience as opposed to an actual event?

A. Most of the time, yes, I can. They're so outlandish that it's not very difficult.

Q. Doctor, when you're talking about hallucinations that are outlandish, you're talking about the sort of things that people describe as pink elephants, or snakes in the corner, or flying buildings, or feeling that you're flying when you're not; correct?

A. And other things.

Q. But with hallucinations of things that are normal, such as conversations, then it is far more difficult to ascertain what is real and what is not real; what was hallucination and what was actuality. Is that correct, sir?

A. It may present a problem because one uses other means to identify it, not only that language itself.

Q. A person being a chronic alcoholic can have a delusion or a hallucination of having a conversation, even about murder, with an individual with whom he did not have such conversation, isn't that correct, sir?

A. That can happen.

Cross-examiner: I have no further questions.

What you've done is logically to reduce the expert by deflating the terms of his art to lay person's language, reduce him to an ordinary witness. At the same time, you've permitted the jury to see and understand exactly what the expert is saying, rather than sitting—usually without admitting it—in a state of confusion because of the same terms of art. Both accomplishments are essential to cross-examining expert witnesses.

DEFUSE THE IDEAS TOO

In addition to defusing the language of the expert, who may not be using those terms merely to impress the jury but, rather, because they are truly the terms of that art, you must also use the same methods to defuse the thoughts and ideas of that expert.

For example, the expert engineer, describing a plastics molding machine that macerated the hand of a worker (the plaintiff), indicates that the steel molding surfaces of that machine were designed to close after an infusion of hot plastic material, with 10,000 pounds of pressure per square inch. He testifies that catching the hand of the worker/plaintiff in the machine, it crushed the same. Obviously, your adversary's theory is, since the plaintiff used that machine innumerable times, his own negligence caused the injury. Your theory is that the machine was negligently maintained and that negligence, not design, caused the injury.

As the prospective cross-examiner, you listen, as does the jury, to the expert's testimony, and you have to think for them, or at least for the points you want them to understand. Can a steel machine be designed to close, and ram into its own parts with 10,000 pounds of pressure, hundreds of times each day? Will that not cause the dies to be smashed, if not on the first blow, perhaps after the hundredth or the thousandth? You rise to cross-examine.

Q. Mr. Engineer, you say the molding surfaces, which molded the hot plastic into dog bowls, closes with 10,000 pounds of pressure per square inch each time it closes?

A. Yes.

Q. Now, this machine has a moving part and a fixed part, does it not? In other words, one part slides open, then closes onto another part that has remained stationary?

A. That's right.

Q. This part that moves and slides, it slides on some sort of track, does it not?

A. It has ball bearings in a slide housing.

Q. And this moving part has some weight to it, does it not?

A. Yes, it does.

Q. How much weight, do you know?

A. No, I was unable to take the machine apart to weigh it. I would say that the part was not too heavy.

Q. It was made of steel, was it not?

A. Yes.

Q. Weighed more than 10 pounds, didn't it?

A. Yes, sure.

Q. More than a hundred too?

A. Yes, I'm sure it did.

Q. And, as it slid forward to meet its mate in molding dog bowls, did it not need some power to propel it forward?

A. Somewhat, not completely, of course.

Q. And of the 10,000 pounds of pressure, wasn't a great deal of that pressure utilized in moving the part forward and in overcoming the inertia and friction of the sliding weight?

A. Yes, I would say so.

Q. So that, by design, the machine required most of that pressure to get the two surfaces to come together?

A. True.

Q. And there is a safety device built into the machine, causing it not to close if the plastic is misfed, misaligned, or anything else that might damage the die surface?

A. True.

Q. You think that hot, melted plastic is harder or softer than a man's hand, the skin and bone of it?

A. I don't know, I never thought about it.

Cross-examiner: I have no further questions.

NOT ALL THE SAME—BUT SO WHAT?

You now have the basic tools you need to cross-examine an expert witness. There are all sorts of experts, in all sorts of fields, and any attempt at cataloging them, or specifically dealing with or treating every possible expert or combination of experts would be impossible and futile. It should suffice, however, that you know that the way to challenge the expert is to make him a mere mortal; no brighter, smarter, or logical a person than any other person in the courtroom. Reduce his language to the jury's language; reduce his logic, the same way you reduce any other witness's logic.

CHECKLIST FOR THE EXPERT

(a) Do you know your subject matter?

(b) Do you know the language of the particular specialty?

(c) Knowing that, reduce the testimony to layman's talk before the jury.

(c) Reduce the logic of the expert's opinion, the same way you reduce that of any other witness.

CROSS-EXAMINATION APPENDIX

As an illustration of cross-examination, particularly of an expert witness, I include hereafter portions of the cross-examination I recently conducted of Dr. Harold Deadman, a supervisory Special Agent of the FBI attached to the FBI Laboratory in Washington, D.C.

Dr. Deadman was testifying on behalf of the prosecution about DNA in a serial rape/homicide case in which the FBI lab, according to its statistical analysis, determined that the probability of the defendant, a 20-year-old Puerto Rican living at the time of the alleged crimes in New York City, being the perpetrator was 49 million to one.

Cross Examination by Mr. Iannuzzi:

Q. Dr. Deadman, please, first of all, if you would be kind enough—and by the way, if any question that I ask you has a tendency to confuse you, would you advise me of that? Because probably I'd be more confused in asking it than you are by the question. But in the event that I don't have it properly, would you let me know that? In connection with the reports that were done by the FBI laboratory, does the FBI laboratory that generated these reports have an independent functioning other than the FBI itself?

A. The laboratory is a division within the FBI.

Q. And is it a commercial venture to the extent that it does reports and analysis for other law enforcement agencies for a fee?

A. No. We're funded by Congress to provide this service to law enforcement agencies.

Q. So, basically, it isn't independent such as Lifecodes or Cellmark or something to that effect?

A. That's correct.

Q. And in connection with the DNA analysis, I believe you indicated—withdrawn. DNA analysis is basically hinged on two aspects of genetics, is that not correct, one being molecular and one being population genetics?

A. Well, both of these fields obviously are part of the procedure that we utilize in a case like this.

Q. And molecular biology basically has to do with the determination of fluids, bodily fluids, and their relationship to each other, wouldn't that be correct, not necessarily an identification, but in reference to medical science? A molecular biologist does research into the correspondence between molecules, parts of the blood and so forth, is that not correct?

A. Well, I would say molecular biology is a science that looks at living things, living organisms, from a molecular approach. And by a molecular approach I mean you're concerned with the chemical reactions that take place, the chemical substances that are involved in life. Molecular biology is an extremely broad field that looks at many different aspects of the chemistry of life.

Q. All right, and they, when I say they I mean molecular biologists, make these comparisons and perhaps draw scientific theorems or theories in connection with the relationship of the molecules to each other and to the other bodily fluids, would that be correct?

A. Molecular biologists generally are not interested in comparing things. They're interested in identifying defective genes or in identifying certain malfunctions in a person's biological processes. But the one thing that is somewhat unique about forensic DNA analysis is the interest in comparing samples to try to determine if there is consistency in two different samples.

Q. So would it be fair to say that the molecular biologist isn't interested in comparisons but rather in identifying certain genes?

A. That's true. They generally are not interested in doing what we're doing in the crime laboratory.

Q. And in the crime laboratory, when you are comparing genes, you're basically comparing genes that may have been identified by, or have in fact previously been identified, by molecular biologists?

A. Yes. All of the probes that we're using have been identified by researchers outside of the FBI, and I would assume most of those would be under the term molecular biologist.

Q. And you yourself, as you've indicated, are not a molecular biologist?

A. I have background in organic chemistry and biochemistry, which is a major part of molecular biology.

Q. Is that answer that you are not a molecular biologist?

A. I have experience in aspects of molecular biology.

Q. Are you a person who has a degree, a Ph.D., in molecular biology?

A. No.

Q. Have you published any papers in connection with molecular biology?

A. I have not.

Q. And that which you—withdrawn. And have you of your own knowledge, not what you've used from other people's research, identified independently the genes as a molecular biologist?

A. That's never been any part of what I've been involved in, the identification of genes.

Q. So that the genes that you compare have been, in fact, identified by others and that you have in some fashion familiarized yourself or been familiarized with them for the purposes of identifying?

A. Well, we have certainly worked with many of these genes and the probes used to detect these genes and have studied them extensively to see if, in fact, they are suitable for our analysis.

Q. And, of course, you've testified that—and it's common knowledge, I believe you've testified to the effect that what ultimately, you cannot—let me just see if I can— when you make your analysis, you can basically get to an ultimate conclusion that certain bands or loci are consistent with others, is that correct?

A. Yes.

Q. In other words, you can't measure with total precision these bands and say, yes indeed, this is exactly the same as the other band, correct?

A. That's correct.

Q. So that when you take a sample and you go through your six-step procedure, and you ultimately end up with an autorad, and you make a visual comparison, that visual comparison can get to the point where you or someone in the lab could say this could be included or could be an inclusion, this could be an exclusion, or it's inconclusive, correct? Are those the three possible results?

A. Well, I would not use the word—I would say this is an inclusion, this is an exclusion, or this is inconclusive.

Q. Right. And those are the three possible results?

A. If you obtain sufficient DNA to work with. In some cases you do not obtain enough to work with.

Q. And, of course, the conclusions have to do—this visual conclusion, that is to say, this is includable as a possible match, correct?

A. Again, it's not an exact match. I'm not sure if possible is the correct adjective. A match is a match.

Q. So basically when—and if perhaps I don't use exactly the proper terminology, forgive me, you can indicate by the visual examination that is exclusion, that is to say for sure this isn't a match, correct?

A. Yes.

Q. Or you can't tell if this is a match, so it's inconclusive, correct, for whatever reason?

A. Inconclusive, yes, is something that comes about for various reasons.

Q. So it could be that it could be inconsistent or that it's not a match, or not that it's an exact match, but this is consistent with a match?

A. That's correct.

Q. And that's about as close as you can get in the science of DNA analysis without statistical interpolation?

A. Yes. Well, I can interpret a match situation without a statistical analysis because—based on my experience, both my own experience and my experience of the forensic DNA analysis community.

Q. However, you cannot indicate to this Court or to any other Court or anybody that that's an exact match of any bands, right?

A. That's correct.

Q. And that goes with all of the power of science that you have at your command in the FBI lab, and all of the other DNA people who work on this cannot say when they see two bands, these are exact matches. Can't do it.

A. That's correct. Nobody can do that.

Q. They can't be measured by machines or by eyes or by anything, right?

A. That's correct.

Q. And within the framework of making determinations, basically what you come down to is that this is consistent with a suspect. When you're doing your work, that is to say identification, and you come down to the match, you say this match is consistent with the subject, as opposed to this *is* the subject. You say this is inconsistent with his blood type.

A. Yes. The results in a case are consistent with this DNA coming from this person.

Q. Not that this is absolutely positively this person, correct?

A. That's correct.

Q. And basically that's because at the status that we're at, or the level that we're at now, this is what would be called the limitation of technology, right?

A. Yes, the technology is limited to the other—we're limited by the technology to the extent that we cannot measure these bands exactly.

Q. Yes. And as a matter of fact, have you not testified that when you do the comparison, that you never get exactly the same correspondence for the location of the loci, when you say we do the blood a second time?

A. It would be very rare to measure two bands with two different samples that are the same samples. It would be very rare to determine that those two bands have exactly the same size because of measurement imprecision.

Q. So that if you had known blood from a known person, because of measurement imprecision, it would be very rare to get the same result two times in a row, right?

A. The same exact size two times in a row, yes.

Q. And that's if you take your own blood and know that it was yours, you still wouldn't be able to, because of measurement imprecision, come up with the same results on your own blood, right?

A. Yes. We have looked at that many times.

Q. And so in comparing the blood of unknown individuals or a known individual with a possible sample, to say with precision that known person and that unknown sample are exactly the same is absolutely nonexistent, right?

A. That's right. You can't say that.

Q. And so, the ultimate bottom line of DNA comparison, after all the charts and all of the everything that we've been through today, is that taking the gels and X-rays and the radiation and everything else, the bottom line is there is not a human being alive who can say this blood exactly and precisely matches that blood, on looking at an autorad.

A. That's correct.

Q. And so, the only way that the FBI lab—and by the way, molecular biologists, scientists who have dedicated their lives to determining the composition of blood in order to perhaps locate the defective genes or genes that affect life, are not in any fashion involved in identification of DNA or DNA for the purposes of identification, isn't that right?

A. Well, we have certainly worked with many molecular biologists.

Q. I understand that, but may I just ask you this: Are molecular biologists who are involved in scientific research involved in DNA identification?

A. Most of them have very little experience in DNA identification and really don't know what's involved.

Q. And as a matter of fact, they've been involved in molecular biology or—I'm sorry, molecular genetics far longer than the 18 months or 24 months that the lab in Washington has been set up using it for identification purposes, isn't that right?

A. That's true, but they have not been involved in forensic DNA analysis.

Mr. Iannuzzi: If your Honor please, could you, so that perhaps we can move along, ask the witness to answer questions, and if there's something else, I'm sure Mr. Girgenti could bring it out in his inimitable fashion.

The Court: Ask your next question.

Q. And the only way the FBI lab and people who are involved with identification, the use of DNA for identification, have to make comparisions of what you have already testified cannot by any means be a precise measurement is to make extrapolation by statistical multiplication, correct?

A. We can assess the significance of our match result in a particular case by conducting a statistical analysis. That's one of the ways of doing it.

Q. Oh. When you say you have a matching result, the fact of the matter is that there isn't a precise match, correct?

A. I never defined match result as meaning that the bands are exactly the same size, if that is what you mean.

Q. I am asking you that there isn't a precise match?

A. Whatever you have defined precise match, I cannot say the two bands are exactly the same size if that is what you mean by precise match.

Q. That's correct. So you can evaluate the assessment of the nonprecise match by multiplication? Is that right?

A. I can assess the frequency of matching bands in a particular case.

Q. But if you take—and perhaps, I am because I am not any kind of a geneticist, I don't even ascribe to having any experience as you do, but if you multiply an imprecise match as many times as you wish, it doesn't make it at the end result more precise than it was before you multiplied it, does it?

A. You're talking about two matching of bands is one operation; statistical analysis of those matching bands is a second operation.

Q. Does the multiplication of imprecise match base pairs we're talking about, imprecise matches we're talking about—what I already asked you questions about—that it isn't a precise match of a piece of DNA one to the other, it's not a precise measurable match. When you multiply it, does that eliminate the imprecision?

A. Again, they don't have anything to do with each other. The matching process is one operation; the statistical analysis of bands that are matching is a second operation.

Q. I understand, sir. What I am asking you is this. And I'll try to phrase it in a way that it makes sense to you as a scientific expert: the imprecise match, no matter how many times you multiply it, it doesn't become more precise? There's no way of making that more precise, just statisically more probable. Is that correct?

Mr. Girgenti: Your Honor, this question had been asked and answered.

The Court: Three times.

Mr. Girgenti: The witness has answered it as best he can. I object.

Mr. Iannuzzi: I object to Mr. Girgenti testifying for the witness.

The Court: I don't think he's testifying. You asked him the same question three times. He's answered the question twice.

Mr. Iannuzzi: I don't think that there has been an answer.

The Court: He has not answered to your satisfaction. He answered the way he believes he can answer that question. If that is his answer to that question, you may not be satisfied with that.

Mr. Iannuzzi: I would like, Your Honor, if it is possible, and I think it is, a simple answer. Does the imprecision that exists inherently in the match disappear by multiplication?

Mr. Girgenti: Your Honor—

The Court: That's the same question,

Mr. Girgenti: Objection.

The Court: Fourth time.

Mr. Iannuzzi: Yes, it is, sir.

The Court: He's answered the question.

Mr. Ianuzzi: Are you directing that the witness not answer the question?

The Court: What I am doing is sustaining the objection.

Q. Is the multiplication basically a method which addresses the statistical approach? Let me do it that way. Does the statistical approach—is the statistical approach necessary to address the limitation of technology that exists today?

A. No the statistical approach is an attempt to assign some significance to matching DNA profiles.

Q. Sir, are you familiar with the treatise, "The Fixed Bin Analysis for Statistical Evaluation of Continuous Distribution of Allelic Data from VNTRA Loci for use in Forensic Comparison"?

A. I am.

Q. As a matter of fact, you participated in putting the document together?

A. I did, yes.

Q. And I ask you to look at page 13 and ask you if that's—if I am reading it corrctly when it says, a statistical approach is needed which will address the limitations of technology, the genetics of VNTR's, and the available data bases. Does that paper that you help put together say that?

Mr. Girgenti: If, Your Honor, I can see the copy that counselor is using. I have a copy here.

Mr. Iannuzzi: Page 13.

Q. Does that paper that you help put together say exactly—let me ask you this. Did I read it correctly7

A. You did.

Q. And in analyzing allels, isn't the analysis that you do in the FBI lab to—and that which you did here, based on a statistical approach, a comparison of theoretical numbers?

A. Statistical analysis is part of the examination procedure used in the FBI.

Q. And after you get the autorad and you get to the point where you make the match which you have already acknowledged can't be measured precisely, from that point you've done all the analysis that is going to be done from the point of view of the physical specimen and the blood, and the radiation, and the X-ray, that's all been done to the point that you're looking at an autorad. There ain't no more scientific analysis of the blood that is going to be done at this point, right?

A. Well, there are measurements made of the autorads after they're developed.

Q. All right.

A. Measurements made on the computer.

Q. And even with the computer, sir, even with the computer, and even with everything else, we're still at the same point, that is to say, there is no precise way to measure by use of a computer, human, android, any other thing, right?

A. You keep using the word precise. There's a precise way of measuring. There's no way of measuring the bands exactly. They can be measured precisely. They cannot be measured exactly,

Q. They can be measured precisely and that precise measurement cannot show that they're exact right?

A. Correct. We cannot measure then exactly. We can measure them with good precision.

Q. You can precisely tell they're not exact, right? Not even a computer can do that?

A. We can precisely measure them.

Q. And you can precisely measure the fact—and you know with all your knowledge of DNA, that they cannot be measured exactly? Right?

A. That's correct.

Q. At the FBI lab you use a window of tolerence, an acceptable shift of 2.5 percent up or 2.5 percent down, in measuring or assessing whether the blood of a known or semen sample of a known compares to an unknown sample? You've a measurement window of 5 percent from top to bottom, right?

A. Well in our—in our laboratory, we know that measurement imprecision can vary as much as 2.5 percent in either direction.

Q. And as matter of fact, by the way, when Mr. Girgenti asked you a question, he asked you whether or not the system that you use is accepted by the other labs across the country. Those other labs don't use as wide a window as the FBI, correct?

A. I would say most laboratories would use the exact same window we use.

Q. Is that right? Is it your testimony that Cellmark uses a 2.5 window, just as you do?

A. Well, I am talking about the laboratories, the crime laboratories, that will be using our procedures. . .

Q. Let me do it this way. I am not asking whether other labs that follow, have been taught to use your system. I am asking whether the people independent of the FBI such as Cellmark use the same window of tolerance. If they give themselves as big a break as the FBI does?

A. Cellmark uses plus or minus 1 millimeter as their window of tolerance. In other words, they use 2 millimeters tolerance when they compare samples generated from different gels.

Q. Is that more or less than the FBI?

A. It probably is less than the FBI. I am not sure of what that 2 millimeter measurement could be in terms of percentages.

Q. And how about Life Codes? They don't use a 2.5 window in any direction either, do they?

A. Their two bands have to be 1.8 percent apart.

Q. So that, basically, the two that have been cited in the documents that you helped put together, Fixed Bin Analysis, both use lesser windows of tolerence than the FBI, correct?

A. As a part of their procedure, their windows are smaller. We believe them to be incorrect.

Q. Regardless of whether you agree or disagree, they, in fact use smaller tolerances than the FBI? Correct?

A. They have a smaller quantitative match criterion than we do.

Q. Let me ask you a question, Doctor, do you know the words yes and no?

Mr. Girgenti: Objection.

The Court: Sustained. Do you know that word?

Mr. Iannuzzi: Yes, sir. I am not intending to be fresh, judge. A little levity doesn't hurt. . .

Q. Now, all of these variables of which we have spoken here several times already, now when you get the final result, all these variables then have to be measured or put through a mathematical computation or statistical analysis to give probability of whether the life fluid that you're measuring belongs to an individual or doesn't, right?

A. One interprets—one develops experience with these variables that we have talked about in working with the system. The variables again have nothing to do with the statistics.

Q. I understand that. But, basically, there are the variables and then there's the statistical analysis of the material that has all of these variables going for or going against it, correct?

A. But the variables in the system have to do with the matching and the variables in the systems have to be understood by the people using that system.

Q. Yes, I understand that. But there are variables and then you get to a point where, now, you cannot say from looking at any one of these charts that the blood that I have on the autorad absolutely, positively belongs to this defendant, right?

A. That's correct.

Q. And that's after all the analysis, all the variables that you did, you cannot, as you sit there right now, testify that this blood that you analyzed, absolutely, positively belongs to this defendant?

A. That's correct.

Q. So, in order to make a determination beyond that, to make your DNA more probable, you do a statistical analysis, correct?

A. We do a statistical analysis to assess the significance. That's one way of assessing significance of a DNA match.

Q. All right. And even when you finished with it, even when you're finished with all of what you have done, and of course the statistical analysis has to do with the data base and sampling of blood from other people in the population, correct?

A. Yes.

Q. And you have to compare the blood of the subject to how many times in our city, how many times in the world this combination of things occurs? Right?

A. We determine or we estimate that by using individuals in a sample of the population, using those individuals, we can generate the DNA frequency that allow us to estimate the frequency of bands in a population.

Q. And even when you finish with all of these probes, with all the computers, and all of the machines that the government of the United States has at its command, you cannot, as you sit there right now, say even after your statistical analysis that this blood absolutely, positively belongs to the defendant.

Mr. Girgenti: Your Honor, I object. This is by my count at least—

Mr. Iannuzzi: This is a different question altogether. This is not about the blood after we have it on the autorad.

The Court: What's your question?

Q. The question is, even after you do your statistical analysis—

The Court: (to Dr. Deadman) You can't say it, just one person in the world that has that? Is that right?

The Witness: That's correct, you cannot make positive matches.

Q. So that basically what you're doing with the statistical analysis is doing probabilities? And trying to do them as spread as possible so as to see that if 1 in 49 million or the 1 in 2 hundred million is about as close as you can get to precision or exactitude. Let me withdraw the word precision—exactitude—right?

A. Again, we can conduct the statistical analysis to assess the meaning of a DNA match. We attempt to do it in a particular way we believe to be an appropriate way of dealing with population samples and dealing with the technology that we have available to us.

Q. By the way, to the extent or to a great extent it has to do with the population base that you're using, correct?

A. The numbers that you develop as a result of a statistical analysis certainly depend on the population samples you're dealing with.

Q. And you have indicated that you have in the FBI determined a Hispanic population base?

A. Yes.

Q. Now, what people have you have included in the Hispanic population base?

A. Our Hispanic population data base deals with individuals from two geographic regions. From Florida and from Texas.

Q. And within the Spanish population base—withdrawn. You are, of course, familiar, I know, with Dr. Lewontin from Harvard University, are you not?

A. I have read some of his writings, yes.

Q. And Dr. Lewontin is a well-known population geneticist in the field?

A. Yes.

Q. Is he well-respected?

A. He is by some people. He's not by other people.

Q. Okay. And does Dr. Lewontin indicate from your reading, let me do it this way. Would you accept Dr. Lewontin as a knowledged individual in the area of population genetics?

A. Yes.

Q. And when Dr. Lewontin indicates that to assign the designation Hispanic to a data base is a biological nightmare, would you disagree with that7

A. Well, I am not sure exactly what he means by that.

Q. Well, when Dr. Lewontin says that the Hispanic data base includes people of Mexican, Puerto Rican, Guatamalan, Cuban, Spanish ancestry, would you disagree with that?

A. That's probably true, yes.

Q. In your FBI data base, have you sampled Mexican, Puerto Rican, Guatamalan, Cuban, Spanish ancestry, people, that is to say?

A. We have sampled people that live in Texas that are Hispanic and people that live in Florida that are Hispanic.

Q. The answer is, if I am not being unfair, that the FBI has not made a determination, within its list of, quote, Hispanic data base of people who are specifically, say, Guatamalan, Cuban, Spanish, or Puerto Rican?

A. Again, we're working with people from two different areas in the United States, and one can talk about individuals and what their ethnic background would more likely be living in those two areas.

Q. Let me ask it this way. In Texas, and in Florida, when you did your data base, did you make any determination as to whether or not the people that you took samples of were from Guatamalan, Puerto Rican, Spanish, Cuban, backgrounds? Specifically?

A. No. Background information of that type is not taken.

Q. And, of course, when Dr. Lewontin suggests to you that Mexicans have large and variable Indian ancestry, would you disagree with him?

A. No, I would agree with that.

Q. And when Dr. Lewontin suggests that Guatamalans are almost pure Indian, would you disagree with that?

A. I don't really know what that would be. Yes, basically.

Q. And when Dr. Lewontin says that Puerto Ricans have little or no Indian ancestry, but considerable African ancestry, would you agree or disagree with that?

A. I would agree with the first part. I am not sure about the second part.

Q. When Dr. Lewontin indicates that Spaniards and Argentinians have no Indian or black African ancestry, would you agree or disagree with that?

A. Well, I could assume that would be true for individuals from Spain. I am not really sure about Argentina. I would assume that they would have quite a mixture in Argentina.

Q. American Indians have gene frequencies that depart from other world populations in an extreme way, correct?

A. In some unconventionally genetic markings, I believe they do, yes.

Q. Indians are extreme in blood group O, many populations being almost pure O, correct?

A. Indians are a different racial group than Caucasians and blacks and they have different gene frequencies for those types of markers.

Q. In your sampling, when you took the samples in Texas and in Florida, did you make provisions to determine whether you were accessing people of Spanish with no black or Indian ancestry?

A. No, we assumed that the Texas population would have a large percentage of Indian blood in them.

Q. That was an assumption, not even scientifically measured in any way to set this FBI standard, correct?

A. I think most people, including Dr. Lewontin, would make that assumption.

Q. You're assuming what somebody else would assume, but do you know, of your own knowledge, whether or not there was a determination in connection with the FBI, quote, Hispanic data base for Spanish people with no Indian or black background?

A. I would assume you'd have to go to Spain to get individuals that would fall into that category.

Q. Is it your testimony that in Texas and in Florida there are no Spanish people from Spain who are descendants of Spanish people from Spain? Is that what your testimony is?

A. Probably very few.

Q. Do you, as a matter of fact, have knowledge to that effect?

A. No. That would be just my guess as to what—

Q. And do you know how many people in your Spanish or Hispanic data base? By the way, Hispanic? What does Hispanic mean to you? Does that mean people who are generally Spanish from around the world?

A. It means to me ethnic groups that are from Mexico, from the southwestern part of the United States, from Cuba, Puerto Rico, those individuals would be considered part of the Hispanic group.

Q. So that Spanish people are not included in the Hispanic data base, Spanish people from Spain or descendents, they are not in your data base, is that correct?

A. Certainly Mexico, Puerto Rico, Cuba would contain considerable Spanish blood since they were colonized by the Spanish several hundred years ago.

Q. So that, therefore, it would seem that, although you don't know for sure, that there are few Spanish people from Spain and descendants of Spanish people from Spain, without Indian or without black blood, in your data base?

A. I would just say since Spanish were here many hundreds of years ago. There are probably very few individuals with pure Spanish blood without admixtures of black, American Indian, in them. . .

Q. By the way, Doctor, what is the makeup of the blood of individuals from Puerto Rico? So far as white, black, and Indian is concerned and please refer to your notes and the specific statistics that you use in the FBI laboratory.

A. Well, I would just say that there's, in fact, probably an admixture of Caucasian, black, and Indian blood in Hispanics from Puerto Rico. Primarily, probably black and Caucasian.

Q. What I am saying is, do you have in the makeup of the FBI Hispanic data base that is used to make DNA interpretations of Hispanic people in the United States? Is there a breakdown of the individuals who have been used in the sample for the purposes of determining their background?

A. No. We know only that there are individuals that are Hispanic from two geographic regions in the United States.

Q. And would you say that the presence of Indians' blood and the measure, which you are only assuming, would it cause gene frequencies quite separate and apart from the gene frequencies of other people?

A. Admixtures are going to cause some differences in gene frequency, with the particular markers we're dealing with, since they're present in all individuals, with not large differences in the racial groups. I would think that some Indian blood here or there would not have a major effect.

Q. Aren't Indians, or Indian blood, doesn't it have an extreme for M? Do you understand M?

A. That's another genetic marker.

Q. And aren't there extremes in connection with M, ranging from 75 to 90 percent?

A. I am really not sure of that particular marker.

Q. And are they not extremely abberant in their RH type, with high frequency of small k, capital DE?

A. I am not familiar with the genetic markers per se in the American Indian population.

Q. In making your Hispanic analysis, you're making a statistical analysis based upon a data base the composition of which, in all charity, you haven't the foggiest idea of what's in it, except that they came from Texas and Florida, right?

A. And those individuals who identified themselves as Hispanic, and we approach the Hispanic population in a way designed to compensate for the unknowns in those two collections of individuals.

Q. The people filled out or responded to the fact that they were Hispanic, correct?

A. That's one of the ways of putting them in the category of Hispanic.

Q. Did they have to fill out some kind of a document to show their background, where their folks came from, where their grandfolks came from, so that you would be able to feed that into the computer in Washington and come up with a specific breakdown of the data base called Hispanic?

A. We do not have that specific information.

Q. So that there's no information whatever as to the makeup of the Spanish people in the Hispanic data base, except that they said they were Hispanic, right?

A. And the knowledge about the individuals that lived in those two particular geographic regions.

Q. The general demographic that in Texas there are probably a lot of Mexicans, and in Florida there are a lot of Cubans, right?

A. That's part of it.

Q. What is the other part of it?

A. There may be Puerto Ricans in Florida.

Q. May be. The words are may be. You don't know because you don't have the information, correct?

A. That is a guess on my part.

Q. There was no effort made by the FBI to make a closer analysis of the folks that were put in the Hispanic data base except for a general demographic: There are a lot of Cubans in Florida, there are a lot of Mexicans in Texas, right?

A. Again, we designed our approach to assessing allele frequencies or determining the appropriate allele or band frequency to use because we know there are different racial groups in Hispanic populations. We designed our approach differently.

Q. Did you in any fashion do a determination of individual groups, let's say, let's do Puerto Ricans and just do them separately so we have some data information as to how Puerto Ricans differ from Cubans? Do you have that in Washington?

A. We have not done that, yet.

Q. Have you anything that tells you how Cubans differ from Guatamalans?

A. No, we do not.

Q. Do you have something that tells you how Central Americans differ from, well, let me ask you, do you consider Argentinians and Brazilians Hispanic, or would it depend on whether they identify themselves as Spanish?

A. It would probably depend on what they identify as; if they're from Germany, they wouldn't be Hispanic. If they were from other—Europe—

Q. If they're Spanish speaking. It depends on how the question was asked of them. Are you Spanish? They would probably say yes?

A. They would say they're Hispanic, yes.

Q. And do you have any determination as to how Puerto Ricans differ from South Americans who speak Spanish?

A. We never compared the two. Again, we did not think there would be anything to suggest significant differences between the two.

Q. Whether you think it would or wouldn't, you have not empirical knowledge or statistical knowledge or computerized knowledge in connection with yes, there is a difference or no, there isn't. Just a guess right now, isn't it?

A. We know we have four population data bases. We know how blacks and whites differ, we know how blacks and Hispanics differ. We know how whites and Hispanics differ. There's essentially very little difference in these different population data bases. These markers are present in all populations. There are frequency differences, but they are not large differences.

Q. And, basically, the reason you're saying that is that because you haven't done any analysis whatever in reference to the Spanish people as to how they differ amongst themselves? That's an assumption on your part, isn't it?

A. We know how the Spanish people differ within the two groups. We look at Texas and Miami, we know how they differ, how whites compare to blacks. There are not large differences.

Q. As a matter of fact, the differences between white and black data bases is sometimes less extreme than, say, between people from Eastern Europe and Italy, isn't that correct?

A. That's possible, but I do not think it likely for these particular markers.

Q. Maybe not for these particular markers, but haven't you seen—and if you'd like to, I'll show you the statistics, that Poles differ more from Italians than they do from other races; that there are fewer differences between white and black than there are between Poles and Welshmen?

A. Well, if you're referring to Dr. Lewantin's [phonetic] data, some say that what he wrote was subject to question, and—

Q. Yes. Would you suggest also that there is some question in connection with M-O-U-R-A-N-T. Are you familiar with his work?

A. I have read references to the book that was written by him. Or her. I'm not sure if it's a he or a she.

Q. And would you say that Mourant and the various studies that were done by Mourant are incorrect?

A. Some of them are probably correct. Some of them are probably incorrect. All that is is a compilation of data from many, many investigators.

Q. Yes. And all your Spanish Hispanic data base is compilation of data from many, many investigators, isn't that right?

A. It's a compilation of data from two locations, one in Texas, one in Florida.

Q. And have you made a determination, sir, or is there any—not you personally, but has there been a determination made within the Spanish data base that you use as to the makeup of Puerto Rican blood, specifically, an individualized—

A. No, we have not set up or have not developed a, quote, Puerto Rican data base.

Q. So that in connection with someone who might be, or have background from Puerto Rico, in making a determination as to the frequency of this blood, you don't know if he's 1 in 49 million or 1 out of every 3 people who live in his neighborhood in Puerto Rico, do you?

A. I guess I don't know for sure, but I can certainly give my opinion as to which would be more likely.

Q. Will it be based on blood sampling from Puerto Rico as opposed to your assumption?

A. It would be based on my knowledge of the tremendous variability of these genetic markers we've been discussing in this particular case in all populations.

Q. Will it be based on scientific information as opposed to your guesstimate, sir?

A. I would say my experience in this particular field of science.

Q. Eighteen or 24 months of it, right? And in this 18 or 24 months you, sir, can make a determination off the top of your head as to the blood frequencies of all 4 or 5 billion people in the world, right?

A. I've been involved in this for four years, and I'm—

Q. I'm sorry, four years as opposed to 2 years—

A. I'm extremely well-read in terms of what other people are doing besides the FBI laboratory. These markers are tremendously variable in all populations, including Hispanics, including all racial groups.

Q. Let me ask you this, sir. Could you make a distinction with medical or scientific certitude that the blood of Carlos Doe is distinct, and I'm talking about of your own knowledge, is distinct from the southern half of the people, the people of the southern half of Puerto Rico? Can you say that it is that distinct without having ever taken a sample of it?

A. I'm not sure what you're asking me. Are you saying do I believe his blood—

Q. No, no. I didn't ask you what you believe. I asked you, sir, because you are a scientist, and that's why you were presented here, as an expert. Can you say with scientific exactitude that the blood of Carlos Doe is indeed quite different than the blood of the people in the southern half of Puerto Rico? Forget the northern half. Without having taken a sample of it.

A. Well, I've never compared it to a population sample from Puerto Rico. But the same multitude of types that exist in all populations are going to be present on the island of Puerto Rico.

Q. When you say that, sir, it's not based on any study that you've done or anybody else has done, it is based on your estimate, right?

A. I would say it's based on my knowledge of the distribution of these markers in all populations.

Q. So is the answer that it's not based on an actual study?

A. That's correct. I have not looked at a population sample from Puerto Rico.

Q. And you will acknowledge that within certain groups, for example, with the Indian group, that there are great variability within certain groups, right?

A. Not necessarily for these markers.

Q. For pure, pure Indian blood, the people who have pure Indian blood, are quite distinct from nonpure Indian blooded people, isn't that right?

A. With respect to some markers, they are. Quite distinct.

Q. And can you say that the same—can you say with scientific exactitude, sir, that the same does not exist in Puerto Rico?

A. Again, I don't think I could testify exactly to anything, but I certainly can give you my opinion based on my own information, the FBI's information, plus the companies that have Hispanic data bases consisting of Puerto Ricans, that there is tremendous variability in these markers. Because the FBI does not have a Puerto Rican data base, that does not mean that Lifecodes, Cellmark, or other companies do not have Puerto Rican data bases. They use the same probes we use. They see the same tremendous variability we see in our populations.

Q. Have you used Cellmark data base to make this determination in this case?

A. No, I have not.

Q. Okay. Have you used Lifecodes to make the determination in this case?

A. No, I have not.

Q. And when, sir, you say that Mr. Carlos Doe is 1 out of 49 million or 1 out of 25 million Hispanics, I want you to answer this question, if you will. Which 25 million Hispanics?

A. I would say that would be an estimate that would apply to the United States, Hispanic individuals in the United States. That would be our best estimate as to the frequency of the defendant's DNA profiles in the Hispanic population of the United States.

Q. And by the way, I'm sure that you are aware of the fact that Mr. Carlos Doe doesn't come from either Texas or Florida, but from New York. Now, that's not a question, and let me base a question on it. Have you done a study of the blood types and frequencies of the Puerto Rican and Spanish population of the city of New York?

A. The FBI has not. Lifecodes, I think, has a population data base of the New York Hispanic population.

Q. And, of course, we've already established that you didn't use Lifecodes statistics, you only used the FBI's, so the answer is that you have not had access to a blood sampling of the Puerto Ricans living in the greater New York area, right?

A. That's true, but I can use Lifecodes data because we do use common probes which recognize the same DNA.

Q. Did you in this case?

A. I have not used the Lifecodes data base, no.

Q. So that when you made the estimate, you made the estimate of a Puerto Rican living in New York without in any fashion checking with any statistical analysis of the blood types of the Puerto Ricans who live in New York, right?

A. That's correct.

Q. And is it your—other than, other than your guess, or your assumption or your probability based on your experience, was there an actual study done to determine if the people who reside in the geographic area of New York and who intermarry with each other or with different groups, if they have similar or different blood frequencies than Carlos Doe?

A. Well, you're comparing an individual to a population. I don't think you can do that.

So much for exact scientific testimony.

18

Summations

Culmination of the entire trial

Right at the beginning of this book, I told you that a trial was a mosaic, with bits and pieces of evidence introduced into the trial in random and various order, to be drawn together at the Summation by your power of persuasion into an irresistible fabric of logic for the jury.

All these bits and pieces were part of the picture that you, and only you, knew, had clearly in mind from the outset. Now, at the Summation, you must assemble the picture that you had in mind; you must draw all the bits and pieces of testimony, of evidence, into a stunning and convincing picture that shall both dazzle and persuade, that shall overwhelm the jury with compelling argument, and shall carry the day for your cause and your client.

Who goes first

In most jurisdictions, Summations are conducted in the reverse order of the Opening, in the reverse order of the named parties in the complaint or indictment.

Thus, as plaintiff was the first to Open, and the defendant followed, at Summation, it is the defendant who first sums up to the jury, and the plaintiff who follows. The same order is applicable to both civil and criminal cases.

The reason for this peculiar order is that the plaintiff carries the burden of proving the case, by whatever measure of proof that is applicable: beyond a reasonable doubt in a criminal case; by a preponderance of the evidence in a civil case. Since the proofs are the burden of the plaintiff, it was determined that it should be the plaintiff who opens, who begins the case, showing what is going to be proven. And, it was also determined by trial and error—no pun intended—that the plaintiff should have the last opportunity to address the jury in his or her task of carrying that burden of proof.

More recently, however, as a result of defendants in criminal cases complaining that it was unfair to have the great power of the prosecution being the last words ringing in the ears of the jurors, there was a change in the classic order of Summations—at least in federal cases.

In other words, defense lawyers were heard to complain that their clients were being prejudiced by the fact that the defense had to Sum up first, that the plaintiff (prosecutor) then had an opportunity to answer the defense summation, that by virtue of the fact that the defense Summed up first, defense counsel had no idea of what the plaintiff was going to argue to the jury and had to respond to imagined or conjured arguments. Such procedure, the complaints continued, was unduly prejudicial to defendants. At least the defendant should have the opportunity to have a rebuttal to the prosecutor's Summation, a mini-second summation, the argument went.

Congress responded and granted the wishes of the defense Bar, at least to the extent of granting a rebuttal summation. A funny thing happened on the way to enactment, however. Congress changed the order of Summations at the same time. Now prosecutors Sum up first, giving defense advocates a chance to hear and respond to the government's charges. But! The prosecutor has been given the opportunity of a rebuttal Summation, with the chance to answer the Summation of the defense.

The second rebuttal/mini-Summation given by the prosecution, of course, is intended only to respond to points that had been made by the defense on its Summation.

Thus, the complaints of the criminal defense counsel were heard and answered. Which result, of course, only reinforces the admonition that you must be very careful about what you wish for, and about the exact words you use to make your wish. After all, sometimes, as we have seen, wishes do come true.

INGREDIENTS OF THE SUMMATION

Summations are made of three segments. The introduction or preface; the middle, or factual argument; and, the Close.

The preface

The preface of the Summation should begin with thanking the jurors, on behalf of your client, for their patience and attention during the trial.

Of course, their keen attention isn't surprising, you can then tell the jurors. After all, they were each handpicked during the voir dire to be just that: attentive and diligent jurors.

You should now tell the jurors that this is the point in the trial that you described to them in your Opening, the last opportunity that you would have to address them, to pull together the entire fabric of the trial; this is the Summation.

Summation is not evidence

You should again remind the jury that nothing that you say, or have said, is evidence. And nothing that your adversary, or even the judge says or has said is evidence.

There are some who think that telling the jurors that what you are telling them is not evidence, in some fashion undercuts your argument; that you are shooting yourself down in anticipation of your adversary shooting you down afterward. I do not agree with this logic. What you are saying is NOT evidence. If you do not have evidence in your case, your adversary is going to point that out to the jurors very clearly in a moment or two. And by telling the jurors that you are willing to live or die with the evidence, you are putting yourself and your case in the light of being forthright, honest, candid.

Thus, tell the jurors that the evidence is that which came from the witness chair, or from the exhibits, however much, or however little there was or is; that they shall soon have the responsibility to weigh that evidence and determine—according to that measure of proof that the Court will instruct the jurors during the charge—which party is entitled to a decision its its favor.

Remind the jurors that you have never asked them to be partisan, but only to weigh the evidence and call out their conscientious decision, exactly as they see or view the evidence, regardless of whom it favors.

Wait until the court's charge

Remind them, as well, that they are not—even now—to make any determination or judgment, not until the Court charges on the law. For there is no way that they can make a determination about the evidence without knowing what law to apply thereto.

The jurors should also be told that they should keep an open mind, but not so open that somehow their brains fall through. They must use their common sense in weighing the evidence, with the same concentration and cerebral effort that they would bring to a matter of vital personal importance to themselves.

Advise the jury that the judge, not you or your adversary, will tell them what the applicable law is. However, just so they have a basis for the discussion, tell the jury that a reasonable doubt is a doubt for which you can ascribe a reason; or that a preponderance of evidence is where one party tilts the scales in its favor with the evidence.

> *NOTE: You must not dwell on the law for long, lest your adversary or the Court, sua sponte, objects.*
>
> *As long as you are right on the money with your thumbnail description of the burden of proof, and as long as you go in and out of advising the jury about the law as quickly as I did here, you may not evoke any objection. Dwell longer, describe the law in more detail, and your adversary will object, and the Court will likely sustain the objection, reserving to itself the prerogative of charging the law of the case.*
>
> *If, of course, the Court sustains the objection even to your thumbnail description of the burden of proof and then later instructs the jury almost verbatim as to that same measure of proof, you ultimately come out looking well, for you were correct and fair in your description of the measure of evidence.*

WITHOUT SYMPATHY OR EMOTION

Now that you've advised the jury on the measure of evidence they should use to weigh the evidence, you can advise them that they MUST, according to their oaths, regardless of sympathy or emotion, call out directly and specifically the weight that they each perceive is on the scale; their verdict must be no more than a recognition, a reporting of the weight of evidence as described by the judge.

Of course, if you've done a good job, that verdict will be in your favor.

PLAINTIFFS—TELL THE JURY HOW MUCH THE SCALE MUST BE WEIGHTED

For the defense, you can remind the jurors that you told them during the voir dire and in your Opening that anything short of the scale weighing down to the point the judge will describe—you will not describe it (not more than a thumbnail), that is the province of the judge—but anything short of that is not sufficient, not enough, not liable, not guilty.

You can advise the jury that this evidentiary determination is a little like pregnancy. Either a woman is pregnant, or she is not. You cannot be 75 percent pregnant, or even 90 percent pregnant. Either you are pregnant, or you are not. Relative to evidence, either there is enough evidence to tip the scale to the point the judge shall describe as preponderance or reasonable doubt, or it is not sufficient, not enough, not liable, not guilty.

This argument, modified slightly, can be used for the measure of proof in either a civil case or a criminal case. Either the scale tips, or it does not. It does not almost tip, it is not an imaginary tipping, it is not an optical illusion. Either the woman is pregnant, or she is not. Either the scale tips, or it does not, according to the measure the judge will describe in his charge.

PROBABILITY IS A FAILURE OF PROOF

Defense advocates can also advise the jury that when they are in the jury room and they hear a fellow juror say the defendant is probably liable or guilty, he or she is not. The plaintiff/prosecutor in such an instance has failed. For probably liable means that there is no proof to point to in order to support plaintiff's theory of liability or guilt.

Advise the jury that if, during deliberation, a juror hears another juror, saying that the defendant is more likely liable/guilty than not, he or she is not; for again the plaintiff's proof has failed.

Tell them that if they hear another juror say, "come on, use your common sense in this situation," without pointing to the evidence that supports the plaintiff's position, the proof has failed.

Make each of the jurors your agents, requiring the other jurors to have articulable doubts for which they have reasons. Doubts for which the jury does not have articulable reasons are a failure of proof.

CIVIL PLAINTIFF ON BURDEN OF PROOF

For the civil plaintiff, of course, the argument is slightly different.

For example, the jurors can be told:

> Now the Court will charge you, advise you of the burden of proof that the plaintiff bears, a preponderance of evidence. I won't define that for you. Instructing on the law is the sole and exclusive province of the Court. However, for the sake of our discussion, if this scale

> that is the jury were to be tipped by the evidence, in favor of the plaintiff, that is a preponderance.
>
> Now the judge will tell you that the plaintiff doesn't have to prove his case beyond that. What the judge will describe as a preponderance is just that, a preponderance. It is does not require evidence that does not permit any other conclusion in the world, nor is it evidence that proves the plaintiff's case beyond a mathematical certainty. It requires just that which the Court will describe, a preponderance, a weighing, at the end of all the proofs, in favor of the plaintiff over the defendant.

PROSECUTION'S BURDEN OF PROOF

The criminal plaintiff's (prosecution) case is different yet again. There the prosecuting advocate might say:

> Yes, it is true, as the judge will describe it, the prosecution has to prove the defendant's guilt beyond a reasonable doubt. Exactly that. A reasonable doubt. But no more. Not any and all doubt, not a contorted, distorted doubt. Not some conjured up, wild, off-the-wall doubt. A reasonable doubt. And proof beyond a reasonable doubt is not proof to a mathematical or scientific certainty. It is and remains just what the judge will describe, a reasonable doubt.

THE FACTUAL MIDDLE

During the factual middle section of the Summation, the advocates on both sides will analyze the facts of the case, blending their arguments with the law that the judge has indicated in a charging conference will be charged to the jury.

> ***NOTE:*** *Prior to the Summations, most of the time, the Court will have a charging conference with the advocates, advising them of what he or she intends to charge to the jury. It is at that time that you can make requests to charge; have a discussion with the Court as to aspects of the charge that you agree with or that you disagree with.*

Knowing what the Court will charge, of course, permits both advocates to blend the law that will be charged into the fabric and logic of their Summations.

The middle phase of the Summation, the factual middle is not intended to be a recitation by rote of the evidence already admitted into the trial; it is not a dull recap of the evidence in shorter version or form. It is here that the advocates for both sides take the evidence—in any order that each advocate wishes—and mount an argument that is intended to show the overwhelming rightness of their cause.

DRAW LOGICAL INFERENCES FOR THE JURY

Take the evidence, seize it, and paint the broad picture, using a piece of the evidence from the first witness, some from the third witness, a bit from the last witness, to show that the logic of your argument, the rightness of your cause is irresistibly supported by the evidence.

In other words, rather than the Summation being a rehash of the evidence, it is a logical, compelling argument by you, it is *your* logic and compelling argument, that you support by reference to the evidence.

HUMOR MAY BE DEVASTATING

Many advocates—including Jay Goldberg of New York, who has been kind enough to provide us with the transcript of one of his major Summations, which appears at the end of this chapter—subscribe to the theory that a laughing jury is a defense jury.

The logic for this proposition is found in the fact that the presentation of the case is serious business, the task of determining a verdict, likewise, is serious. When remarking about the evidence, if defense counsel can get the jury to laugh during the trial, particularly during Summation, that jury can be persuaded that the evidence is not serious, should be taken lightly, and, should therefore not be that upon which to hang liability/guilt.

You will have the opportunity to read at length Mr. Goldberg's humor-blended Summation, gathering therefrom any points that you think will be useful in your future endeavors.

CRIMINAL DEFENSE FACTUAL MIDDLE

The defense advocate in the criminal case may handle the factual middle of the Summation as follows:

> Now, what is the evidence on which the prosecution will argue he has proven his case beyond a reasonable doubt?
>
> Well, that's a good question? What is there indeed?
>
> If you really analyze the evidence, which is what I want to do with you, you'll see that there isn't any evidence; there is a great deal of guess, surmise, conjecture, a lot of people who have told you what they didn't see. But there isn't any proof that the defendant committed

the crime. Surely there isn't evidence to convince you beyond a reasonable doubt.

CIVIL DEFENSE FACTUAL MIDDLE

The defense advocate in the civil case can use pretty much the same factual middle approach as the criminal defense advocate, except for the modification of the argument concerning the burden of proof:

> Now the plaintiff is going to argue to you that she has proven her case by a preponderance of the evidence. That is, that the scales of Dame Justice have been weighted in the plaintiff's favor, with evidence that shows that the plaintiff is entitled to judgment. With what evidence you might rightly ask? And that would be a very difficult question to answer.

OF COURSE THERE IS SOME EVIDENCE AGAINST THE DEFENDANT

Of course, there is evidence against the defendant, the defense advocate should tell the jury.

> We're not here totally to waste the time of this learned Court, you jurors, and everyone else involved in the justice system. Of course there's evidence. The real question, at the end of the proofs, is, is there enough; is it sufficient to find in favor of the plaintiff? Let's look at what evidence there is. Let's look together at the evidence and then you make up your mind, if indeed, there is enough evidence to prove the case to a preponderance in favor of the plaintiff.

DEFENSE UNDOES PLAINTIFF'S CASE

At this point, the defense advocate starts to take the evidence apart, a piece at a time, to show that there is not enough to satisfy the burden of proof.

Let's start with the criminal defense advocate:

> The prosecutor presented 12 witnesses altogether. And of all of those witnesses, one, only one, even mentioned the defendant. And that one witness, by her own words, previously lied about this defendant, about this case, told other and different versions of how this crime occurred, told the police during the investigation stage of the case that she didn't know anything about this case or the defendant.
>
> Then Miss Witness is paraded in here during the trial and tells completely contradictory things about the defendant.

What is the truth? What, if anything, did Mary Smith know about this case? Nothing, as she said to Detective Donnelon on the morning after the crime when he first interviewed her? Or that she was home in bed, in Rita's apartment at the time of the occurrence, as she told her mother? And remember, Rita has come in here and told you that Mary Smith was, indeed, in Rita's apartment at the time this crime occurred.

But we'll get to that.

Or was Mary Smith telling the truth in this courtroom? I don't know. They're all her words, each version is hers, flows from her mouth. Each rendition came from the same mouth. Which one is correct? Is any one of them correct?

While you're deliberating about this case, after the judge charges you with the law, you'll have to ponder those questions. But, remember this: The judge is going to submit to you the question of whether or not Mary Smith is someone that the law calls an accomplice. You will have to decide as judges of the facts whether Mary Smith's activities make her an accomplice in this case.

If you decide that she was an accomplice—as the Judge will describe that term to you—then our law in this jurisdiction says before you can convict—regardless of what Mary Smith said—you have to find other, independent evidence that tends to connect the defendant to the crime.

The judge will tell you that if you find Mary Smith was an accomplice—as the judge describes that term to you—then this defendant CANNOT be found guilty unless there is independent corroborative evidence that tends to directly connect this defendant to the crime.

The judge will tell you that this independent evidence must not rely on the story of Mary Smith for its meaning or relevance. The evidence, in order to be corroborating evidence, must, standing by itself, independently, tend to connect the defendant to the crime.

Well, okay then, since Mary Smith's testimony CANNOT, standing alone, convict the defendant, perhaps her testimony is not the place we should start our search for the truth.

Since there must be corroboration from an independent source—which doesn't rely on Mary Smith's story—let's see if there is, indeed, corroboration.

For the moment, I'm not even going to talk about Mary Smith's testimony, about the fact that she's told different versions to different people about this case, about the facts of this case. Which version is correct, when was this woman telling the truth? I won't go into that for the moment.

For Mary Smith's testimony standing alone may be totally inadequate—even if she's testified for two weeks solid on the stand—to convict the defendant.

Nor will I go into the fact that during the moments after the homicides, according to her own testimony, Mary Smith took the wallet of the deceased, the silencer from the death weapon, and left the scene of the crime with the defendant.

Just as an aside, if Mary Smith's testimony about the defendant is true, so is her description of her own activities. And, those activities make her chargeable with crimes under our law, crimes of facilitation, possibly robbery.

Now the judge is going to define the law of accomplice to you. An accomplice doesn't have to be chargeable with the crime with which the defendant is charged. She can be considered an accomplice if, on the same facts of this case, or some of them, she can be charged with ANY crime.

I'm not going to talk about the underlying facts concerning Mary Smith's activities. She's admitted to them. If her current version of the story is true, then all of that activity about taking the murder weapon, and taking the wallet of a deceased, is true.

If her current version of the facts, her testimony isn't true, well then, we don't have to even consider the rest of this case.

But if she's an accomplice, according to her own present version of the case, then let's look for the corroboration, without which there is no case whatever against the defendant.

Maybe I shouldn't say, let's look at it.

Maybe I should say, let's look for it. Because if you look at each and every one of the other witnesses to see if in their testimony they mention anything that tends to directly connect this defendant with the crime, you must answer that these other witnesses never even mentioned the defendant and that there is NO CORROBORATION WHATEVER.

That's it. That's all she wrote. There is no corroboration whatever.

Look at the witnesses, see what they said about this defendant. Nothing! I asked them specifically, what could they tell you, the jury, about the defendant. And each one of them, each one of them said "NOTHING."

If that isn't right, and I mean this, if that isn't right, if my recollection of the facts differs from yours, then you just throw what I say in the garbage can, because, as I've already told you, what I say is not evidence.

The judge will tell you that if you consider Mary Smith to be an accomplice—and you measure that by whether she can be charged with ANY crime based on the facts, or some of the facts, that have been introduced in this case—then you CANNOT convict this defendant unless some *other* evidence connects this defendant with the crime.

And nothing else does. Nothing.

And, by the way, the reason for that is very simple. Mary Smith is not telling the truth here. She is telling something that is very convenient for the prosecutor. Mary Smith was afraid that she was going to be charged with a crime—the crime for which the defendant is on trial—and for that reason, she agreed to testify against the defendant. She agreed to change her story once again to benefit the prosecutor. So she wouldn't be charged with murder.

And that's why you know she's an accomplice. Because she changed her version of the case to hide from prosecution.

Isn't that just about where it is on the question of accomplice status? Mary Smith is shielding herself from prosecution by ingratiating herself with the prosecutor, by testifying against the defendant.

And because of that accomplice status, her story needs corroboration. And there isn't any. There simply isn't any.

In connection with a civil Summation, as we shall see in our Summation Appendix, you basically gather your evidence together in the same way, making, I hope, a logical and forceful presentation on behalf of your client.

THE CLOSE

The Close of the Summations is just a final reminder to the jurors that they must do their duty, that they have a responsibility, and that all they need do is keep an open mind, follow the law as the judge gives it, and vote their conscience, whether it favors the defendant or the plaintiff.

It is where the jurors are told that the decision that they make is important, that, more than likely, the Court shall advise them in sum or substance that they should use that degree of care in deliberating about their verdict as they would in a matter of significant importance to themselves personally.

You should advise them that this matter is of significance to them personally, for it is only through the evenhanded administration of justice, both civil or criminal, that all citizens can live by the rule of law.

AN ANALOGY

Here, I often tell the jurors that not even a President of the United States is above the law. The law is paramount; that this system works only because those who are involved with the implementation of the law—the judges, the lawyers, and, yes, the jurors—apply the law exactly as it should be applied, without sympathy and emotion, just weighing the evidence and calling out the true verdict exactly as they see it, no matter who or what it favors.

Oftentimes, I tell the jurors an analogous story, helping to draw inferences concerning the evidence in the case by casting the same witnesses and the same evidence into a slightly different scenario, a scenario in which each juror must make a most significant personal decision concerning whether or not a close relative of the juror requires major surgery.

I tell the jurors that the chief of the hospital will tell the juror that they must decide if there should be such an operation and that if they decide there should not be an operation, the patient won't die, that the hospital will find another method for dealing with the patient. I tell the jury further that the chief of the hospital shall tell them that they can talk to the doctors, the anesthesiologist, the nurses, in order to make up their minds.

At this point, I introduce each witness as Doctor so-and-so, or nurse so- and-so, and supply the same kind of factual (or unfactual) medical report concerning this fictitious operation as the witness gave on the stand concerning the case on trial.

At the end of that recitation, I ask the jurors if they would permit their loved one to have such an operation based on the stories told them by the various doctors and medical personnel who testified in the case. In their heart of hearts, would they let someone who is important to them go under the knife? Well, if they wouldn't—and if you've told the story correctly, they wouldn't—then they should decide the case before them in the same fashion.

The reason for this, you tell the jury, is that the plaintiff, or defendant, is important to them. He or she is a brother or sister citizen, standing before the bar of justice. And it is this bar of justice that sets our way of life, our life under the rule of law, apart from other places where there is no such freedom of choice, freedom of decision making, where a jury of peers decides the significant issues for the government.

Being a Juror Is a Serious Responsibility

Thus, for some, the responsibility of being a juror is the most significant role in support of their system of life and their government that most jurors have ever been called upon to exercise.

You may suggest to them that at the very minute that you talk to them, in different parts of this country, other jurors, in other cases, are being exhorted by other attorneys. No one wants those jurors, in those cases, to give an edge to either side, to any person. And so, too, no one wants this jury to do anything except to be fair and impartial and to call the verdict exactly as they see it, letting the chips fall wherever they may.

Summation Appendix

The following are Summations by two prominent trial attorneys taken from the minutes of actual trials.

The first is by the Honorable Jacob D. Fuchsberg from the case of *Ergas v. Barricini* which resulted in the first "million dollar" verdict in the history of the United States.

Judge Fuchsberg, one of the preeminent negligence and aviation trial lawyers in the United States, later became an Associate Justice of the Court of Appeals of the State of New York, New York's court of highest jurisdiction.

Judge Fuchsberg is now back in private practice, overwhelming juries with his tried and true advocacy.

The second Summation is by Jay Goldberg, from the case of *U.S.A. v. Bess Meyerson, et al.* In that case, Ms. Meyerson, Hortense Gabel, a Justice of the Supreme Court of the State of New York, and Andy Capasso (Mr. Goldberg's client) were tried in the Federal District Court, Southern District of New York, on charges that Ms. Meyerson bribed and influenced Justice Gabel on behalf of her friend and companion, Mr. Capasso, to bring about a favorable result in a matrimonial action in which Mr. Capasso had been the defendant.

The trial ended in an acquittal for all, not in small measure based on Mr. Goldberg's Summation, in which he introduced humor to amuse the jurors and ridicule the prosecution's case. Mr. Goldberg's theory, ascribed to by many prominent criminal trial lawyers, is that a laughing jury is not a hanging jury.

Apparently there is much to this theory.

Ergas V. Barricini

Mr. Fuchsberg: Mr. Justice Suozzi, Mr. Berman, Mr. Konheim, Mrs. Wendling, gentlemen of the jury! I am going to allow myself the privilege of very few personal references. I am not going to give you any testimonials. I am not going to vouch for things for you. I am not going to tell you how honest I am, and, therefore, anything I say must be so. I am not going to tell you how late or early I went to bed last night.

But I am going to make just one little preliminary reference, and it is in that spirit that I am going to ask you to be patient with me, as you have been patient throughout this case, and for which patience I thank you. And I am going to ask you to forgive me, because I am going to try to be as restrained as possible if I may sometimes seem just a little tremulous, perhaps, in my restraint. I say that almost as a little brake on myself as I stand here before you.

Now, I haven't been trying cases as long as my friends here, both of whom are amongst the peers of our profession, but I do not pretend to you that I am an inexperienced lawyer. And though they were great and famous when I came out of law school, the years have crept on pretty rapidly, and I am beginning to feel them now. But I hope I'll always have a little bit of naivete, if you wish, that makes me approach this discussion in this case with you—as I do, I would say, in almost every case—like, if you will, maybe the ancient priest—it could be a minister, it could be a rabbi—who approaches the altar with the same degree of tremulousness that he felt when he said his first mass.

> ***AUTHOR'S NOTE:*** *The jury is told of its importance, its uniqueness, to have them undertake their important task seriously.*
>
> ***ANOTHER NOTE:*** *Gone are the days when a 4-week trial was extraordinarily long.*

I say that and that's the only personal reference I will make because I am a little conscious of your position here in this case. Everybody has told you on all sides that this is an extraordinary situation, nothing like it ever before. I don't remember the time when a jury in an accident case—plain, ordinary accident case—served for four weeks. Everybody admits that. But, you know, you as a jury are not 12 or 14 people—you are no longer 12 or 14 people, you are now a jury. A jury is something different. You see, it has 800 years of tradition as an arm of justice behind it, and you are a body, like members of Congress. They are not just 400 or

500 people. They are capable of declaring war and making peace and passing legislation.

You have the power assembled in a proper case—not the power of 14 people, but the power over life and death. And you have power in a case of this sort—and I want to impress you with that—to decide something that may be even more important than life and death, because it is the question of the rights of people in our community, our fellows, to be secure in their right to pursue life, liberty, and happiness. That is what we are talking about in this case, and why I rose to make the only objection that I did. We are not here concerned with what was not taken away and what was left—and this is what my friend talks about—we are here to discuss what was taken away and what was destroyed. This is the issue that we are here to decide.

We are here to decide whether we—you as jurors and we as officers of this Court—are capable of participating in a process which can right a wrong, which can take the destruction of the life, liberty, freedom—freedom from disability, freedom to live a normal life, pursuit of happiness—and whether we have the power and the capacity in a case of this unprecedented size to do justice nevertheless.

Let me just make one or two reflections on this matter of pain and disability, so we can put it a little in the perspective our society regards it. Somebody used the word "maturity" and "adulthood." But, you know, it is not the possession of him who mouths it, it is the possession of the facts. Let's put this matter of pain and death, disability and death, in proper perspective.

THE ADVOCATE HAS THE JURY FOCUS ON PAIN AND SUFFERING

You know, the American Constitution permits punishment as far as death, but it does not permit cruel and inhuman punishment. No pain, but you can take a man's life. You cannot torture him. The supreme punishment in our morality, if you do something wrong, is not death; it is to go—if I don't appear blasphemous—to hell for pain and punishment. Let me only tell you this: I don't know how long each of you have lived in life, but I have known people, and so have you, who have wished death for themselves, but I have never known anyone who wished pain for himself. So let's get this thing in some proper perspective, because the value of this hasn't even been suggested by anyone. I am the one who summoned the blackboard, and I am the one who is going to use the most exact, dullest, the most boring, the least emotional of all our sciences—mathematics. Mr. Berman, who saw me with this book, with the quickness for which he is nationally renowned, was quick to warn you against the emotion that might come, believe it or not, by mathematics. You will have to tell that to your kids, what a romantic and exciting subject this is.

THE ADVOCATE SPEAKS OF CONCOCTED DEFENSE TESTIMONY BEING A THEFT

Now, you know, if this process that you and I are jointly engaged in is as important as everybody tells you, then I am personally a little humiliated. In fact, I am very much distressed, and so should you be, at the posture of the conduct and the references of these defendants. I am not talking of the lawyers to one another. I wrote down these words, I'll say them quietly: "Lie, contrived, concocted, perjury."

Well, let's see what we are talking about, because I am going to make some references to the proof as to the happening of this accident and I think we must put it in proper perspective, too. You know, we all know it is wrong to lie, to contrive, to commit perjury—which, in plain language, means false swearing under oath by our God. But, you know, our law alone doesn't say it is wrong. I don't care what your religion is, and certainly in our basic religions in America, the Ten Commandments is fundamental to all of it—when you lie, when you tell an untruth—you violate the precept. Not the representatives, but at least one of these principles for whom such noble words have been said here is certainly guilty of that in this case beyond question—when you lie you not only violate that admonition in the Good Book, "Thou shall not lie," but if you are doing that in order to take away from somebody his legal right to be paid by you for the wrong that you have done him and to do him out of his just due, then in my book, and in the simple text that my parents taught me, you violated another commandment, and that is, "Thou shall not steal." This is how fundamental to the morality of our entire society this case is in the posture in which it presents itself to you. . . .

THE ADVOCATE BEGINS TO CALCULATE DAMAGES

Let me put it to you this way—give you an example. You all promised that you wouldn't be scared by the immensity of the case—we haven't talked about the child yet. Isn't that what you all promised? You took your oath on that. Nobody asked you to promise big or small. Now, you as a jury that has the power of life and death, all these things we talked about, you have got to rise above yourselves. I don't care what your economic position is. I don't care what you earn, I don't care if you are rich or poor. By the way, I don't understand this argument my friend makes as to how the boy will be able to get along. This would assume, for instance, if you were the son of a rich man and somebody dropped a sign on you and paralyzed you from the chest down, you get nothing. Because your parents are well able to take care of you, you don't have to worry about that. That's not our law, and we are not here for anarchy for their pleasure.

Now, let me just talk to you about the immensity of the injury and your approach to this. Suppose when this sign fell it hit a truck on a street. It bounced out a little further and it did to this truck, let's say, $400 worth of damage. None of you would have any problem about awarding the $400, if that was it, would you? Because we are dealing with small things. And nobody is going to try to give you some malarkey, and I use the word advisedly, about making some kind of quick overall justice. You know, say to you, "Well, this fellow driving this truck, he has a few bucks in the bank, he doesn't need it. He can go out and buy another truck." That's what he is saying. You wouldn't want to be treated that way.

Well, now, suppose instead of the truck being empty it had a cargo of golf balls in it. The golf balls didn't get damaged because they are harder than the sign that fell down. Suppose instead of golf balls they were eggs crates of eggs. They got smashed. If the eggs were worth $100, you would give him $380 for the truck and $100 for the eggs, right? No problem about it. If somebody said to you, "Well, $480 damage, but give him $380 and forget about the eggs." This is asking you to cheat the man. You know, assuming it's the other fellow's fault and everybody admits it's the other fellow's fault. Nobody can argue with that.

Suppose in that truck instead of golf balls or eggs—I forgot the name of the famous stud horse, Nashua, I think it was. Sent out to stud and sold at the time, I think for $1,200,000. Well, it's on the way to being delivered and the guy was supposed to collect $1,200,000. I don't think you would have any difficulty just because it was a horse instead of a boy in seeing that the man got paid for what was done.

You remember all that publicity a couple of years ago because the Metropolitan Museum of Art—I guess they know their business—bought a painting, something by Rembrandt, I think it was "Aristotle Looking at the Bust of Homer" or something. All the papers had it, and it sold for 2 million. I am not going to talk to you about the Mona Lisa—they brought that over—God knows what that's worth. Suppose this sign had fallen down on this "Aristotle"—Parke-Bernet Galleries, they were delivering it. They showed us what they were supposed to get. No businessman or anybody else would hesitate to state they are entitled to it.

I want to know whether in our society—I want to tell you this was a little boy to whom this happened. And what kind of a boy? As we know, 139 I.Q., three-and-a-half-year mentality beyond his age, and in a healthy—you know, a good brain and a healthy body, a prize little athlete, even. You see the spirit and courage.

Then the hospital record tells us—it's in the record or I wouldn't say it—that he had intelligent parents. And certainly we know they were devoted parents, parents who would encourage him. What a future this boy had. What kind of an art object was this? This is the big item of damages.

But before I discuss money, I want to run through—this is pedestrian, boring. I have taken more time than the other lawyers have and I am going to take some more of your time. We haven't finished. We have hardly talked about something in some ways. Don't get scared because some of it is repetitious as to the types of argument. But it's facts. I don't think I have repeated myself as to any of the items, really. . . .

Lady and gentlemen, I hope you will forgive me for having to weary you this way, but I guess the whole experience of life is wearying in some ways, and the experience of being a juror is wearying. I am going to try to give you a little summary. As I have already given you the method for which I have arrived at some of the figures, I'll try to give you the product of some of the figures with respect to the boy. And then as to two of the items which I recognize can be controversial, I will discuss it with the hope that my approach to it is as I think it should be approached—will be well-received by you as being a fair approach. And I hope you pay me the compliment.

As I said, I am not going to tell you I am honest or dishonest. I am merely going to ask you to believe this, that I would be stupid if I tried to talk to you about anything that I thought didn't make sense. Because if it didn't, I would figure you wouldn't accept it; you would throw the baby right out with the water. So I am trying, really, as I said a few times when I said "13 cents of the quarter, give that to them," to be really conservative and bend over to be fair.

Although I say I want you to realize that by everything that's fair the boy should be given the benefit of the doubt; number one, because they imposed this trouble on him and, Number 2, because some of these figures on which we base our calculations are uncertain, and the uncertainty, where it exists, and there is a range, should be one that should not work against him.

THE LIMITATIONS OF LIFE EXPECTANCY TABLES

Now, I am going to give you one illustration of what I mean. The judge is going to give you the different life expectancy tables, the one that they are working to and the ones that Uncle Sam said should exist and that I have therefore brought to the Court's attention. Therefore, at best, I have said to you if you take Uncle Sam's table, or the other—I have had two tables and I have asked you to take the smaller one, which is a 61-year life expectancy and take off the year, which would make it 60 years.

I want you to know that I may be, and you may be, doing the boy an injustice, because the judge is going to tell you that you are not to accept these tables as the gospel; that these tables are only a guide.

You see, everybody who is 13 doesn't die 60 years later; the whole population doesn't get wiped out. We don't know what life will bring. With some there may be an earlier death, and some may live to 80 or 90. This is a sort of average. It may turn out—because we know that this boy's heart and lungs are all right, and we know that he comes of stock that's long-lived, as witness his father—that in his particular case his expectancy will be longer.

In other words, it might be 10 years longer, less a year, and since nobody knows, we are averaging it.

Also, these averages are conservative. They are based on our past experience. You see, since they are based on our past experience—like, for instance, one of the tables that I gave the judge was concluded at the end of 1949 and then I have the '55 table and I finally got the '60. We all know that by reason of the increase of science, medicine, and so forth, our longevity is constantly increasing. So this is, in the first place, a conservative figure, and, secondly, it may turn out—suppose you were sitting here saying, "Well, I am sure you wouldn't intend that if the boy turned out to live 10 years longer at the end of that period to say: 'I am sorry, the tables didn't say you were going to live longer.'"

You know, it's a debt they owe, and the debt is for the balance of the boy's life. There is no reason why he should ever feel devoid by less than full justice.

I am not necessarily suggesting to you, therefore, that you should exceed the tables, but what I am trying to point out to you is that they represent a fairly conservative approach. I don't know the language the judge is going to use. I have never tried a case before Judge Suozzi in which he has had occasion—because I have never tried this kind of case before—to explain these tables. But I am sure, because I know what the law is, that he is going to have to tell you basically, and in other words, what I have pointed out to you. I think it is well you have it before you while we discuss it.

Now, taking that in, let's see Martin's out-of-pocket expenses. I have taken it from the age of 21, which would actually mean an expectancy of 52 years. He has a 60-years expectancy, less eight from now to 21, which is only 52 years. And if you take the nursing item—of course, we are not allowing for any inflation at all, which is very unrealistic, and the fact that people will be earning more money, which is unrealistic, too. But I guess that's sort of balancing out if you forget about the discount factor. But, anyhow, those 52 years at $9,464 come to a neat little sum, if you please—and if it is large, my friends, and I make no hesitation and saying it is large—but remember, this a large sum that he will have to pay out, that's $492,128. And I am sure that some nurse 40 years from now, if he is unable to pay her because you followed the dictates of my friend, will not be interested in "Well, a jury didn't allow me the full amount that I need to pay for the nurse."

Now, that's exactly, precisely, the amount. You know, even a fellow earns a fairly modest sum of money, when you start figuring out what the earnings are over a lifetime, as we sometimes do when we read magazine articles or spend money for various things, it comes to quite a sum. What we are dealing with here is practically, really, a whole lifetime of a boy with special and extraordinary needs that they have brought about.

Now if you take the discount factor on this, then you only take 57 1/2 percent of that, and that reduces that item to $283,973.60.

Let's take the next item, that's the cystography, pyelogram, and urology—even they bear witness to the fact that that's needed. That, for 60 years, or 52 years, rather, comes to $62,000 roughly, and reduced it's $35,900.

Future appliances at $410 a year—assuming that the price doesn't go up, which is ridiculous really, 52 years—$21,320, or reduced, it is $12,261.

And then future neurological and orthopedic care, $175 a year, including X-rays twice a year. $175 times 52 is $9,100; reduced that's $5,232.50.

Before I total these items, which, of course are quite substantial—I'll give you the total all at one time.

We now deal with the vocational loss. You know, if a fellow has a job, suppose he was a doctor, engineer, carpenter, a lawyer, and he could tell us what he was earning, and he already arrived at his maturity, say 30, 35, we have a pretty good idea what his position in life was going to be. It would be simple arithmetic, more or less; at least the uncertainty would be out of it. Now, this is one of two items that I said presents a problem. But because it presents a problem it doesn't mean it isn't real and it doesn't mean that the loss isn't definite there.

Now, talk about the losses here—and I might say, perhaps right at this point, I heard the protestations of one of my friends here when he talked about the victim very politely and also talked about "Mr. Fuchsberg's client." I was thinking at the time—and I am a rather, maybe, silly fellow, but sometimes the best way to get my thoughts out is just say them, you will excuse me for my boldness. I wanted to say to him—it goes something like this, in the words of the immortal Fitzgerald—some of you no doubt are familiar with it. I think it says, "The moving finger writes, and, having writ, moves on: Nor all your pretty piety and all your wit and charm will alter half a line, nor can all your tears wipe out a word, for you have done the damage."

Now, what would this boy have earned? Their doctor—oh, no, I think originally one of the other doctors on questioning by my friend said this boy could at least have been a doctor. And, you know, as their doctor admitted, there are even greater things than that. Doctors will pardon me for saying so, and I mean no disrespect. What do you think that kind of vocation is worth? We have to guess and speculate a little. It's not our desire to speculate. It's speculation they force us into. Dr. Covalt wasn't prepared to say that $25,000 for an average, successful doctor was other than reasonable. Is it fair to say that this would have been this boy's intention?

You see why you have to be tough and you have to lift yourself above being a juror? Maybe there are one or two of you who make more than that, then it's easy for you to see the perspective of $25,000. But maybe some of you, I am sure, make a lot less and it is not hard to say: "This is all I make and look what we have to give this fellow." But, you know, somebody steals $10,000, or destroys $10,000, the fact that you have no money doesn't mean you are going to do an injustice. You know this isn't Moscow. So, therefore, is that a fair figure? Well, I don't know. Shall we cut it and make it $20,000? During the course of this trial the teachers were, by and large, given $11,000 a year, and they are notoriously underpaid by all the advertising that's done for educated people. Skilled laborers earn more money these days than they used to, as they should. We come to appreciate skills. Incidentally, I am not going to take the time to read the record, but it says this boy was not good with is hands, by the way, and his rehabilitation occupational therapy was very poor. I don't think you need me to read it. As a matter of fact, I have it marked out right here in the record to read, and in case my friends want to challenge it, it's on page 99 of the record. So it's probably not at all being unrealistic. We are probably being unfair to the boy—it's a gamble. But we are probably taking a gamble against what his potential would have been under the circumstances, giving you the average kid, good family, interest in schooling, I.Q. like this, a good healthy body, nice personality. Would you doubt that he would at least achieve that? So this is what they took from him.

So let's give him the benefit of the doubt, let's make it 20, not 25.

So they say, "Maybe he will do some work." Well, I suppose some hours of the day, other than telephone, people coming to him, special equipment, special places, maybe. You know, I don't go for some of this stuff. For instance, I didn't dispute that maybe they will someday teach him to ride a special car. But I wonder how he would do with heavy traffic, bad parking spaces, icy days, moving the stuff in the back. And then I really wonder—you know, it's like "Let him eat cake instead of bread," you know, and it's "Give him an ice cream soda instead of steak."

I didn't ask him what the car would cost. What's a couple of thousand one way or another in this kind of picture?

I tell you what I was wondering about: How much value it really would be, from a practical vocational standpoint of view, to me if I rigged up the kind of car that maybe I would get to learn to drive. But, you know, I couldn't get out of the bathtub myself, I couldn't get out of bed without somebody helping me on with my braces, I can't bend my feet without pulling up the legs manually, I can't exercise my normal functions of urination and defecation without diapers and smelling and all kinds of things. I can't get down a set of stairs except through all kinds of convolutions.

You remember, I went over that with the doctor and he said, it's better off not to encourage him because they get too tired in most cases and hardly worth it. You know there are different kinds of gaits; don't compare this with fellows you see using crutches. So I just wonder how much value this thing really has. And as I tried to analyze it with you earlier, a partial little disability, if you get educated and so forth, may be the same as practically none. And if you want my own personal judgment of it, only in the sense that I suggest to you objectively the reality of it, I don't think you can expect this boy to ever be employed except spasmodically in some kind of special—maybe some kind of hobby sort of job. And certainly he is not going to earn special money, except if a miracle happens, and we have no right to figure miracles. We have a right to figure probabilities.

I say to myself, "Let's give them every benefit of every doubt." Let me suggest even a situation that goes beyond what I think common sense tells us would happen. Let's say he earns some kind of money. But with his limitations, with his handicaps, with his troubles, with his tiring, with the disposition—there is a whole emotional string of problems that I read from the record, the anxiety neurosis and the antagonism in the hospital, things of that kind, you think if we figured that as against $20,000 that this boy will earn $5,000 a year? I am probably doing him a crass injustice.

Let's figure he will earn—-

HAVE THE JURY CONSIDER THAT SOME OF THE MONEY WILL BE TAXED

Incidentally, a lot of things I haven't figured. When I said, for instance, let's allow them the discount on the income on some of these items, I didn't mention the fact that, of course, the 3 percent or 2-7/8 percent that his money may earn, that would be a taxable item as distinguished from the principal. In other words, my friend here was quick to point out to you that the award wouldn't be taxable but he didn't tell you, of course, the income from the award would be taxable. He wouldn't really be holding onto that money. I didn't make an allowance for that.

Would it be fair for us to figure $15,000 a year? If we figure $15,000 a year—I am not figuring that, of course, from 13 or 7. I'll say from 21 until—and not his full life expectancy if he has 52 years. Let's say only to social security age of 65, that's 44 years.

Now, there again I am erring on the conservative side, because particularly a man who is in a profession, some of his most glorious years are after he is 65—you got the wisdom of the old sage. You don't have to retire at 65.

I think I saw in the *Times* the other day that even in industry the average actual age of retirement is only 67, in professions and business. Even if we work with our hands, as my father did—as I said, he wanted me to be a lawyer—we can appreciate what it means to have an education. There isn't one of us who didn't wish for himself an ability to have it. And so I wonder whether 44 years, where you automatically assume he would have to quit at 65, we are giving the benefit of the doubt there. That's why it comes to such large sums, even if we give them the benefit of the doubt, which shows you the reality of it.

So if you take 44 years, $15,000 a year, that kind of round figure, it's exactly $660,000. Now, we discount it down to $379,500.

Now, suppose we total these together, all the figures I have given you. Do you know what the boy's out-of-pocket expenses and losses will be? Fairly realistic—maybe erring on the side of the conservative approach a little bit, of guessing, but only guessing in the sense they force us to make predictions—he didn't ask for the predictions, he didn't want any of their money. He would have been perfectly satisfied to earn it himself and probably a lot more, and not have to worry about how much he is going to earn 10 or 20 years from now, or 30 or 40, because he is going to be awarded now when money values may change.

Can you imagine if you had to give him an award thirty years ago in terms of wages then. And I don't have to tell you, it's only twenty years ago, you used to go out and buy a Ford for $500; you pay $3,000 now. When I earned my money to go through college, it cost me $300 a year. I want to send my kid to college, cost closer to $3,000. Figure it out yourselves.

Well, the total is exactly—hold your hats, folks, hold your hats—this is what they have taken from him. Don't hold your hats because this is what he is asking. He didn't ask to ask. Hold your hats—this is what they did to him—$1,244,948. And if you take the discounts—they are big—would be only $715,877.10.

Now, you know I haven't yet asked you for a dime for the pain, for the suffering, for the injury, for the humiliation, for everything—not for a life expectancy from now until 61 years or work expectancy of 44 years. You know, as we analyze these figures—none of these were touched by my friend. I don't understand what kind of game—somebody mentioned a game this courtroom is supposed to be. For the whole lifetime from seven on.

EVALUATING PAIN AND SUFFERING

And in this connection I am not going to talk to you a word about sympathy or pain or humiliation. I am not going to give you any of the gruesome details because I think I heard some psychologist say people don't like to be troubled by the cares of others and so it is the wrong psychology to do it. So please remember, first, when I talk to you about it, it is because I have to, and, secondly, please don't get so numbed by it that you can't be sensitive enough to fully respond and give full justice.

Let me just remind you and just itemize some of the things—any one of which could in themselves, without regard to any out-of-pocket expenses, be the subject matter of a major award in any other case—and you see whether I am wrong.

Paraplegia from T7 down, bilaterally. I guess you can write books on that and talk about it for days. We have been here for weeks. No questions. This is beyond dispute. It's just like the stipulation, almost.

Incidentally, you might be interested in knowing—and I have the page reference—Dr. Deaver, he says—this is page 10 and 59, that sensory loss is up to D5. I think maybe I should make sure and not misquote him. Yes, here it is. Yes.

"The hypethesia," that's the sensory loss, not the motor loss, "is between D5 down." Now, if you remember, the T or D, it's the same thing—thoratic or dorsal. Seven is up at the nipple line. In other words, from here up he can't feel, from here on he can't move, on both sides—all of his body.

As I mentioned earlier, if he didn't have any legs—if a fellow lost two legs, not up to the knees, up to the hips, that is terrible. You wouldn't consider the body or anything. He might be better off in a way, as I see it, than with the flesh and bones left to him as a source of troubles. You wouldn't have to worry about the stuff spilling on you and rotting you and cleaning. You cover it up with trousers anyhow. You say, "Oh, my!" It's only the beginning here. Well, if there was nothing else in the case, what's that worth, my friends?

THERE ARE NO EXPERTS FOR PAIN AND SUFFERING

I went to law school and I was a fair student, maybe not as bright as my friends here. I had some bright professors there, and I am sure when His Honor went to school and when these men here did—none of us—because I didn't either—ran across a professor who was smart enough to tell us what injuries are worth. You know there is no law on this thing. It just tells you, use your common sense and experience. If you had nothing else in this case, what would you think that's worth?

Suppose it happened to a 50-year-old man, think how much it would be worth. Fifteen years of work ahead of him. This happened not to a 40 or 35, 25 or 20 or 18, 15, 10—to a 7-year-old boy. I mean, that's the length. You have to measure it differently. Did you hit the golf balls or did you hit the eggs? Did you do it to somebody who is 70 or did you do it someone who is 7? It's a completely different thing. Did you destroy the Mona Lisa or did you destroy some junky painting that I did? That's it. Well, that's one item.

Then you had a sensory and motor loss, complete, on both sides. Then you have a complete loss of urinary control. If we had only that alone. You are able to collect and squeeze some of it and the doctor said he thinks we'll be able to get through with some of this excreting—one of my friends brought out. And I said, "Are you sure of it." And he said, "It's in the heavens."

I said, "Well, if the heavens don't shine on him, then what's going to happen?" He said, "Well, then he will be wetting all the time. He just won't be collecting as much."

You know you don't have really too much of a wonderful choice day in and day out.

Suppose you had a case of loss of sexual power alone, not to a man of 60 or 70 or even a man of 40 or a man of 30, or married—or maybe he gets the rare woman who doesn't care. I am being realistic about it. It happens to a boy of 7. Obviously, on top of his other things he is never even going to get married; it would be ridiculous to figure it. And it isn't just not getting married. There are jokes—people who aren't married play around more than people who do—all this kind of stuff. I am speaking to you like men and women now, as grownups—somebody said "adults." Well, nothing in this life of any kind is for him. And everybody around him in one way or another is going to participate in the natural functions of living.

Let me get a little more conventional. Never for him will be the pleasures of being a father. There are all kinds of reasons. I mean, let's say he will never hold a child in his lap; for one thing, he really has no lap—I am not joking—and secondly, it's full of urine, and thirdly, he will never have a baby. Just think about it. Suppose it was nothing else but that in the case, what would the case be worth? No damages. Doctors can't do anything. You don't need any nurses. All you have done is just lost your sex function completely. No nursing, no loss of earnings, no medical. Doctors say, "We can't do anything for you." What's it worth? Just think about it, taking out of the literature of Dr. Charles Ney, he had to agree: "Bowel control is not easy. Hours may have to be spent at the toilet. The bowels may not move at regular times." And incontinence, you know, droppings, occurred and they couldn't work it out at the hospital. And you remember, his last statement was; "Well, every case is different."

He didn't know this case. Every one is different, but he gave you a pretty definite judgment. How would you like him to come in and make the judgment for you? A thousand dollars a blow.

Well, there are the multiple fractures he had, compound and simple, of the legs. Bones sticking out, shattered, legs twisted. You remember that "varus" business, and so forth. Maybe it doesn't really make any difference. Since it's on top of the paralysis, I suppose it doesn't matter whether it turned out a little more or not. What would that be worth if it just existed in a case by itself?

THE JURORS TOOK AN OATH TO FACE THE REALITY AND DO JUSTICE

Facts. Undisputed facts. You want to escape it? You want to run away from it? Would you rather have sat in only one of these many cases instead of all put together? Fine. You took the oath, not I. The oath was not for partial justice, it was for full justice. It was not for partial injustice.

Now, I am not bothering with the small things. You remember the skull fractures, parietal region, base of the skull—long time, weeks. I forget some other part of the skull, one of them running—the doctor said: "I see the X-ray running as far as the top of the skull. I can't see the other side." With the stuff dribbling out, the cerebro-spinal life fluid dribbling out of the nose and ears and mouth because the bottom of the skull that holds the brain was cracked. Well, you can hurt the case, shatter it. Maybe you cracked all the egg shells, but the egg didn't pour out, and if you are very careful you can make scrambled eggs out of it. Maybe that's what happened when it fell on the truck. Well, here, unfortunately, the egg, the brain, got hurt. Why do I say it? I don't say it. The good doctors at the St. Clare's Hospital, all of them, say that almost every neurological sign was affected—remember that—reflexes, the eyes, the Babinski—this famous sign at the bottom of the feet—everything.

And in case anybody had any question about it—he didn't have to be a doctor—he was unconscious for seven days.

Now it's cleared up outwardly. And maybe you think that Dr. Marks when he said to you, "Well, there is a greater exposure to epilepsy here," maybe you figured, well, I don't know, nobody asked him what he was getting. Maybe you figured he is a professional witness. I don't know him from Adam. Coming here to give us a hand. Maybe he is sorry for the boy or something.

You know, it's helpful to find out what a doctor would say who is just busy in the hospital making entries in order to do an errand of mercy, day-to-day work, and not with the prospect of Court in mind. So says a Dr. Gruber: "It will be important to watch for signs of an organic brain syndrome as time goes by, with the real possiblity of a seizure disorder or its equivalent being borne in mind." See, that nailed everything down.

Well, what's that kind of a brain damage worth? Think about it. You got to think about it. I told you I don't really have a figure.

As a little incidental thing—I don't know how it crept in here, I don't know if I mentioned it during the trial—glancing through the record I saw it, perforated ear drums. One of the few pleasures is his father dumping him in the water for a little swim. I forgot to ask him what kind of special precaution he even has to take then.

Then, of course, there is the spinal cord contusion, all-over paralysis, and so forth. Then he has a right lung collapsed with operative procedure; blood and fluid and air all had to be pumped out. Seems to have done all right in that. And I guess that would be a relatively minor case, just a collapsed lung. I guess some of the sign must have struck him and crushed the kid. I mean, I have to remind you of this because it's weeks later. I wouldn't even bother if the testimony went in a day or two ago.

Then he has seven breaks of the spine, seven fractures of the vertebral bones, and a few dislocations. Can you imagine if you just had a case with seven breaks of the neck and the upper chest and some bones dislocated, compressed fractures? I guess it must have crushed his skull, that's the cracks, and then taking the spine one bone on top of the other and crushed them—compression. The doctor explained once compressed, always compressed.

And one of the medically skilled lawyers here brought out that "Well, the nerves are not affected in the arms." Well, that's true. I guess, fortunately, when the bones collapsed that way, to stay collapsed forever, they didn't happen to squeeze against the column at that point. Because if the same thing happened that happened a couple of inches lower, then I guess the breathing apparatus and the heart would be knocked out, and I guess we wouldn't be here discussing a live boy. So he brought this out, and the doctor says yes. But, said the doctor, from the point of view of future arthritis, this boy is going to have trouble with these troubles already and is going to do as he gets older.

You remember, all the doctors, including their Covalt, because I asked him, said that as you get older your endurance gets weaker and you feel the effects of this more.

Well, what's the seven broken bones worth alone? How about the emergency tracheotomy so he could breathe to survive—suppose that was by itself?

Well, I have a few others, but—let me say this, my friends, the only thing I am going to ask you, because I am going to be as practical as possible—would you say that all these hurts are without precedent? It's almost hard to conceive of their being more in one human being who is still here or ever will be here. Would you say they are worth as much again, at least, as the money that's got to be laid out to keep him alive?

I think somebody said we live for the pleasures we get out of life. Somebody may work at his job all day long and find a certain amount of drudgery and look forward to playing pinochle or bowling or going to a ball game or listening to TV—that is his pleasure. And in work itself that is pain-free and happy, without the exasperation of knowing that you have certain capacities and you are frustrated because you can't achieve them, you get pleasure out of your work. A fellow who is a fine tool and die maker, he not only gets paid but most of them love their work. And I don't care whether you are a salesman or mechanic or an office worker, if you have the right feeling, that's so. But if you can't get the right job and you are pushed and you are pressed and so forth, what are the pleasures in life worth?

It isn't just the working hours, it's the living hours. It's the nonfamily hours in this case. Always having—and this is what they would deprive him of—having to buy most of the pleasures in life that you and I just take for granted. Want to go somewhere casually, you need somebody around you in order to be safe. Things can't really be done—you know, you can't rely on doing everything yourself. Suppose you want to make a trip. You and I, we might save up and take a little trip somewhere with our wives. He would have to get somebody to come with him and pay him for the time, and then maybe pay for transportation, and see him being boosted up a plane or into something.

Every little pleasure in life—and maybe he should have more of them to divert him than you and I—everything in life as free as air for you and me—great expense. He can't live in just any house, he can't work in just any job, he can't park in just any place. Everything in life within his limitations, within the limitations—what is it?—"activities of daily living."

So I wonder, my friends, whether the out-of-pocket estimate, which is only the conservative way to give him as best we can measure what they have taken away and will have taken away financially, whether the good health that the Lord gave him that they took from him, under our system of equal justice, which you are sworn to uphold—because your decision has more effect than just in this Court, it has an effect, really, on the whole system of justice and the need to uphold it—whether big or small. Can we say our American system of justice is only good for ordinary large cases only, where you are not allowed to have all these 12 things happen to one person and you have to divide them into 12 cases? But we didn't make the choice, they did.

So I say to you, my friends, as a very minimum—you may disagree with me—$1,244,000 or $715,000 for the boy, depending on which figure you take, discounted or not discounted, on this out-of-pocket part of it, special damages, we lawyers call them, and whether actually it isn't unfair to the boy to allow him the so-called general damages, the pain, the suffering, the injuries, at least once again that amount. And you can multiply by two just as well as I can.

There are many other things I would like to talk to you about, but I am not going to do it.

Mr. Berman: Excuse me. Just a minute, please. I respectfully except to an argument which is far in excess of the *ad damnum.*

Mr. Fuchsberg: In fact, I might tell you that when I was first retained in this case five years ago I had no idea at the time, just like you, you had no conception, no matter what we told you when we picked the jury. You remember, I spoke in a general way how serious and unprecedented—and my friends were telling you in advance so as to deaden the blow a little bit. I don't think any of you really conceived that it was quite as awful and as bad as you heard it here. I didn't think it was that way either. So, frankly, when I started this suit it was for an amount which you may find was really insufficient and under the circumstances where maybe—I have to confess this because I suppose I should have done like some lawyers and sued for—taken all possibilities. I am no seer. I am not clairvoyant. It may turn out to be unjust to this boy.

But you know what the losses are, anywhere from approximately 2-1/2 million dollars to a million and a half dollars in the boy's case, if you take this conservative approach that I have suggested to you, and there are about 200 to 250 thousand dollars which is mostly out-of-pocket losses for the father—$182,000. That's actual moneys going to have to be spent. Otherwise, I don't know, you and I are going to have to pay it by way of charity, I suppose.

I am merely going to say this, my friends: You come here to do perhaps one of the most important duties—perhaps the most important as far as in the sense of the case is concerned, as one of them right here suggested, that's ever been requested of any jury in this country. I am glad we are talking today and the judge is charging you tomorrow, because I am not talking with you with emotion and I am perfectly satisfied for you to let all this cool down overnight. Because when all this cools down, it is still there. You see, like that Fitzgerald quotation I gave, the hand has writ, you have done the damage.

I am going to suggest to you—I am sort of glad I am turning the responsibility over to you. We sit and jest and joke and are casual, but, please believe me, it's been an awful burden.

HE ASKS THEM TO BE ADVOCATES ON BEHALF OF THE PLAINTIFF

I would merely suggest to you two things—three things: One is that I know when I sit down, realizing, even as I do now, there are some things I have forgotten to talk about, I am going to ask you to please supply any voids that I have allowed to exist from your own memories and your good judgment and your good intelligence. I have talked to you from the head and not from the heart because you have been sitting here the same as I have.

The second thing I want to suggest to you is that if somebody says to you, and of you, and 12 different people eventually—if we all survive by tomorrow—God willing—the alternates are excused—somebody may say to you, "Well, it's all right, it's all correct, it's all logical, it's all sensible, it's all reasonable, the result of reason"—you reasoned with me—"but, you know, that's an awful lot of money, and money doesn't grow on raspberry bushes." I want to suggest to you, if that is going to be the approach of anyone, please remember that when this case is over, if you want to go home and lay your head peacefully down on your pillow with a conscience clear that you have fulfilled your obligation as men and women and your oath as citizens, and that you have preserved the sanctity of our right to life, liberty, and the pursuit of happiness in seeing that full justice is done and a wrong is righted for one of our fellows, then you must see to it—and understand that when you give 20 percent less, you are not doing 80 percent justice, you are doing 20 percent injustice.

It's like the fellow who says, "I owe you a dollar, but I am giving you 80 cents." He has deprived you of 20, he hasn't given you 80. And if you cut 10 percent because you want to see what a swell guy you can be, you have done 10 percent injustice. The cup of justice is to be full pressed down, and if not overflowing in a case of this kind, with all that's been imposed on this boy, it should certainly not be poured below the top.

And for all of us I would like to perhaps close on this note: It's nice not to be practical and maybe a little foolish, but I would like to envision this cathedral of justice in which we find ourselves—because it is in a sense. Like today we have Lincoln's stories. It isn't the words, it isn't even the place. It's the idea. I like to view the law in its majesty, which we as civilized beings live, as a cathedral with the spire reaching up to the heavens. I would like to feel that any time a lack of insight and strength of purpose and fulfillment of obligation of either our judges or our jurors permit less than full justice to be done, that spire just gets pulled down a little bit more closely to earth; and every time you walk out of here with a proud feeling of full justice done, wherever it leads you, that spire has just reached a little more heavenward. And that's why I say your verdict here is important beyond the reaches of this courtroom.

U.S.A. v. Meyerson

Mr. Goldberg: May it please the Court and ladies and gentlemen of the jury, good morning to you.

We have now reached the point where I am going to have some time this morning and perhaps in the early afternoon to share with you my thoughts on what has been, I guess, by my calculations, close to a two-month trial with some 34 witnesses and a number of documents.

AUTHOR'S NOTE: *He explains some of the procedures.*

I think you should know that with respect to the defense lawyers, this is the last time that I'll have an opportunity to speak with you. This is the only time that the law provides me an opportunity to share with you and reason together with you in the course of our analysis of the case.

The law, on the other hand, in its wisdom, provides the government an opportunity to speak with you two times. The prosecution may sit there pen in hand, yellow pads, and then when they speak in their rebuttal they may say, for example, that I have misstated the case or I have overstated or understated some aspect of the case. I have, as you should know, no opportunity to respond, and I don't want you to think that because I don't get up and I don't speak to you again, that I am agreeing with what they say.

I can assure you that my function before you will be to show you how wide of the mark the government is in its efforts to prove the charges to the required point beyond a reasonable doubt; how utterly deficient the proof is; how absolutely void the evidence is as the government tries to fulfill its obligation—the obligation which remains with it all throughout you deliberations—and that is to bring to you, if it can, solid, credible, believable evidence to a point beyond a reasonable doubt.

We say that if you search the record in this case you will conclude that, despite the presence of a staff of three prosecutors and an investigation that we learned commenced some two or two and a half years ago, the prosecutors have failed—have failed—in their obligation to present solid proof to a point beyond a reasonable doubt.

It matters, then, to me not one whit that they have two chances to speak to you because two times zero will still turn out to be zero.

That's where the government is in its claim that Justice Gabel was corrupted, so the charge goes, in rendering her decisions in the matrimonial case *Capasso v. Capasso.*

Now, yesterday Mr. Abrams made use of a number of charts. And there was a certain vice in the use of those charts that I want to share with you. It is one thing, I suggest, to blow up an exhibit, it is one thing to blow up testimony because those things are evidence, those things you may consider, can have with you during deliberations, ask that portions of testimony be read back to you. So, at times, lawyers blow up exhibits or they blow up portions of testimony.

My recollection is that except in one limited area, Mr. Abrams steered clear of quoting any testimony in this case, referring you to any sworn testimony of a witness except in one area when there was a question of whether Hortense Gabel either embraced or did she hug Bess Myerson.

The only exhibit, as I recall, that he presented to you was the letter that Bess Myerson sent to Mayor Koch.

What he did in the use of those charts, complete with the colors and the graphic display, was to give you an incomplete picture of testimony in an inaccurate version of what the witnesses said, and those charts could, if you don't realize the use to which he put them, could divert you from the task that's yours, and that is to search the records to see if he satisfied his burden to a point beyond a reasonable doubt.

Here he uses the record to support this argument.

I am going to give you a couple of graphic examples of how that chart and those charts used by the prosecutor were designed to mislead you in your search for the truth. You recall that one of the critical areas touched on by Mr. Abrams yesterday was Shirley Harrod's supposed witnessing of a celebration which he listed on his chart as having occurred in September.

Now, that was for some reason important to the government. They wanted you to believe that after Justice Gabel restructured—restructured—the payments that Mr. Capasso had to pay in September, which amounted to a reduction for Nancy Capasso of $500 a year—and that's what this federal case involves, $500 a year by the restructuring of the June order by the September 1983 order—they wanted you to believe that when that happened in September of 1983, that Shirley Harrod witnessed a celebration. So they listed on the chart: September: Shirley Harrod witnesses a celebration.

If they took the time, as I will later on, to read to you the testimony, you will see that Shirley Harrod, while she said on the direct examination, questions put to her by the prosecutors, that she recalled that it was September, it was during cross-examination that she rethought her position and said she was now clear that it was June or July; that her husband Ray Harrod was fired on August 5. So it was now June or July. But Mr. Abrams didn't tell you that on the chart. He construed it in a light most favorable to his position because, after all, he is an advocate.

He is not required to be impartial. Those charts are not prepared by a team of referees. Those charts are prepared, because we have an adversary system, by a group of partial, biased advocates. Biased in favor of the side that they represent.

Those charts do not represent the true picture of the testimony you heard because, if that chart truly reflected what you heard, it would have indicated that Shirley Harrod now says that this supposed celebration did not take place in September, when there was a restructuring of the award, but it took place in June or July.

You know, it has been said by a legal scholar that the most effective tool in the search for truth is cross-examination. It is so easy to prepare a witness for some 44 working rehearsal sessions, one witness 44 times, another witness 18 to 20 times, and then put them as wind-up toys, asking them questions that have been rehearsed.

But it's the art of cross-examination that's designed to search out the truth.

Mr. Abrams, on the other hand, prepares a chart, containing incomplete versions of the record, based solely on the answers of witnesses who have been prepared, without any thought given to the cross-examination.

Another point—because I don't intend to get bogged down on attacking his charts—but just to give you an example of how you cannot rely on the graphic, colorful display that was presented here yesterday. It was important to the government, so desperate were they to try to inject Andy Capasso into this that on the chart they said: Birthday party, August 30.

Why was that important?

They had a credit card slip for Andy Capasso, signed by Bess Myerson, for August 30. They wanted Sukhreet Gabel's birthday party to be August 30, but there was a problem. Not one single witness had said that the birthday party took place on August 30. And there was in the record substantive proof—substantive proof—a document that I will show you later on, that indicated that the birthday party was August 24.

That didn't stop the government in preparing its case to show some nexus or connection to Andy Capasso and Sukhreet Gabel. Even though he wasn't at the party. They wanted it to be August 30; the fact that there was documentary proof it was August 24 didn't matter one bit to a partial, biased advocate. So the listing on the chart was August 30.

So, too, yesterday—these are by way of examples—yesterday the government wanted you to believe that the party couldn't have been August 24 as the document reflects because Justice Gabel's diary reflects that she came back on August 29. That is what Mr. Abrams said, leading you to believe, no doubt, "coming back" meant coming back from Mattituck. But that wasn't accurate. That was most disingenuous by the prosecutor.

August 29 was the day she came back to work in the courthouse at 60 Centre Street, not the day she came back to New York.

But Mr. Abrams presented the case as though August 29 was the day she came back; but he didn't complete the sentence, leaving you to opine, perhaps, that that's the day she came back from Mattituck so she couldn't be at the party.

He didn't show you an exhibit—because exhibits played no part in his Summation yesterday, nor did actual testimony—he didn't show you an exhibit that was marked in evidence as 165, the telephone bill of Mr. Justice Thompson out in Mattituck, that showed that Hortense Gabel and her husband made no calls from that Mattituck house after August 18. No calls made by the Gabels after August 18, leading to the conclusion that it was more than likely that after August 18 she was no longer in Mattituck and was available, as Sukhreet Gabel testified on two occasions, for the party to have occurred on August 24.

But the government had no credit card for Andy Capasso on August 24, and it didn't want to accept the notion that the birthday party took place on August 24, so it simply picked a chit from Andy Capasso's credit card slips—so desperate, such an effort to stretch—and said that the birthday party took place on August 30. . . .

Now, as you know, I stand here on behalf of one person, Andy Capasso, who—and I believe the judge told you this at the beginning of the trial—who but for the convenience of the government would have a separate trial, be on trial alone, and that a joint trial in which you are to consider a number of defendants is for the convenience of the government. But even though it is conducted as a joint trial, more than one person, you are still required as part of your obligation to give Mr. Capasso a trial as though he were here alone, focusing on what the proof does or does not show as to him now.

While the indictment will be before you and will speak for itself, and the judge will fully explain it to you, you will conclude that stripped to its essentials the charge in this case is that a scheme supposedly existed to victimize the City of New York of moneys that were paid to Sukhreet Gabel for her employment at the Department of Cultural Affairs between the period of August '83 to June of '84, and the second victim is claimed to be Nancy Capasso, who the proof will show, through the restructured order of Justice Gabel, lost $575 a year prior to city and state taxes.

I haven't picked this number out of the air. If you recall towards the end of the trial, I put in, with the government's concurrence, Nancy Capasso's tax returns. I also put in the 1983 tax tables, and together we will do her tax returns and figure out her taxes. Very simple. You will see that this million-dollar federal case involves a claim when reduced to its essentials, that through the restructured order of Justice Gabel in September of 1983, this supposed victim, Nancy Capasso, lost—and properly so, you will conclude—the grand sum, considering city, state, and federal taxes, of less than $500 a year.

The claim is that the city was victimized, and Nancy Capasso was victimized because Justice Gabel, in rendering her decision of September 13, 1983, was corrupted because a job had been given to her daughter.

Mr. Goldberg reminds the jurors of their obligations.

Now, you know we are here, obviously, because the defendants have pleaded not guilty, and once they did that a number of principles came into effect. Principles this country was founded on, principles which make the American system of justice a unique system among world governments.

First and foremost is that the defendants now and during your deliberations are presumed innocent and that this presumption stays with them throughout your deliberations and falls only if the prosecution has come forward with solid, credible, believable proof to a point beyond a reasonable doubt.

We say they have failed to do that. We say no amount of conjecture, no pleas about coincidences, are substitutes for the burden that rests on the prosecution to prove its case, if it can, to a point beyond a reasonable doubt. If you should conclude, as I say you will, at the end of your deliberations that despite the efforts of Mr. Abrams, his fellow assistants, and the support staff of investigators and FBI agents, that they have failed to prove their case to a point beyond a reasonable doubt, the defendants are entitled to an acquittal, whatever suspicion remains, whatever conjecture there might be or surmise on anyone's part.

So, you see, in recognition of this heavy burden that always stays at the prosecution table, the law in its wisdom, no quarrel, gives them two chances to speak with you.

It was yesterday when the learned Court told you the role that you play and he will have more to say about it, but in our system we have two sets of judges. Judge Keenan is supreme on the law. No one here may question it. When he rules, that is the law of this case.

But just as he is supreme, so you as the jury are supreme within your sphere. You are what we call the supreme judges of the facts. Factual questions are yours and yours alone for all time to decide. No one may question your factual determination. Just as you may not intrude into Judge Keenan's province, neither he nor anyone else has the power to intrude into yours.

When you think about it, when you think that you, as a group, exercise the power to decide the fate, the future of three people, that you hold that enormous power in your hands, you understand that it is no overstatement to say that for you this is an extraordinary occasion.

A doctor may operate on a patient. You, when you deliberate, you will be operating on the lives and future and fate of three people. That's the heavy responsibility that you have as the supreme judges of the facts; and with such a heavy responsibility comes a number of challenges. Because nothing is easy in life. With the enormous responsibility that is yours, you have to meet a set of challenges. I will propose a few of them to you and see how you measure up.

Is there anyone—the first challenge—who cannot look upon my client, Andy Capasso, or for that matter the other defendants and not now say that they are presumed innocent?

Is there anyone, who because of anything that Mr. Abrams may have said when he misused the facts on the charts that he crafted, is there anyone who can say that they are influenced to a point that they cannot presume the innocence of Andy Capasso?

If you cannot presume the innocence of Andy Capasso and the two other defendants, you would be violating your oath.

Now, there was proof in this case that in February of 1983—Mr. Abrams alluded to it—that Mr. Capasso wrongly struck his wife. There is no excuse for that, but each of you were separately questioned by his honor and asked eyeball to eyeball when you sat as close as two feet from the Court in the robing room on another floor, when the judge said to you, there will be proof in this case about that incident, do I have your pledge that you could deal with that by laying it aside and not letting it influence your consideration in this case? Some people couldn't do that. They were excused. You, on the other hand, gave the Court and counsel your solemn pledge. If you could not, then, lay aside that incident, you would be violating your oath.

Finally, you learned that in January of 1987 Mr. Capasso pleaded guilty—he asked for no trial by jury—he pleaded guilty to a tax violation. You learned that. He said in a prepared statement that he was pleading guilty because he was guilty. He didn't need a trial. He didn't have to take the time of jurors on that tax matter. When he was guilty, he pleaded guilty. But not so this case. Nonetheless, the judge gave you an instruction that you cannot hold against him in your deliberations, the fact that he pleaded guilty to a tax case.

Let me read to you what the judge said because I suggest it applies to every other prejudicial matter in this case whether it be the pretrial publicity, whether it be the alleged striking of the wife, these words that I am going to read to you apply to all of those unduly prejudicial matters. The Court said to you in connection with the tax situation—listen to the words that the Court used:

"I charge you unequivocally, without any hesitation, without any reservation whatsoever, that to in any way hold against him in this case anything about a tax case would be grossly unfair and would be a violation of your sworn oath as jurors and would in a real sense be absolutely unAmerican."

He is not on trial for anything having to do with his taxes, and that has nothing at all to do with this case. So if anybody during jury deliberations ever says that or ever thinks that, well, he pleaded guilty, that had something to do with this, you would be violating your oath and you would be acting absolutely improperly.

You know, you jurors, I think there are 17 jurors, were culled from a group of 150 people, because counsel thought that you had the discipline and the commitment to abide by the instructions of the Court, to focus on what is the real issue in this case: have they satisfied their burden of proof to a point beyond a reasonable doubt—and you could lay aside prejudicial matter that has no place in the decision making necessary to your verdict.

To that extent you are a chosen, select group of people exercising this enormous power.

Now, before I get to the nuts and the bolts of this case, which I have divided into three parts—the decision making of Justice Gabel in the Capasso case; the hiring of Sukhreet Gabel; and what the proof shows or does not show with respect to Andy Capasso—I want to make some general observations with respect to so much of the proof of this case.

Mr. Goldberg begins to poke fun.

I suggest that when you analyze the 34 witnesses in this case, and the 35 or so trial days, you will be convinced that the government sought to divert your attention from their lack of proof. They gave you so much smoke and dust that you have to ask yourself why was it, why was it necessary that we hear this proof? What desperation was there on the part of these adversaries that caused them to present this kind of material to us that has no real bearing on the issues in this case?

I am going to run off some examples for you.

Was it important, for example, for you to know through the testimony of Sukhreet Gabel that Bess Myerson tried on Nancy Capasso's bathing suits?

Or that Bess Myerson threw out—as the government chose to bring this out—Bess Myerson threw out Nancy Capasso's potted plants? That was some part of the proof in this case.

And then it became necessary for Mr. Hafetz to show that, well, instead of the potted plants she had a list of silverware she had brought, Bess Myerson, perhaps as a substitute for the potted plants and for her payment of the use of Nancy's bikinis. That was one aspect of this case that took some time. . . .

Or that through Sukhreet Gabel, Bess Myerson fell on a tennis court? He even has it on his chart: Bess Myerson fell on the tennis court. Sukhreet Gabel says she witnessed it, she bruised her knee and she bruised her face. And he went to the trouble of making an entry to that effect on his chart, so important it is to the case. . . .

Or was it really important, was it really important to Mr. Lawrence, who was the examiner, that Edward I. Koch thought that Mr. Capasso's home was an estate? Do you remember that? He put the question to the honorable Mayor, "Now, at the estate of Mr.—" That was the question, when the Mayor interrupted him and said, "No, hold it."

You see, the fatal flaw committed by Mr. Lawrence, if I may be so bold as to correct him on trial strategy, is that one question earlier he had said to the Mayor, did you know the housekeepers—obviously the Harrods—and the Mayor obviously—I know his head—the Mayor, obviously, thinking back to the steady diet of hamburgers, remember, hot dogs, macaroni salad, that he had gotten at the hands of the Harrods, said to himself, listen, this was no estate. This was a home. I've gotten better meals at Popeye's 44th Street and Eighth Avenue. . . .

Before I discuss the case in detail, aside from my observation that there is this smoke and dust diversionary material thrust at you, I make also the observation that this case had an inordinate amount of Herbie Rickman.

He was a go-fer with half a brain, someone to whom the oath meant very little. The preservation of his job—it is not civil service—was all-important, and he was intent on preserving that job. There is a document that you are going to have before you that puts the lie to Herbie's testimony. It is Exhibit V of Hortense Gabel. It spells out just when this "whatchamacallit" or "what's his face" conversation took place. It never occurred on May 23. There was no proof in this case that Bess Myerson ever asked or suggested or intimated that Justice Gabel should compromise her decision, and she never did with her $358,000 award. There is no proof that prior to September 14 this justice of the supreme court knew of Bess Myerson's relationship with Andy Capasso.

Injecting more humor

Before I discuss the case in detail, aside from my observation that there is this smoke and dust diversionary tactics, and a whole raft of biased, disgruntled, disturbed people who the government used to try to make up for its lack of proof, witnesses who—well, in the old vaudeville days when a person performed very badly from the side of the stage there would be a hook, and the person would be whisked right off the stage, or off center stage.

I don't know if you people are this old, but *Amateur Hour with Major Bowes*, when a person there was utterly terrible he would ring a bell and off the person would go. Then in the seventies you remember we had the *Gong Show*. when a person was on center stage and was really bad, Chuck Barris, remember, gong, and that was the end of the performance. This is the only new addition I can make to the Court structure, that jurors should have at their chair a button that could sound the gong. I'm going to give you a few as we go along. You see if I overstate it.

You see, so much of this case—I told you 34 witnesses—had so little to do with Andy Capasso—I think I examined by my own count about 5 or 6 out of the 34—and, quite frankly, I don't know whether I examined those witnesses because they were really relevant to Andy Capasso or I wanted my picture drawn by the artists.

So I had a lot of time to think about this case. How and why were we here, and what were we doing? What were we trying in this case? What TV or daytime serial could I put this case into?

Well, believe me, the first one that came to my mind early in the trial was the dispute. I could see it emerging, Nancy's claim that her potted plants had been wrongly discarded, and her bathing suit had been used, that was a perfect case for Judge Wapner. Any question about that? That was a *Peoples Court* case, clearly.

With Shirley Harrod you had the PBS program, right, *Upstairs Downstairs*.

Look what Shirley Harrod told you. She was the first one for which the gong would be in order. She would have you believe the following. She would have you believe that her husband, Ray Harrod, was fired because Barra Reilly, that's Bess Myerson's daughter, and Bess Myerson's son-in-law, traveled 6,000 miles, 3,000 from California to Westhampton, 3,000 back, 6,000 miles, and rather than enjoy the sand and the surf at Mr. Capasso's home, rather than play tennis and enjoy the pool, the only pleasure, the one pleasure that Barra Reilly had in life was that when Ray Harrod went into the kitchen to his meal, the Reillys would come into the kitchen and stand there—this was their thrill—just to watch him masticate. Wait a minute; that's to chew. Chew? That was the joy that the Reillys had. That was the only reason, she says, that there was a dispute. After all, she says, we are fascinating people. That is the reason that there was this dispute.

Now, look, ladies and gentlemen, a little more on Shirley Harrod, a critical witness, appears on the chart, a number of entries. Exhibit 535 was the picture of the rear end of a Mercedes automobile Shirley Harrod took. Do you remember that?

She took a picture of the rear end of a Mercedes automobile. Was that Mercedes automobile in some way helpful to Nancy Capasso?

Well, let me read you what Mr. — she took this picture one month after she meets Nancy Capasso. Was that Mercedes important to Nancy Capasso? Let me read you what Mr. Leventhal, the judge's law clerk says. "Here's the question: 'By the way, did you ever make a statement that you believed that Nancy Capasso from the papers that you read was more interested in getting a Mercedes for herself than support for the children? Did you ever say that?'

"Answer: 'Yes, sir.'"

What did you mean by that?

This is what the law clerk says about this Mercedes that Shirley Harrod would have you believe she just took.

"Answer: 'From the papers before me I could think of at least three separate occasions, three separate motions, where she asks the Court for exclusive use of a Mercedes vehicle which seemed to be a fixation with her.'

"Question: 'Fixation?'

"Answer: 'Yes, sir.'"

Shirley Harrod would have you believe that she took a picture of the rear end of a Mercedes, not at the urging of Nancy Capasso, who she secretly met a month before, and she kept this rear-end picture of a Mercedes for five years and then turned it over to the government because in her own words she is fascinated with tail pipes. Now, tell me, you couldn't see a hook come right out, whisking her, poof, right off?

She is hooked on tail pipes!

But then there was more. You heard about Sukhreet Gabel's hospitalization, and her 15 shock treatments, and her care by a psychopharmacologist—I'm sure a nurse on the jury could tell us what that is, a psychopharmacologist.

And then you had that sterling special assistant Herbert Rickman's hypochondriasis, right? His fear, according to special agent St. Germain, that he is in the beginning stages of Alzheimer's disease. And his obvious stomach cramps and frequent trips to the bathroom at the mere sight of Fred Haefitz. I don't know if you remember that as soon as Mr. Haefitz got up to cross examine Mr. Rickman, he had to run to the toilet up and back. Do you remember that?

That was only because Mr. Hafetz was trying to get the truth, but you remember what happened. I said to myself that this took on shades, right, as I sat there, because I had very little to do, that this did take on shades of General Hospital, and the government didn't need a paralegal like Joan Alexander, it could have used a paramedic.

And even the defense was a part of it, too. Justice Gabel, unfortunately, there was proof had suffered a heart attack, she had been hospitalized for a stroke. Bess Myerson had endured ovarian cancer, chemotherapy, and a stroke herself.

What a tragedy, what a tragedy, that we are here. What a tragedy that we are here because Nancy Capasso has sold the government on a bill of goods that just won't hold up once I analyze the nuts and bolts of the case.

And, finally, as I opine what this case could be all about, David Lawrence stood up here, my learned and esteemed adversary, and he had the Mayor on the witness stand, and there had to be, it had to be the consideration given by the government to the Mayor for having made the walk over from City Hall, the Mayor's political future hanging in the balance, the matter of his health somewhere looming largely.

Do you remember David Lawrence standing here and saying, Mayor, how is your health? And state to us how you are feeling. That had to be the Mayor's consideration for having walked over. I, of course, objected, concerned as I was that as desperate as the government is to bring Andy Capasso into this case, who the heck knew whether his elevated cholesterol and his stroke might somehow be related to the hamburgers, hot dogs, and macaroni salad. Luckily for me, the judge sustained my objection.

That's where we were in this case. . . .

There was some testimony that when Shirley Harrod was interviewed, Mr. Capasso was concerned about security. Do you remember that he was concerned about security? Well, look how intelligent the man was. While Shirley Harrod worked for him, Nancy Capasso arranged to secretly meet Shirley Harrod at the home of the Ponterelli's.

Shirley Harrod said it wasn't a prearrangement, she came to the Ponterelli's, Nancy was just there. Nancy only realized that she worked for Mr. Capasso because her name was Shirley. Do you remember that?

I said to her "You mean the mere mention of your first name, there was something so distinctive about the name Shirley that once Mrs. Capasso heard that you had the first name of Shirley she knew that you were Andy's housekeeper?"

And of course this woman said "yes."

That's baloney. That was a meeting arranged by Nancy Capasso while Shirley Harrod was working for Mr. Capasso.

Shirley Harrod also told you that Tony Bailey, Mr. Capasso's chauffeur, was Nancy's key informer and would do anything for Nancy. Mrs. Capasso called Shirley Harrod six times long distance in Maryland, called her in Armonk, and Shirley Harrod says all they talked about was social things. Do you believe that?

Mr. Hafetz asked, in many areas, we only have your word for it, Mrs. Harrod? The government—I am not saying the government is required to bring any number of witnesses, no such requirement, but the government didn't bring Nancy Capasso to this stand so that you could learn her true role in orchestrating this case.

Shirley Harrod was on a first-name basis with Nancy Capasso. Shirley Harrod takes the picture that we talked about, Exhibit 535, which you can conclude was for Nancy Capasso. We know of at least one meeting in the living room between the government investigator and Nancy Capasso at the beginning of this investigation. The claim that Shirley Harrod—and this is critical for the government—the claim that Shirley Harrod supposedly saw Mr. Capasso throw papers down and say, "can't you do something about this, Bess?" is something that occurred only after Shirley Harrod had met numerous times, spoken numerous times, with Nancy Capasso.

You may conclude that since Shirley Harrod had been grilled intensively for two days by the Tyler Commission and never ever said, in over 12 hours of interviews, that she ever saw Mr. Capasso throw down papers and say to Bess Myerson, "can't you do something about this," you may conclude that that in-Court testimony of Shirley Harrod was not based on what she saw or heard at the Capasso residence, because she never told that to the Tyler Commission, never told that to Tony Lombardi before she went to the Tyler Commission, never told that to the United States Attorney before she went to the Tyler Commission, but did say it only after she and Nancy had conferred over a half a dozen times.

You know, of course there is a reason the government called Mayor Koch. The government alleges that the City of New York—erroneously alleges that the City of New York was a victim—so they called the mayor, but there is reason that they didn't call Nancy. Why—why—has Nancy Capasso's emotions so turned to hatred to the point where she is the orchestrator, I suggest you will conclude, of this prosecution?

I told you in my opening, something which I hate to quote, something I said, but it bears repeating. I said there was no fury as intense and mean spirited as Nancy Capasso. No rage as venomous as that of Nancy Capasso once her love for Andy Capasso turned to hate. Even at the expense of the two small children. Even if it meant destroying her husband, the father of her two children and person who by all accounts was a wonderful father to the three-step children. Why was that? Why was it that there was such rage? It couldn't be because there was a $500 difference to her in the two orders out of which this whole case is fabricated and concocted. Well, Andy left her for another woman, an older woman. Nancy was rejected by her husband for an older woman. But you know something? This is lucky for Mr. Herbert. Andy and Bess did to Nancy what Nancy really did to Mr. Herbert when she left him, three children, and ran off with Andy. . . .

Now I don't think there is a more interesting person to discuss than our friend Herbie Rickman, the man who obviously owns a patent on how to shriek in a courtroom, right? A performance that stands unique among the 34 people that you saw in this courtroom. He finds a place on the government's chart; the government wants you to believe that Justice Gabel knew Andy Capasso was going with Bess Myerson as early as May 1983.

Well, that, ladies and gentlemen, you will conclude is just false. What does the government do? They call Herbert Rickman. We know the following: We know that he lied before you when he said that he didn't tell Special Agent St. Germain that he was concerned about the fact that he was in the beginning stages of Alzheimer's disease. That is their witness.

He falsely told you that he never raised the prospect of a job for Sukhreet Gabel in the eight weekends he spent with Bess Myerson. That's just not believable. Think about it. Hortense Gabel meets him every six weeks, has lunch with him at the Hunan Garden, talks to him about a job for Sukhreet Gabel. Bess Myerson is now new to the administration. He is a special assistant to the mayor and a freeloader. And he's living in "Herbie's room" out in the Capasso home, and he never even raised the issue of a job with Bess Myerson because to him work at the DCA pasting pictures of museums on a map, DCA, was just too taxing for Sukhreet Gabel. He tries to make you believe that the DCA is the CIA. It's too hard. It is just too hard. He would never think of suggesting that she should work in this agency. Probably three-quarters of you jurors never even heard of it. And it seems to be the most perfect spot for her with all due respect. Never even raises it with her and claims that he never tried to get her a job with Ambassador Saltzman, even though we were able to learn that he had to have discussed a job with Saltzman in June or July because Saltzman left in July.

He tries to distance himself from this whole scenario by saying once he came back from his mid-eastern trip, 6 countries, to try to work out discrimination, obviously he was laying the predicate for explaining why he didn't pick up the bill himself and traveled at the taxpayers' expense. Because you could just see the politician's mind working. When he was asked why he went to Europe, he gave you a litany of supposed business reasons. You can be sure that he didn't pay for it, it was his way of covering himself, but he said that he was livid when he found out that Bess Myerson had hired Sukhreet Gabel, so he immediately ran in and spoke to Patrick Mulhearn. He lied.

You saw that witness Patrick Mulhearn. Never happened. It just didn't happen.

Did Herbie Rickman look like the kind of self-restrained, self-contained person who could keep a secret? Forget it.

But let me tell you what he did. Let me tell you what he really did. We know that he was interviewed by the government. I don't know whether it was—I can stand corrected—I have 28 times. It may be 18 times—I may have the number wrong, but it was a lot of times—and never once did he ever say that more than five years ago he remembered that on May 23, 1983 Hortense Gabel said at the Bess Myerson reception, "is what's his name here?" or something like that, "whatchamacallit?" which Mr. Abrams puts on his chart as May 23, ignoring the fact that there is documentary proof in this case that he attributes that remark to Justice Gabel not in May of 1983 but well after the *Post* article came out in September of '83 or even '84.

But now, for the first time, he supposedly remembers Hortense Gabel saying to him more than five years ago, this man in the beginning stages of Alzheimer's disease, "is what's his name here?"

Let me run through very quickly with you how it came to him, how this vision came to him. "How, Herbie, did you suddenly remember more than five years ago, despite your 28 other contrary statements, that Hortense Gabel ever said that to you in May?"

"Well," he says—watch this, this is a few months ago—"I went to a reception. I sat on a bench—I sat on the bench that I sat on when I sat there with Hortense Gabel five years before, and that refreshed my recollection from sitting on the bench."

So my question to Herbie is, I've heard of people who have had their recollection refreshed when an idea popped into their head, but I have never until this trial, in my life, heard of a man's recollection being refreshed through the seat of his pants!

But then there was a kicker to all of this. I believe it was the judge who said this to him—you know, it is like you want to know if somebody is hard of hearing and you say, are you hard of hearing, and the guy says, what's that you said? The actions tell the story. But here's the kicker—this is a question that was put by the learned Court: Now you say you remember something—I am not quoting, by the way—you say you remember something that occurred five and a half years ago?

"Yes," says Herbie.

"You say this was at a recent reception that you went to just a month or two ago?"

"That's right."

Well, if you can remember what you say happened five and a half years ago from sitting on that particular seat cushion, what reception was that that you went to just a couple of months ago? You know, testing the man's memory.

He said he couldn't remember!

Mr. Goldberg continued this Summation and moved the jury to a rousing acquittal on all counts.

INDEX

I

J

P

Q

R

S

T

V

W